JOHN CAM HOBHOUSE

JOHN CAM HOBHOUSE

A Political Life, 1819–1852

R O B E R T E . Z E G G E R

U N I V E R S I T Y O F M I S S O U R I P R E S S

C O L U M B I A , 1 9 7 3

ACKNOWLEDGMENTS

Many individuals helped me at various stages in the preparation of this political biography. Among them, Sir Charles C. Hobhouse, sixth Bart., must be especially noted because he kindly allowed me to examine some forty volumes of John Cam Hobhouse's diaries in his possession. I recall with great pleasure the hospitality Sir Charles and Lady Hobhouse extended to me during the time of my research at The Manor, Monckton Farleigh, Wiltshire. I am also grateful to John Murray for granting permission to examine the Byron-Hobhouse correspondence in his possession. Doris Langley Moore shared many insights she derived from her own study of Hobhouse, which appeared in *The Late Lord Byron; posthumous dramas* (London, 1961). Russell Ellice, Esq., of Invergarry, Aberchalder, Invergarry, Inverness-shire, kindly allowed me to examine the Edward Ellice Papers at the National Library of Scotland. Hobhouse's correspondence with Lord Palmerston became available by permission of the Trustees of the Broadlands Archives. I am likewise indebted to Earl Spencer for making the Althorp Papers available. Viscount and Lady Lambton granted permission to examine the papers of the first Earl of Durham, and the staff at the National Register of Archives provided most valuable help in locating other sources indicated in the Bibliography. Portions of Chapter V first appeared as an article, "Greek Independence and the London Committee, Revolution in the 1820s," *History Today* (April, 1970), 236–45. The article is incorporated by permission of the editors, Peter Quennell and Alan Hodge. Some Hobhouse letters in the Royal Archives, Windsor Castle, were made available by gracious permission of Her Majesty the Queen.

In the United States I am especially indebted to Professor Robert K. Webb of Columbia University for his valuable advice and his many comments upon points of detail. Professor Trygve Tholfsen of Teachers College, Columbia University, also read various drafts and gave valuable suggestions, as did Professor James Shenton of Columbia University. The late Professor Archibald S. Foord of Calhoun College, Yale University, was kind enough to furnish me with a transcript of his work, *His Majesty's Opposition, 1714–1830* (Oxford, 1964), and Professor Walter L. Arnstein of the University of Illinois, Urbana, offered excellent suggestions and criticisms of various chapters. A New York State research grant helped defray research expenses over a number of years. I was able to complete this work during a sabbatical leave from Northeastern Illinois University (Chicago) during the academic year 1971–1972. My wife helped me greatly by proofreading and improving the manuscript. The final handiwork is necessarily my own.

I am also grateful for the help provided by the staffs at many libraries and record offices on both sides of the Atlantic. These include Columbia University and the main branch of the Public Library in New York City; the Newberry Library and the University of Chicago Library in Chicago; the British Museum, the Public Record Office, and the Guildhall Library in London; the National Library of Scotland in Edinburgh; the County Record Office in Wiltshire, Staffordshire, and Hertfordshire; and the National Library of Greece in Athens.

R.E.Z.
Wilmette, Illinois
December, 1972

CONTENTS

INTRODUCTION

John Cam Hobhouse, Lord Broughton, was a witness to many great events of his day—so observed the writer of an obituary article in the *Edinburgh Review*.[1] The article included many passages from the five volumes of reminiscences that Hobhouse had extracted from journals and memoranda in his possession and had privately published in 1865, four years before his death. Decades later, his daughter, Lady Dorchester, included portions of her father's work, together with hitherto unpublished excerpts from his diaries, in preparing *Recollections of a Long Life* for publication.[2] This edition has illuminated for posterity many obscure parliamentary and ministerial episodes and has provided insights into some of the nineteenth century's leading figures. Napoleon's Hundred Days witnessed in Paris, or events in London society viewed by an inquisitive and cultured man; Radical meetings at Westminster taverns, or weekends at Windsor as Queen Victoria's guest; ministerial deliberations during the crisis over parliamentary reform, or the ill-fated decision of the Melbourne Government to invade Afghanistan; Byron and Lord Holland, Canning and Peel— Hobhouse was able during his long and varied career to observe a great span of history and those who shaped it.

The *Recollections* are an accurate, though by no means a total, reflection of Hobhouse's mind and personality. There are flashes of wit and insight, a redeeming streak of humor, an inclination to be prim and proper, anxieties and fears that often blocked him from action, much social reportage and trivia, some close analysis, and occasional lapses into mawkishness. There is also a tendency to gloss over compromising episodes in his career and a reluctance to disclose his innermost thoughts to the public. Fortunately he also left behind extensive unpublished diaries written with a candor that permits a fuller, more sustained evaluation of the man and his career.

1. "Lord Broughton's *Recollections of a Long Life,*" *Edinburgh Review*, 133 (April, 1871), 287–337.

2. Lady Dorchester, ed., *Recollections of a Long Life, by Lord Broughton (John Cam Hobhouse) with additional extracts from his private diaries.*

Such a study can be fruitful because Hobhouse's mind and motives remain so poorly understood, despite his published memoirs and the many references made by others to one or another aspect of his career. Also, his career and his concerns touched upon so many major issues of his day: radicalism in the London borough of Westminster, the nature and function of His Majesty's Opposition in Parliament, state regulation of factory labor, Greek independence, personal freedoms and minority rights, legislation affecting local government (Hobhouse's Vestry Act), parliamentary reform, and the administration of India during the Melbourne and Russell ministries.

A major portion of this book will be devoted to Hobhouse's association with the Radicals of Westminster from 1818 to 1833. No constituency was known as more radical than this London borough, and those who heard Hobhouse's speeches at the hustings agreed that no politician was more typically radical than he. In 1819, when Hobhouse had lost his first bid to enter Parliament after a virulent contest that had received the entire nation's attention, he told the multitude, "Parliament will never reform itself, but the people will break through their unnatural bondage with as much ease as Samson broke through the green withes with which the Philistines tried to bind him. The bloated carcase of the present corrupted political system is about to burst." [3] From Italy, Lord Byron expressed his dismay that his friend had issued such harsh attacks upon aristocrats—Whigs and Tories alike—and that, worst yet, he was now consorting with raw and threatening Radicals in Westminster's taverns and back-street committee rooms. Reform, Byron thought, was one thing, reformers another! Before the year was out Hobhouse made himself even more conspicuous in politics when he wrote an inflammatory pamphlet that provoked the House of Commons into committing him to Newgate prison on contempt charges. His fortunes then turned dramatically. George III's death in January of 1820, by dissolving Parliament, automatically released him from prison and brought a general election. This time he easily defeated his Whig opponent, George Lamb; most Westminster voters apparently believed that the ill-treatment Hobhouse had suffered was the best guarantee that he would indeed be a tribune of the people.

3. *Morning Chronicle*, May 22, 1819; *The Champion*, May 30, 1819.

Others were far less enthusiastic over Hobhouse's success. One Tory newspaper urged the Commons to disqualify "the convicted libeler" from joining their ranks.[4] A rumor heard in various political circles implicated Hobhouse in the Cato Street Conspiracy—he had allegedly agreed after a meeting with Thistlewood to lead a provisional government after the assassinations. The Duke of Wellington, for one, had no doubt that the interviews had taken place and that Hobhouse would willingly place himself at the head of any revolutionary government.[5] The Whig aristocracy regretted ever having opened their doors to such a notorious demagogue, a friend of Byron besides, while the younger generation of liberal Whigs—Lambton, Russell, and Ellice among them—looked forward to unseating Hobhouse at the earliest opportunity. Henry Crabb Robinson was not at all pleased with the appearance Hobhouse had made at the "ridiculous and disgusting" hustings at Covent Garden, but Sydney Smith conceded that he had "some talent for addressing the mob," [6] and John Galt, the Scottish novelist, at least held out some hope for Hobhouse at the time he and Sir Francis Burdett were returned for Westminster:

Hobhouse speaks more correctly [than Burdett], but he lacks in the conciliatory advantages of personal appearance; and his physiognomy, though indicating considerable strength of mind, is not so prepossessing. He is evidently a man of more education than his friend, that is, of more reading, perhaps also of more various observation, but he has less genius. His tact is coarser, and though he speaks with more vehemence, he seldom touches the sensibilities of his auditors. He may have observed mankind in general more extensively than Sir Francis, but he is far less acquainted with the feelings and associations of the English mind. There is also a wariness about him, which I do not like so well as the imprudent ingenuousness of the baronet. He seems to me to have a cause in hand—Hobhouse *versus* Existing Circumstances—and that he considers the multitude as the jurors on whose decision his advancement in life depends. But in this I may be uncharitable. I should,

4. *Morning Post*, March 26, 1820.
5. Frances Bamford and William Arthur Wellesley, seventh Duke of Wellington, eds., *The Journal of Mrs. Arbuthnot, Vol. I: 1820–1825*, 15.
6. Thomas Sadler, ed., *Diary, Reminiscences and Correspondence of Henry Crabb Robinson*, I, 404; Sydney Smith to Lord Grey, February 19, 1819, in Nowell C. Smith, ed., *The Letters of Sydney Smith*, I, 321.

however, think more highly of his sincerity as a patriot if his stake in the country were greater; and yet I doubt, if his stake were greater, he is that sort of man who would have cultivated popularity in Westminster. He seems to me to have qualified himself for Parliament as others do for the bar, and that he will probably be considered in the House for some time merely as a political adventurer. But if he has the talent and prudence requisite to insure distinction in the line of his profession, the mediocrity of his original condition will reflect honour on his success, should he hereafter acquire influence and consideration as a statesman.[7]

At the time of Galt's description, the radical politician was thirty-four years old, short in height, and stocky in build. He had dark and sharp eyes, full cheeks, a touch of primness about the mouth, and a generous forehead that became ever more prominent as his curly, dark hair receded and greyed in later years. His most noticeable physiological feature was a large, hooked nose, "compared with which that of the Duke of Wellington is the Roman beau-ideal," according to one contemporary. Beau Brummel at Calais kept a pet macaw he named Hobhouse, and he often commented on how the man and his namesake looked so strikingly similar. A close study of his portrait conveys the feeling of a conventional, somewhat anxious man, perhaps less sensitive than solidly intelligent.

Hobhouse's reputation underwent a total transformation through the years, a transformation shown by the comments of political observers and the changing image projected by political cartoonists. George Cruikshank, for example, caricatured him sitting glumly in a Newgate cell with lines from his libelous pamphlet *A Trifling Mistake* placarded on the wall; again in 1820 he presented Hobhouse, "The Radical Quack," administering a big tricolor bolus to an ailing John Bull. Cartoons continued in such a vein for some years: Hobhouse plotting England's ruin with Queen Caroline or, wearing his *bonnet rouge* and dagger, associating with Thelwall, Cobbett, and other prominent Radicals.[8] After a decade, however, many Radi-

7. John Galt, *The Ayrshire Legatees*, 194–95.
8. M. D. George, ed., *Catalogue of Political and Personal Satires preserved in the Department of Prints and Drawings in the British Museum*, X, cartoons 13501, 13714, 14139; XI, cartoons 16318, 16818, 17304, 17325. Joseph Grego, *History of Parliamentary Elections*, 334–42.

cals who supported him in 1820 had concluded that Hobhouse, while not an opponent of reform, was at best lukewarm in his approach. Francis Place, after increasing disagreement, severed all ties and urged the Westminster electorate to reject at the polls one who had so shamelessly betrayed every Radical principle. During the same decade Hobhouse's standing among the Whigs had risen to the point that he entered Lord Grey's Ministry on the eve of parliamentary reform. John Doyle (H. B.) commented on the appointment in a cartoon that depicts Hobhouse turning on the steps of the War Office to give Burdett the castoff cloak of radicalism. Next came a Cabinet appointment from that most eminent and typical Whig patrician, Lord Melbourne. Thus, from the notoriety of a Newgate imprisonment Hobhouse had ascended in less than two decades to high ministerial office as President of the Board of Control for India.

Hobhouse's career baffles current evaluators, just as it did his contemporaries. Some say that during the time he represented Westminster, he was a Benthamite Radical; others, a Whig.[9] He is so identified on the basis of isolated events or his dealings with the leading personalities of his age. Some observed, as did Disraeli, that Hobhouse had risen to high office by sacrificing conscience to ambition. James Grant, however, writing in 1836, thought Hobhouse was "one of the most upright and straightforward men" in the Commons. Throughout the 1820's, Grant asserted, Hobhouse had "never shrunk from an open avowal of his opinions, at a time when the word Reform was considered synonymous with everything that was low, unprincipled, and degraded."[10] However interpreted, Hobhouse's career invites certain questions about the nature of his radicalism during his Westminster years and the extent to which it was a matter of rhetoric or of specific plans for how society

9. Elie Halévy includes Hobhouse among the Philosophical Radicals in *The Growth of Philosophical Radicalism*, 511 ff. He is described as a Benthamite Radical in Edward P. Thompson's *The Making of the English Working Class*, 468–69. Hobhouse is discussed also in S. Maccoby, *English Radicalism, 1786–1832*, and William Harris, *The History of the Radical Party in Parliament*. He is identified as a Whig in G. I. T. Machin, *The Catholic Question in English Politics, 1820–1830*, 40.

10. Disraeli's comments appeared in *The Times*, March 2, 1836, under the pseudonym of Runnymede; James Grant, *Random Recollections of the House of Commons, from the year 1830 to the close of 1835*, 208–9.

should be changed. Did he change his political affiliation because his earlier radical views mellowed with time, as some have assumed, or were Hobhouse's views consistent and eventually fulfilled as reform brought the social and political changes he wished? Perhaps in his own mind differences between Radicals and Whigs were not nearly so great as others thought; hence, he may have tried to bridge the gap between the two groups, essentially because he found points of agreement with both. How successful was he in courting the masses without alienating middle-class and aristocratic support? And what can Hobhouse's career reveal about English radicalism and Whiggism, especially during the 1820's?

It would be well to trace the history of Westminster radicalism in order to understand Hobhouse's constituency and his relationship to it. This London borough, the seat of Court and Parliament, was a center of the resurgent radicalism that accompanied the distress after the Napoleonic wars. Henry Hunt went forth from Westminster to popularize the goal of political reform; there too William Cobbett published his weekly *Political Register* for the working masses; an aged Major Cartwright resided in the borough, as did Jeremy Bentham at Queen Square Place. Francis Place and other members of Westminster's electoral committee had rallied voters behind Sir Francis Burdett and Lord Cochrane, whose return to Parliament in 1807 was an open defiance of traditional political groups. These and other Radical leaders were the inheritors, as well as the creators, of a rich, diverse tradition of protest that provided the referents for dealing with postwar challenges. This tradition was deeply rooted in the past—the constitutional struggles of the seventeenth century, the Wilkes affair, the various parliamentary reform movements of the 1780's, and the working-class agitation that arose during the French Revolution. Observers found Westminster radicalism bewildering in its diversity. Lord Holland, for example, referred to "the faction of Levellers, Jacobins, or radicals" and held various Westminster figures—Hunt, Cobbett, and Cartwright—responsible for postwar tumults.[11] However, Radicals in Westminster and elsewhere had pursued divergent goals and continued to

11. Lord Stavordale, ed., *Further Memoirs of the Whig Party 1807–1821, with some Miscellaneous Reminiscences, by Henry Richard Vassall, Third Lord Holland*, 253.

do so. Some vigorously opposed Hobhouse when he became a candidate for Parliament in 1819.

Westminster Radicals addressed the matter of governmental organization, as well as those of agitation and political theory, during the famous episode of John Wilkes and the Middlesex elections. The Commons tried to dispose of Wilkes by declaring him ineligible to sit in their midst; the smaller Middlesex freeholders and merchants, tradesmen, and shopkeepers, who formed the bulk of his supporters, insisted just as adamantly that Parliament had denied them a fundamental right of choosing their M.P. The controversy aroused the Rockingham Whigs, and other parliamentary opposition groups, to the threat that Crown influence posed against the independence of Parliament. The Rockingham Whigs alleged that George III was intent on reviving absolute power, destroying party opposition, and corrupting Parliament through his resources of patronage. Indeed, those who conspired against an excellent and balanced constitution had already captured the government: At their bidding, the ministry and the Commons had overridden the voters of Middlesex. The Whig reformers intended to settle political issues within the arena of Parliament, but the Middlesex voters set out on a bolder course that challenged some assumptions upon which the eighteenth-century constitution rested. In 1769 some fifty of Wilkes's prominent City supporters, among them John Horne (who later added the surname Tooke), formed the Society of the Supporters of the Bill of Rights. It was their original intent to help pay off Wilkes's debts, but they soon began promoting more ambitious goals outlined in various resolutions for political reform and for exacting pledges from parliamentary candidates. By 1774 both newly elected M.P.'s for Middlesex and three from the City of London had pledged themselves to an eleven-point program prepared by the Society. Henceforth, a band of M.P.'s from the metropolis was committed to such items as annual elections, a "full and equal representation of the people in parliament," redress of grievances before granting supplies, and an inquiry into the expenditures of public money. The program as a whole repudiated the notion that Britons enjoyed a matchless mixed government and a balanced constitution, with adequate weight given to all the important interests within the country. Rather, the program implied that the Crown had encroached upon other branches of government, that Parliament did not sufficiently express urban interests, and hence that virtual representation was a fiction. Wilkes, who was finally permitted to take his seat in Parliament, made some effort on behalf of his followers' program by proposing a parliamentary reform motion in 1776. It was unwelcomed and untimely; the American colonies were in open revolt, and neither Parliament nor the nation was in any mood to grapple with political reform and popular rights.[12]

The Wilkes affair did stimulate a minority to encourage further critical assessment of English politics. James Burgh, a member of the "Honest Whigs," a group that met periodically at Ludgate Hill, drew upon recent events to write his *Political Disquisitions*, which he published from 1771 through 1775. Burgh went significantly further than the Society of Supporters of the Bill of Rights: Its members trusted to a traditional parliamentary expedient of withholding money; he proposed as a lever against Parliament a national association of representatives elected at various regional levels. The impact of Burgh's work was evident in Major Cartwright's pamphlet *Take Your Choice*, published in 1776. Cartwright, who openly sided with the American colonists, reproduced Burgh's plan of association and added a proposal to include all Englishmen in it. He also challenged the social assumptions other reformers had hitherto accepted by proposing literal universal suffrage. Previously, requiring some amount of property, which would ensure the "free agency" of an individual, was an appropriate part of proposals for "universal" or "full and equal" suffrage. Besides granting the vote to every man, Cartwright's Radical program included annual elections, the secret ballot, electoral districts of equal size, and payment for members of the Commons. Cartwright's belief in the myth of Anglo-Saxon democracy enabled him to maintain that his reforms were in no way innovations, but merely the means of restoring ancient English rights. He also derived many of his ideas from successive generations of writers and political philosophers who had transmitted liberal

12. See Lucy S. Sutherland, "The City of London in Eighteenth-Century Politics," in *Essays Presented to Sir Lewis Namier*, ed. by R. Pares and A. J. P. Taylor, 49–74; George Rudé, *Wilkes and Liberty*; and I. R. Christie, *Wilkes, Wyvill and Reform; the Parliamentary reform movement in British politics, 1760–1785.*

thought from the Restoration of Charles II up to his own day. Known as the Commonwealthmen, they had likewise influenced Burgh, the Real Whig group in London, and many Dissenters who had converted to reform.[13] One of them, Dr. John Jebb, took the occasion of a Radical victory in the Middlesex election of 1779 to propose a national organization composed of county delegates that could conceivably supersede Parliament itself. His idea proved timely as Englishmen pondered the example afforded by the Irish Volunteer Movement, and it focused attention upon public economy or upon a ministry too long associated with the American war. This rampant discontent gave radicalism new dimensions as another decade opened.

The lead in organizing massive public support for reform came from Yorkshire, where the Reverend Christopher Wyvill stirred up the freeholders against the Government and encouraged similar associations elsewhere. Economic reform was the immediate object, although Wyvill ultimately sought a parliamentary reform compatible with property representation. Early in 1780 Sir George Savile presented to the Commons the Yorkshire petition denouncing sinecures, pensions, and Crown influence. The Opposition rose to the attack in the months that followed; the House of Commons rang to the eloquence of Edmund Burke, Savile, and Dunning. The cry went up against all forms of corruption and influence: Burke first introduced his measures of economic reform; Savile demanded the publication of pension lists; Dunning in April carried his famous resolution against the growing influence of the Crown. But the Opposition had to await the fall of Lord North's Government two years later before reform could be implemented. Burke's Civil List Act, the disfranchisement of Crown revenue officers, and reforms in financial administration all contributed to the waning of royal power, a fundamental development in English government that many politicians did not immediately comprehend. The very success of Burke's economic reforms and Pitt's subsequent financial measures alleviated the discontent of county reformers, many of whom became indifferent to the need for changing parliamentary representation. Some, like the

---

13. See Caroline Robbins, *The Eighteenth-Century Commonwealthman;* for Cartwright's political career, see Naomi H. Churgin, "Major Cartwright: A Study in Radical Parliamentary Reform, 1774–1824" (Ph.D. dissertation, Columbia University, 1963).

country gentlemen of Yorkshire, were still willing to concede that the electoral system was too narrowly based, but their aristocratic allies of late echoed Lord Rockingham's sentiments that "the country at large does not care for these kinds of objects." [14] Upon the defeat of Pitt's proposals in the 1780's, widespread interest in parliamentary reform ebbed.

Among the counties and boroughs that had supported the Association movement, Westminster demonstrated the most fervor for reform. There, a committee was created early in 1780 to promote the plan of association and to carry on the necessary correspondence. Unlike its counterpart in Yorkshire, the Westminster Committee welcomed into its membership politicians from both Houses of Parliament, and among the one hundred names on the initial list was a sprinkling of Rockingham Whigs who wished to safeguard their interests in all matters. Honorary memberships were also extended to chairmen of committees in other constituencies. The program drawn up at the Association convention in March was a compromise among the Rockingham faction, the county members, and the Radicals on the Westminster Committee inasmuch as parliamentary reform was endorsed, but not to the extent the Radicals wanted. They favored an extension of the franchise and a redistribution of parliamentary seats, whereas the propertied majority of Associationists endorsed annual elections and the addition of one hundred county members to the Commons. The national convention over, a subcommittee of the Westminster group—Cartwright, Jebb, and Thomas Brand Hollis—framed a program almost identical to that described in Cartwright's *Take Your Choice*. Once more England was offered a Radical program for taking government away from a minority of landed and mercantile people and placing it in the hands of a majority of its citizens.

As the man responsible for appointing the subcommittee, Charles James Fox appeared to cast his lot decisively with the Radical camp. During the several months preceding the national convention he had advocated a vigorous and carefully planned public agitation to remedy the ills within the nation.

14. Quoted in Philip A. Brown, *The French Revolution in English History*, 15; see also Eugene Black, *The Association, British Extraparliamentary Political Organization, 1769–1793*, and Carl B. Cone, *The English Jacobins: Reformers in Late Eighteenth Century England*.

One address in February mentioned the proposition, which had been recently introduced in a pamphlet by Jebb, that the people must employ sanctions if Parliament continued to ignore their wishes. There was an infectious excitement as Westminster was swayed by Fox's oratory and he was carried away by the popular response. Respectability and property were wedded to radicalism as "The Man of the People" became Westminster's M.P. after the 1780 election. Fox was an extremely complex person in whom the impulsive, generous man of feeling and the ambitious schemer were combined. He saw how popular forces could be exploited against Lord North's Ministry, and he reaped the rewards of office when that government did fall. In 1783, however, he formed the "infamous coalition" with North, a union of convenience that shocked the Radicals and yet failed to win over the Crown. The Government's downfall in 1783 brought on the general election the following year in which Fox contested Westminster against Admiral Hood and Sir Cecil Wray, who had the Crown's support. It was one of the most celebrated and violent of eighteenth-century elections, with the Duchess of Devonshire's intercessions for Fox and pitched battles that raged throughout the borough until the polls finally closed after some forty-five days, with Fox victorious. In 1790 Fox and Hood agreed to avoid another expensive contest by dividing Westminster's seats, but they were forced into a contest nevertheless as Horne Tooke came forward himself and obtained 1,679 votes as an independent candidate. Tooke, who had joined Cartwright and Jebb in founding the Society for Constitutional Information, the main purpose of which was to publish tracts on the traditions and doctrines of liberty, held that Fox's blatant opportunism and ministerial intervention had undermined freedom in Westminster itself. "The Westminster public is both willing and able to teach the government," Tooke declared, "that it has other and more important duties to perform besides the levying of taxes, the creation of Peerages, compromising of counties, and arrangement of boroughs." [15]

The French Revolution and its impact in England cast Tooke and Fox in unexpected and unwelcomed roles—one a near

---

15. Francis Place Papers, Additional Manuscripts 27849, f. 130–31, British Museum. (Subsequent references to Additional Manuscripts in the British Museum are cited as Add. MSS.)

martyr to liberty, and the other the leader of a hopelessly out-numbered opposition group in Parliament. Radicals exulted in this "dawn of liberty" while others watched events in France at first with reservations, then with suspicions, and finally with frantic hostility. Reform societies flourished before public opinion swung round to reaction. At Tavistock Street, Covent Garden, a reinvigorated Society for Constitutional Information commended parliamentary reform as an activity within the best tradition of English liberty; youthful aristocrats at the Society of the Friends of the People endeavored to keep agitation within safe limits by moderate proposals to replace venal borough nominees with more county members; and at the Bell Tavern off the Strand, Thomas Hardy and his friends founded the Corresponding Society, chapters of which rapidly proliferated throughout the country. The Corresponding Society alone was truly a working-class organization with democratic goals. Its shoemakers and shopkeepers, its journeymen and tailors, were nurtured on the writings of Paine; they resented aristocratic patrons as much as they did gentleman intellectuals dispensing doctrines of liberty from a safe distance. Faith in the common man gave them high hopes for the future. Through an expanded franchise and annual parliaments, they believed, government by minorities of powerful interests would cease, and working men would get their due. But reaction, not reform, marked the remaining years of the century. Burke's and the Duke of Portland's desertion to Pitt was a severe blow to the Friends of the People and to Fox, who wished them well. Hardy, Tooke, and other Radical leaders barely escaped with their necks in the famous treason trials. Parliament rejected Grey's moderate reform proposals, and eventually the corresponding societies were suppressed. A patriotic England, geared for war, had little sympathy for those who criticized its institutions.

Tooke lived to see Westminster return to Parliament two avowed Radicals, Sir Francis Burdett and Lord Cochrane, in the general elections of 1807. It was a stunning triumph for reformers who had been designated as Jacobins and revolutionaries for so long—Radicalism had captured the seat of Parliament itself. The victory of 1807 was entirely the work of a new Westminster Committee, many of whose members had participated in Radical politics of the 1790's. "We were laughed at for our folly, and condemned for our impudence," Francis

Place recalled; however, the boldness and courage of the committeemen were matched by their electoral skills. They provided the nation with a striking example of voters using modern election techniques to withstand every ministerial resource employed against them. A detailed canvass of Westminster was prepared in advance; handbills and placards articulated commonly felt grievances; voters were asked to contribute their pennies and shillings, for the cause of reform depended on the peoples' contributions, as well as on their exertions.

Tooke's platforms of 1792 and 1796 became the rallying point of the committee.[16] It denounced the restrictions placed upon political liberties and supported parliamentary reform. It condemned Whigs and Tories alike as members of "the system": One party constituted the "Ins" and enjoyed the political spoils; the other self-seeking "Outs" tried to oust them, but not in ways threatening an arrangement that kept power in the hands of an oligarchy. Clearly, the committeemen said, the interests of Westminster's citizens were disregarded in a structure of politics that accommodated only landlords, borough patrons, and their servile appointees. Whigs and Tories tried to bribe or coerce voters; they made many promises and always broke them. The committeemen commended Westminster's voters for rising up and severing all ties with both parties. Radical Westminster was now in the forefront of a reform movement that would transform England by restoring "purity of elections" and a "full, free and equal share" in electing parliamentary representatives.[17]

By earliest nineteenth-century standards, when any urban center of over 50,000 constituted a large city, Westminster was a metropolis in itself, with over 165,000 people residing in its nine parishes.[18] The population would reach 202,080 by 1831. Saint Paul, Covent Garden, and Saint Clement Danes were de-

16. Tooke had again become an independent candidate for Westminster in 1796, when he received 2,819 votes. See *An Exposition of Circumstances which gave rise to the election of Sir Francis Burdett, Bart. . . . and of the Principles which governed the Committee who conducted that election;* Thompson, *Making of the English Working Class,* chap. XIII.

17. *Exposition of Circumstances,* 3, 4.

18. *Comparative Account of the Population of Great Britain in the Years 1801, 1811, 1821, 1831, Parliamentary Accounts and Papers,* 1831 (348), XVIII. Westminster's nine parishes were: St. Anne, Soho; St. Clement Danes; St. James; St. Margaret; St. John; St. Martin-in-the-Fields; St. Mary-le-Strand; St. Paul, Covent Garden; and St. George, Hanover Square.

clining in wealth as those who could afford to moved west to the fashionable and growing parishes of Saint James or Saint George, Hanover Square. There, the small tradesmen and artisans were outnumbered by wealthier merchants and tradesmen, aristocrats and politicians, Court and Government officials, landowners and members of various professions. Radicalism was unwelcomed where the wealthy resided comfortably in elegant Georgian houses near spacious squares. Populous Saint George parish voted conservative by a wide margin, Saint James and Saint Margaret by a slightly smaller one, and a Radical candidate had to offset the adverse vote by a strong showing in the other parishes. Hobhouse, like Burdett before him, could also appeal to moderate voters everywhere, but so doing incurred the risk of alienating the extremists, many of whom lived east of Saint Martin's Lane and in Saint Anne.

Early nineteenth-century Westminster was a scot-and-lot constituency where some twelve thousand householders who paid the local rates were eligible to vote. Elections repeatedly gave rise to disputes about exactly what payments of rates involved. Some polling officials held a voter liable for payments up to a certain date, while others disqualified an elector at the polls for failing to bring his payments up to date. Francis Place described Westminster as a "court borough" even after the 1807 Radical victory because many aristocrats and government employees "all possessed considerable influence, which, whenever it became necessary, was exerted without any attempt to disguise it." [19] Place recalled earlier degrading spectacles like the screaming mob kicking and fighting its way to a table where servants of the Duke of Northumberland distributed beer and food on election day. Other tactics were designed to intimidate voters. Place alleged that many tradesmen ran considerable risk to their businesses by violating the dictates of wealthy patrons at the polls. Radicals charged that voters were physically assaulted by hired gangs of Whig or Tory "bludgeonmen." Conservatives answered Place by claiming that the sober, self-respecting tradesman of the Westminster Committee's image was not above hiring ruffians to attack gentlemen and destroy property. Such violence remained a feature of Westminster elections involving Hobhouse.

19. Francis Place Papers, Add. MSS 27849, f. 89.

"Westminster's pride and England's glory" was Sir Francis Burdett, a disciple of his late Wimbleton neighbor Horne Tooke, whose bust stood prominently in Burdett's London home. This "plain, unaffected, unsophisticated English gentleman," as William Hazlitt described him, was by birth a member of an old and wealthy landed family, and he was by marriage connected with the banking family of Coutts.[20] From the time he entered Parliament, Burdett enhanced his popularity among his constituents by denigrating the war against France as the Government's pretext for stifling basic freedoms at home, by constantly assailing government expenditures and the crushing burden of taxes, and by urging abolition of the Civil List. One of the most theatrical episodes in Westminster politics occured in 1810 when officers, sent to arrest Burdett for a breach of parliamentary privilege, burst into his house where he stood reading Magna Charta to his son. Like Tooke, he harkened back to the days of Magna Charta and "the ancient constitution," to an idealized past free from Whigs and Tories who had usurped power and destroyed the freedom Englishmen once enjoyed. "His love of liberty is pure, as it is steady," Hazlitt wrote, "his humanity is unconstrained and free." Other Radicals were less favorable. Samuel Bamford, for one, felt he submitted to, rather than sought, conversation with members of the working class.[21]

Burdett's views on reform did not suit various Westminster Radicals. He had joined Thomas Northmore in founding the Hampden Club, which in 1813 came to support Burdett's program of household suffrage. Three years later Burdett categorically opposed Henry Hunt's attempts to insert universal suffrage in the club's reform program. Hunt and Cobbett never forgave Burdett for refusing to participate in the Spa Fields meeting of 1816 and for not seconding a motion opposing the suspension of habeas corpus. Burdett thought the motion was futile. He advocated only household suffrage in a parliamentary speech of 1817, whereupon Cobbett began vilifying "Old Glory" Burdett for having abandoned the Radical cause. Burdett did use Bentham's more radical *Resolutions on Parliamentary Reform* as the basis for a reform motion he introduced in June,

20. William Hazlitt, "The Spirit of the Age" in *Complete Works of William Hazlitt*, ed. by P. P. Howe, XI, 140–41; see also M. W. Patterson, *Sir Francis Burdett and his Times (1770–1844)*.
21. Samuel Bamford, *Passages in the Life of a Radical*, I, 21.

1818, knowing full well, he told Bentham, it would be defeated because "of the prejudices to be surmounted." [22] Still, he hoped the extremist proposals—annual parliaments, universal suffrage, the ballot—would prod Parliament into accepting moderate reforms. Burdett may also have wished to repair his sagging reputation as the parliamentary Radical leader, especially among the Westminster extremists.

Many Westminster Radicals involved in the issue of parliamentary reform were similarly concerned with making vestry government in the parish more representative. The controversy over local government became intense during the 1820's, at which point Hobhouse intervened by securing a parliamentary committee of inquiry into the state of parish government throughout Britain. Hobhouse's Vestry Act of 1831 followed, with many Radical innovations accepted by the House of Lords even though it had rejected parliamentary reform only days before. Reformers from every Westminster parish paid tribute to Hobhouse for having crowned with success their efforts of over a decade.

The ecclesiastical parishes formed one unit of local government throughout Britain. Numbering over ten thousand in England and Wales, they presented every variety of size and population, from little hamlets tucked away in the countryside to populous urban areas like London's Saint Marylebone or Saint Pancras. The Tudor Government had provided for each parish a legal framework for ensuring the maintenance of local order and institutions and had made service to the community obligatory, but the Royal Council in London was unwilling to entrust responsibility to the parishioners themselves. They could meet in vestry, perhaps to elect a churchwarden or to decide upon a church rate; on all other matters, however, they were to obey appointed parish officials, such as the overseer of the poor, the constable, and the surveyor of the highways. Parishioners could be indicted and brought to trial before local magistrates, who also saw to it that the parish responsibilities of repairing the roads and caring for the destitute were fulfilled. Thus, local

22. Halévy, *Growth of Philosophical Radicalism*, 261–63. The perceptive Sir Denis Le Marchant, Brougham's secretary, observed that Burdett "reverenced the Monarchy, maintaining that even the Monarchy was the natural protector of the lower class against the higher," in Sir Denis Le Marchant, *Memoir of John Charles Viscount Althorp, Third Earl Spencer*, 120–21; Cobbett quoted in *Political Register*, September 13, 1817.

government rested in the hands of unsalaried parish officials who were in turn responsible to local magistrates.

Changing circumstances threw this arrangement completely out of gear. One factor was the removal of an over-all supervisory body fulfilled by the Royal Council in London. Officials were left to their own devices, and Parliament rarely intervened. Another problem arose with the growth of industrial towns and of London itself, where hundreds of parishes had to work with obsolete laws devised centuries earlier for small communities of a few dozen families. The normal recourse was for the principal inhabitants of a community, aided by their M.P., to press for a local act granting additional powers to the vestry.[23]

Vestry government in some large urban communities had assumed a wide variety of powers by the early nineteenth century. It levied rates for maintaining the church, for administering poor relief, and for various municipal services, such as disposing of sewage, paving, lighting, and policing. Through innumerable laws prohibiting public nuisances the vestry could regulate traffic, abate street noises, and control public houses. The London vestry of Saint Marylebone controlled weights and measures, and it had compelled the purchase of property in the public interest, mainly for enlarging the more heavily traveled parish streets.[24] The municipal services and facilities so urgently needed in rapidly growing communities were elaborate and expensive, and required a staff of salaried officials to perform onerous tasks involving appointments, inspections, planning, supervising, and complex bookkeeping. All too often misuse of parochial authority entailed waste, extravagance, and corruption. The London parish of Bethnal Green was for many years controlled by a political machine headed by Joseph Merceron, a magistrate who dispensed favors to a coterie of supporters. Liverpool provided one example of an efficient and democratic local government evolving with the growth of the city. There, vestry meetings were conducted according to rules of procedure that worked to everyone's satisfaction.

23. See Sidney Webb and Beatrice Webb, *English Local Government from the Revolution of 1688 to the Municipal Corporation Act*, Vol. I, *The Parish and the County;* B. Keith-Lucas, *The English Local Government Franchise.*

24. See F. H. W. Sheppard, *Local Government in Saint Marylebone, 1688–1835.*

Liverpool had vestry meetings that were open to all rate-payers, but such meetings elsewhere often occasioned turbulent disputes among political and religious antagonists who took sides for the perennial vestry brawl. "Here is a ministry, and here is an opposition," Henry Fielding wrote in describing the vestry meetings he knew. "Here are plots and circumventions, parties, and factions, equal to those which are found in courts." [25] There was little change a century later, or so one writer for *The Westminster Review* concluded, after noting how "the affairs of the parish necessarily fall into the hands of the jobbers." Confusion and discord began when "the meeting called to pass a motion for a rate is adjourned; another is called, and a thousand persons assemble to rave, storm, wrangle, fight, and perhaps, if they get through no such business, vote certain strong resolutions against the Churchwardens and Overseers." [26]

Such meetings, where antagonists often came to blows, were at times owing to local political tensions, but more frequently, they were the result of differences between opponents and supporters of the church rate and the ever-rising rate for poor relief. The national expenditure for poor relief had twice doubled between the years 1785 and 1818, and the landowning classes bore most of the expenses. Parochial democracy enabled the poorer citizens, who contributed little or nothing to the rates, to exercise a decisive voice in the operation of the Poor Laws. The remedy most often prescribed was to encourage a policy of economy and restraint in the parish by enabling wealthier residents to manage vestry affairs. Such was the intent of Sturges Bourne's Vestry Act of 1818, which applied to all parishes not controlled by private Acts of Parliament. The measure enabled wealthier parishioners to have as many as six votes. The following year Bourne tried to bring order to chaotic open vestry meetings by allowing parishioners to appoint annually a committee to control the application of the Poor Law. An itemized agenda for all parish meetings was made mandatory, and any increase in the poor rate beyond one shilling in the pound was to be submitted to a referendum of property owners. Within a decade, 2,736 vestries in England and Wales had adopted the measure.

25. Henry Fielding, *Tom Jones, a Foundling*, The British Novelists (London, 1810), XIX, 174.

26. "Local Government in the Metropolis: a sketch of Municipal Institutions of London," *The Westminster Review*, 25 (April, 1836), 96.

But Sturge Bourne's Acts did not apply to the many parishes governed by select, or close, vestries established by Parliament. Westminster had several: Saint Giles, Saint John, Saint Anne, Saint James, and Saint George, Hanover Square. Select vestries also emerged through other ways in Westminster. Saint Martin's-in-the-Fields had evolved by immemorial custom, and other vestries became select through "Bishop's faculty"—under terms made by the bishop of the diocese when he transferred land or authority to the parish. There were about sixty close or select vestries throughout the London area by 1800. *The Times* described such a vestry as "a close corporation, self-elected so often as vacancies occur, responsible to no power but itself, and possessing what the House of Commons does not, unbounded control over the fortunes of the public." The editorial added, "It is the most terrible prerogative committed to the most unassailable agents; a rotten borough erected in the heart of each parish, exercising a sway at once unbounded and irresponsible." [27]

Reformers fully agreed, especially after exposés of scandals in the Westminster parishes of Saint Margaret and Saint John and allegations of abuse in Saint Marylebone, Saint Pancras, and Bethnal Green. Quite typical were the practices of a select vestry governing Saint Paul, Covent Garden, which had had this form of government for over a century without any specific legal authority. On August 1, 1826, the vestrymen held a dinner on the occasion of a visit to the pauper children at suburban Norwood. The total cost of the dinner came to £34.12.6. The chief item of expense was not the £9.9 for the dinner alone, but the cost of wines and liquors consumed by the eighteen vestrymen. The four bottles of champagne cost £2.8; twelve bottles of port added another £3.12 to the bill; rose water, sauterne, bottles of bucellas, and soda water accounted for £6. The vestry's mode of travel befitted its feasting, for included in the voucher was the sum of £8.11.6 for coach hire and turnpike tolls. [28] James Corder was the vigilant parishioner who procured the receipts for what he called the rose-water repast. He also brought legal action against the vestry in the Court of King's Bench, but on the eve of the trial the vestrymen consented to a verdict against themselves and agreed to open all future meetings to the public. Corder and other reformers eventually obtained a local Act of

27. *The Times*, March 20, 1828.
28. *The Examiner*, March 16, 1828.

Parliament empowering ratepayers of £20 and over to elect a standing committee in which all parochial authority was vested. The parishioners of Saint Paul were fortunate in that the parliamentary act establishing their parish during the seventeenth century made no mention of a select vestry system, but those select vestries whose claim rested upon immemorial custom, upon "Bishop's faculty" or formal appointment, or upon a local act were more difficult to change. More often than not, efforts to open these vestries failed in the law courts or in Parliament. For instance the select vestry of Saint James parish, established by Parliament in 1685, was the center of a reform movement in 1828 and 1829. Even after a parliamentary committee discovered a startling imbalance of £15,000, Parliament voted to postpone action on a bill to create an open vestry, one that would be elected by those taxpayers assessed for at least £50 and that would be required to have its accounts open to public inspection. William Beckett, who had led the reform movement in the parish, saw Hobhouse about introducing legislation in Parliament. Corder, Robert Fenn of Saint Martin's, and several members of the Westminster Committee did likewise. A drastic overhaul of local government could be delayed no longer.

Many reformers in Westminster and elsewhere maintained that reform of the vestries and other institutions could not be implemented under the party system of government. The Westminster Committee had been created in protest against Whig and Tory party men, and opposition to party remained an article of their Radical creed. Then as now, a debate took place about the nature and functions of political parties in Britain. Did the party system help or hinder constructive legislation? Did it exist, or was it in the process either of growth or decay? Canning's coalition government, the breakup of parties in the years following his death, and the inability of the Whigs to provide a strong leader in either parliamentary chamber all suggested the extremely loose and weak nature of the party system during the 1820's.[29] This situation is reflected in Sir Lewis Namier's assertion that the modern party system did not fully emerge until after the Reform Bill of 1867; "intermediary forms" of party

29. Donald Read, *Peterloo: The "Massacre" and Its Background*, 198; Arthur Aspinall, *Lord Brougham and the Whig Party*, 100; Robert T. McKenzie, *British Political Parties*, 1. See also Austin Mitchell, *The Whigs in Opposition, 1815–1830;* Donald Southgate, *The Passing of the Whigs, 1832–1886;* F. O'Gorman, *The Whig Party and the French Revolution, 1789–1795.*

that existed during the early nineteenth century corresponded to the "mixed government" of the time.[30] George IV retained certain executive powers, however circumscribed they were by parliamentary forces and by the primacy of Downing Street in decision making. The Crown's persistent role in politics continued, Namier suggested, because all elements comprising an alternate system of constitutional monarchy had not yet replaced eighteenth-century royal government, in which the Crown's influence harmonized relations between the executive and legislative branches of the government. Namier listed among the essential elements of constitutional monarchy a sovereign placed above party and politics; a Prime Minister and Government received, rather than designated, by the Crown; and an unpolitical civil service unaffected by changes in government.

Extensive discussions concerning the relative merits and defects of a party system posed a fundamental constitutional issue for politicians under a "mixed form of government." There was a basic conflict between the royal prerogative and a party system in which politicians contended for office, thereby depriving the King of a right to choose his ministers. There was no consistent defense of party within the framework of the mixed constitution. The exponents of the party system asserted, as had Edmund Burke, that it served the entire community and acted in the Crown's best interest, but Burke implied a diminution of royal power in his *Thoughts on the Cause of the Present Discontents* (1770). In it, he interpreted the royal prerogative as the instrument for effecting popular government: the King must defer to party leaders attuned to national sentiments and needs. Thus, party served as a constitutional balancing force. However, those who thought party men acted at variance with broader national interests championed the royal prerogative. Hobhouse, for instance, who opposed the party system in 1819, alerted the Westminster electorate to the usurpations of party retainers, who had "appropriated to themselves all the honours of the Crown and all the powers of the people—have robbed the one of its just prerogatives, and the other of their undoubted rights." [31]

Westminster, with its sizable electorate and sophisticated

30. Sir Lewis Namier, "Monarchy and the Party System," The Romanes Lecture Delivered in the Sheldonian Theatre, May 15, 1952.
31. Westminster Committee appointed to manage the Election of Mr. Hobhouse, *An Authentic Narrative of the Events of the Westminster Election which commenced on Saturday, February 13 and closed on Wednesday, March 3, 1819*, 173.

political techniques and organizations, did not typify the nation as a whole, where voters numbered under half a million and most constituencies remained uncontested at election time. Electoral arrangements normally retained a casual and informal air among a closely knit society of influential families and friends. There were regional meetings, such as the annual Fox Club dinner, to cement local ties. In lieu of a formal political apparatus, traditional ties among landlord and tenants, manufacturer and worker, prevailed in many localities. Yet on occasion, public support for party principles and programs was enlisted through more organized, formal channels. Such was true among the opposition Whigs during the 1780's, or to a lesser extent after Peterloo and during Queen Caroline's divorce trial, when party leaders organized addresses to the Crown and parliamentary petitions. Party propaganda was disseminated through the *Morning Chronicle* in London, various local newspapers, and nationally through the *Edinburgh Review*.

Whig parliamentarians of the 1820's had recourse to various forms of a modern party apparatus created by their forebears during the late eighteenth century. A central party fund no longer existed, although on occasion Whigs subscribed to an electoral fund for special purposes. Thus Whigs who were aroused by attacks from Radicals during the 1819 Westminster contest contributed on behalf of Hobhouse's opponent out of a sense of obligation to the party. The Whigs proved just as adept as their adversaries in forming an electoral committee and canvassing the Westminster voters. Various functions, such as circulating information and providing seats for deserving party members, were more informally arranged than they had been when Whigs had William Adam serving as a central party manager.[32] At the same time, the activities of the party Whip had increased in scope. During the 1820's Lord Duncannon's organizational skills were deployed in planning party strategy, mustering strength for parliamentary divisions, and giving lists of opposition voters on divisions to various newspapers.

It can be suggested that the "mixed government" of George IV's reign had taken many strides toward constitutional monarchy. It can also be urged that emphasis be placed on positive

32. See Donald E. Ginter, ed., *Whig Organization in the General Election of 1790; Selections from the Blair Adam Papers.* The introduction is most thoughtful in its discussion of party.

strengths, instead of apparant weaknesses, within the "intermediary forms" of party politics then existing. Namier himself did not equate a "two-party system" with a "modern" party system,[33] and Austin Mitchell, who finds qualifications of "modernity" irrelevant in appraising the impact of party upon politicians of the early nineteenth century, accounts for such factors as factions and neutral groups, the independent M.P., and the existence of nonparty divisions throughout the 1820's. Ultimately, there was a dichotomy between Ministerialists and Opposition on a wide range of issues; it was a fact of political life Hobhouse noted on several occasions in Parliament.

Hobhouse could not ignore party once he entered politics. He was in a dilemma between adhering to the Radical stand against parties, but thereby becoming an almost solitary voice in Parliament, and cooperating with liberal Whig party men, but thereby jeopardizing his relations with the Westminster Radicals. Although he proclaimed himself an independent, eventually he had to join one side or another—Tory Ministerialists or Whig Opposition—in Parliament. He did, and in the process he came to appreciate more fully the role of party and party opposition within the constitutional framework.

Hobhouse worked not only for political reform but also for various social reforms while representing Westminster. He donated generously to various charities, supported institutions of learning, and took an interest in law reform, as had his Westminster predecessor, Sir Samuel Romilly. Throughout the 1820's public-spirited men with disparate ideologies and backgrounds were united to achieve specific improvements. John Stuart Mill recalled in his *Autobiography* that the decade was one "of rapidly rising liberalism," when people who had confidence in man's powers of self-government and self-control sought common goals. They wished to promote tolerance, free discussion, and education; they envisioned humanity's general progress through the growth of wealth and production, science and reason. Out of a humanitarian spirit bred in the eighteenth century came the impulse to combat human suffering in the nineteenth, and toward this end Evangelicals, Utilitarians, and Liberals were all committed. With prison reform, the creation of philanthropic institutions, and the abolition of the slave trade

33. Namier, "Monarchy and the Party System"; see also Mitchell, *Whigs in Opposition*, chaps. I, II, XI.

already implemented, reformers shared hopes for still more improvements—and soon.

Much work remained to be done. A harsh criminal code meted out capital punishment for approximately two hundred offenses, but it was haphazardly and ineffectually applied. Conflicting statutes perplexed judges; jurors proved reluctant to return a guilty verdict; an efficient police force was needed. Civil law was in an equally lamentable state. Many suitors abandoned their cases rather than submit to the costly and interminable proceedings Dickens described in *Bleak House*. Hobhouse paid special attention to the laws on libel, which so affected publishers and booksellers in Westminster, especially in the early 1820's. And before the decade ended he was the leading parliamentary spokesman for state intervention in the management of factory labor.

Undoubtedly the most puzzling episode in Hobhouse's career was his resignations in 1833, by which he abruptly gave up his Westminster seat and his post as Irish Secretary. He disappeared from the front rank of rising statesmen, although he resumed public life and held high office. For the next two decades he encountered India as President of the Board of Control during the Melbourne and Russell ministries. During these years, which preceded the Great Mutiny, he participated in important policy decisions that affected educational, legal, and social reforms; imperial expansion; the ill-fated Afghan expedition; and the role of the Mogul Dynasty. His Indian career was bound up with some of the most eminent names in imperial history: Macaulay and Palmerston, Auckland and Dalhousie.

CHAPTER I

PROFILE OF A POLITICIAN

John Cam Hobhouse evoked diverse responses from many people. Byron immortalized his friend so "true in counsel and trusty in peril" by dedicating Canto IV of *Childe Harold's Pilgrimage* to him. Lord Althorp and Sir Francis Burdett esteemed him highly. Lord Melbourne admired his learning, and Queen Victoria found him charming company. But Lord Hardinge thought he was vulgar, Francis Place doubted his sincerity, and William Cobbett called him a Sancho Panza to his colleague Burdett. Lord Duncannon felt Hobhouse lacked courage, although he was a good, honest man. Some people found him warm and open-minded, generous and kindly almost to a fault; others concluded he was callous and dogmatic. He struck many acquaintances as a man of considerable humor and force; others thought him too strait-laced, too prone to moralizing, and too downright disagreeable. Hobhouse in fact displayed all of these qualities in various situations: He was a dandy in Regency England, the fiery Radical hero of Westminster, the John Bull incarnate in early Victorian times.

A number of close friendships Hobhouse maintained throughout his life provide insights about himself. Then as now, his name remained linked first and foremost to Lord Byron's, so that upon his death in 1869 *The Times* recalled when "60 years ago, there were among the students of Trinity College, Cambridge, 2 young men of good birth and more than average talents; fast and firm friends, and bound together by the tie of more than 'advanced' Liberal opinions. George Gordon Byron and John Cam Hobhouse; the one already a peer of the realm, the other a wealthy country gentleman's eldest son." [1] They were contrasting personalities in many respects. Hobhouse, undoubtedly more sober and less daring but possessed with sound judgment and much common sense, provided a stabilizing force for his brilliant and erratic friend. Yet the enthusiast lurked behind Hob-

1. *The Times*, June 4, 1869.

house's stiff armor of reserve. He loved hunting and shooting, books, good food, and erudite conversation. His taste for writing verse first drew him to Byron; they wished to enjoy life and the art of living; they shared a sense of hero worship for Napoleon, the towering figure of their early lives. Hobhouse admired Byron most of all for his spirit: "He gallantly defied each petty act, each paltry aim," he recalled in 1825, "I should have been very fond of him had he been a much less personage than he turned out to be." [2] But Hobhouse was never fully aware of the complex motives behind Byron's wayward behavior. Most often he felt an affectionate indulgence for a good and charming fellow.

Occasionally Hobhouse discussed Byron's measure of human weakness: While they were at college, he observed that Byron gambled too much and urged him to be "more earnest in abstaining from it"; years later he found earlier cantos of *Childe Harold* too full of "morbid sentiments"; and in 1819 he tried to persuade Byron to delete some stanzas from *Don Juan* because "the licentiousness, and in some cases downright indecency of many stanzas and of the whole turn of the poem, from the flings at religion, and from the slashing right and left at other worthy writers of the day is unworthy of you." [3] The poem was too sensual—"a whole stanza on pox"!—and he advised the "*total suppression* of *Don Juan*." He was not preaching to Byron about the deeds themselves, he said, "but merely of the inexpediency" of writing about them: "Our English world will not stand that." *Cain* was a poem even more "foolish" for assaulting the delicate area of religion. Hobhouse counseled, never censured, yet his well-intentioned advice to Byron too often had a patronizing tone that revealed a more self-sufficient, conventional person using his own standards to judge another who did not accept them.

Hobhouse was inclined to take himself too seriously. Byron recalled how the high-spirited Charles Skinner Matthews, another close friend at Cambridge, once affronted Hobhouse at a

2. Hobhouse to Burdett, January 20, 1825, Sir Francis Burdett, Correspondence, f. 29.

3. Hobhouse to Byron, January 5, 1819, John Cam Hobhouse, Correspondence, John Murray Collection; John Cam Hobhouse, Proofs of Letters from John Cam Hobhouse to Lord Byron, set up in type in connection with an edition of Byron's correspondence projected by Charlotte Carleton, Baroness Dorchester.

party at Newstead Abbey by threatening to throw him out the window. Hobhouse came up to Byron and announced he would leave the next morning, and, Byron wrote to John Murray, "He did. It was in vain that I represented to him that the window was not high, and that the turf under it was particularly soft. Away he went." [4] Years later Hobhouse felt gravely offended because Byron had a laugh at his expense with a poem lampooning his imprisonment in Newgate. Even worse, various versions went the rounds of London society, and one appeared in the *Morning Post*.[5]

Possessive, as well as chivalrous, qualities in Hobhouse's friendship for Byron made him protective about Byron's honor and reputation in life and fiercely loyal to Byron's memory afterwards. He foresaw no good in Byron's marriage and observed after the surprisingly slow journey to the Milbankes' that "never was lover less in haste." [6] As best man, he sought in vain for excuses to explain their late arrival. A year later he was a party to all separation proceedings; for a moment even he was shocked by rumors of his friend's conduct and found it "difficult to account for his wishing to deceive me," but that same day, in 1816, he reported getting Byron "to admit much of what I had heard." [7] Nevertheless, he resolved to stand by Byron after London society ostracized him, and in contrast to private comments, his published memoirs never even hinted that Byron was at fault. He resolutely insisted as the years passed that nothing prevented Byron from returning to England. As one of his executors, he helped arrange for the funeral at Hucknall Torkard, where Byron "was buried like a nobleman, since we could not bury him as a poet." Hobhouse next witnessed with approval the burning of Byron's memoirs at Murray's office, and throughout the years

4. Byron to Murray, September 19, 1820, in George Gordon Byron, sixth Baron Byron, *The Works of Lord Byron; A New, Revised and Enlarged Edition, with Illustrations: Letters and Journals*, ed. by R. E. Prothero, V, 123–24.

5. Byron, *Works: Letters and Journals*, IV, 423. The poem was sent to John Murray and appeared in the *Morning Post* on April 15, 1820; ibid., Appendix XI.

6. Hobhouse, diary, December 26, 1814, John Cam Hobhouse, Lord Broughton, Papers, Add. MSS 47232, f. 48.

7. Hobhouse, diary, February 12, 1816, Berg Collection. On the same day Hobhouse reported having learned "what I fear is the real truth that Byron has been guilty of very great tyranny, menaces, furies, neglects, & even real injuries such as telling his wife he was *living* with another woman & actually *in fact* turns her out of the house."

he never could approve of others writing about Byron for a curious public.

If at times Hobhouse complained about "the thousand and one squabbles" that Byron's affairs heaped upon himself, he yet tried to settle differences as well as the individuals involved permitted. He continually tried to win for Byron a place in the Poet's Corner, and at one point stood up in the House of Lords to protest the refusal by Church authorities. He wrote *Remarks on the Exclusion of Lord Byron's Monument from Westminster Abbey* in 1844 to reprove those who had inferred from Byron's works that he was an atheist, the basis upon which a monument in the Abbey was denied. Hobhouse's retrospective evaluation of Byron made him a man any Victorian could admire, as his conclusion suggests:

In mixed society Lord Byron was not talkative, neither did he attempt to surprise by pointed or by humerous remarks; but in all companies he held his own, and that, too, without unbecoming rivalry with his seniors in age and reputation, and without any offensive condescension towards his inferior associates. In more familiar intercourse, he was a gay companion and a free, but he never transgressed the bonds of good breeding, even for a moment. Indeed he was, in the best sense of the word, a gentleman.[8]

The unquestioned loyalty Hobhouse displayed toward Byron was extended to other friends who later entered his life. At the end of his political career he stood by Lord Palmerston when both the Court and the Cabinet were resolved to remove him from office. He was a kind person. Many political exiles from the Continent received his financial aid to tie them over; his brothers and sisters leaned upon his support at some troubled points in their lives; he was a solicitous friend for a widowed Lady Holland long after the brilliance of Holland House had faded; and Hobhouse consoled a bereaved Thomas Love Peacock upon the death of his only surviving daughter.

He enjoyed the extrovert—Byron, Sir Francis Burdett and Lord Durham while representing Westminster, and Brougham and Palmerston later. Sydney Smith was a great favorite, even if his jokes "were not exactly suited to his cloth." Finally, there

---

8. John Cam Hobhouse, *Remarks on the Exclusion of Lord Byron's Monument from Westminster Abbey*, 48.

was his ministerial colleague Macaulay, who had censured the British public for driving Byron into exile through "one of its periodic fits of morality." Hobhouse usually found it impossible to get a word in edgewise when Macaulay conversed, but he appreciated his great talents, and wrote Peacock after his death:

I read over again Macaulay's four volumes of History. The premature death of that man is a great loss to civilized society —as he got older he got more tolerant and less paradoxical— When I first knew him I thought him rather overbearing and over fluent—Latterly he was just as a very superior & most successful writer ought to be—easy, unaffected, ready to teach, but not unwilling to learn—I hope some one who knew him well, and is equal to the task, may give a good biographical memoir of him.[9]

Hobhouse's interests ranged widely. His diary is filled with engagements for theatres, concerts, dinners, balls, and travels abroad. He was a scholar of Ancient and Renaissance Italy and published in 1859 his *Italy: Remarks Made in Several Visits from the Year 1816 to 1854.* Wonders of the modern age fascinated him—new machinery, a journey to Scotland by steamship, or a first trip by railroad: "I think I was more affected by this display of power than by any other work of art, the Simplon Road or Menai Bridge not excepted." [10] He read modern novels and admired those of Dickens and Thackeray most of all. He thought Hawthorne had some merits, although the "wild, fantastic, and unintelligible" author could not be placed "on the same level with Cooper and Irving." [11] He found Carlyle's style "most suffocating and detestable"; even his friend Macaulay's tended to be "all flash, dash, and splash." [12] Hobhouse was devoted to Ancient and Neo-classic authors and throughout his life entered comments in his diary after re-reading their works. He would discuss with Lord Holland just where the stress fell in a line from Pope; with Peacock, the quality of ancient Greek wine—"Some pure; most Greek wine generally abominable—

9. Hobhouse to Peacock, October 7, 1860, Lord Broughton Papers, Add. MSS 47225, f. 57–58.
10. Hobhouse, diary, August 20, 1834, Lord Broughton Papers, Add. MSS 47227, f. 123.
11. Hobhouse, diary, October 8, 1862, Lord Broughton Papers, Add. MSS 43765, f. 43.
12. Hobhouse, diary, June 12, 1854, Lord Broughton Papers, Add. MSS 56566 (unfoliated).

mixed with resin in large quantities."[13] He put his classical
training to frequent use in Parliament by ending a speech with
a Greek or Latin flourish, and he often caught another M.P.'s
misquote. On one occasion, however, he spent a sleepless night
thinking about his own "blunder in the Latin." He was also fond
of collecting anecdotes about such famous men as Sheridan,
Johnson, and Napoleon. In order to improve his public speaking
he spent hours "reading aloud of Pitt and Fox, till I called them
Pot and Fix."[14]

Obviously a life of such refinements and leisure needed the
financial means to sustain it. This, Hobhouse had in abundance.
The value of his father's landed property and financial investments in 1831, the year of his death, amounted to just under
£250,000. That year Hobhouse inherited the family shares in
Whitbread's Breweries amounting to some £25,000, in addition
to a share of £14,000 in his stepmother's settlement.[15] A will
made out in 1836 listed, besides £40,000 in the hands of his
father's executors, some £69,000 in interest-bearing mortgages,
£29,000 worth of shares in Whitbread's, £7,000 in surplus
capital, and a marriage settlement of £4,000.[16] Five years earlier
he had married Lady Julia Tomlinson Hay, youngest daughter
of George, seventh Marquis of Tweeddale, "a compatriot and
neighbor," so Hobhouse informed Sir Walter Scott.[17] It was a
well-connected marriage inasmuch as Lady Julia's brother married into the Gordon clan, which in turn was connected to the
Dukes of Richmond.

Hobhouse took great pride in his political and social advancement, especially when it required considerable effort on his part.
He never had that effortless knowledge of the world, that easygoing assurance possible only to those born and bred to an assured social position. As a result he was too concerned about

13. Hobhouse to Peacock, August 15, 1857, Lord Broughton Papers, Add.
MSS 47225, f. 86.

14. Hobhouse, diary, February 8, 1816, Berg Collection.

15. Hobhouse, diary, August 14, 1828, Add. MSS 56553.

16. Hobhouse, diary, March 5, 1836, Add. MSS 47227, f. 191–92.

17. Hobhouse to Scott, July 14, 1828, Sir Walter Scott Papers. Lady
Julia died of tuberculosis in 1835. Another tragedy in Hobhouse's domestic
life occurred in 1849 when his eldest daughter, Julia, died of the cholera.
His second daughter, Charlotte, who edited the *Recollections*, married Dud-
ley Wilmot Carleton, later Lord Dorchester. Sophia, his youngest daughter,
married the Hon. Strange Jocelyn, afterwards Earl of Roden.

the opinions others had of him and noted, "My difficulty is a sort of nervous sensibility about reputation which may go far to prevent my having a reputation."[18] Success came, but a complete sense of personal security eluded him, as he noted much later in life:

I went to Lady Holland's, where was a party. I cannot get rid of my shyness at entering or going from a room full or half full of company; and any man, much more woman, can disconcert me at once by a cold or equivocal look just as much as when I was twenty. In fact, I have neither the air nor the spirit of society, for I want that self-confidence without which complete social tact is unattainable. This deficiency makes a man either too reserved or too familiar, either too silent or too talkative, and generally both on the course of the same evening. At least, it makes me so, and neither experience nor good resolutions will ever cure me.[19]

Hobhouse had his complex side. He was stiff and ill at ease as a public speaker. He was subject to anxieties and bouts of severe depression. Periodic fits of self-doubt left him paralyzed in the face of demands for action. Lord Melbourne never understood why he vacillated between a wide and narrow outlook, between a tolerant, congenial acceptance of life as it is and an acceptance limited by moral prejudice. Too often Hobhouse confused morality with manners—not that the conduct of his own life could entirely withstand the closest scrutiny of the most strait-laced moralist. In 1827 he proposed marriage to Sophia Burdett, only to suffer the mortification of an emphatic refusal. Months later he began a furtive affair with a married woman, the wife of a close Wiltshire friend, which caused some awkward moments after his engagement to another woman: "Went to a great assembly at Grosvenor House & was in a most ridiculous embarassment between a lady who is my X & another who I wish to be my wife."[20] The liaison ended a few weeks before Hobhouse's marriage, whereupon he expressed great relief that

18. Hobhouse, diary, November 15, 1821, Lord Broughton Papers, Add. MSS 56544.

19. Hobhouse, diary, June 21, 1845, Lord Broughton Papers, Add. MSS 56565; Lady Dorchester, ed., *Recollections of a Long Life, by Lord Broughton (John Cam Hobhouse) with additional extracts from his private diaries*, IV, 150–51.

20. Hobhouse, diary, May 30, 1828, Lord Broughton Papers, Add. MSS 56552.

a "turbulent, agonizing" year was over and his life could become more regular.

Hobhouse had a fondness for moralizing. Lord Dalhousie, who found him so gracious in London, was deeply offended by the sermonizing tone of some letters Hobhouse sent to him in India. It was Hobhouse who undertook on behalf of Tom Moore and Douglas Kinnaird to caution Byron against offending respectable taste in his poetry. Throughout his life Hobhouse was preoccupied with resolving how one with strong beliefs and solid principles should cope with the compromises and corruptions of politics. He thought Canning was the prime example of the unprincipled political adventurer and in 1828 refused to vote for pensioning his family. The debate furnished him with "another proof of the utter impracticability of speaking all the truth in parliament." "Some private reason, some fear of offending delicate tastes, or of maintaining unpopular propositions," he wrote, "silences men even of the most disinterested and individual characters." Politics exacted a price, and Hobhouse did not know "how this is to be avoided by those who have lived together at school, and at college, and the gathering of social life." He ended his reflection with the admonition, "If you enter into all the schemes of a clique, you become a mere tool, and lose the representative character altogether." [21]

Some insight into Hobhouse's personality helps to understand his public career. He was indolent and energetic, capricious and yet capable of sustained application, humorous as well as serious. He had much common sense but was also impulsive and displayed an enthusiast's lack of balance. He appreciated genius and at the same time had a passion for the second-rate. He led the usual life of other men of his class, but he was conscious of the need for public leaders to feel a sense of urgency in reforming postwar Britain. He craved respectability yet began his political career an outcast from established society. On some issues—parliamentary reform, civil rights, and independence for subject peoples—he was firm in his convictions, defied social ostracism, and was emphatic in asserting his principles. On other matters—factory legislation, the Afghan expedition, and the ballot—he sacrificed principles to expediency. He occasionally shrank from commitments, preferring instead to await a

21. Dorchester, ed., *Recollections*, III, 262–63.

lead given by others, and although his courage rose up, it often lacked stamina. His career involved a constant struggle between a desire to press for change and innovation and an inclination either to accept things as they were or to yield before prevailing beliefs or forces. Especially in later years Hobhouse became less aware of the art of the possible in politics and more concerned with the possible adverse consequences a rash measure might cause. He was not a leading personality of his age, but his responsiveness to its inner momentum and his wide range of interests made him reflect contemporary tensions more clearly than did men of greater eminence.

CHAPTER II

PREPARATION FOR A
POLITICAL CAREER

The fortunes of the Hobhouse family were linked with the growing wealth of the city of Bristol.[1] Bristol's overseas commerce enabled John Cam Hobhouse's forebears to build a substantial fortune during the eighteenth century. The earliest recorded notice of the family name was an obscure entry in the court rolls of Milverton, a small town west of Taunton in Somerset, where a warrant was issued in 1371 against a William Hobhouse to answer a plea of trespassing. Investigations made by members of the family [2] trace the name from 1541 to 1688 in the parish of Holcombe Regis in north Devon, near the Somerset border. A branch of the family then moved north to Minehead, where a Capt. John Hobhouse attained some local prominence as a constable, a churchwarden, and a principal leaseholder in this port town. His younger son Isaac later set out to establish a career elsewhere, and in 1717, he chose the larger commercial world of Bristol. Isaac Hobhouse's mind for business and his previous experience with commercial matters enabled him to establish the family fortune. He profitably invested in the Joseph Percvell Copper Company, and within a decade of his arrival he was a partner in the Bristol firm of Hobhouse, Ruddock, and Baker, with a fleet of ten ships and agents in Jamaica, Barbados, and Virginia.[3] Profits soared through such ventures as the slaving voyage of the ship *Freak*, which in 1749 delivered 329 African slaves at West Indian ports of call at a gross profit of £6,207.[4] Isaac Hobhouse was a commercial agent and banker

1. See W. E. Minchenton, "Bristol—Metropolis of the West in the Eighteenth Century," *Royal Historical Society Transactions*, 5th Series, IV (1954), 69–89; also Bryan Little, *The City and County of Bristol, A Study in Atlantic Civilization*, 154–96.

2. Henry Hobhouse, *Hobhouse Memoirs*, and Charles P. Hobhouse, *Account of the Family Hobhouse and Reminiscences*.

3. W. E. Minchenton, ed., *The Trade of Bristol in the Eighteenth Century*, 18.

4. Henry Hobhouse, *Memoirs*, 22.

as well; he performed such various personal services as attending to the education of children sent to England by his West Indian clients. Childless himself, he invited his two nephews, John and Henry, to come from Minehead to Bristol as partners in his own firm. Upon his death in 1763 Isaac bequeathed to them a portion of his holdings estimated at £70,000.[5] John Hobhouse also inherited Isaac's Westbury College estate, where his first wife, born Mary Medley, gave birth to their second son, Benjamin.

Benjamin attended the grammar school in Bristol before going to Brasenose College, Oxford, where he received his degree in 1781. The Society of the Middle Temple called him to the bar, and in 1796, he stood for Bristol but withdrew from the contest after polling only 102 votes on the first day of the election. He entered Parliament the following year as member for Bletchingley, Surrey. He successfully stood in 1806 for Hindon, Wiltshire, which he represented for over a decade. His manner of speaking was "unembarrassed, fluent, easy, and eloquent," reads a contemporary profile, "his delivery graceful and neither too tedious nor too rapid. He rather advised and persuaded than commanded." [6]

Benjamin Hobhouse was a moderate reformer of some reputation before the end of the century. One of his chief concerns was removing the Test Act and other discriminatory measures against Dissenters. He described anyone who upheld civil inequalities on the basis of religion as "affronting the majesty of heaven" by usurping "an authority over the judgement of his fellow creatures." [7] He praised the work of the Constituent Assembly in France and pleaded for parliamentary reform in his own country. As developments across the Channel got out of hand, however, he became disenchanted, and when "the spirit of riot and insurgency" had erupted at home, he warned Englishmen not to be taken in by "those deluded rioters" from various patriotic societies who, "by crying out for Equality . . . mean that no one individual shall have a greater share of prop-

5. Ibid., 21–22.

6. Quoted in Charles P. Hobhouse, *Account of Family*, 13.

7. Benjamin Hobhouse, *An Address to the Public, in Answer to the Principal Objections Urged in the House of Commons against the Repeal of the Test Laws*, 15.

erty than another." [8] He then clarified his own political position as the situation at home grew more menacing:

I offer you the sentiments, I will dare say, of an honest mind, neither influenced by a sense of interest, nor attached to party, nor fear of danger. I am still an enemy to civil exclusion on account of religious or any other opinions. I am still ready to promote any proper and peaceable schemes, for correcting the unfair and unequal representation of the people . . . but I am still a friend to order, and to peace.[9]

He was, like others, shocked by the Reign of Terror in France and by the aggressive nationalism of the regicide revolutionaries. He subordinated his interest in reform to William Pitt's call for national unity, but he could not condone the repressive policies that the frightened Government introduced during the war. He supported Grey's motion of 1792 for parliamentary reform, condemned the treason trials of 1794, and supported Fox's motion of 1797 against suspension of habeas corpus.

Benjamin Hobhouse first held office under Henry Addington as Secretary to the Board of Control for India, a position he left when the Government resigned in 1804. The following year he became Chairman of the Committee of Supplies, which reviewed the annual estimates for all Government departments. He was later appointed First Commissioner for investigating the debts of the nawabs of the Carnatic. He received the baronetcy in 1812; six years later he retired from public life.

Benjamin Hobhouse was living on the outskirts of Bristol when his first wife, the former Charlotte Cam of Bradford, gave birth to their first child in 1786. They honored both sides of the family by naming the boy John Cam. He was five years old and the eldest of four children when his mother died. A year later his father married Amelia Parry, daughter of the Reverend Joshua Parry, a Unitarian minister from Bath. Amelia's brother John became a renowned physician and father of the explorer Sir Edward Parry. Hobhouse never indicated in his memoirs that his relations with his parents were other than perfect, but among his private notes was this rather chilling comment about his stepmother:

8. Benjamin Hobhouse, *To the Patriotic Societies in London and its Neighborhood*, 2.
9. Benjamin Hobhouse, *To the Patriotic Societies*, 4.

She was a handsome, healthy woman, and in due time added some dozen children to the family—she was not without good qualities—but she also had little judgement, and being fondly devoted to her husband, encouraged rather than corrected, his failings. She had no fortune and was of penurious habits, which operated injuriously upon her step-sons, myself and my two brothers who were sent to very inferior private schools, with a few halfpence in our pockets, and with none of the little indulgences which were bestowed upon most of our school fellows.[10]

Benjamin Hobhouse had converted to Unitarianism shortly after his first marriage and worshipped at Lewin's Mead in Bristol. The congregation of some 250 persons had recently built its new chapel, a stately classic building designed by the London architect William Blackburn, which is now in a state of blackened disrepair just off the reconstructed central area of the city. Their minister at the time was the Reverend Dr. John Prior Estlin, who was highly esteemed among Unitarian circles. Estlin entertained often, and John Cam recalled having met when he was a young boy many noteworthy people at the Estlins' home: "Amongst them I saw some political opponents of Mr. Pitt's administration and some very good patriots—Southey, Coleridge, Lloyd, and Lamb frequented the doctor's house and partook of his modest suppers." The Estlins also invited Benjamin Hobhouse to stay with them when he ran for Parliament in 1796. Coleridge recalled that he "spent about two thousand pounds in Beer and Cockades—that is—in making the Mob filthy and fine—and then found that *it would not do.*"[11] Coleridge described Hobhouse as a man "of great abilities & uncommon Probity" who had written several "ingenious tracts" about Unitarian doctrines.

John Cam attended Dr. Estlin's Unitarian grammar school and years later described his headmaster as "a most worthy man." According to Mrs. Barbauld—herself the daughter of John Aiken, a headmaster at Warrington—"Dr. Estlin treated his students with great liberality" and provided an excellent education. "Their sense of the happy hours they had spent under

10. Hobhouse, notes for *Recollections*, John Cam Hobhouse, Lord Broughton, Papers, Add. MSS 47230, f. 129.
11. Coleridge to John Fellows, May 31, 1796, in Earl Leslie Griggs, ed., *The Letters of Samuel Taylor Coleridge*, I, Letter 131.

his tuition was expressed by the annual meeting which was held on his birthday, by the gentlemen who had been under his care." [12] Hobhouse continued to see Dr. Estlin long after he had left the school. His diary records several visits in 1810, upon returning from his journey to the Near East, to discuss what he termed "spiritual necessities." [13] Another entry in 1814 refers to a dinner at the Estlin home: "He talks of stirring the soul of the human mind, and read to me part of his prayer in a tone of rapture." [14] Dr. Estlin died a few years later, but Hobhouse remained close friends with his son John Bishop, who became a noted eye surgeon. Throughout his life he never did sever ties with Bristol Unitarians.

An early dissenting background had some influence on Hobhouse. Clearly, he felt the sharp stigma of being a Dissenter as a youth. "I was insulted and laughed at—and questioned as to what god was worshipped at my chapel," [15] he remembered about his years at the Westminster School in London. He remained sensitive to religious and political restrictions on Dissenters and voted to repeal these discriminatory statutes in later years. But he took no active part in the cause of dissent and was reluctant to discuss his own background. How, then, can the impact of dissent upon Hobhouse's outlook be interpreted? Of course, dissent was only one of a multitude of forces that influenced Hobhouse's point of view, and an admittedly indirect approach is to suggest the impact of Dr. Estlin's beliefs and the position of Unitarianism in English society.

Dr. Estlin had joined the Bristol congregation upon leaving the academy at Warrington in 1770. The most complete expression of his beliefs appears in his *Familiar Lectures on Moral Philosophy*, published shortly after his death. He described moral philosophy, which involved observation, reasoning, and experiment, as a means of understanding God and His "purposive activity" on earth. Estlin was deeply influenced by the doctrine of Necessarianism, which held that the natural and

12. Mrs. Barbauld, "Recollections of Dr. John Prior Estlin," *Monthly Repository*, 12 (October, 1817), 573–74.

13. Hobhouse, diary, November 26, November 28, December 8, December 9, 1810, Lord Broughton Papers, Add. MSS 56529.

14. Hobhouse, diary, September 14, 1814, Lord Broughton Papers, Add. MSS 47232, f. 19.

15. Hobhouse, notes for *Recollections*, Lord Broughton Papers, Add. MSS 47230, f. 131.

moral universe operated according to laws established by God. Basil Willey observed in his study of eighteenth-century intellectual life [16] that thinking men were caught between the doctrine of a deterministic divine will and the notion of man shaping his destiny through his conscious efforts. Estlin was aware of this dilemma because Necessarianism saw human action and matter thought as functions of matter and hence subject to natural laws. A firm belief in the essentially benevolent nature of God, however, rescued him from any sense of fatalism. "It is the goodness of the Deity," he wrote, "which renders Him the object of our love." Mankind, he thought, must realize that "a divine plan is calculated to promote the highest happiness of the whole universe of intelligent beings." [17] How could man best advance the divine plan? Estlin answered, "There is deeply rooted in the mind a steady propensity towards its own highest happiness. This proceeds from the will of God through habit and association." [18] He was, in effect, linking John Locke's and David Hartley's theories on knowledge and the workings of the mind to Providence. Man had the task of understanding God's laws and applying them. It was necessary to improve life on earth in order to implant the most beneficial sensations on the mind. Progress was assured, but the tempo of progress was left to man.

Estlin enjoined not the passive notion that "whatever is, is right," but a doctrine requiring man to work actively for his predestined happiness. Religion was a matter "not so much of speculation, as of practice," and Priestley's greatest-happiness principle he paraphrased as "Every man owes it to himself, to acquire and enjoy the greatest sum of good, and to suffer the least evil he can, consistently with the duties which he owes to others." [19] The discrepancy between present shortcomings and divinely willed potential Estlin attributed to the deviation of mankind from the path of reason and improvement, whether through ignorance, prejudice, or superstition. A tide in the affairs of men would flow on to fortune and limitless perfection,

16. Basil Willey, *The Eighteenth Century Background; studies on the idea of nature in the thought of the period* (London, 1950), 153.

17. John Prior Estlin, *Familiar Lectures on Moral Philosophy*, I, 176, 190.

18. Ibid., 26.

19. Ibid., 78; John Prior Estlin, *Evidences of Revealed Religion, and Particularly Christianity, Stated, with Reference to a Pamphlet called "The Age of Reason,"* 7.

he thought, should the nature of God and God's laws become understood. William James termed such a creed the religion of "healthy-mindedness," which placed its emphasis not upon mysticism or resignation, but upon adjustment and improvement of life on earth. Surely, their having a frame of mind that stressed the vast potential of life goes a long way toward explaining why so many persons of a Unitarian background participated so vigorously in British intellectual and public life during this time.

At Lewin's Mead, Hobhouse heard Dr. Estlin proclaim his optimism for the future in sermons that were later printed under the title *Discourses on Universal Restitution*, a work that held Coleridge's interest through five readings, proclaiming as it did the final salvation of all mankind.[20] Estlin described the idea of an eternal hell as "the principal ingredient in the composition of the Bigot, the Persecutor, the Inquisitor." [21] He announced in his third discourse that his ideas had secured the agreement of his friend Dr. Priestley before the latter's death in 1804. The doctrine of universal restitution had a practical significance in Estlin's estimation, for divine benevolence indicated the way in which a man should deal with his fellow men. For example, the brutal nature of English criminal laws offended his humanitarian sentiments, and Estlin looked forward to legal reform "in proportion to the improvement of human society." [22] The ultimate end of justice was not the punishment of the criminal, but his reformation. It would be well to remember that Hobhouse learned of the need for legal reform from his Unitarian master before he came into contact with Jeremy Bentham's ideas. In Hobhouse's case, as with certain other reformers of the early nineteenth century, Benthamism strengthened humanitarian impulses originally derived from Unitarianism. The Unitarians added the factor of divine sanction to Bentham's declaration that the aim of justice is the largest possible balance of pleasure over pain or the greatest happiness of the greatest number of people.

Hobhouse's dissenting background influenced him in several other ways. Unitarians believed that the exercise of a free con-

20. John Prior Estlin, *Discourses on Universal Restitution delivered to the Society of Protestant Dissenters in Lewin's Mead, Bristol.* Coleridge praised the work in a letter to Estlin, April 5, 1814, in Griggs, ed., *The Letters of Coleridge*, III, Letter 911.
21. Estlin, *Discourses*, 115.
22. Ibid., 31.

science was the foundation of all individual and social improvement, and Dr. Estlin affirmed the right of everyone to think and speak as he wished, whatever the nature of his creed, outlook, and personality, when he defended the publication of Thomas Paine's controversial *Age of Reason* during the French Revolution. "Let every subject be discussed; let every difficulty be urged and examined; let every opinion be fairly and honestly proposed," exhorted the minister, although he disapproved of Paine's attack upon divine revelation.[23] Hobhouse used much the same language a generation later when the Government decided to prosecute Richard Carlile for reprinting Paine's blasphemous work. Hobhouse thought that the pretended alarm for religion was the alarm of men without any of the faith or morality of religion.[24] The use of censorship or any other form of coercion to deprive one person of the right to express himself was to Hobhouse a denial of a fundamental religious tenet he had learned at Lewin's Mead, namely, the ultimate triumph of truth in the world. Hobhouse continued his fight against censorship and libel laws when he became a Member of Parliament during the reign of George IV.

Unitarians also believed it was not enough to proclaim equal rights in the eyes of the law; they demanded equality of opportunity as well. Unfortunately, they found themselves an oppressed minority in what Joseph Priestley had called the "capital branches" of civil liberty—religion and education, and all Dissenters looked forward to the day when the Anglican policy of exclusion would end. William Hazlitt, who came from a Unitarian background, echoed the sentiments of Dissenters when he noted that "religion cannot take on itself the character of law without ceasing to be religion."[25] The Dissenters had led an intermittent campaign throughout the eighteenth century against the Test Act and the Corporation Act, which aimed at preventing them from holding public office.[26] They also protested against contributing to a church to whose articles they did not subscribe.

23. Estlin, *Evidences of Revealed Religion*, 7.
24. John Cam Hobhouse, *A Supplicatory Letter to Lord Viscount Castlereagh, K.G. on the bills introduced into Parliament for preventing seditious meetings*, 21.
25. Quoted in Herschel Baker, *William Hazlitt*, 14.
26. Dissenters who held public office evaded the penal law through the Indemnity Acts. This annual measure forgave dissenting officials for failing to meet the terms of the Test Act and the Corporation Act during the year.

Dissenters had little hope for receiving full civil rights without parliamentary reform, a change many Englishmen found revolutionary once the prolonged war against France began in the last decade of the eighteenth century.

The cause that aroused the most enthusiastic response from Unitarians, however, was education. For them, learning was the key to all human improvement, the means by which men broadened their minds and broke down the barriers of prejudice in order to progress according to divine will. Unitarians therefore found their exclusion from the nation's two universities especially onerous. It seemed outrageously unfair to them that a Dissenter who received a good education in one of their academies should be barred from higher education—A student at Cambridge had to belong to the Church of England in order to obtain a degree, and Oxford required all students upon admission to subscribe to the Thirty-nine Articles and to take the Oath of Supremacy. No doubt Hobhouse's dissenting background caused him to take a keen interest in establishing the nondenomonational University of London in 1827. He was a member of the provisional committee established at the beginning of 1825 to take care of all business details, and he actively promoted the project, selling shares and helping to prepare a deed of settlement.

Hobhouse continued his association with the Unitarians, even though he had affirmed his membership in the Church of England before taking his degree at Cambridge. Besides occasionally visiting Dr. Estlin in Bristol, he apparently kept up with the activities of the Bristol congregation. A letter from his sister Charlotte, with whom he was always on the closest terms, answers his inquiries in 1823 about the various religious controversies involving the Unitarians of Bristol. She expressed her regrets that a mutual friend, a Dr. Stock, had turned Calvinist —"And what is worse than all," she lamented, "he has given up the doctrine of Universal Restitution"—and that another acquaintance, Dr. Pritchard, remained obstinate and was "by no means to be brought over to the true faith, as preached at Lewin's Mead." [27] Her candid reply to her brother indicates that he still discussed Dr. Estlin's ideas with her and most probably retained the Unitarian doctrines he had learned as a child.

27. Charlotte Hobhouse to Hobhouse, January 5, 1823, Lord Broughton Papers, Add. MSS 36461, f. 1.

The reasons for Hobhouse's subscription to the Church of England are to some extent obscure and personal. He may well have been unwilling to have creed stand in the way of a university degree and a promising chance for a high place in the Establishment, and this essentially pragmatic decision may have been made easier by his father's earlier resolution to send him to the Westminster School. His subsequent conformity—a willingness to accommodate to an established order—is surely not characteristic of the uncompromising Radical.

Benjamin Hobhouse made an important decision about his son's future in 1799 when they visited Bowood, the Wiltshire estate of Lord Shelburne, the first Marquis of Lansdowne. The Marquis urged him to send John Cam off to the Westminster School for many reasons. No advantage could be gained, he asserted, by enrolling the boy in one of those dissenting academies, which many now denounced as breeding grounds of sedition. Dissenters would remain a despised and oppressed group; the previous decade had witnessed the failure of a parliamentary motion to repeal the Test and Corporation Acts, and it was unlikely these discriminatory measures would be repealed while the war against France continued. Benjamin Hobhouse heeded the advice. In 1800 he sent his son to the Westminster School, where the headmaster, Dr. Vincent, placed him in the upper shell, which ranked next to the sixth form.

At Westminster, Hobhouse grappled with Greek, Latin, and Hebrew texts—quite successfully, judging from a commonplace book filled with notes on Ancient and Classical readings. He relished historical memoirs and lengthy narratives and took notes on various anecdotes or memorabilia from which worthy lessons from the past could be derived: Henry VII's honest rule increased his revenue; Queen Elizabeth's wisdom and tolerance earned her the admiration of all Englishmen; liberty of conscience had brought great prosperity to the Netherlands. He quoted Racine and Montaigne, Algernon Sydney and Bacon; from a book on art he found that "nothing is great which is unnatural and effected"; and from a now-obscure work he learned that "in New Holland they copulate promiscuously and by way of ornament or from nature never have either the two upper front teeth." He thought Adam Smith gave "a convincing argument favoring commercial freedom." [28] Westminster also

28. Hobhouse, Commonplace book, Lord Broughton Papers, Add. MSS 36482, f. 58.

enabled Hobhouse to become a parliamentary observer, because the galleries of Saint Stephen's Chapel were open to the students. He never tired of attending the debates during his five years at school.

Hobhouse entered Trinity College, Cambridge, in 1806, took his bachelor's degree in 1808, and received an M.A. three years afterwards. Byron recalled Hobhouse doing "great things" at college.[29] He hunted, acted in theatricals, joined a debating society that periodically met in Lord Palmerston's rooms at Saint John's, and founded the Amicable Society, which dissolved because its members constantly quarreled. He also founded the Cambridge Whig Club, which had ten members who, according to Byron, sought to maintain the principles affirmed by the Glorious Revolution.[30] Hobhouse thought the Revolution of 1688 was the outstanding example of Whig aristocrats uniting with the rest of the nation to resist arbitrary government. He felt that the Whigs of his own time provided poor leadership because they concerned themselves with only their selfish interests. He frequently voiced his dissatisfaction with political events of the day before his fellow club members, among them the future Lord Ellenborough and the heirs to the dukedoms of Devonshire and Bedford. Another club member was Douglas Kinnaird, fifth son of the seventh Baron Kinnaird, who became a close friend of Hobhouse. Kinnaird later became a partner in the Westminster banking firm of Ransom and Morland and was Lord Byron's banker and business adviser. After a by-election in July, 1819, he was returned to the Commons for Bishops Castle, Shropshire, a seat he held until the general elections of 1820. Kinnaird was for a time an influential figure in Westminster politics; he unsuccessfully stood for the borough in 1818 and later helped Hobhouse launch his own political career there.

At Cambridge, Hobhouse collaborated with Byron and others to produce a miscellany of poems. He contributed several translations from Juvenal, Horace, and Voltaire, besides a witty version of some Boccaccio stanzas. Early in the same year, 1809,

---

29. Byron to Murray, September 19, 1820, Letter 847, in George Gordon Byron, sixth Baron Byron, *The Works of Lord Byron; A New, Revised and Enlarged Edition, with Illustrations: Letters and Journals*, ed. by R. E. Prothero, V, 123.

30. Byron to Murray, September 12, 1820, quoted in Thomas Moore, *Memoirs, Life, and Journals of Lord Byron*, 60.

he saw published his college prize-winning *Essay on the Origin and Intention of Sacrifices*—"your essay upon entrails," so Byron called it—an inquiry into the role of the sacrificial ritual among the religions of the ancient world. Hobhouse's Hebraic and Classical scholarship led him to conclude that Christ's death had rendered any mode of sacrifice unnecessary. Christianity "enjoins no outward ceremonies, but only an observance of justice, mercy, and humility." [31]

Hobhouse disliked some features of Cambridge life. He thought it absurd to inflict on some student offender the task of memorizing portions of the Greek testament or attending chapel daily. Religion and learning too often became associated with suffering and disgrace. He found a wide difference between "the social treatment of the pupils" at Westminster and at college:

At the former there was very little distinction of rank—at the latter a difference was made not only with reference to the parentage but the wealth of the pupils. The dress, the diet, the social privileges of one class distinguished them from those of another class, but this applied only to them as students under the eye of their tutors—and the consequence was that the idlest & the most profligate were not unfrequently to be found amongst those whose parents, thinking to secure their good behaviour & occonomical [*sic*] habits, had placed them in the common & humble rank of Pensioners. Some of these having lived when at school on terms of perfect equality with the grandees of the fellows table, could not be reconciled to a separation from their former play mates and, in order to maintain their old position, joined in amusements and adopted habits far beyond their means. [32]

Hobhouse himself was a pensioner, and he resented it. He asked many years later whether "there ought to be any such distinctions," then decided it was a moot question, "which seems at first sight easy of decision—but the answer to which must depend upon the institution & the state of society in the community itself." Although mindful of such issues as a retired Victorian gentleman, he never thought of airing such searching questions in his youth. He simply felt his father was at fault for not pro-

31. John Cam Hobhouse, *Essay on the Origin and Intention of Sacrifices*, 72–73.

32. Hobhouse, notes for *Recollections*, Lord Broughton Papers, Add. MSS 47230, f. 135–36.

viding him with funds sufficient for his high social position. Relations with his father continued to remain strained for a number of years. Hence he had his own family in mind when he observed, "It was a great mistake . . . of parents with adequate means, and of a certain condition, to send their sons from public school to college as pupils of an inferior class to that of their former associates." [33]

Hobhouse spent many years abroad during the decade following his graduation from Cambridge. First came his famous grand tour as Byron's companion across the Mediterranean to Albania, Greece, and finally Constantinople. This finishing touch to a young English gentleman's education was no longer as common as it had been before the war with France. Hobhouse and Byron sought uncommon adventures in areas and among people most Englishmen knew only through legend. Hobhouse was especially intent on compiling material for a book, and Byron bemusedly observed, "100 pens, two gallons of Japan ink, and several volumes of the best blank is no bad provision for a discerning public." [34] The two set out for Lisbon in June, 1809, the first stop in what became *Childe Harold's Pilgrimage*. Hobhouse's companion work, *A Journey Through Albania and other Provinces of Turkey in Europe and Asia to Constantinople during the years 1809 and 1810*, is a record of his travels. The book was a great success, partly because *Childe Harold* had swept readers off their feet and partly because Hobhouse's account of exotic lands and novel situations provided war-weary, isolated Britons just the diversion they wanted. Travel books on the Near East had become a well-established literary genre by the time Hobhouse's work appeared. [35] Treatments differed, of course, but the well-received travel book included many strange or exotic episodes, descriptions of "romantic" landscape, descriptions of, as well as historical digressions on, ancient ruins, and comments on the manners and customs of other cultures. It helped Hobhouse's book that he and Byron were often entertained by local dignitaries who told them the history and legends of the areas. The Balkans seemed to abound in exotic tribes.

33. Ibid., f. 137.

34. Byron to Henry Drury, June 25, 1809, quoted in Moore, *Memoirs, Life, and Journals of Byron*, 89.

35. See Wallace C. Brown, "The Popularity of English Travel Books about the Near East, 1775–1825," *Philological Quarterly*, 15 (1936), 70–80.

One of them, the Suliotes of Greek ancestry, had been recently conquered by Ali Pasha. Barbarism and chivalry mixed at his court, which Hobhouse and Byron visited. Hobhouse told one tale about the Pasha ordering the death by drowning of fifteen women, each of whom, his daughter-in-law claimed, had stolen her husband's affections.[36] His book related the hardships and perils of journeying through rugged Greek mountains, and his description of a fierce thunderstorm read like a Gothic thriller. There were many thoughtful reflections about the decay of ancient empires: The ruins of Athens presented "a grand, but melancholy spectacle, where you behold, not only the final effects, but the successive progress of devastation, and at one rapid glance peruse the history of a thousand ages."[37]

Hobhouse contrasted modern Greece with its splendid past and offered little hope that the Greeks could recover some of their ancient greatness. An Athenian had told him, " 'Your Excellency will find but poor fare in our country; but you are not in Christendom. What can be done amongst those beasts the Turks?' " Hobhouse, however, also emphasized the inherent goodness of the Turkish character: "Ingratitude is a vice unknown to the Turks, whose naked character . . . belongs to those whom nature has formed of better clay, and cast in her happiest mould." The institutions of government and religion were at fault, not the people, and he gave Englishmen who knew so little about Turkey the opportunity to read about the seclusion of women, the closer relationship between mother and child than that which prevailed in the West, opium eaters and coffee houses, the seraglio and Santa Sophia, the kindliness and the cruelty of "these people of contradictions."[38]

Hobhouse returned home in 1812 £5,000 in debt. His father eventually agreed to pay the creditors on the condition that his extravagant son apply for a captaincy in the militia. Six months later Hobhouse was on duty in Ireland with the Royal Cornwall and Devon Miners. He loathed army life, with "boys over your head, and brutes under you, mess, country quarters, courts-martial, and quelling riots." Early in 1813 he secured a tem-

---

36. John Cam Hobhouse, *A Journey Through Albania and other Provinces of Turkey in Europe and Asia to Constantinople during the years 1809 and 1810*, I, 122.
37. *Ibid.*, 290.
38. *Ibid.*, II, 585–86, 912.

porary leave to attend to the final details of publishing his book in London, and a few months later he resigned his commission. Throughout the next few years Hobhouse's life revolved around the fortunes of Napoleon. He and Byron had long shared a sense of hero worship for the once-obscure man who had created an empire that defied all of Europe's sovereigns. Their patriotism was interwoven with sympathy because the Imperial Army that threatened Britain's very existence also seemed to be a reforming force against a despised *ancien régime*. Hobhouse was eager to take a closer look at the Empire and its enemies, so early in 1813 he again left for the Continent as a diplomatic courier to Sweden's Crown Prince Bernadotte at Stralsund on the southern Baltic coast. He and other Englishmen received a warm welcome at Berlin, for at long last an allied coalition appeared to be getting the better of Napoleon. Officials in Vienna were cordial, as were the Russian officers at Czar Alexander's headquarters near Breslau, where Hobhouse delivered official dispatches. Hobhouse recorded his impressions upon meeting the Czar:

His neck rather short & bullwise—his face round, full and rather flat—his nose a la Calmucke & his cheek bones—eyes rather small, and of a light blue—his forehead high and round, his hair light. He had no hat in his hand—when speaking he put his head near the person addressed & looked rather eagerly & uncomfortably in his face. He is deaf in both ears, particularly the left. His voice is coarse and unmusical.[39]

Some Russian officers toured the battlefields of Leipzig with him, after which Hobhouse crossed Germany in the wake of the shattered *Grande Armée*. He returned briefly to London before heading off again, this time to witness the Bourbon Restoration in Paris. His diaries for the next several months tell of balls and receptions in the French capital and later in Britain, where an overjoyed nation celebrated and welcomed the victorious allied leaders. Then in 1815 came the startling news of Napoleon's return from Elba: "England wears a melancholy air . . . all is to be done over again, we have lived in vain for 25 years—We are bankrupt as it were of power and must recommence our struggle for life." Intent on witnessing events in Paris, Hob-

---

39. Hobhouse, diary, March 4, 1813, Lord Broughton Papers, Add. MSS 56532.

house hoped to procure a courier's assignment, only to be told at the Home Office by Henry Addington, Viscount Sidmouth, that the Government had no intention of entering into diplomatic exchanges with Napoleon. He therefore left on his own the first of April, and two weeks later he was looking out onto the courtyard of the Tuileries, unable to resist joining in the cheers when the Emperor appeared:

I positively found my eyes moistened at the sight of the world's wonder—the same admiration of great actions which has often made me cry at the trait of Greek or Roman virtue caused this weakness; but I do not know that if Napoleon had not then stood before me as a man against whom all Europe was rising, and as the single individual to dethrone whom, or rather to destroy, a million of men were rising to arms from the banks of the Tanais to the Thames, that I should have felt such a sensation. No; there was something of pity, however unreasonable and unnecessary perhaps, which made me look upon him with such gratification and melancholy delight.[40]

Hobhouse was convinced that Europe had nothing more to fear from Napoleon inasmuch as the French people themselves were opposed to war and the Emperor had promised to preserve peace. Also, as he informed Byron, the free press and free speech that flourished prevented any immediate renewal of military despotism.[41] Napoleon's decision to invade Belgium proved the incorrectness of his impressions. The Hundred Days over, Hobhouse returned to Paris as the city prepared once more to greet Louis XVIII. A few days later some officers from an English regiment encamped in the Bois de Boulogne informed Hobhouse of his brother's death at Waterloo.

Hobhouse returned to London and settled down to write a book on the Hundred Days and its significance for Europeans. He rushed the work to completion in order to warn Englishmen that the Congress of Vienna would use Napoleon's last bid for power as an excuse for imposing a harsher absolutism upon Europeans. Writing in epistolary form as an anonymous Englishman in Paris, Hobhouse dealt with the last months of Louis XVIII's reign, the Hundred Days, and Napoleon's final abdica-

40. Lady Dorchester, ed., *Recollections of a Long Life, by Lord Broughton (John Cam Hobhouse) with additional extracts from his private diaries,* I, 256.

41. Hobhouse to Byron, April 16, 1815, John Cam Hobhouse Correspondence, John Murray Collection.

tion.[42] He criticized sharply the restored Bourbons: Louis had had an opportunity to create a strong and popular regime by accepting some changes instituted in France during his long exile; instead, he defamed the great revolution that had benefited so many of his subjects. He partially restored the hated *ancien régime* by conferring odious privileges to the Church and Aristocracy, and it seemed only a matter of time before those elements would regain all their lost lands. He violated his own constitutional charter by imposing special law tribunals and rigid press censorship. Bitterness infested the royal family, who saw in every Parisian a regicide. It was no wonder, he wrote, that the French people rejected an imposed sovereign and turned once more to Napoleon. In his fourth letter Hobhouse took issue with Englishmen who viewed Louis' dethronement as an act of daring conspiracy and who supported Britain's foreign policy of the past several years. Napoleon's return had in fact the full approbation of the French people, and Britain's foreign policy had been "staked to the maintenance of a certain system and making good those bargains driven with the sovereigns." Thus, England had starved Norway into obedience, agreed to Polish slavery, and delivered Genoa to the King of Sardinia. He likewise attributed the return of the Inquisition in Spain and monkery at Rome to English influence. He went so far as to propose an alliance between a peaceful Napoleonic France and a liberal British Empire. Thus, two traditions of reform would become one force sufficiently strong to bring a more just and enduring peace for all Europeans.

Not surprisingly, this suggestion was abhorrent to the vast majority of Englishmen, and Croker pounced upon the work as one of the most infamous libels ever written. Wordsworth had accurately expressed the sentiments of his countrymen when he wrote *Ode* (1815) to celebrate Britain's victory over "France, humbled France, amid her wild disorders." To Hobhouse and Byron—both members of a later generation that had not experienced first disillusionment, then horror, about unspeakable Jacobin deeds—revolutionary ideals seemed praiseworthy, particularly in an age of Metternich. Also, Hobhouse assumed that the Emperor's professions of liberalism were genuine, and his was

---

42. John Cam Hobhouse, *The Substance of Some Letters written by an English resident at Paris during the late reign of the Emperor Napoleon.*

one of the first works to revive the cult of Napoleon for the nine-teenth-century world.[43]

Benjamin Constant declared himself satisfied with the facts presented in the French edition. Henry Bickersteth, later Lord Langdale, and Lord Holland, however, advised Hobhouse to alter certain passages lest he be convicted for libel. He refused, claiming the book must remain unsparing because gross imposture, ignorance, and passion had misled Parliament and the public into the late war against Napoleon. Hobhouse saw himself as only transmitting to paper the indignation every Englishman in Paris felt over his Government's policy during the past spring. Furthermore, it made no difference that the Whig beau monde would ostracize one so unpatriotic: "I have already made a much greater sacrifice than that of the intimacy of these gentlemen or the approbation of their associates and approvers," Hobhouse informed Lord Holland, "I mean that of the assent and support of my own family in any projects I may form for public life and consequently of all chances of immediate activity." [44]

By the summer of 1816 Hobhouse had rejoined Byron, now living abroad since his unfortunate separation, at Villa Diodati, on the Savoyard side of Lake Geneva. With the wars over, other writers and public figures from all over Europe converged upon the shores of the lake. Mme. de Staël's salon at Coppet was a chaos of languages and haphazard dinner parties for any number of arrivals. Hobhouse found his book on Napoleon well received, for many guests shared his own unfavorable views about the Vienna settlement. He and Byron then toured Switzerland before proceeding to Italy, where Hobhouse stayed over a year researching in Rome and in Venice. He had his companion volume ready by the time Byron handed him Canto IV of *Childe Harold's Pilgrimage* on January 1, 1818.

43. See "An Englishman's Letters on Napoleon," *Edinburgh Review*, 26 (February, 1816), 215–23, and [John Wilson Croker], "Letters from Paris," *Quarterly Review*, 14 (February, 1816), 445–52. The first observed that while the work displayed an "exhuberant zeal" for Napoleon, it was yet a good thing to see a writer of ability "go a little too far on one side of the question." Croker found it "so tedious, so dull, and withal so laboriously impudent that our contempt for the author's talents . . . almost equal our abhorence of his principles." The French Government fined and imprisoned both the publisher and translator.

44. Hobhouse to Lord Holland, January, 1816, Holland Papers, Add. MSS 51569, f. 58–59.

Hobhouse was especially proud of his *Historical Illustrations*, which in its discussions of the past and present Italian scene can well compare with the journal on Italy later compiled by his friend, Samuel Rogers. Like many of his Protestant countrymen, Hobhouse was both awed and repelled by the scenes and ceremonies of Catholicism. Saint Peter's struck him as "glorious"; however, "religious sentiments are, perhaps, the last it inspires," [45] with fashionable crowds promenading along the nave, past the confessionals and vendors. Now that the French had departed, miracles were reported everywhere, and "when the images do not declare themselves against the government, their animation is rather encouraged than forbidden, and superstition is allowed its full play." Unfortunately, the future held out little hope for Italy because its people were held down by reactionary Austria. To Hobhouse, it was a deplorable example of "sedate ignorance" establishing "her leaden throne" by virtue of the peace settlement at Vienna.[46]

Hobhouse's classical scholarship was impressively put to use in his discussions of Roman antiquity, but there is a section that he did not write: Six biographical-critical sketches of contemporary poets were written by Ugo Foscolo, an Italian writer Hobhouse had met when he returned to London in 1818. By agreement, Foscolo's authorship was concealed, lest the public make the awkward discovery that he had written a favorable review about himself. The deception, as Professor Vincent explains,[47] seemed innocent enough to the writers in question, but it was quickly discovered among literary circles in Italy.

Hobhouse was by now a prominent social figure both on the Continent and in England. Byron had seen to it that he and Hobhouse both shared the social ascent following publication in 1812 of the first two cantos of *Childe Harold's Pilgrimage*. Hobhouse continued to mix with the charming and talented set that frequented Lansdowne House, Holland House, and Melbourne House in Whitehall. Hobhouse's fellow alumnus from Cambridge, the Marquis of Tavistock, introduced him to the Rus-

45. John Cam Hobhouse, *Historical Illustrations of the Fourth Canto of Childe Harold: containing Dissertations on the Ruins of Rome; and An Essay on Italian Literature*, 316.

46. Ibid., 326.

47. Eric R. P. Vincent, *Ugo Foscolo, an Italian in Regency England*, 86–92; see also Vincent, *Byron, Hobhouse and Foscolo; new documents in the history of a collaboration*.

sells, John George Lambton, and Edward Ellice, who belonged to the younger generation of rising Whigs. A friendship was renewed with Henry Bickersteth, who was destined to enjoy a distinguished career in law as Lord Langdale. By 1818 Hobhouse had also met Sir Francis Burdett, the Radical M.P. for Westminster, and found him "a perfectly fascinating and irresistible person."

Although Hobhouse always had a strong interest in politics, the idea of launching his own political career first attracted him in 1812, when Byron made his few appearances in the House of Lords. He claimed to have had a sizable share in preparing Byron's maiden speech attacking a Government bill that specified the death penalty for frame breaking. Hobhouse was more critical of Byron's next speech in April on the Catholic question in Ireland because he felt the points of dispute had been totally ignored. Byron's parliamentary interests quickly subsided, but even while recalling his brief political ventures with great distaste he yet urged Hobhouse to start a career of his own, especially in view of the strong interest in politics he had always shown.[48]

Hobhouse turned his attention to the possibility of representing Cambridge in 1814, when it was rumored that Lord Palmerston would vacate the seat by becoming a representative peer. Henry Bickersteth tried to discourage him by warning about the "pusillanimous corruption" of Cambridge politics.[49] The venture came to nothing, however, and Hobhouse had to await a dissolution of Parliament or an unexpected vacancy. Perhaps he would get the nod from an influential Whig borough patron inasmuch as his ties to the party were so strong and various. Holland House had drawn him ever closer within its orbit. He was thoroughly steeped in the cult of Charles James Fox, which was tirelessly propagated there by Holland, Sheridan, and other Whig luminaries[50]: Fox the scholar-statesman, the humanitarian who had abolished the slave trade, "The Man

48. On Byron's political career, see David V. Erdman, "Lord Byron and the Genteel Reformers," *PMLA*, 56 (December, 1941), 1065–94. See also Leslie A. Marchand, *Byron, A Biography*, I, 319–51.
49. Bickersteth to Hobhouse, June 19, 1814, Lord Broughton Papers, Add. MSS 36456, f. 101.
50. Hobhouse, diary, 1814 and 1818 make frequent mention of Fox; Hobhouse, note, Lord Broughton Papers, Add. MSS 47233, f. 62–63 relates Sheridan's discussions of him.

of the People" who had championed popular rights and assailed the abuse of ministerial power. His career invited close study for anyone concerned with postwar Britain. But Foxite principles had survived only among Lord Holland, who was Fox's nephew and disciple, and his Whig associates. Hobhouse also saw that the younger Whigs he knew were similarly inclined to divest the party of its narrow proprietary and family connections and to have it adopt a more popular stance. His own political future now came more sharply into focus; he would join those liberals who were, like himself, at odds with traditional Whiggery. Reformers would eventually carry greater weight among the Whigs, especially if they acquired support from the professional and middle-class public. Hobhouse accordingly took a significant step to further his political career by joining Brooks's on May 11, 1818.[51] Now he could hope to participate with aristocrat and commoner alike at party councils in the Whig club. More than ever, his political future seemed set with the Whigs.

The influences upon Hobhouse's life thus far were many. He had the example before him of a long line of ancestors who had built a substantial fortune through resourcefulness and hard work. His father was now concluding his parliamentary career as a moderate reformer; his cousin, Henry Hobhouse, had just enhanced his own by being appointed Under Secretary of State for the Home Office. John Cam had grown to manhood amidst revolution or perpetual wars that had changed the world about him. An older generation dwelled upon Jacobin horrors; his focused upon the incredible Napoleon. His earlier dissenting background had made him conscious of the political and social disabilities many people endured. His tastes and inclinations were at one with the liberal and well-born Whigs he had met at Cambridge and later in London, yet he felt at odds with the dominant conservative Whigs. He was socially uneasy in 1818 and felt sharply his rejection by the Establishment. A sense of alienation, he confided to Lord Holland, extended to his own family because he had championed Napoleon's right to the throne. A threatening future loomed as distress and repression intensified at home and abroad. Hobhouse's response to these matters began to take shape when he commenced his political career soon after returning to England in 1818.

51. *Memorials of Brooks's*, 84.

Chapter III

WHIGS AND RADICALS AT WESTMINSTER, 1818-1820

The political career Hobhouse sought upon his return from abroad began at Westminster. He assisted his friends Burdett and Kinnaird in the 1818 election, stood and lost as the Radical candidate the following year, and finally entered Parliament in 1820. During these two eventful years Parliament imprisoned him in Newgate, and Whig politicians severed all ties with him.

Hobhouse frequently conferred with Burdett after returning to England in the spring of 1818. The two agreed it was an opportune time to criticize the Government and to disseminate reformist ideas. Protest was clearly needed against a ministry that had panicked into a policy of repression. Beset with growing public unrest, the Government had returned to its traditional role of preserving law and order. Ministers saw the shadow of revolution hanging over the violent Spa Fields meeting in December, 1816, after which Lord Sidmouth obtained suspension of habeas corpus and issued proclamations against public meetings. The repressive measures only widened the gap between the Government and reformers who prescribed simple remedies that had been advanced in earlier, less complex times. English society was shifting from an agrarian and mercantile to an industrial base. An old world was being lost, and almost no one knew how to cope with the unprecedented tempo of change, let alone devise creative solutions for the pressing political, economic, and social problems created by the new industrial age.

Hobhouse and Burdett agreed that protest must be sound and wise; it must appeal to propertied, educated, yet confused citizens. It must refrain from the incendiary utterances of Radical demagogues like Henry Hunt. Hobhouse found Henry Bickersteth and Douglas Kinnaird thinking along similar lines. The trio joined Burdett and Sir Robert Wilson, who had a distinguished military record during the Napoleonic wars, in forming the Rota, a political dinner club named after James Harrington's debating society. They scheduled bimonthly meetings during the parliamentary session. Reform resolutions were drafted and speeches written for various candidates, among them

Wilson, who was standing for Southwark. The Rota also directed its attention to some remarks Canning made in the Commons during a discussion of the Habeas Corpus Suspension Bill. Grey Bennett, M.P. for Coventry and a friend of Hobhouse, had presented a petition from an aged Manchester printer, William Ogden, who was in prison for libel. The House heard first an exaggerated, piteous tale of an old man weighed down by chains and shackles, then Canning's satire upon the "ever to be revered and unhappy Ogden." [1] *The Times* declared that Canning's brutal speech should never have been delivered, let alone applauded by members of the Commons. [2]

The Times also published the Rota's commentary, which Hobhouse had prepared in the form of an anonymous letter. The sarcastic, brilliant Canning was highly vulnerable to attack; he was distrusted by Tories for having betrayed them in the past, and Whigs wished to avenge his constant ridicule of themselves. Many politicians therefore welcomed Hobhouse's letter, which began

Sir—I shall address you without ceremony, for you are deserving of none. Ask if people have any regard for a mountebank? Your jingling, and chattering, and balancing, were all inimitably performed and admirably becoming; perhaps some of the younger Senators, transported by low ambitions, envied, one instance, yourself. In plain words, there was not a member in the house, not a stranger, or doorkeeper, who had a higher opinion of you after than before your speech, or felt more inclined to change characters with Mr. George Canning: not one. [3]

Hobhouse included some attacks at "the gulled, the gaping Sidmouth" and the Home Office's employment of spies before concluding with additional comments on Canning: "On no one occasion have you ever evinced that sincerity, either of principle or capacity, which the lowest amongst us are accustomed to require from the pretenders to excellence." Hobhouse's letter delighted friends of the Rota, who chuckled over Canning's retort that the anonymous writer lacked only the courage to become an assassin.

Bickersteth next entrusted Hobhouse with the task of prepar-

1. *Hansard Parliamentary Debates*, 1st series, XXXVII (1818), col. 1026.
2. *The Times*, April 16, 1818.
3. Ibid., April 14, 1818.

ing for publication the manuscript of Jeremy Bentham's *Book of Fallacies*. Bentham, whose *Parliamentary Reform Catechism* was published the year before, wished to rescue radicalism from a Jacobin taint given it by such spokesmen as Henry Hunt. Bentham's work would serve the aims of the Rota by teaching "the lower orders how to avoid mixing up absurd and dangerous notions as in their cry for reform," Bickersteth informed Hobhouse, "and deprive their enemies of the powerful fallacy of depriving reform . . . under the pretext of fearing danger." [4] But Hobhouse never completed his editorial assignment, which eventually passed into the hands of James Mill and Francis Place, who edited the work in 1824. His mind dwelled instead upon greater things, for Burdett and Bickersteth had asked him whether he would stand for Westminster. [5]

Hobhouse learned from Burdett that Lord Cochrane, who had been imprisoned and expelled from Parliament for a stockmarket swindle in 1814, had quit politics to assume command of the Chilean Navy in Chile's fight for independence. Hobhouse then met with several members of the Westminster Committee to assure them that he would pledge himself as required, but they quickly dashed his political aspirations by nominating instead Douglas Kinnaird. Hobhouse could not conceal his disappointment. "Had I first obtained the support of my Whig friends," he wrote in his diary, "my nomination would have been assured." [6] Having missed the chance to represent Westminster, he nevertheless became an active participant in the borough's politics by joining the electoral committee supporting Burdett and Kinnaird.

The Westminster Committee claimed an active membership of several hundred supporters. Its ruling core consisted of about twenty artisans and tradesmen who met to plan policy and strategy whenever the need arose. Francis Place, the tailor of Charing Cross, is now the best-known committeeman because he was involved with many national issues and because he kept detailed records of Westminster politics. Yet Place did not al-

4. Bickersteth to Hobhouse, May 5, 1818, John Cam Hobhouse, Lord Broughton, Papers, Add. MSS 36456, f. 25.

5. Bickersteth to Hobhouse, May 22, 1818, Burdett to Hobhouse, May 22, 1818, Lord Broughton Papers, Add. MSS 36457, f. 30, 31.

6. Hobhouse, diary, May 27, 1818, Lord Broughton Papers, Add. MSS 47233, f. 11.

ways exercise the decisive voice in the committee's deliberations; Samuel Brooks, a glass manufacturer in the Strand, was the highly respected committee leader until his death in 1822, and William Adams, a coachmaker in Long Acre, also had considerable influence. Place's flair for organization and detail, however, was unrivaled. It was he who did most of the work in canvassing voters, raising money, writing campaign literature, and planning the meetings and rallies that were all important factors in the Radical victory of 1807.

Place's experience and wide range of political contacts were very important in Hobhouse's Westminster career, although their relationship was a stormy one. A native Londoner, Place had experienced hardship as a young journeyman, especially during one year when he despaired of finding work because employers knew he had organized an unsuccessful strike by the Breeches-Makers' Benefit Society. Better times followed, and Place, as the prosperous tailor of Charing Cross, believed that the factors that had contributed to his success applied to the working masses as a whole. Self-taught, he believed education held the key to all improvement, hence his early interest in Lancastrian schools, the Mechanics' Institutes and other institutes of learning. Industrious, serious, purposeful, he believed that self-help, guided by the inexorable laws of Malthusianism and Utilitarianism, would bring material rewards. Place felt the uneducated London rabble, so prone to riot and license, was not yet ready to exercise its role in changing a society whose organization was indefensible on any rational grounds. He also thought too many public men from outside the working class were indolent and bored by details. Burdett, according to Place, was such a one—an "amateur" politician who was "too rich, too high, and too lazy." [7] Place had lost faith in the immediate efficacy of universal suffrage and unlimited popular agitation for reform, a conviction nurtured by reading Paine and Godwin that had motivated him to join the London Corresponding Society in 1794. In 1818 he was a gradualist with high hopes for the future: The "march of intellect" by the masses was everywhere evident, and the collapse of oligarchic rule was imminent. Westminster radicalism pointed the way to cooperation by the middle

7. Place to John Wright, December 8, 1820, Francis Place Papers, Add. MSS 27843, f. 306.

class and the working class. When such cooperation was achieved, he thought, and with reformers able to act as preceptors of the people, the monopoly of aristocratic power would cease to exist.[8]

He was destined to be disappointed. Urban Westminster was not England, and for many years the committeemen remained in a political wilderness, despised by Whigs and Tories alike as dangerous revolutionaries who had dared question the leadership naturally belonging to their social superiors. Only Samuel Whitbread and Henry Brougham considered working out a common strategy against the Government, but they found other liberal Whigs scandalized by any overtures to the tradesmen of Westminster. The Radical hold on the borough was becoming increasingly precarious because wealthy voters, hostile to any form of extremism, were moving into parishes like Saint James and Saint George, Hanover Square.[9] Internecine quarrels plagued the Radicals as William Cobbett, Henry Hunt, and Major Cartwright opposed the committeemen at one time or another, thus diffusing leadership in the very borough trying to provide a clearer direction for the Radical cause. James Mill and Jeremy Bentham, both Westminster residents, supported the committeemen, and Place, who had met Bentham through Mill in 1812, found confirmed his view that the ruling classes would never surrender voluntarily to the people. Hence, they thought, the masses might justifiably hold the threat of violence over the heads of their masters, forcing them to realize that ultimate self-interest dictated a surrender of power.[10]

At a public meeting on June 4, 1818, several voters warned the committeemen about the opposition they could expect from both Whigs and dissident Radicals in the coming election. The Whigs soon entered the contest by proposing the candidacy of Sir Samuel Romilly, who had attained a reputation for penal reform. Romilly received firm support from James Perry, editor

8. See W. E. S. Thomas, "Francis Place and Working Class History," *Historical Journal*, 5, 1 (1962), 61–79 for an analysis of Place's career and motives.

9. Edward P. Thompson, *The Making of the English Working Class*, 464, places Westminster safely in the Radical camp for decades after the 1807 election.

10. See Joseph Hamburger, *James Mill and the Art of Revolution*, chaps. 1–2, and his *Intellectuals in Politics: John Stuart Mill and the Philosophical Radicals*, chaps. 1–3.

of the *Morning Chronicle*, and Brougham paused during his own campaign in the north of England to praise Romilly while comparing the Westminster "junto" to the corrupt Lowthers of Westmorland, who sent eleven nominees to Parliament.[11] The committeemen got support from Bentham, who prepared a bill dismissing Romilly for being "no better than a Whig."[12]

Dissensions within the ranks of Westminster's Radicals added to the confusion of the 1818 election. Cobbett scorned Jeremy Bentham for "the bombast of his books," which Cobbett found "puzzling and tedious beyond mortal endurance." Following his flight to America in 1817 Cobbett wrote a number of letters to Hunt attacking the "rump" Westminster Committee dominated by "Old Glory" Burdett and utterly at variance with the true feelings of most Westminster voters.[13] Cobbett deemed Cartwright the only genuine champion of the common man in Westminster. Place, however, never had a high opinion of the Major, finding him "in political matters exceedingly troublesome and sometimes exceedingly absurd," and Cobbett's ally, Henry Hunt, he found "a turbulent mischief-making fellow."[14] Place therefore backed Kinnaird's nomination at a public meeting of June 4 before Hunt disrupted all proceedings to announce his own candidacy. Major Cartwright likewise declared himself a candidate on June 14, four days before the polling began.

The committee's candidates fared poorly from the first day of the election. Romilly and Sir Murray Maxwell, a former naval officer who was the Tory nominee, were well ahead of Burdett after three days, while Kinnaird had scarcely any votes at all. Kinnaird and Cartwright then withdrew from the contest in order to secure Burdett's election. The final returns on July 4 had Burdett placing behind Romilly, while Hunt received a mere 84 votes.

This first contested Westminster election since 1807 embittered many. Hobhouse had asked Lord Holland to keep the Whigs from attacking Kinnaird and the Westminster Com-

11. *Morning Chronicle*, June 17, 1818.
12. John Bowring, ed., *The Works of Jeremy Bentham*, XI, 61.
13. Cobbett's attacks appeared in the *Political Register*, 33, January 3, January 17, March 14, 1818. Burdett's and Cobbett's estrangement discussed in J. Jackson, *The Public Career of Sir Francis Burdett: The Years of Radicalism, 1796–1815*, 198–203.
14. Place Papers, Add. MSS 27850, f. 108, Add. MSS 27789, f. 296.

mittee.[15] Holland had done nothing. Brougham's article in the *Edinburgh Review* purposely warned Englishmen against the foolish Radical notions that served "in shaking the people's confidence in their natural leaders, and in branding rank, station, long service, and liberal accomplishments as tokens of hostility to the cause of liberty." [16] Brougham extended a helping hand to those he considered respectable reformers, but Westminster Radicals were not among them. What was worse, the Whigs had stopped at nothing to humiliate Kinnaird, so Hobhouse informed Byron, starting with the last-minute "scurvy trick" of making Romilly his opponent.[17] Hobhouse found himself snubbed by Lord and Lady Holland and other eminent Whigs who attended Romilly's chairing in Pall Mall. The Marquis of Tavistock explained: Hobhouse, a member of the publicity committee in the late election, allegedly was responsible for a poster describing the Whigs as "the basest of factions." Hobhouse hotly denied having anything to do with the offensive poster. Indeed, when asked to join the committee, he had "distinctly stated that if by enrolling my name I was to make myself a party to the abuse of the Whigs, I would not be put upon the said committee." Hobhouse then added that, because of his personal attachments to certain Whigs, he had refused to participate in activities involving any hostile word about the party. He, for one, wanted honest Whigs to unite with the people, and abuse would give the Whigs "an excuse for their deserting the people and thinking only of themselves." [18] Abuse there was, but Hobhouse thought it came from Brougham, not the Westminster Radicals. Thus Hobhouse had indicated just where he stood in 1818: He esteemed the Radicals, was attached to individual Whigs but suspicious of the party as a whole, and still had hopes of uniting Radicals and Whigs.

There was no immediate chance of reconciling Whigs and Radicals, but Hobhouse thought dissensions among Westminster reformers could be ended. He strongly favored a dinner to

15. Hobhouse to Holland, n.d., Henry Richard Vassall Fox, third Baron Holland, Papers, Add. MSS 51569, f. 17.

16. "State of Parties," *Edinburgh Review*, 30 (June, 1818), 202.

17. Hobhouse to Byron, June 25, 1818, John Cam Hobhouse, Correspondence, John Murray Collection.

18. Tavistock to Hobhouse, August 6, 1818, Hobhouse to Tavistock, August 12, 1818, Lord Broughton Papers, Add. MSS 36457, f. 73, 80–81.

honor Cartwright, who had publicly accused Burdett and the members of the committee of having defeated "my just and natural expectations" of receiving the Radical candidature in the last election.[19] The dinner was held, and after Hobhouse delivered a lengthy tribute, which Cartwright much appreciated, the Westminster Radicals spent an evening in mutual admiration.

The status of his own career thoroughly depressed Hobhouse. Westminster hardly took notice of him. An earlier chance of standing for Chippenham failed to materialize. Tavistock suggested a family pocket borough, but such an enterprise cost money. "I am sick of my vagabond life, and of wandering as it were on the wrong side of the Styx,"[20] Hobhouse wrote to his father, but his father replied that family expenses prevented him from giving anything beyond a minimal amount toward election costs.

Then the unexpected happened. At the beginning of November, Hobhouse was discussing business with Byron's agent, John Hanson, when he heard the news about Romilly's suicide, which followed the death of his wife a few days before. The tragic event provided Hobhouse the opportunity to stand for Westminster in another election. Burdett asked and obtained his consent to nominate Hobhouse, but Place was suspicious about Hobhouse's radicalism.[21] He favored Kinnaird as a man of extremer views who did not mind what he would undertake to do for the Westminster electors. Place had ordered to be printed an anonymous handbill calling for Kinnaird's candidature and had shown the proof to Bentham, who approved, as did Bickersteth in principle.[22] Hobhouse had seen the handbill, and he acted to prevent a *fait accompli* when the committee met on November 5 at Brooks's house. There, he called for a public meeting of electors to nominate the Radical candidate, and the idea was put into a motion by a committeeman, George Parr.[23] It was a move

19. Lord Broughton Papers, Add. MSS 36457, f. 76; *Black Dwarf*, July 15, 1818.

20. Hobhouse to his father, May 26, 1818, Lord Broughton Papers, Add. MSS 36457, f. 38.

21. Place to Edward Adams, November 12, 1818, Place Papers, Add. MSS 27842, f. 40.

22. Place, notes on election, Place Papers, Add. MSS 27842, f. 20. See also, Hobhouse, diary, November 5, 1818, Lord Broughton Papers, Add. MSS 56540.

23. Place, notes on election, Place Papers, Add. MSS 27842, f. 39, 43.

to gain time until Burdett and others could advance Hobhouse's nomination. The committee agreed to the proposal despite Place's dogged support of Kinnaird and his warnings about the folly of a public meeting, which could become a forum for Hunt's and Cobbett's supporters. Opposition to Kinnaird then began to mount. James Mill wrote to Place expressing doubts about him and favoring cooperation between Whigs and Radicals lest the results of the 1818 election be repeated.[24] James Perry, the Duke of Bedford, and Henry Grey Bennet, the reformist Whig and friend of Hobhouse, also made known their disappoval of Kinnaird. Bickersteth next told Place that Hobhouse was "more likely to fulfill the wishes of the people" and assured him that Hobhouse's motives were quite sound.[25] By this time, Kinnaird had misgivings about his own candidature because it had obviously been Place's idea and was so widely unpopular. Two days before the public meeting he withdrew his name, and Place reluctantly shifted his support to Hobhouse.[26]

Burdett's masterful chairmanship at the public meeting of November 17 secured Hobhouse's candidature without too much disruption from dissident Radicals. He first read a letter from Kinnaird announcing his withdrawal from the contest and then ruled out of order one elector who wished to nominate Lord John Russell. Thomas Thelwall, a Radical hero since the famous treason trials, gave Hobhouse's nomination a good send-off by declaring he was entirely satisfied with his principles. The nomination was challenged by Henry Hunt, who pointed out that Hobhouse's father had made a fortune as a Crown appointee, and T. J. Wooler, editor of the *Black Dwarf*, who then proposed Major Cartwright's nomination. After that, supporters of the various nominees began shouting at one another, and a riot threatened until Burdett brought proceedings to an end by calling for a show of hands. He declared an overwhelming majority for Hobhouse. The dissident Radicals withdrew and began a campaign to run Cartwright, who did stand for election when the polls opened.

The Westminster Committee then went into action. An elec-

24. James Mill to Place, November 6, 1818, Place Papers, Add. MSS 27842, f. 49–50.

25. Place, notes on election, Place Papers, Add. MSS 27842, f. 44, 58.

26. See William Thomas, "Whigs and Radicals in Westminster: The Election of 1819," *Guildhall Miscellany*, 3, 3 (October, 1970), 174–217.

toral committee, composed of members from each parish, organized meetings and distributed campaign literature. Place and Brooks headed a managing committee of five to coordinate efforts and record election details. Brooks informed the committee that as of January 1, 1819, contributions to the electoral fund totaled £1,780, with Burdett having donated £1,000 to pay expenses.[27] The managerial committee reported completion of the canvassing some weeks later. Hobhouse undertook a round of speechmaking; beginning at the Crown and Anchor Tavern, he repeated his plea for "thoroughgoing" reform and "a full, free and equal share in the choice of representatives." Next came the parish meetings—at the Gun Tavern, Pimlico; the assembly rooms in Brewer Street, Saint James; the Five Courts in Saint Martin's. The Tory *Morning Post* found in a meeting with the electors of Saint Anne, Soho, a veritable conspiracy:

Mr. Hobhouse was the chief speaker, and as usual with all candidates who court popularity, he was very liberal in professions and promises. As a proof of the political principles of the ceremony, the Marsellois [*sic*] Hymn, the great symbol of revolutionary triumphs, horror, and carnage, was twice sung, amidst the loudest shouts of applause. Surely such a person as a Major in the British service, who was present, ought to have recollected the dreadful events which occurred in France at the time when this dreadful anthem of anarchy first defamed all loyalties, and outraged every human heart! [28]

Byron thought Hobhouse did well to stand for Westminster because he would undoubtedly win the election and go on to achieve political fame. Hobhouse was more cautious; he stressed in one of his own letters the importance of Whig support, which he had busily courted for some weeks.[29] He had asked Lord Holland to restrain other Whigs from running a rival candidate after the *Morning Chronicle*, in a violent attack on the Westminster Radicals, urged them to do so. Tavistock, with whom he was on the closest of terms, saw no reason against his apply-

27. Place, notes on election, Place Papers, Add. MSS 27842, f. 10.
28. *Morning Post*, January 28, 1819.
29. Byron to Hobhouse, December 12, 1818, Hobhouse to Byron, January 2, 1819, Lord Broughton Papers, Add. MSS 42093, f. 134, 178. See also Hobhouse to Holland, n.d. [late November, 1818], Lord Broughton Papers, Add. MSS 47223, f. 55, Hobhouse, diary, December 3, 1818, Lord Broughton Papers, Add. MSS 56540.

ing to Lord Lansdowne and Lord Devonshire for support. Thus, when it was rumored in December that the Whigs would nominate young Whitbread, Hobhouse told Tavistock he was "rather astonished" at the hostility of the Whigs, especially since he had carefully avoided uttering anything that could be construed as an attack upon themselves or their principles. Tavistock replied that he never heard an angry word against Hobhouse personally, but because the party had grave reservations about his Radical associates, it would never support him. Hobhouse retorted that the party's reluctance to support him was a testament to his political independence. "But independence does not suppose hostility," he added, "and I have drawn that line in all I have said both in public and in private." [30] Hobhouse's hopes rose when Whitbread's candidacy failed to materialize, but still his closest Whig friends refused their active support. Lambton, for instance, found the Westminster Radicals too offensive:

I can not contribute to the success of a party whom have been foremost in their abuse of those with whom I am politically connected and whose watchword during the late contest was hatred against the Whigs. [31]

Lambton counseled a policy of neutrality when he consulted Grey about the approaching election. He felt Hobhouse was no threat to the Whigs and more popular at Westminster than Russell, who could not stand the fatigue of a long contest. Edward Ellice informed Grey that Hobhouse "had resisted the pressure of the radicals" and therefore merited active support from the Whigs. In another letter he spoke of Hobhouse being "as good a Whig as I am." Hobhouse, Ellice pointed out, had pledged himself to no more than the resolutions of the Friends of the People in 1798, and besides, he had backing from the influential Bedfords. Brougham, who had never forgiven the Westminster Committee for having spurned his overtures to them in 1814, took the opposite position by urging the Whigs to present a candidate of their own inasmuch as Hobhouse was a Radical "of the Cartwright school." Brougham felt Hobhouse's duplicity made

30. Hobhouse to Tavistock, December 3, December 10, 1818, Tavistock to Hobhouse, December 8, 1818, Lord Broughton Papers, Add. MSS 47223, f. 3, 7, 8.
31. Lambton to Hobhouse, n.d. [December, 1818], John George Lambton, first Earl of Durham, Papers.

him worse than Kinnaird; Hobhouse "shewed us the smooth side of his tongue" by acting friendly to the Whigs, who should not be taken in "by so gross a trick" of one who was "among the most, if not the very most bitter enemy we had." [32] The party leaders finally agreed on the policy that they would not oppose Hobhouse but would make quite explicit their opposition to the Westminster reformers. A round of speeches at the Newcastle Fox Club dinner on January 8 left no doubts about the latter point, with Lambton following Lord Grey's invective by scorning the Westminster Radicals as "brawling, ignorant, but mischievous quacks" who were associated with the lowest of the rabble. [33]

Hobhouse was dismayed by such scorching remarks, but Place decided to meet fire with fire by preparing a report for the public meeting of electors on February 9. It reviewed the way in which Westminster had extricated itself from the "two great family confederacies" of Whigs and Tories. Place severely censured Lord Grey and claimed that Grey's joining the 1806 coalition with those unrelenting persecutors of reformers, the Grenville faction, had been an act of shameless "apostacy." The Whigs were further aroused when Hobhouse declared at the meeting if sent into Parliament, it would be as "one of those extravagant reformers" Mackintosh had criticized recently in the *Edinburgh Review.* [34]

Place had committed a grave error in political tactics because the Whigs found his report an insufferable affront that they could not ignore. Lambton immediately called on Hobhouse, who said he had tried in vain to have the offensive portions removed. Lambton replied that the Whigs must vindicate Lord Grey's honor and that of the party as a whole by setting up a rival candidate; besides, Maxwell's earlier retirement from the

32. Lambton to Grey, November 21, 1818, Ellice to Grey, n.d., December 11, 1818, Charles Grey, second Earl Grey, Papers; Brougham to Lambton, January 2, 1819, quoted in Henry Peter Brougham, first Baron Brougham and Vaux, *The Life and Times of Henry, Lord Brougham Written by Himself*, II, 340; Brougham to Grey, late November, 1818, Henry Peter Brougham, first Baron Brougham and Vaux, Papers.

33. *Morning Chronicle*, January 13, 1819.

34. Westminster Committee appointed to manage the Election of Mr. Hobhouse, *An Authentic Narrative of the Events of the Westminster Election which commenced on Saturday, February 13 and closed on Wednesday, March 3, 1819*, 56–63. Mackintosh reviewed Bentham's *Plan of Parliamentary Reform* in "Universal Suffrage," *Edinburgh Review*, 31 (December, 1818), 165–203.

contest provided an added incentive because the Whigs now had an excellent chance of capturing the moderate and Tory vote. Lambton left to confer with Holland, Sefton, Duncannon, Macdonald, and Abercromby. They found their candidate in George Lamb, brother of the future Lord Melbourne. "All were unanimous," Lambton wrote Grey, "that it was advisable after the Radicals' atrocious faults and calumnies." [35] Even Hobhouse's staunchest Whig supporter, Edward Ellice, saw no other alternative:

You could not keep your promise to me of remaining quiet, and I see the consequences of your speech at the Crown & Anchor in the Papers of this morning; an advertisement from George Lamb, for which I was rather prepared, from some hints given me last night in the House of Commons. It is impossible to expect people will sit tamely to receive abuse, and you have certainly only to thank yourself for an opposition, which the Whigs were compelled in their own defence to attempt, a most troublesome & expensive contest, and a *doubtful issue*. As you know, there was more than a disposition not to intervene against your election; and why in God's name should you go out of your way to provoke an opposition? & why put off your enmity to all who profess *Whig principles*, or consider it essential to obtain their ascendancy, to act with the opposition party, till the last moment? And till just when it ought to be supposed you had made your declaration of being secure from any contest? I . . . had some hope my influence would have been sufficient even to protect you, against what I have always dreaded most, with all your talents, the consequences of your own indiscretion. It has not however been sufficient.[36]

Unfortunately, Hobhouse had no easy explanation to offer. From the start he had tried to reconcile the Whigs to his candidacy. He had been careful to advocate reform in phraseology calculated to give them no offense and had emphasized in letters to various Whigs how he wished to bridge the gap between themselves and the Radicals. After the slanderous assaults from Newcastle and Place's provocative reply, Hobhouse, whose situation was extremely precarious and whose political inexperience

35. Lambton to Grey, February 12, 1819, Grey Papers. William Hazlitt thought Place cost Hobhouse the election; see William Hazlitt, "On Jealousy and Spleen of Party," in *Complete Works of William Hazlitt*, ed. by P. P. Howe, XII, 382.
36. Ellice to Hobhouse (copy), February 13, 1818, Edward Ellice Papers.

was no help, then managed to follow Place's inexpedient action by adding insult to injury.

The Westminster contest began on the morning of February 13, when Arthur Morris, the High Bailiff, appeared at the hustings—a covered wooden platform that was in front of the portice of Saint Paul's Church in Covent Garden and that was divided into seven parts, corresponding to the parish electoral divisions. Morris became the Sheriff during elections. He and other inspectors watched the proceedings and dealt with disputed votes. The candidates themselves had inspectors and clerks who could register each vote, so any elector could have his qualifications questioned at the polls. An elector could either "plump" his two votes down for one candidate or else register his second choice for another. Because the parish rate books served as electoral rolls, the candidates sought the aid of the indispensable rate collector.

The virulence of the nineteen-day contest, with its speechmaking, processions, banquets, and doggerel song and verse from Grub Street, drew the attention of the press throughout the country.[37] From the outset Hobhouse found himself under cross fire from Whigs and extremist Radicals who portrayed him as the nominee of a "rump committee" opposed by most Westminster voters. The pro-Whig *Morning Chronicle* and the Radicals favoring Major Cartwright repeatedly asked in public letters just what Hobhouse meant by "radical reform." Did he mean a radical reform of the House of Commons? If so, did he consider as radical any reform that fell short of annual parliaments and universal suffrage? Surely, the questioners said, he must do more than adopt the Westminster Committee's ambiguous formula for a "Full, Free, and Equal share in the choice of representatives" and "parliaments of a short duration." [38] Pressed by his opponents, Hobhouse tried to clarify his position on reform by reading this statement on nomination day:

Annual Parliaments and Universal Suffrage have been mixed together for the sake of confounding the subject; but they are distinct and separate, and upon each of them I claim your separate attention. Upon the latter of the two . . . I consider the extension of suffrage to be not only of second, but even of

37. Newspaper clippings, Place Papers, Add. MSS 27842.
38. *Morning Chronicle*, February 9, 1819; Westminster Committee, *Authentic Narrative*, 71.

third-rate importance. The first object for the people of England to obtain is equality of the right of suffrage; in other words, that there be one and the same, be that what it may, for every Elector in the commonwealth. The second object is, that equality of numbers elect each representative. These objects attained, then, if I am then asked whether security from misgovernment by a real representation may be preserved by an extension of suffrage, short of universal, I answer Yes, by an extension far short of universal. How far short is a question for fair discussion, and honest difference of opinion. With regard to annual parliaments, I should think myself the greatest coxcomb were I to say that twelve months is the precise golden age within which elections must periodically recur in order to secure your liberties.[39]

Place and other committeemen could only shake their heads over Hobhouse's equivocal statement. The Radical Sir Charles Wolseley walked away convinced that Hobhouse was a humbug. The *Gorgon* reflected the puzzlement of reformers in a tortuous analysis of the speech "which gave us much pain because of the way it would be misconstrued." [40] The Whigs gleefully offered a reward to anyone who could unravel Hobhouse's views on reform. Of course Westminster reformers had expressed a variety of opinions on just how far the franchise had to be expanded to ensure responsible government. Burdett, for instance, had similarly tried to reconcile various views by claiming that uniformity of suffrage would achieve the same beneficial results as any extension of the vote and with less controversy. But no Radical spokesman had dismissed an extension of the franchise as a matter of "third-rate importance" and then stressed that suffrage be made "far from universal." Obviously, the reformers thought, Hobhouse did not feel bound by any Radical program whatsoever; his declaration was much too complicated and confusing. Moreover, it failed to placate the Whigs and antagonized further the extremists.

After such an unpromising start, Hobhouse began to sound like the Radical candidate he was. He had to, with Hunt openly supporting Lamb, who was five hundred votes ahead after the fourth day of polling. Hobhouse described himself as "a leveller of the pretensions of an usurping aristocracy . . . which the

39. Westminster Committee, *Authentic Narrative*, 78.
40. *Gorgon*, February 16, 1819.

systems of feudal barbarism, pernicious as they were, would never have deigned to admit." Aristocrats, he charged, had gained too much power by "intrigue, subserviency, illegal gains and the baser arts." After an outraged Lambton reminded voters of past Whig reforms, Hobhouse retorted that present Whigs "would unite with the meanest and most atrocious of mankind" to prevent a genuine reformer from entering Parliament. Indeed, he said, Whigs had tried "to crush the inclinations of the people of the metropolis" since the time of Wilkes.[41]

These and other statements that were widely circulated gave Hobhouse the reputation for being an extreme Radical. A truer insight into his outlook, however, is obtained from his patterns of thought, not from isolated statements. It is significant that he displayed a backward-looking stance by repeating what other reformers before him had said. The Whigs had long deplored the Crown's unconstitutional influence as "fatal to the liberties of this country"; the Commonwealth man of the eighteenth century, Cartwright, and Burdett had all referred to "ancient liberties of Englishmen"; Tooke and other urban Radicals had supported "a full, free and equal representation of the people"; Jeremy Bentham's *Resolutions on Parliamentary Reform* spoke of restoring "a community of interests between the governors and the governed." [42] And most of the eighteenth-century gentry would have nodded approvingly when Hobhouse proudly defended his political independence:

I am not arrayed in the attractions which belong to many of the candidates for popular confidence: I am allied to no great family either by blood or connexion: I am the child of no party: I am the champion of no individual interest.[43]

His specific proposals were far from extravagant. He mentioned the usual Radical demands for ending lavish pensions and sinecures, curbing excesses of monopoly and privilege, lowering the burdensome weight of taxes imposed by a corrupt government, and above all—"the paramount object of my exertions"—reforming Parliament and thus rendering government more responsive to public opinion. Only then, from his point of view, could

---

41. Westminster Committee, *Authentic Narrative*, 173, 283, 105.
42. Ibid., 146, 157, 173; *Morning Chronicle*, February 18, 1819.
43. Westminster Committee, *Authentic Narrative*, 13.

dangerous divisions between the masses and the rulers be ended, and traditional institutions made workable.

Hobhouse's comments about the Whigs probably provide the most instructive clues for understanding him. Despite his many harsh attacks, he evidently remained a Whig at heart. The legend of Charles James Fox still had its hold over him. He evoked a Fox who was a Radical reformer on all counts: the defender of popular freedoms during the French Revolution, Westminster's "Man of the People" for a time, the generous-minded individual who hated intolerance or oppression of any sort. With Fox in mind, Hobhouse declared on the last day of the contest that "my principles have been those of the Whigs of 1798 in contradistinction to the Whigs of 1819." [44] Before the election he had confided his views to Lambton: "My views on reform are similar to those of the Society of the Friends of the People—uniformity of suffrage and possibly triennal parliaments." [45] Unfortunately, present Whigs had failed to consult their own reformist tradition in which Fox featured prominently.

Some of Hobhouse's remarks about the Whigs and other matters were a source of deep embarrassment to the Westminster Radicals. Thus the *Authentic Narrative* of the election, which Place later prepared, was a highly selective compilation of events and speeches, some of the latter polished up for posterity. The manuscript version of Hobhouse's final hustings speech reads, "My Whig friends know that up to the very last election I had not altogether given up the hope of seeing a union between the Whigs and the people." A candidate referring to his "Whig friends" on the final day of a heated contest hardly suited Westminster's Radicals, so the *Authentic Narrative* reads:

I have concealed from no associate that I have long thought that the Whigs have been gradually detaching themselves from the people: but I have equally openly confessed, that up to the last election in this place, I had not lost all hopes of seeing an union between that party and the people. [46]

Hobhouse mounted the hustings for the last time, on March 3, to acknowledge his defeat by George Lamb. [47] He attributed the

44. Ibid., 282. Other references to Fox appear on pp. 119, 238, 246.
45. Hobhouse to Lambton, n.d., Lambton Papers.
46. Westminster Committee, *Authentic Narrative*, 282. The manuscript version appears in Lord Broughton Papers, Add. MSS 36457, f. 247.
47. Hobhouse obtained 3,861 votes; Lamb, 4,465; and Cartwright, 38.

outcome to "the combination of almost the whole Aristocracy of Great Britain" and "the union of the two great parties of the day." *The Examiner* declared Hobhouse owed his defeat to the provocation he gave to the Whigs, his ambiguous statements, the notion that Burdett wanted to dominate Westminster, and opposition from Radicals like Cobbett and Cartwright.[48] An analysis of the polls reveals that Hobhouse lost to Lamb because he did so poorly in the conservative parish of Saint George, Hanover Square. There, Lamb's plurality was 851. Hobhouse also lost Saint James parish by 60 votes, and Saint Margaret–Saint John by 34. His best showings were in Saint Martin and Saint Anne, where voters always backed the Westminster Committee's nominee.[49]

The afternoon the polls closed, the crowds that packed Covent Garden began to riot. They fought a band of Whig celebrants, among them the Russells, Lambton, and Lord Nugent. Then the mob made a shambles of the Whig committee rooms facing Henrietta Street, before moving on to the offices of *The Courier* and the *Morning Chronicle* whose editor, James Perry, the next day denounced "leveller" Hobhouse for inciting the mob to riot. Hobhouse immediately replied that Whig ruffians had instigated the deplorable event.

The contest left a legacy of embittered personal feelings. Major Cartwright, who fancied himself insulted by some of Hobhouse's remarks at the annual Westminster dinner in May, challenged him to a duel. The misunderstanding was quickly settled, but Cobbett continued to champion Cartwright and denounce both Burdett and his "nominee," Hobhouse.[50] Lord Grey remained gravely offended by the Westminster Radicals and warned Robert Wilson against associating with them. "Look at the men, at their characters, at their conduct," he lashed out, "What is there more base, more detestable, more at variance with all taste and decency, as well as all morality, truth, and

---

48. *The Examiner*, March 7, 1819; Westminster Committee, *Authentic Narrative*, 281.
49. Place, notes on election, Place Papers, Add. MSS 27842, f. 610–24. The pollbooks are in the Greater London Record Office and are analyzed in Thomas, "Whigs and Radicals in Westminster," Appendixes A and B, 215–17.
50. *Political Register*, May 22, August 21, 1819.

honour." [51] Lord Byron from Italy expressed annoyance about Hobhouse's attacks on aristocrats and Whigs; Hobhouse, he wrote, should know better than to involve himself with "those blackguard reformers" and Cartwright's "midsummer madness." [52]

Lord Erskine defended the Whigs and their principles while Place and Hobhouse criticized them in a number of pamphlets written during the next several months. [53] The first of the series, Erskine's *A Short Defence of the Whigs*, tried to refute various charges made by Westminster reformers during the past election. Whiggism, he argued, was enshrined in the Revolution of 1688, which established a principle of obligation between the enlightened upper classes and the people. Since that time Whigs had remained "instinctively at their posts" to resist whatever threats to liberty arose. Even extremists who had rashly attacked the Whigs found protection when prosecuted by the Government. Erskine proposed a modest plan of parliamentary reform that would "fairly and judiciously" extend the franchise to a propertied minority. The proposal, he argued, was consistent with a long tradition of moderate Whig reforms that protected property and liberty but avoided the tumult of revolution. His main point was that Radical schemes were unsound and impractical while Whig proposals were wise and stood a better chance of implementation.

First Place, then Hobhouse, answered Erskine. Place's reply was a capsuled version of *An Authentic Narrative* that emphasized the ways in which the Whigs had opposed the Westminster reformers. Hobhouse's *Defence of the People* was a more sophisticated and ambitious work—he expended much time revising and researching and drew from Bolingbroke and other writers—that dealt in large part with Whig traditions and prin-

51. Grey to Wilson, October 24, 1819, Sir Robert Wilson Papers, Add. MSS 30109, f. 56–58.
52. Byron to Hobhouse, June 26, 1819, Hobhouse Correspondence, Murray Collection.
53. Place first answered Erskine's *A Short Defence of the Whigs* with his *Reply to Lord Erskine by an Elector of Westminster*. Erskine then wrote *A Letter to an Elector of Westminster*. Hobhouse contributed *A Defence of the People in Reply to Lord Erskine's Two Defences of the Whigs*, which Erskine rebutted in *A Preface to the Defences of the Whigs*. Hobhouse had the last word with *A Trifling Mistake in Lord Erskine's Recent Preface*.

ciples. He assailed Erskine's Whig interpretation of history, which viewed the inexorable triumph of liberty through the agency of various party heroes. Hobhouse argued that Erskine erroneously tried to connect the merits of the nineteenth-century Whigs with those of the Revolution of 1688, whereas in fact the event was the work partly of Tories. The Whigs had neither liked King William nor cared for the people, except as appendages to their own power. Some Whigs, Hobhouse reminded Erskine, even wanted James II restored. He moved on to Hanoverian times and stated that during the reign of the first two Georges, the Whigs assumed that the system of corruption they had organized so effectively would secure their power and keep the Crown forever in their hands. The very perfection of the machinery, however, rendered it easily transferable to other hands, which had happened under George III. It was at that time, Hobhouse continued, that the rejected families began to court the people as a means of intimidating the Crown, just as they had previously upheld the royal authority to overawe the people. Hobhouse spared no Whig leader, not even Fox, who allegedly typified his associates by following the devious path of corruption. His coalition with North was "odious"; his motion in 1805 enabling Lord Grenville to retain his sinecure offices showed "that the Whigs despised all public opinion, and were, for the sake of ministerial arrangements, quite careless how soon they gave a proof of their contempt." [54]

Hobhouse maintained that Erskine's portrayal of Whigs continuing to support their reformist traditions by striving to protect the interests of the people was one of sheer fancy. Whiggism was a "fantastic, obsolete name" rarely invoked by present party members who were too hopelessly divided to constitute an effective opposition. Hobhouse wanted to know just who the Whigs were who Erskine defended: "Were they Foxites, Fitzwilliamites, or Tierneyites?—Were they old or new Whigs?—Friends of revolution or decriers of revolution?—Radical Reformers—moderate Reformers—or no Reformers?" [55] No one knew, for Whiggism meant "any thing, every thing, and nothing." Hobhouse thought Erskine should realize the pitiful spectacle the parliamentary Whigs had provided since the Ministry of All the Talents fell.

54. Hobhouse, *A Defence of the People*, 152.
55. Ibid., 45, 14.

The medley of men who occupied the opposition benches never, as I heard, were guilty of the absurdity of calling themselves Whigs. They seldom contrived even to vote together upon the most important points. Who knew or who cared for the principles of Mr. Ponsonby? Did he agree with Mr. Whitbread? Did Mr. Whitbread agree with Mr. Sheridan? And where was Mr. Sheridan too? What did the party for the last of those who reminded the nation, that the Whigs could once boast of genius, eloquence, and taste? Did not Messrs. Lambton and Ferguson, and Bennet, seem to form a little squadron apart from all? Could any one divine which way Mr. Brougham was likely to vote? Did the language of Lord Milton accord with that of Sir Samuel Romilly? Mr. Grattan too, did not he promote to the utmost the last war with France, which Lord Grey strained all his ability to prevent? [56]

Hobhouse was especially effective in refuting Erskine's idea that Whigs were a band of high-minded and like-minded men who were the inheritors of a distinct reformist tradition, but he offered no specific proposals to deal with current economic and social problems. Instead, he stressed the "paramount necessity of reform" and reminded Erskine that the Radical proposals of 1819 hardly differed from those he and Grey had favored in 1793. The Westminster Radicals had thus taken up the mantle of popular leadership that a body of men called Whigs had long since discarded. Hobhouse also defended his ambiguous declaration on nomination day of the 1819 election by claiming that the Radicals "never were for annual parliaments and universal suffrage in the pure, bigotted, exclusive sense of the phrase." [57] If they had been, they would have given Major Cartwright more than a mere 38 votes and Hobhouse less than nearly 4,000. What Westminster wanted, he declared, was a reformer who would more urgently try to cope with popular distress, a moderate man like himself, but the Whigs, out of the enmity that had always marked their conduct toward Westminster since the Radical triumph of 1806, had employed all their corrupt tactics to defeat him.

Hobhouse's reply to Lord Erskine was marred by some inconsistency and other flaws. It began by stating that the Whigs

56. Ibid., 42–43.
57. Ibid., 67.

never acted in concert because their opinions, like their traditions, varied so, and it ended by picturing Whigs as a corporate body hostile to Westminster reformers. Hobhouse also indulged in personal insults, which constituted the weakest portions of his work. Leigh Hunt, *The Examiner*'s editor who favored a Whig-Radical alliance, regretted that Hobhouse had "come to regard the Whigs not as a part of the people, but as an aristocratic clique whose tricks were to be exposed." [58] In spite of its shortcomings, James Mill found the work praiseworthy both as a critique and as a statement of Hobhouse's reformist position, and Hobhouse recorded Mill's remark that "there is not a sentence of it of which he would not be proud to be the author." [59]

That summer Hobhouse turned his attention to the economic crisis that plagued the country. "The distress here is beyond all imagination," he wrote Byron, "the poorer class of manufacturers can earn no more than three shillings & six-pence a week —thousands of them are starving in all the manufacturing districts." [60] Lord Sidmouth had already begun to take steps against any possible disorders when, on August 16, the incident at Peterloo occurred. The response of both the Government and its critics was instantaneous. Sidmouth congratulated the local authorities and prepared repressive measures for parliamentary approval in the autumn, and an outraged Burdett wrote a violent letter to his constituents, comparing England to Nero's Rome and warning the King that he risked the fate of James II. Hobhouse, realizing that Peterloo was an issue on which Whigs and Radicals could unite, prepared a resolution suitable to both groups. He consulted James Mill, who insisted on mentioning reform, and Lord Holland, who cautioned against mentioning it at all.[61] Burdett, Hobhouse, and Thelwall were the principal speakers at the public meeting held at Palace Yard, where a resolution condemning Peterloo and calling for immediate par-

58. *The Examiner*, November 7, 1819.

59. Hobhouse, diary, August 31, 1819, Lord Broughton Papers, Add. MSS 56540.

60. Hobhouse to Byron, June 16, 1819, Hobhouse Correspondence, Murray Collection.

61. Hobhouse, diary, August 31, 1819, Lord Broughton Papers, Add. MSS 56540; Hobhouse to Holland, n.d., Lord Broughton Papers, Add. MSS 47224, f. 66, 67; Tavistock to Hobhouse, October 13, 1819, Lord Broughton Papers, Add. MSS 47223, f. 29.

liamentary reform was passed.[62] Other meetings were held with various Whigs in attendance, a sign that some *rapprochement* was possible in such troubled times.

As the excitement mounted, Hobhouse published his *Supplicatory Letter to Lord Viscount Castlereagh, K. G.*, which objected to the impending Six Acts. He asked what more the ministry could gain by the total humiliation of the people, by legislation that would destroy at a single blow the Constitution. Already the people were at the Government's mercy: The Tories had a compliant Parliament, a vast ecclesiastical establishment to do their bidding, and an orderly and obedient military that had "cut the people to pieces" at Manchester as "40 flurried yeomen drove away like sheep" thousands of demonstrators. Hobhouse ridiculed the ministers trembling from fear of impending revolution; "prudent" Sidmouth apparently saw armed men "laying about in various holes and corners of the United Kingdom," and his Cabinet colleagues saw more danger "in the quiet of the People than in their tumults." [63] Such men would suspend the remaining liberties Englishmen enjoyed. Hobhouse then made it quite clear that the anonymous author was not a Radical reformer; rather, the letter represented the opinions of "those who never lose an opportunity of attacking the abominable trash and impious nonsense" that Radicals spluttered forth in their taverns.[64] This pamphlet, the author asserted, showed that even moderate Britons would be driven to desperation by measures that dimmed all hopes for future reforms.

When Parliament passed the Six Acts in December, Hobhouse published another pamphlet in the series of exchanges with Lord Erskine. *A Trifling Mistake in Lord Erskine's Recent Preface* was less a critique of the Whigs than an angry attack on ministerial policies. He showed the work to Francis Place, who changed a few lines just before the conclusion.[65] As pub-

---

62. Home Office, Internal Disturbances, series 41, vol. 5, f. 5, September 2, 1819.

63. John Cam Hobhouse, *A Supplicatory Letter to Lord Viscount Castlereagh, K.G. on the bills introduced into Parliament for preventing seditious meetings*, 13.

64. Ibid., 32.

65. Hobhouse, diary, October 27, 1819, records, "Place has added a thundering note to my *Trifling Mistake*." Lord Broughton Papers, Add. MSS 56540.

lished, the pamphlet claimed that force had replaced the rule of law since passage of the Six Acts, and it asked:

What prevents the people from walking down to the House, and pulling out the members by the ears, locking up their doors, and flinging the keys into the Thames? Is it any majesty which hedges in any members of that assembly? Do we love them? Not at all,—we have an instinctive horror and disgust at the very idea of a boroughmonger. Do we respect them? Not in the least. . . . Their true practical protectors then, the real efficient anti-reformers, are to be found at the Horse Guards, and the Knightsbridge barracks: as long as the House of Commons majorities are backed by the regimental muster roll, so long may those who have got the tax power keep it, and hang those who resist.[66]

The strong language did not remain unnoticed. On December 9, Stuart Wortley, M.P. for Yorkshire, read some extracts from the pamphlet before the House, and within a few days the Commons passed a motion condemning the pamphlet as a scandalous libel in contempt of the privileges and constitutional authority of Parliament. The Commons thereupon found Hobhouse guilty of contempt and, by a majority of sixty-five, committed him to Newgate.[67]

Hobhouse's arrest was in the best tradition of Westminster radicalism, but a tame affair compared to Burdett's imprisonment in 1810. He went off quietly when parliamentary officers came to arrest him at Edward Ellice's home.[68] He obtained a hearing before the Court of King's Bench, where he contended that a court of law could set aside the Commons's illegal action of sentencing a man *in absentia*. Chief Justice Abbott refused to interfere with the Speaker's warrant and dismissed him. Hobhouse wrote a lengthy protest from Newgate,[69] citing many

66. Hobhouse, *Trifling Mistake*, 49–50.
67. *Hansard*, 1st series, XLI (1819), cols. 917, 989, 1010.
68. Hobhouse, diary, December 14, 1819, describes the arrest. He told the parliamentary officer he would go peacefully: " 'I am not going to shoot you,' I said. 'Oh,' replied the officer, 'you are too much of a gentleman I am sure.' This made us both laugh." Lord Broughton Papers, Add. MSS 56540.
69. John Cam Hobhouse, first Baron Broughton, *Proceedings in the House of Commons and in the Court of King's-Bench, relative to the Author of the "Trifling Mistake", together with the argument against parliamentary commitment, and the decision which the judges gave without hearing the case . . . Prepared for the press by John Cam Hobhouse.*

precedents and quotes arguing against his treatment. At least his prison quarters were comfortable, and Burdett, who awaited his own trial for libel, sent many cheerful letters. Expressions of outrage and sympathy poured in from all over Britain, and his visitors were many—James Mill, Cartwright, Place, Ricardo, Sir Robert Wilson, and delegations from Liverpool and Manchester. Imprisonment had made Hobhouse a popular hero.

The king's death on January 29 dissolved Parliament and thereby automatically granted Hobhouse his release from prison and brought a general election. He left Newgate the end of February, knowing the Westminster Committee had again chosen him to stand for Parliament. His letter of acceptance promised every effort "to procure for the People that constitutional control in the legislature, to the want of which I attribute all our calamities." [70] The contest began on March 9, and this time the Radical cause was not marred by disagreements. Henry Hunt's arrest at Peterloo had removed him from the scene, and the dissident Radical press was shocked into silence by the Cato Street Conspiracy and at least mollified by Hobhouse's martyrdom at Newgate. There was also a resurgence of support for Burdett, whose conviction for libel at the Leicester Assizes was announced before the election ended. The Westminster Committee took the precaution of nominating Hobhouse in secret, lest there should be a repetition of 1819, when the public meeting erupted into a near riot.

The effort of the only other candidate, George Lamb, was weakened by several factors. According to Mrs. Arbuthnot, the Tories refused to help him because he had repaid their earlier support with abuse. [71] Also, three months earlier, in January, a decision in the Court of King's Bench, Cullen vs. Morris, denied the High Bailiff's right to disfranchise voters because they had not brought their payment of rates up to date. Radicals lauded the decision because they believed that the old ruling had cost the votes of many supporters. Henceforth, householders remained eligible to vote if they updated rate payments at the time of polling. William Lamb also noted the lack of preparation on the canvass and a lack of funds as reasons for his broth-

70. John Cam Hobhouse, *A Letter to the Independent Electors of Westminster, 26 February 1820.*

71. Francis Bamford and William Arthur Wellesley, seventh Duke of Wellington, eds., *The Journal of Mrs. Arbuthnot,* Vol. I: *1820–1825,* 10.

er's defeat.[72] Against strong odds, Lady Caroline Lamb did all she could for her brother-in-law, but Princess Lieven believed the Radicals would owe their victory to "that made woman" who had "made no bones about going into taverns and dancing and drinking with the electors; what else she did is shrouded in obscurity." [73] The common cry whenever George Lamb tried to speak from the hustings was "Where is Caroline?"

The Radicals won; Burdett led the polls with 5,327 votes, Hobhouse followed with 4,882, while Lamb received 4,436 votes. An analysis of the polling reveals that Hobhouse improved over his 1819 showing with retailers, smaller tradesmen and artisans, and such subprofessional people as printers, booksellers, and clerks. Lamb was still strong in prosperous Saint George's parish, with a plurality of 744 over Hobhouse, but this showing was more than offset by returns from every other parish, including Saint James, which Lamb had captured in 1819 by a slim majority. It was not an outstanding triumph, considering that many of Lamb's supporters were out of town campaigning for friends, but Hobhouse was delighted to be returned by "the most enlightened, the most independent, and the most numerous body of electors in the Kingdom." [74] The Radicals prepared an elaborate ceremony for April 5, when Burdett and Hobhouse were chaired. A parade began at two o'clock after the parish delegations, each with its colored banners and bands, had assembled in Sloane Street, Knightsbridge. Headed by the standard-bearers, who displayed dark blue flags bearing the inscriptions "The People" and "Reform of Parliament," the procession proceeded to Hyde Park Corner, down Piccadilly, and on to Charing Cross Road. Four trumpeters heralded the two victors, who waved from a Roman chariot; a retinue of fifty men on horseback followed. The procession continued along the Strand to the Crown and Anchor Tavern, where toasts and speeches lasted till late that night.[75]

72. William Lamb to Frederick Lamb, May 3, 1820, quoted in Thomas, "Whigs and Radicals in Westminster," 212.

73. Princess Lieven to Prince Metternich, March 11, 1820, in Peter Quennell, ed., *The Private Letters of Princess Lieven to Prince Metternich, 1820–1826,* 13.

74. Hobhouse, diary, March 25, 1820, Lord Broughton Papers, Add. MSS 56541.

75. *Order for the Procession on the Chairing of Sir Francis Burdett and John Cam Hobhouse,* Broadside 6.95, Guildhall Library.

The past two years had been eventful for Hobhouse. He had started his political career hoping to unite Radical and Whig reformers because he found points of agreement with both groups. His efforts had failed. Instead, the bitter 1819 contest drove him into the Radical camp, and a year later he was still sharply critical of the Whigs who had rejected him. His anger flared up in a letter to Byron:

If you want to find a true blackguard, chimney-sweep-seeking politician, a truly mean mob-hunting master of the dirty art, commend yourself to a Whig, but do not expect to find him amongst the Reformers. It is all very well for such pitiful patriots in petticoats as the Duchess of Devonshire and Lady Crewe to kiss butchers to get votes for Charley Lamb Fox, but those days are gone by, and I am convinced that the proudest of all politicians and the most uncondescending is the man of principle, the real Radical Reformer.[76]

Hobhouse also defined Radical reform as he understood it in 1820:

We know that we mean no more by radical reform than has been expressed by the first men whom the country ever produced. We mean only the rooting up of that tree of corruption which, like the Upas, has grown to such height, that it extends its branches and sheds its pestiferous dew over the land. Are our principles to be branded with the name of revolution, because we wish to strike at the root of the tree? No, we are rather entitled to be regarded by our fellow-countrymen as those who endeavour to remedy an evil by which all are affected.[77]

Unlike other Radicals who placed their faith in political programs, Hobhouse felt that principles provided the most reliable guides for dealing with present challenges. His statement interpreted radicalism in the literal sense of returning to roots or first principles. It was a backward-looking concept, a hankering for return to a pure state of affairs that presumably existed before encrustations of corruption appeared. Finding perfection in the past, Hobhouse's radicalism had little sympathy for new

76. Hobhouse to Byron, March 31, 1820, Hobhouse Correspondence, Murray Collection.
77. John Cam Hobhouse, first Baron Broughton, *Some Account of a Long Life*, I, 126; Hobhouse, diary, March 27, 1820, Lord Broughton Papers, Add. MSS 56541.

ideas and aspirations. Hence, Radicals who embraced the democratic programs enunciated by Cartwright or by the Corresponding Societies could not recognize in Hobhouse a spokesman for the masses. Like the Yorkshire reformers or urban Radicals of the past, he attributed all the evils in the state to powerful interests that held sway in an improperly balanced Constitution. True, he shared the moral indignation common to all Radicals—and other reformers—who surveyed the sorry state of England after Peterloo. If anything, Hobhouse was in a political no man's land on the eve of his parliamentary career: Parliament had imprisoned him for defending popular liberties; he had severed ties with the unprincipled Whigs; he had rejected democratic notions of universal suffrage, annual parliaments, and equal electoral districts; and Westminster waited to see just how far he would live up to the Radical principles he professed.

CHAPTER IV

HIS MAJESTY'S OPPOSITION
1820–1830

Hobhouse's position in politics shifted considerably during the reign of George IV. The Whigs he once criticized so bitterly began to esteem him highly, but the Westminster Radicals, whose cause he once championed so ardently, began to find fault. He discovered growing areas of agreement with one group, growing areas of discord with the other. However, Hobhouse's disputes with Francis Place and other Radicals did not preclude cooperation on specific issues as they arose.

Hobhouse and Place could agree on most things as a new decade and a new reign began. Both wished to rescue England from the clique of corrupt politicians by which they saw it enslaved. Both sympathized with the desire of the masses for self-improvement through education and economic advancement. Both wished to detach the masses from the influence of violent demagogues. They favored libertarian movements abroad and feared the Government's postwar foreign policy. Hobhouse valued Place's practical experience and his many contacts with working-class leaders; Place appreciated the way in which Hobhouse's solidly respectable background could win adherents to the Radical cause from among propertied and professional Englishmen. Both saw England divided as never before between the angry masses and the privileged minority who had closed ranks in self-defense. If anything, tensions had arisen before the new Parliament convened. There was shocking news of the plot by Thistlewood and his accomplices to assassinate the entire Cabinet and proclaim a republic—a desperate effort to strike out at the thousand evils that existed. Protected landlords reaped huge profits while factory workers starved; the penal code was barbarous; libel laws curbed all protest; Catholics were unemancipated and Dissenters restricted by statutes; every form of corruption was practiced in public life; parliamentary representation preserved an elaborate system of privilege enjoyed by a minority. These and other grievances awaited the attention of Radical reformers, and Place was eager to assist Hobhouse as Parliament met.

Both thought England's leaders were primarily responsible for the country's ills, and both believed the parliamentary Radicals could function most effectively by directing attacks against them. The issue of Government spies provided the occasion for Hobhouse's maiden speech, in which he recommended an investigation into rumors that agents of the Home Office had lured Thistlewood and his accomplices into the Cato Street Conspiracy in order to pocket a reward by betraying them. Hobhouse realized that the extremists, besides having prejudiced the reformers in the eyes of many, might provoke the government into passing more repressive measures in order to forestall any portents of revolution. He therefore sought to quiet the alarm by dismissing as a lunatic fringe those dozen or so men who had plotted in a hayloft to upset the nation. Why then the need for an additional 11,000 troops, which the Government proposed in June? Would force be used even more indiscriminately against guilty and innocent alike? Hobhouse saw in the Mutiny Bill a further affront against the civilian population, already justifiably angry over Peterloo and military outrages at Oldham and elsewhere, as well as by the quartering of more troops in London itself. The repressive measures of 1819, the heaven burden of taxes, the economic and foreign policies, the imprisonment for libel of many journalists and publishers—he raised these issues in Parliament during the year, confident that if he won sufficient support, the Government would abandon or at least modify its disastrous policies of the past several years. The country needed new directions, not measures engendered by fear.[1]

However, nothing shook Lord Liverpool's Government quite so much in 1820 as Caroline of Brunswick's return to claim her rights as Queen. Domestic quarrels within the House of Hanover, a recurrent theme of eighteenth-century politics, returned to plague the Ministry as Opposition members rushed to Caroline's defense. Brougham served as her attorney, Thomas Denman her Solicitor-General, and Alderman Wood of London her most enthusiastic supporter. Other Whig and Radical poli-

---

1. *Hansard Parliamentary Debates*, 2d series, I (1820), cols. 255–60, 334, 668–70, 1084–93.

ticians soon received public acclaim by championing the "injured Queen" over her unpopular husband. Most significantly, many political opponents forgot past grievances while fighting for Caroline. In terms of Hobhouse's political career the episode brought about his *rapprochement* with leading Whigs, an event that profoundly affected his relations with the Westminster Radicals.[2]

Times had changed since a pro-Whig Prince had instituted the "delicate investigation" into Caroline's personal behavior in 1806. Then it was the Opposition Tories who rallied to the defense of the Princess. The situation altered within a few years when the Prince broke with his Whig allies, who now inherited the role of an Opposition eager to exploit trouble within the royal family. The Whigs could do little for Caroline, who soon wearied of the constant humiliations she encountered in England. Her conduct became a public scandal after she left to reside on the Continent, and her husband was only too eager to verify the gossip by sending the Milan Commission to investigate. Two years later he was obsessed with divorcing Caroline before the Coronation took place. At one point he threatened to dismiss his ministers; only reluctantly did George IV consent to a compromise plan they submitted. Lord Liverpool asked Brougham to inform Caroline that she would receive a lifetime annuity by renouncing her claims as Queen Consort and consenting to remain abroad.

The ministers soon realized Caroline had not hastened through France in order to negotiate, for she crossed the Channel with Alderman Wood and prepared to face divorce proceedings. Her procession of June 6, 1820, through London to Wood's house on South Audley Street in Mayfair was that of a returning heroine. The Government acted promptly on the same day by sending evidence to both Houses of Parliament. The trial itself finally began on April 17, and for weeks afterwards the peers heard the testimony of sailors, servants, and valets from every corner of Europe.

Hobhouse took up Caroline's cause with enthusiasm, even if he found it hard to be sincere about her innocence, as one letter to Byron suggests:

2. On the Queen's trial see Frances Hawes, *Henry Brougham*, Chester New, *Life of Henry Brougham to 1830*, chap. XI, and Roger Fulford, *The Trial of Queen Caroline*.

You should really, if you can, come over to do an act of justice for this "Mob-led Queen." It would be a great thing if a person like you, who has lived so long in Italy, and might speak to manners, & etc., would lend your powerful assistance against this most odious persecution. There is no saying but such an additional weight might break down these villians, who bend now most woefully. They have been forced to give up the coronation; indeed, they could not have crowned him without cannon. You have no conception of the popularity of the Queen's cause—even the Clergy are for her—in the country. The little creatures called the great are, to be sure, behaving with their usual meanness, but all below the exquisites are for Her Majesty. Poor creature! she has been shamelessly used. She lives at a little lodging, 22, Portman Street. . . . Burdett and I went up with the Westminster address to her the other day, She received us alone in her little room, and, I must say, with a dignity as tranquil as if she had been at Carlton House in her own court. We don't care a fig about her guilt, as they call it.[3]

Hobhouse shared neither Denman's chivalrous sentiments about her being "the most wronged and insulted of womanhood" nor Brougham's outrageous opportunism, which he dismissed with the comment that "he does this sort of thing always." [4] He preferred to discuss the sordid nature of the trial. When Viscount Castlereagh moved on June 26 for a secret committee to investigate the papers relating to Caroline, he tried to end proceedings then and there. He urged rejection of the motion in order to preserve the dignity of the Crown. The King should realize, Hobhouse argued, that he was injuring his own best interests by allowing the substitution of a secret committee for the common law of the land. Did he want to establish a precedent for allowing future sovereigns to be plagued with sleuths hiding under tables or in palace corners and eagerly jotting down any gossip? Hobhouse again tried to rescue the Crown by moving in September to prorogue Parliament. The trial had already tarnished the royal family's reputation, and it degraded all the peers in Britain who were sent to pry into foul clothes-bags and hear the gossip of disreputable characters. Hobhouse

3. Hobhouse to Byron, June 14, 1820, John Cam Hobhouse, Correspondence, John Murray Collection.
4. Hobhouse, diary, August 25, 1820, John Cam Hobhouse, Lord Broughton, Papers, Add. MSS 56541.

declared the trial was a ministerial device to discredit the King, his wife, and Parliament. Someday, the culprits would be summoned before the Commons, he warned, "and God send them a good deliverance." [5]

The Government had barely squeezed the bill of divorce through the Lords. Unwilling to risk defeat in the Commons, the Ministry called off proceedings on November 10 and prorogued Parliament until after the new year. Hobhouse went over to Caroline's residence the next day to offer Westminster's congratulations. There followed a thanksgiving service at Saint Paul's at which Caroline and her supporters found a most suitable expression of their feelings in Psalm CXL: "Deliver me, O Jehovah from the evil man; Preserve me from the violent man." Caroline appeared deeply moved, but the Earl of Donoughmore found the ceremony "a burlesque on everything good and holy." [6] Caroline consented to accept an annuity after her supporters failed to have her name restored in the liturgy. Finally, an indifferent multitude looked on when she unsuccessfully tried to force her entrance into the Abbey on Coronation Day. Although Hobhouse continued to bring her news of public sympathy, the affair of Queen Caroline had run its course.

Many politicians speculated about the ultimate significance of the trial. The Duke of Bedford thought the public clamor during the year foretold the doom of the British Monarchy. Hobhouse thought the trial had diverted the public's attention from Radical reform, an interpretation true in itself but failing to account for the easing of tensions because of an economic upswing at the end of the year. Lord John Russell assessed the effects more accurately in terms of party politics when he told the poet Thomas Moore that "the Queen's business had done a great deal of good in renewing the old and natural alliance between the Whigs and the people and of weakening the influence of the Radicals with the latter." [7] Russell hoped the lesson would not be lost among fellow Whigs: Only by preserving popular

---

5. *Hansard*, 2d series, I (1820), cols. 1383 ff., III (1820), cols. 54–58, 804 ff.

6. The Earl of Donoughmore to Sir Benjamin Bloomfield, November 29, 1820, in Arthur Aspinall, ed., *The Letters of George IV, 1812–1830*, I, 396.

7. Sir Spencer Walpole, *Life of Lord John Russell*, I, 122. New, *Life of Brougham*, 261–62, sees the trial as a watershed in the politics of the decade as the Whigs emerged the popular party.

support could his party provide effective opposition in the months and years ahead.

Hobhouse welcomed a reconciliation with the Whigs. He spoke to his constituents about "a new epoch making for the forgetfulness of all minor differences" among reformers.[8] He began consulting with Lambton and Russell, advised Grey through Russell and Ellice on the urgency of supporting parliamentary reform, and even had a long and cordial conversation with Lord Erskine. By 1823 he and Burdett were once more dining at Holland House after a five-year absence. The accord with liberal Whigs pleased and surprised him. "What a change since last year," he wrote in April, 1821, "when scarcely a Whig would speak to Burdett and me!"[9]

Two weeks later Hobhouse supported Lambton's motion for parliamentary reform with a carefully prepared speech that ended with a withering attack on Canning, who was described as a man who had sacrificed all virtue and character to ambition and had by turns "insulted, derided, betrayed, and crouched to every party" and politician in the country.[10] Hobhouse reported that all the Whigs at Brooks's were pleased with the speech, particularly with the profile on Canning, which was intended as a reply to some insulting comments he had made weeks earlier. After Lambton's motion was easily defeated, Hobhouse and various Whigs acted in concert on another motion to investigate Peterloo. Burdett introduced it in May, after serving a prison term for his libelous letter on the massacre. Hobhouse spoke at length on "the massacre of the innocents" and condemned the Government for the atrocity.[11] This time the Tory majority was 124, but Hobhouse noted the wide range of backgrounds represented by the 111 members who had supported Burdett's motion. The bloc included the representatives from the London area, Joseph Hume among the Radicals, and those Whigs who had become Hobhouse's close associates in Parliament—Lord Nugent, the Marquis of Tavistock, Coke of Nor-

8. Hobhouse, diary, April 22, 1821, Lord Broughton Papers, Add. MSS 56542.

9. Ibid., April 4, 1821, Lord Broughton Papers, Add. MSS 56542. See also Lady Dorchester, ed., *Recollections of a Long Life, by Lord Broughton (John Cam Hobhouse) with additional extracts from his private diaries*, II, 139–40, 160–72.

10. *Hansard*, 2d series, V (1821), cols. 425–26.

11. Ibid., cols. 799–823.

folk, Viscount Milton, Viscount Ebrington, and Thomas Denman. They joined Lambton, the Russells, Ellice, Duncannon, and Brougham, who were also party liberals and who had been conferring weekly with Hobhouse since the session opened. William Smith, chairman of the Dissenting Deputies and the influential M.P. for Norwich, supported the reformers, as did David Ricardo, the economist, who was at this time M.P. for Portarlington. Here was the nucleus of an effective Opposition, confined to no particular class or creed, although the bulk of its members were Whigs.

Hobhouse proposed to Lord Liverpool's Government a program of retrenchment in government expenditure that accorded with both Whig and Radical programs. He repeatedly denounced pensions, appropriations for church building, and the creation of additional ministerial posts as wasteful and unnecessary items in the annual budget. Another target was the size of the military force, which exceeded anything the nation had ever known in peacetime. He described London itself as "an armed camp"; soldiers jostled civilians in the streets, and reckless troops fired on innocent bystanders in 1821 when Queen Caroline's funeral cortege passed through Hyde Park. In the interest of public safety, as well as economy, Hobhouse opposed the construction of military barracks at Charing Cross and recommended removing the Horse Guards from the capital. In 1826 he obtained 34 votes for a motion to reduce by 77,000 the size of the Army.[12]

Hobhouse also advocated a lowering of taxes as soon as the Government announced a surplus of revenue for 1821. He singled out the assessments on houses and windows for special consideration. Hobhouse had chosen well because these taxes were unpopular to rich and poor alike. He pointed out that an increase in the assessments from 150 per cent to 200 per cent during the past twenty years had caused a national calamity. Anyone who traveled through the English countryside, he said, could not fail to observe innumerable instances of houses abandoned by old and respected families who had succumbed to the "tax gathering plunderer." The country householder was driven to the town, the town householder to a smaller dwelling. Property deteriorated because when a person rented a house he

12. Ibid., VI (1822), cols. 32–36, X (1824), cols. 546–48, 862–64, XI (1824), cols. 332–41, XIV (1826), cols. 1192–95.

checked on the number of windows, and mindful that each one would cost him about fifteen shillings annually, he insisted on a reduced rent. The landlord in turn resorted to walling up windows, thus excluding light from staircases and cellars, and causing the damp and dry rot to set in. Hobhouse also claimed these taxes were especially unfair and onerous to the small tradesmen, who usually needed a great deal of light for working and displaying goods. Furthermore, as the levy did not distinguish between rich and poor, wealthy banking firms on Lombard Street paid no more for each window than did the wretched artisans living in low-rental houses in back alleys. The artisans, Hobhouse recounted, let lodgings to meet taxes, and squeezed their families into some dark, ill-ventilated rooms at the back of the houses. Rural depopulation and urban overcrowding, disfigurement of stately homes and urban blight, soaring poor rates and epidemics—Hobhouse found the house and window taxes partly responsible for all these misfortunes each time he proposed repeal.[13] Each time, his proposal was defeated.

Hobhouse discussed general economic and fiscal policies whenever he introduced his tax-repeal motions to the Commons. He took a dim view of the national economy in 1822, when he drew attention to the rising poor rates. He attributed much of the poverty in London and other cities to the high cost of food, yet he knew that abolition of protective prices set by the Government would force the farmers to sell their produce at disastrously low rates. How then could the agricultural and urban interests be reconciled? Hobhouse realized that many members of the Whig Opposition were staunch protectionists; he therefore dodged the controversial issue of the Corn Laws and proposed a reduction of taxes as the only possible way of diminishing the hardships felt by the urban population.[14]

Hobhouse summed up his views on fiscal policy in 1822 by depicting England as "the house of a spendthrift running to ruin."[15] The severe economic crisis that seized the nation in 1825 bore out his predictions. When he and other M.P.'s were

---

13. Hobhouse's discussions of the House and Window Taxes, ibid., VII (1822), cols. 1458–91, X (1824), cols. 652–67, XIII (1825), cols. 771–76.

14. Ibid., VII (1822), col. 1471.

15. Ibid., VII (1822), col. 1469.

beset by frantic bankers and investors in highly speculative joint-stock enterprises who all expected some economic miracle or solution, Hobhouse could only offer remedies to prevent future economic disasters. "Unless something was done to strike at the root of the present banking system," he told Parliament, "the country would be exposed to the constant recurrence of those evils under which it now suffered." [16] Hobhouse proposed to avoid an overabundance of bank notes in the future by requiring banks to deposit with the Government a security in proportion to their currency issue. He also suggested that country bankers report monthly on the amount of their notes in circulation, thereby enabling the Treasury to check on the nation's banking operations. [17]

The Government tried to reform the banking system by increasing the size of the banks and by decreasing their note issue. It also ended the monopoly of the Bank of England by permitting joint-stock banks to issue larger notes outside a radius of sixty-five miles from London. But the Government was not prepared in 1826 to introduce the regulations against joint-stock companies that Hobhouse wanted. He later recalled that in 1826 Parliament had given its approval to some of the wildest schemes after "gentlemen had come down to that House, lauding to the skies the wealth and riches of the South American states, and setting forth the vast advantages likely to result from the . . . speculations." [18] The Commons were awed as those men spoke of gold and silver in such abundance that the natives hardly knew what to do with all the precious metal. Investors eagerly purchased shares in Peruvian Mining and other ventures in the lands described as El Dorado; indeed, M.P.'s were among the first to run out and purchase stock. Hobhouse then proposed to protect future investors by having the Government reintroduce another Bubble Act covering all joint-stock enterprises. [19] Thus, while the Government adhered to its policy of economic liberalism and allowed the public to pay the consequences of its folly, Hobhouse proposed an alternative policy of reintroducing governmental regulations in

16. Ibid., XIV (1826), cols. 884–86.
17. Ibid., cols. 863, 1188.
18. Ibid., XVI (1826), col. 264.
19. Ibid., XII (1825), cols. 1048 ff., XIV (1826), col. 644–47, XVI (1826), cols. 263–64.

banking and finance. He refused to accept laissez faire in its entirety.

Hobhouse maintained that his regulatory program did not necessarily violate the doctrines of influential political economists. He pointed out in 1826 that David Ricardo had not upheld absolute economic freedom. "Advocate as he was for free trade," Hobhouse observed, "he deemed it necessary for the government to interfere with the dealings of the traders in paper-money, and to secure for the community a guarantee against loss." [20] Hobhouse felt that political economists had to ask a fundamental question: Did the natural identity of interests come about spontaneously by the actions of natural laws, or was it attained through the deliberate efforts of men? Obviously, the policy of economic freedom was disastrous to many men, he asserted, and principles or dogmas notwithstanding, the nation needed practical and specific remedies. He could see no foundation in actual experience for theories like nonintervention.

Hobhouse's efforts to offer reasonable alternatives to the Government's economic and political policies did not entirely satisfy the Westminster Radicals. Specific matters, such as the redress of taxes, retrenchment in Government expenditures, or a condemnation of Peterloo, greatly pleased his constituents, but his equivocal stand on the Corn Laws and above all his reconciliation with Whig reformers strained his relations with them, particularly with Francis Place. The occasion of the annual committee banquet in 1822 revealed the rift between the two men. Hobhouse, eager to cement ties with other reformers, wanted to change the date scheduled to suit those prominent Whigs who were planning to attend and suggested, "Perhaps on this occasion when the scoundrels [the Tories] are tottering it might be worth while to strain a point in order to show a union between public men." Place bluntly refused. The *volte-face* of the man who had spent the better part of 1819 denouncing the Whigs simply astonished him, especially since Place could detect no significant moderation of the Whigs' hostility toward the Westminster Committee. The banquet commemorating the victory of 1807 was held as scheduled on May 23, but Place had been angered further by Hobhouse's refusal, in advance, to toast "radical reform." To Puller, Place wrote:

20. Ibid., XIV (1826), col. 885.

So—our anniversary is to be a Whig dinner; at least Whiggery is to be the leading feature. And Why? Because Mr. Hobhouse says that to drink *Radical Reform* will be to offend the Whigs. Only think of this as a reason for our "turning our backs upon ourselves." Who was it that pulled down the Whigs? Was it not Sir Francis Burdett and Mr. Hobhouse and the last 3 Westminster elections? And now the same parties are to attempt to set them up again. Depend upon it Puller the time for such humbuggery to be successful is gone by, and the attempt if it be made will bring nothing but disgrace. What was it but *Radical Reform* that made Mr. Hobhouse a member for Westminster; what can endanger his seat so much as Whigising.[21]

Hobhouse, who prided himself on principles, wanted to "strain a point"; but Place, an excellent political tactician, asserted that he had betrayed the principles of Radical reform. Such disputes over tactics and principles suggest the complex nature of their partnership. They also suggest fundamental differences of opinion that would ultimately prove fatal to their political alliance.

Place maintained that Whig and Tory oligarchs would continue to protect their special interests, whereas the Westminster Committee wished to put government in the hands of the people. He allowed for no compromise: A public man sided either with the privileged and titled ranks or with the rest of the nation, and Hobhouse, by associating with the Whigs, had violated the principles and goals of his Westminster constituents. Hobhouse, for his part, thought human ties and relationships too complex for such a standard formula and neat solution. He maintained that honest men of principles were everywhere to be found; they were not confined to a particular class or group. Hobhouse differed from Place by wanting to broaden the reform alliance to include aristocrats and workingmen, Whigs and Westminster Radicals.

Place invested the term "Radical" with special meaning. He identified the Radical movement with the courageous, self-made artisans and tradesmen of Westminster and other urban com-

21. Hobhouse to Place, Place to Hobhouse, May 12, 1822, Francis Place Papers, Add. MSS 27843, f. 347, 348; Place to Puller, May 22, 1822, Place Papers, Add. MSS 27843, f. 349. *The Times*, May 24, 1822, reported J. B. Monck, Peter Moore, H. G. Bennet, Lords Nugent and Ebrington, Wilson, Alderman Waithman, Hume, Russell, Lambton, and Tavistock among the participants.

munities who defied the patronizing aristocrat. They were the vanguard of a movement that aimed to overthrow the existing political and social order. Place's indignation was directed against the privileged classes on behalf of the underprivileged and exploited masses. He thought a Radical was essentially an "outsider" who must appeal to the people by stressing how a Radical had different attitudes and goals than did other reformers. A Radical sought fundamental change; he wanted to uproot everything standing in the way of the common man's economic and social betterment. Whig reformers, by contrast, merely wished to tinker with the political system. Hobhouse was "Whigising" by bending over backwards to accommodate the Whigs at the Westminster banquet. His regard for their feelings was nothing less than a repudiation of Radical principles.

Hobhouse did indeed give wider latitude to just what was meant by a Radical. Speaking about himself and his associates in 1819 he recalled: "We were all Parliamentary Reformers, but were by no means agreed as to the extent or general character of the change which ought to be made in the representative system. The term Radical, used as a substantive, had not yet come into use, but was commonly applied as an epithet." [22] His statement dwells solely on political matters, though accurate in the sense that the term Radical had just become widespread in the political vocabulary and lacked precise definition. He felt Westminster Radicals and Whig reformers, while differing in manner and degree, held views that overlapped on particular issues. It was wrong to insist on distinctions that the complex political scene of the 1820's had blurred. How should one describe Durham, Russell, Wilson, or other Radical-Whigs whose aid was needed to implement change? Bentham had written *Radicalism Not Dangerous* (1819–1820) urging Radicals to meet other reformers half-way in the interest of attainable improvements. In this spirit Hobhouse voted with Russell's motion of 1821 on the disfranchisement of the rotten borough of Grampound and expressed gratitude for what little Russell had achieved.[23] Hobhouse did emphasize on other occasions in Parliament how the Whigs had to take up reform with greater

22. Dorchester, ed., *Recollections*, II, 113.
23. Ibid., 128, 141.

urgency in order to suit the Radicals, but generally he considered all reformers Radicals. He noted how "we had a Radical party" [24] at the Speaker's dinner on the eve of the 1821 parliamentary session, a party to which Russell and Wilson were invited. Earlier he wrote that the Duke of Sussex "begins to be Radical." [25] Evidently Hobhouse understood Radical to mean simply a politician who evinced a more than average concern about remedying the political and social ills of the nation. Anyone could be a Radical, even dukes and baronets.

Hobhouse found great merit in his views because the all-important question of leadership was satisfactorily resolved. As did any patrician reformer, Hobhouse thought in terms of ranks or orders of social classes. He was bound too closely by the milieu he knew—a milieu of the university, of exclusive clubs, of fashionable society—to think otherwise. He and Place had agreed that power must be taken away from a hereditary clique and assumed by people who could be expected to use it wisely; both agreed that the "middling ranks" had a legitimate claim to authority by virtue of their commercial and industrial wealth.

They disagreed about the value of the aristocracy and the status of the masses. At the apex of Hobhouse's social pyramid stood the aristocracy, traditionally the link between the masses and the King that had vital functions in Hobhouse's plan for a reformed, hierarchical England. Hobhouse made this point quite clear when he "positively asserted" to the Westminster Committee that his "propensities were towards the Whigs as to their principles." [26] He made this statement in 1818, when Whiggism denoted rigid social ranks over which an aristocracy presided. Place, however, disdained the aristocrat, and Jeremy Bentham and James Mill had reinforced his antipathy to the point that he thought all social and political ills resulted from aristocratic influence. He decided Burdett and Hobhouse were "little better than mere drawling Whigs" [27] for objecting to a committee resolution condemning aristocratic influence during the 1826 elections. The following year he expressed delight because such

24. Ibid., 140.
25. Ibid., 138.
26. Hobhouse to the Westminster Committee, November 19, 1818, Lord Broughton Papers, Add. MSS 47226, f. 41.
27. Place to John Gale Jones, June 1, 1826, Place Papers, Add. MSS 27843, f. 390–91.

aristocrats as "Lambton the Prig," "Lansdowne the Soft," and "the supercilious Lord Grey" would cease to rule once "the march of intellect" had prepared the masses to become their own masters.[28] To be told by Hobhouse that his remarks were simply "foolish" confirmed for Place his suspicion that Westminster's M.P.'s were attempting to direct a formidable Radical movement into channels controlled by the aristocracy. As for the masses, Place had never resolved throughout the 1820's whether they had sufficiently elevated themselves to merit the vote, but he welcomed any signs that "the march of intellect" had progressed because political and social distinctions would sooner cease to exist. Place's egalitarian society of the future was inimical to Hobhouse, who believed that the rights of the masses should at least be preserved, if not extended, but who also believed a politician had the equally important task of preserving certain privileges and ranks in civilized society. If anything, his faith in a tempered aristocracy was stronger in 1832 than it was in 1820, whereas Place was more democratic. The thinking of both had evolved differently.

Hobhouse viewed his own role as a politician within a hierarchical framework. He believed the Westminster electorate had given him a mandate to vote as he wished and to decide upon the measures he would present to Parliament. An M.P., he thought, ought to give great weight to his constituents' opinions, but never at the expense of his own mature judgment. Place found such a politician unacceptable. Hobhouse's "aloofness" and want of "business habits," his growing closer to the Whigs, as well as his taste for fashionable society, were all called into account when Place informed him in 1826 that "very few persons come to you of parliamentary matters." [29] In a confrontation at Saint Stephens, Place emphasized that Hobhouse could regain Westminster's confidence only by becoming a businesslike functionary who implemented decisions reached by his constituents. Hobhouse expressed his contempt for such a politician in a letter of reply:

What one man calls "habits of business" another looks upon as restlessness and a silly desire of always doing or appearing

28. Place to Hobhouse, December 19, 1827, Place Papers, Add. MSS 35148, f. 5–9.
29. Place to Hobhouse, December 2, 1826, Lord Broughton Papers, Add. MSS 36463, f. 66.

to be doing something no matter what. It is certain that when a public man acquires this latter character he will have his hands full in a very short time—Petitions about nothing—individual cases where no cases are made out—anonymous letters—visitors whose names are no recommendation to them. All will flow in upon him, and if he has a little credulity and a great deal of variety—and moreover is not extremely nice in distinguishing right from wrong—he will turn out a most accomplished man of business, and at the end of a laborious life, equally disatisfied with himself, and disagreeable to others, and will discover that he has attempted everything and done nothing.[30]

Hobhouse and Place ultimately found their social and political outlooks irreconcilable after the enactment of many reforms that they had advocated. Partial success raised the question of ultimate purposes behind the Radical program, and although Hobhouse wanted many sweeping measures that would abolish injustice, exploitation, human misery, and political corruption, he was committed to the traditional social structure. Like Burke, he wanted to repair the foundations and adapt to new conditions. Within a decade he became Place's political opponent because he would not reject traditional institutions and authorities and replace them with new social bonds.[31]

The summer of 1822 produced some totally unexpected political developments that affected both the Tories and the Opposition. Lord Castlereagh's suicide in August enabled Canning to assume charge of both the Commons and the Foreign Office. With the unpopular Sidmouth's being replaced by Peel as Secretary of the Home Office and William Huskisson's subsequent promotion to the Board of Trade, the reform wing of the Tory party was strengthened. Peel employed his administrative talents in a series of important reforms that changed the criminal law and legal procedures. Huskisson meanwhile reorganized the nation's finances and began to liberalize economic and commercial policies. The parliamentary Opposition at that point had

30. Hobhouse to Place, December 4, 1826, Lord Broughton Papers, Add. MSS 36463, f. 69–70.

31. Graham Wallas, *The Life of Francis Place*, chap. 5, relates Place's disenchantment with Hobhouse but gives little information about the reasons. See W. E. S. Thomas, "Francis Place and Working Class History," *Historical Journal*, 5, 1 (1962), 61–79, for an analysis of Place's career and motives.

to contend with ministers whose talents and imagination were effectively employed to meet the nation's needs.

The reforming spirit of Lord Liverpool's Government aroused Francis Place's approval and surprise in 1824, when the ministers permitted the repeal of the Combination Acts of 1799 and 1800. Place had begun a campaign for repeal as early as 1818 when he secured the financial support of Jeremy Bentham and Henry Bickersteth for the *Gorgon*, a weekly working-class paper. Place eventually found an ally in Joseph Hume, who obtained a parliamentary committee of investigation in February, 1824. Place worked energetically, gathering data on various trade societies and instructing various witnesses who appeared before the committee. He and Hume planned the investigations so effectively that the committee, which included both M.P.'s for Westminster, approved a series of resolutions favoring labor combinations. Parliament accordingly repealed the Combination Acts with scarcely any debate before the close of the session.

Place's satisfaction gave way to apprehension during the following year as strikes and labor disturbances swept the country. The appeals of the powerful Liverpool shipping interests, together with reports of labor outrages from Manchester, from Glasgow, and from industrial centers along the Tyne, all convinced the Government that the labor unions had to be curtailed. Huskisson therefore moved for a committee of inquiry, which the Commons established under the chairmanship of Thomas Wallace. Place and Hume sensed disaster, for Huskisson's appeal to Parliament included a strong attack upon the repeal measure which Hume had "smuggled" through the Commons.[32]

Place then asked Hobhouse and Burdett to resist the Government's new labor bill when it reached the committee stage in the Commons. In committee, Hobhouse defended the work of Hume's previous committee by charging that the Government's proposed bill was much too vague; its clauses about "molestation" and "intimidation" could be used to destroy the unions. Hobhouse also recommended that representatives of the workers'

32. For accounts of the controversy over the Combination Acts, see Sidney Webb and Beatrice Webb, *The History of Trade Unions*, chap. II, and G. D. H. Cole, *A Short History of the British Working Class Movement, 1789–1947*, 61 ff.

interests appear before Wallace's committee; otherwise, he, for one, would "produce the most strenuous opposition to the bill." Burdett supported him by giving a short address in which he noted that none of the recent strikes warranted the revival of Combination Laws.

Hobhouse's protests in Parliament were really more routine than heartfelt. He found the Government's bill quite reasonable and justifiable. The violent attempts during the past year to form labor unions were often aimed at intimidating the workingmen themselves, and he found no objection to imposing a maximum penalty of three months imprisonment on any workman who threatened fellow workers or employers. When Place voiced his suspicion that the magistrates would indiscriminately convict labor leaders under the common-law charge of conspiracy, Hobhouse discussed the point with the Attorney-General and with Hume and then informed Place that even Hume thought the Government's bill in no way altered the power to indict on a conspiracy charge. "For my own part," Hobhouse avowed, "I do not think much harm is done, after all, by the enactment as it stands now." Place disagreed entirely and predicted the disappearance of all unions within six months after Parliament passed the bill of 1825. He saw more violence looming in the future. The workers of England, he predicted, in order "to evade the terrible consequences of this act will resort to illegal and secret oaths." [33]

Hobhouse felt the application of the law in the course of time would determine whether any further revisions were necessary. His optimism proved well founded; the measure in no way made the existence of unions a crime, nor was the workers' right to bargain collectively with employers at all curtailed. Place was again shocked at what seemed to be Hobhouse's reversal of attitude. That Hobhouse should credit the Government with anything but a willingness to serve the interests of employers was bad enough, but worst of all, Hobhouse's ambivalent attitude toward the labor unions had seriously undermined any chances of attaching a working-class following to the Westminster Committee and its parliamentary allies.

33. Hobhouse to Place, July 2, 1825, Place to Hobhouse, July 2, 1825, Place Papers, Add. MSS 27802, f. 42, 44. Cole, *Short History of Working Class*, 61, states belief that Hume's bill did not obtain complete immunity for workmen on the charge of conspiracy.

By now, the issue of party had added to the growing area of disagreement between Hobhouse and Place. Hobhouse had at first agreed entirely with the Westminster Committee that the very term "party" was one of opprobrium. "I say the country is sick of party," he declared in 1819, "I say it is so sick of party, that it will no longer take promises for performance, no longer prefer persons to principles, no longer be caught by names instead of examining into things." [34] Party politics destroyed integrity and understanding, and it was a serious mistake to think that "party cooperation renders necessary a sacrifice only of minute differences"; it required a sacrifice of vital principles, a price beyond what Hobhouse declared he would ever pay.

Principles served Hobhouse well in appraising politics from afar, but once in office he realized that a Radical M.P. could achieve little in the long run, outnumbered as he was in the pre-reform Parliament. "Better far to tell the truth at once," he observed in 1826, while paying tribute to the small Radical contingent solidly united behind Joseph Hume, "no attendance, no efforts of ours, in this place, can make us a match for ministers." Throughout 1820 and 1821 "if ever opposition despised hunger and thirst, and watchfulness for conscience sake, it was the opposition that wasted by my honorable friend [Hume] during those never-ending sessions." But were not the Ministerialists equally on the alert? "We had, indeed, the satisfaction of fatiguing them, as much as ourselves; but that was all," Hobhouse concluded.[35] Obviously the deadlock could be broken if Radicals, such as himself, joined forces with others. An outward orientation similarly prevailed among most Whigs. Denied power for so long, some party leaders sought to make the Whig vote in Parliament more consistent and cohesive in order to attract waverers over to their side, while other, more liberal-minded Whigs proved willing to step outside the bonds of their immediate connections to find a basis for cooperating with "respectable" Radicals. The question remained about the extent to which the Whigs could resolve differences among themselves on a series of issues and thus assume a reformist stance in Par-

---

34. Westminster Committee appointed to manage the Election of Mr. Hobhouse, *An Authentic Narrative of the Events of the Westminster Election, which commenced on Saturday, February 13 and closed on Wednesday, March 3, 1819*, 60–61.
35. *Hansard*, 2d series, XV (1826), cols. 692–93.

liament. A Grenville group was opposed to reform, and Grey
endorsed in 1819 only a "moderate and cautious policy of gradual improvements founded in whig principles." [36] Even on as
fundamental an issue as parliamentary reform, the Whigs were
at odds in the early 1820's. Abercromby, Milton, and Honywood
all came out against Lambton's motion of 1821, which Hobhouse had supported at length. Whig patricians were also quick
to remind others of their superior social pedigrees whenever the
question of cooperating with them arose. Aristocratic leadership
was for Brougham the very essence of any effective Opposition
to the Crown. "The power of great families," he argued in
1818, "is indeed a most necessary part of the array to which the
people must look for their security against misgovernment. It
is vain to stigmatise this cooperation as the influence of a domi-
neering aristocracy." [37] Essentially, the Whigs were grappling
with the difficult problem of somehow recruiting wider support
without sacrificing their hereditary power.

Yet despite their varying degrees of liberalism, the Whigs
as a group advocated various principles that Radicals favored,
and both groups were committed to many similar goals. Both
took pride in a tradition of opposition to the Crown; both welcomed public opinion as a force against a ministry that had
all the influence of government at its disposal. Of course the
Whigs claimed to be more discriminating inasmuch as they
would defer to the sentiments of only educated and propertied
segments of society, but they still claimed, as did the Radicals,
that the postwar tumults were the result of certain legitimate
popular grievances that had to be resolved lest agitators be
driven to further extremes. Whigs and Radicals made perennial
demands for economical reforms, tax reductions, and retrenchment in all areas of government. During the 1820's, they were
spokesmen for the civil rights allegedly threatened by repression. Ministerial reforms invited bolder, more effective alternatives on their part. Hobhouse, still identifying himself in 1821
as a Radical, worked to cement closer ties between the Whigs
and the London Radicals. "We radicals will help the Whigs
when the Whigs will do anything," he wrote in connection with
arranging a series of reform banquets. He noted that "all the

36. Grey to Robert Wilson, October 24, 1819, Robert Wilson Papers,
Add. MSS 30109, f. 56.
37. "State of Parties," *Edinburgh Review*, 30 (June, 1818), 192.

Whig reformers" attended a reform dinner in April arranged by the Westminster Committee.[38] The problem, the Radicals thought, was the Whigs' lack of action. Hobhouse prodded them in Parliament by recalling the party forebears who had so actively supported reforms. Hesitant Whigs of 1821 should consult, he suggested, the examples of Portland, Fox, Shelburne, or the Friends of the People on the issue of parliamentary reform.[39] Brougham had espoused Opposition unity under Whig leadership, and Hobhouse realized that reform stood a better chance of implementation through concerted efforts. Place, however, was disturbed that Hobhouse should invoke a Whig reformist tradition that he had assailed in *A Defence of the People*. It was obvious to Place that Hobhouse, the equivocating Radical whose motives he always suspected, was moving back to the Whig camp. An ideological affinity, as well as considerations of strategy, was bringing about what George Lamb had foretold in 1820:

If Mr. Hobhouse was returned, the moment he entered the House of Commons, from that moment he must become a Whig; for his services in parliament could only be rendered available by voting with the Whig party in opposition to the measures of government. If he did not do that he could do nothing.[40]

Hobhouse was discovering a workable approach to politics through party, but not party in the sense of a closely disciplined group whose members acted concertedly in Parliament and had ties with a formal nationwide organization. Parliamentarians of the 1820's often proclaimed their independence or else disputed with fellow party members, which produced a wide range of opinions often decided along nonparty lines. Hobhouse had earlier pictured Whigs and Tories as two organized bodies of like-minded politicians having a corporate existence. Upon entering Parliament, he began to appreciate the wide variety of outlooks and temperaments found among his fellow M.P.'s. The political situation was fluid, yet the future held promise because reformers were making headway, especially among the Whigs.

38. Hobhouse, diary, March 20, April 4, 1821, Lord Broughton Papers, Add. MSS 56541.

39. *Hansard*, 2d series, V (1821), cols. 413–14.

40. *Morning Chronicle*, March 14, 1820.

"The Russells, the Cavendishes, the Grosvenors, and the Vanes have only to be joined by the other monopolists of the elected franchise," [41] he thought, and the reformers would predominate. Hobhouse, who was so distrustful of the Whigs when the decade began, was if anything overly optimistic by 1825. A solid core of Whigs were intransigent, and the possibility that the Government might fall produced a resurgence of support for the Tories from among uncommitted M.P.'s. He more accurately assessed a primary feature of politics in 1822, when he pointed out the Whigs' need of a leader to tighten the reins on the loosely organized adherents. Followers of Brougham and Lambton, the party liberals, strained relations almost to the breaking point with party conservatives. An uncertainty prevailed in the Lords as Grey gradually withdrew from politics and Lansdowne proved unwilling to take up the mantle of leadership. Tierney withdrew in 1821 as leader in the Commons, and the inability of the Whigs to agree on a replacement left the position vacant until Althorp assumed the leadership in 1830. The enduring Tory Government gave the illusion of stability, but here, too, fundamental differences of opinion existed. Lord Liverpool's great political attribute was his ability to mediate between High Tories and party reformers, Peel and Huskisson among them, who sought economic and administrative improvements. Party politics provided situations involving bold and disruptive personalities—Brougham or Lambton among the Whigs, and Canning their counterpart among the Tories in his quest for leadership in the Commons and later for the post of Prime Minister.

Hobhouse reinterpreted constitutional practices in light of changing views about party. He discovered that in party struggles, an individual politician like himself could obtain parliamentary support for various proposals. Throughout the 1820's the Tories decided while the Whigs criticized policies, but both groups had to appeal to the nation for support. More than ever before, public opinion acted as a check upon both Government and Opposition members. Hobhouse was well aware of the importance of well-organized and politically conscious voters in his own constituency. Many more newspapers brought parliamentary matters to the reading public. The decade also featured

41. *Hansard*, 2d series, XV (1826), col. 705.

many committees of inquiry, which enabled citizens to present their views in person. This participation of the public in the political scene helped to dispel Hobhouse's earlier belief that party men operated in a political vacuum, preparing their intrigues and practicing their deceptions against the outside world. He slowly swung around to accepting the idea of party, but Place remained convinced that party politicians were evils.

Hobhouse and the Westminster Radicals thus pursued different tactics after appraising the concept and the operation of party. The complex workings of party, which allowed for a great deal of consultations and negotiations, convinced Hobhouse that he could work with party politicians without sacrificing principles. Party, so conceived, was not only tolerable but desirable; it respected the independent politician in Parliament and offered support for his bills. The party system presented another advantage by offering the public alternative policies and leaders. During the reign of George IV, the Tories had the task of remaining in office by presenting a legislative program able to withstand criticisms and counterproposals from the Opposition. Hobhouse referred in 1826 to Tory measures of the past several years when he commented, "I have lived to see many surprising reforms which had I dared to foretell, I should have been ridiculed as the wildest and most enthusiastic of dreamers." [42]

Although Tory measures may have differed only in points of detail from those proposed by their parliamentary opponents, it was to Hobhouse's credit that he recognized the importance of the Opposition in the conduct of the Government, giving it a name that would prove enduring. In an 1826 debate on the separation of the office of Treasurer of the Navy from President of the Board of Trade, Hobhouse declared in his speech rejecting the proposal, "It is said to be hard on His Majesty's Ministers to raise objections to this proposition. For my part, I think it no more hard on His Majesty's Opposition to compel them to take this course." [43] Canning's and Tierney's use of the phrase confirmed the acceptance of opposition within the constitutional framework of nineteenth-century Britain. The Monarch no longer had cause to think the Opposition wanted to drive his

42. Ibid., col. 703.
43. Ibid., cols. 135, 137, 149; see also Archibald S. Foord, *His Majesty's Opposition, 1714–1830*, chap. 8.

ministers from office, whatever had been their accomplishments and however disastrous might be the consequences to the nation. Opposition members acted in the best interests of the Crown by endeavoring to implement the wishes of his loyal subjects.

That same year, 1826, Hobhouse assessed the voting lists for nine important divisions during the 1821–1822 session.[44] These revealed that 320 members had voted with the Ministry, 226 against it, 23 both ways, and 89 not at all; 546 M.P.'s had voted consistently one way or the other, and 89 salaried officers of the Crown accounted for the ministerial majorities on each division. Furthermore, the bulk of the Opposition votes were recorded by members from cities and boroughs where elections were open, whereas almost half the ministerial votes came from cities and boroughs with a negligible electorate. Thus, despite both groups' agreement on some issues, Hobhouse still believed that ultimately there was a popular and a corrupt party. The Whigs evidently belonged in the former category, because Lord John Russell and other party members had proposed to remedy the unfortunate dichotomy through parliamentary reform.

An awareness of many issues on which they concurred drew Hobhouse closer to the Whigs. His involvement in party councils and organization strengthened his ties to them as he participated in discussions about strategy and tactics at Brooks's and elsewhere. Hobhouse began employing the term "our party" in his communiques to Durham, Tavistock, and others, and Grey thought most highly of him for having refused to support the unequal coalition with Canning in 1827. The Grand Whiggery opened their doors to him once more; visits to country estates and houses kept him further in touch with party news. The political independence Hobhouse affirmed on the eve of the Reform Bill does not eclipse the fact that he had worked and voted with the Whigs on most parliamentary divisions for over a decade. There remained parliamentary reform itself, and after the Whigs' action on the matter, Hobhouse's close alliance ripened into what became a formal party membership.

At times he regretted the lack of party unity, especially among the Whigs. The Catholic and Irish debates of 1825 furnished one such occasion. The Opposition had agreed to introduce the

44. *Hansard*, 2d series, XV (1826), cols. 697–99. Hobhouse's figures were extracted from a pamphlet written by a Mr. Marshall entitled *Alphabetical List of the Members of the House of Commons* (London, 1823).

Catholic Emancipation Bill, to which were added two supplementary "wings," or measures designed to reassure the public and reconcile some waverers or opponents of emancipation; one restricted the franchise in the Irish counties while the other aimed at curbing militancy among the Irish Catholic clergy by providing them with a government subsidy. The Opposition first had to offer stiff resistance against the Government's proposal to outlaw the Catholic Association, which had spread rapidly from the time of its founding in 1823. Hobhouse was among the Opposition members to urge that O'Connell and other Association leaders be allowed to state their case to the Commons inasmuch as only they truly represented the Irish people.[45] Their proposal rejected, the Opposition then introduced Catholic Emancipation, which carried by a majority of 17 on its first reading in February.

Some Tories had supported Burdett's Emancipation Bill in order to force Canning to take a stand on the issue. When Canning declared himself against the measure, which he said was "fraught with calamity to the country," a disappointed Brougham angrily assailed Burdett for not choosing a more opportune time to introduce emancipation. The Opposition was even more divided when Littleton proposed to disfranchise the Irish forty-shilling freeholders, a proposal that, despite O'Connell's prior consent, caused Lambton to rise up in protest. Hobhouse and Brougham then expressed their dissatisfaction with him on the floor of the House and urged him to reconsider his objection to disfranchisement and his declared intention to vote against the Catholic Emancipation Bill as well.[46] Lambton eventually abstained from voting on both measures, and Hobhouse confessed to experiencing "a more painful struggle within myself than I have ever experienced since I have been a public man" over the various Catholic bills, as his voting record indicates. He "reluctantly left the House, and did not vote" on the Irish franchise and the Catholic clergy bills; he likewise abstained from the Catholic Emancipation Bill's second reading but was among those approving final passage on May 10 by a majority of 248 to 227.[47] A week later the peers rallied around the Duke of York to reject the measure. All in all the Irish debates proved

45. *Hansard*, 2d series, XII (1825), cols. 84, 554–57.
46. Ibid., XIII (1825), col. 477.
47. Dorchester, ed., *Recollections*, III, 98.

a fiasco for the Opposition: Not one of their proposals was enacted, and they had failed to prevent suppression of the Catholic Association for at least two years; also, as Hobhouse commented, "differences among supporters of Catholic Emancipation were nearly breaking up the opposition." [48]

"Whig and Tory, Foxite and Pittite, Ministerial and Opposition have ceased to be distinctions," Lord Holland wrote Lord Grey at the end of 1826, "but the divisions of classes and great interests are arrayed against each other—grower and consumer, lands and funds, Irish and English, Catholic and Protestant." [49] Holland's appraisal of politics was well founded. Canning had no choice but to side reluctantly with fellow Tories against the pro-Catholics, once he had spurned Brougham's offer of a coalition. He led the Tories in the Commons, and yet any party member who suffered defeat during the 1826 general elections over the Corn Law constituted a victory for his free-trade principles. His parliamentary opponents supported his foreign policy; Hobhouse, for one, went so far as to praise Tory achievements in general. Issues were transcending party ties, and old assumptions were becoming less true as a more fluid political situation was emerging.

At a December parley Hobhouse and Place could foresee no major reforms in the immediate future. The Catholic question and parliamentary reform would be shelved indefinitely by the Liverpool Government, and the 1827 parliamentary session would be generally uneventful. But the political scene was suddenly altered on February 17, when Lord Liverpool suffered an apoplectic fit. After some hesitation, the King chose to ask Canning to head the Government. Canning had reckoned upon his indispensable role within the party and his immense popularity at large when he refused any subordinate position under Wellington or Peel. They were equally adamant in refusing to serve under Canning, a controversial figure and the son of an actress besides. Leading Tories greeted the King's decision with dismay and deserted the new Government, but Canning remained master of the situation. Acting the part of Achitophel, he persuaded the King to renounce the Tory deserters and allow his Chief minister to seek support from the Whigs.

48. Ibid., I, 165.
49. Lord Holland to Earl Grey, December 21, 1826, quoted in Keith Feiling, *The Second Tory Party, 1714–1832*, 401.

Brougham hailed Canning's offer of a coalition as the realization of his long-cherished goal. Moderate reformers would unite at last against conservative and Radical extremists, and with a high office for Brougham. Brougham's plans, however, suddenly evaporated when Lord Lansdowne ended negotiations with Canning because the latter could not surmount royal opposition to the appointment of a pro-Catholic Irish Lord Lieutenant and Chief Secretary. Lansdowne left London for his Bowood estate, whereupon Brougham summoned a meeting of Whigs and prevailed upon them to send to Wiltshire a deputation favoring a coalition. The deputies succeeded in persuading Lansdowne to reopen negotiations, in which he wrung the concession of a pro-Catholic Irish Secretary. Canning had formed his coalition Government, with Lansdowne, Carlisle, and Tierney representing the Whigs.

Reaction to the short-lived coalition was sharp and varied. Burdett told Hobhouse that he would support Canning in order to keep the High Tories out of office. Francis Place disapproved, as did Jeremy Bentham, who deplored Burdett's hankering for a high position among the Tories. William Cobbett was angrier than anyone. He turned the annual Westminster dinner of May 23 into a free-for-all before the several hundred guests. Just after Lord John Russell proposed a toast to Hobhouse, Cobbett jumped on a table and began screaming insults at Burdett and Hobhouse, who he called "my dear little Sancho" and who seized one of the steward's wands and threatened Cobbett. Fighting broke out, and disputants barricaded themselves behind chairs and tables. Hobhouse mounted the high table to speak, but it gave way and he came crashing down along with decanters, glasses, and all.[50]

Hobhouse could claim unjust treatment by Cobbett because he had emphatically disapproved of Burdett's decision to support Canning, whom he still regarded as "the arch-enemy of Reformers." [51] He commented ironically to Tavistock upon the "generosity and disinterestedness and the easy confidence which have induced our friends" to support Canning.[52] Indeed, the Whigs who had joined his Government had obviously lost their

50. Dorchester, ed., *Recollections*, III, 195–97; *Political Register*, May 26, 1827.
51. Dorchester, ed., *Recollections*, III, 187.
52. Hobhouse to Tavistock, May 3, 1827, Dukes of Bedford Papers.

senses. There was no guarantee even for Catholic Emancipation, and it was doubtful that the Whigs carried enough weight to tip the balance toward other reforms, even though the High Tories opposed Canning. Hobhouse agreed with Lord Grey that those Whigs who had welcomed the coalition had sacrificed all party principles to gain a subordinate status in the Government.[53] He thus refused to transfer to the Government benches in early May and declared he would vote for or against certain measures as an independent. A small Whig group led by Althorp, and including Tavistock, Duncannon, Russell, and Ebrington, took a similar position. Weeks later Hobhouse felt obliged to refuse Canning's dinner invitation at the close of the parliamentary session.

Canning was Prime Minister for only a few months longer. Earlier in the year he had caught a chill while attending the Duke of York's funeral, and late in July, he contracted a fever at Lord Lyndhurst's home. On August 6, Hobhouse rode to Chiswick to pay his respects to the dying man. Two days later, he assessed Canning's career and unfulfilled opportunities upon learning of his death:

Great things were expected from him, and he had certainly commenced a noble career, with respect to foreign politics, and it is believed he meant to do his utmost for Ireland. Yet his foreign politics were, according to his confession, the consequences of the changes which had occurred in Europe, and such as Castlereagh himself had resolved upon and had partially initiated. All was to be done for Ireland: nothing had been done. He had not time to show his sincerity to the world, and private conviction in these cases is not enough for a politician to act upon.[54]

Politicians parleyed until the void left by Canning's death was filled by a new Government. Hobhouse learned from Tavistock, who forwarded some letters, that Lord Holland, who expected a Cabinet post, had deplored Hobhouse's unwillingness to "sacrifice a doubtful opinion" by supporting the coalition. Hobhouse retorted that it was Holland and other Whig leaders who had deserted reformers to become ministers without power and poli-

53. Hobhouse to Ellice, May 3, 1827, Edward Ellice Papers; see also Tavistock to Hobhouse, April 30, 1827, Lord Broughton Papers, Add. MSS 36463, f. 307–8.
54. Dorchester, ed., *Recollections*, III, 216–17.

ticians without principles. "My great objection to Lord Lansdowne," he wrote, "is that he is trying to act without his friends
and has reduced himself to impotence by so doing." [55] He denied
the rumor that he and other independents were trying to form
an official neutral party. Such efforts, he thought, would prove
abortive and would only add to the political confusion.

The year ended with the Whigs once more the Opposition.
Never satisfied with their share in Canning's Government, the
coalition Whigs had pressed for Holland's admission into the
Cabinet, and the King had refused, whereupon Lansdowne resigned as Home Secretary. When Parliament reconvened in early
1828, the Duke of Wellington had established an administration after Lord Goderich had briefly tried to lead the Government. "Individuals were so dispersed, and of such varied opinions," Hobhouse recorded, "that they could not be brought to
meet or even to consult on immediate measures." [56] Anything
was possible while the political situation remained so fluid.

Hobhouse did not agree with Holland, Francis Place, and
others who felt the return of the Tories was the greatest of evils.
"It would be unwise as well as unfair to oppose his [Welling-
ton's] administration at once, without giving it a trial," he wrote
Place.[57] Hobhouse thought it very likely Wellington would appoint liberal ministers, and he included Peel among them because he was "anxious to try his popularity." Besides, no Government could ignore the sentiment for reform that prevailed.
Hobhouse did not become concerned until Huskisson's resignation increased the prospects of a conservative ministry. He then
declared his first choice to lead the nation would be Althorp or
Bedford, who had both resisted the blandishments of office under
Canning, because "if they would do nothing one should then
know that goodwill could do nothing." Place thought Althorp
and Bedford were "as good as any in their class" but lacked any
popular support. Place, who was aghast at Hobhouse's comments about the Tories, declared that Peel "would make a despotism if he could" and that Wellington "would cut the throat

55. Hobhouse to Tavistock, January 8, 1828, Bedford Papers.
56. Dorchester, ed., *Recollections*, III, 234–35.
57. Hobhouse to Place, December 18, 1827; see also January 7, January
12, January 15, 1828, for other exchanges, and Place to Hobhouse, December 19, 1827, January 7, January 12, January 15, 1828, Place Papers, Add.
MSS 35148, f. 5–15.

of any one who stood in the way of his supreme ignorance." And did Hobhouse, he asked, not realize that most parliamentarians had no interest in serving the people? Place discerned events moving slowly but inexorably to the point at which the entire antiquated political system would be superseded by one responsive to the needs of most Britons. The masses had watched as public men made spectacles of themselves disputing over offices and forming ministries. There was a time when such slogans as " '45" or "Wilkes and Liberty" had made "the silly people mad," but since then the people had learned much, and the "march of intellect" assured that the present state of affairs could not continue much longer. He thought it regrettable that Hobhouse did not see the future dispensation coming.

Place later expressed surprise when Wellington's solidly Tory Cabinet proceeded to shatter party unity by undertaking the reforms its predecessors had refused to touch. One measure was the repeal of the Test Act and Corporation Act. Hobhouse, who had been too ill to participate in the debates, attended a Dissenters' banquet on June 18, 1828, as did many Catholics who thought the festivities heralded emancipation.

Their expectations were reasonable, because the King's speech opening the 1829 session stunned the Protestant party by referring to Catholic Emancipation. Peel and Wellington had convinced the Monarch that only concessions to the Catholics could avert civil war in Ireland. The Irish people had united the previous year to defeat a minister at the polls in County Clare; also, their Catholic Association had risen like a phoenix that summer, and the stark reality of its power could no longer be overlooked. The anti-Catholic party nevertheless presented many petitions to Parliament during the course of the debates, hoping to impress upon the Government the public's opposition to emancipation. On one occasion Hobhouse told the Commons he was not a fit member for Westminster if so many householders had actually signed one anti-Catholic petition presented by Mr. Palmer of Surrey.[58] The bill passed its third reading on March 30, and the next day Hobhouse joined others to witness its submission before the Lords. "Thus was consummated this great act of national justice and saving policy," he recorded when Catholic Emancipation received the King's assent two weeks later.[59] The

58. *Hansard*, 2d series, XX (1829), col. 1327–28.
59. Dorchester, ed., *Recollections*, III, 318–19.

High Tories pledged a fight to the finish against Peel and Wellington, who they characterized as reprobates who had betrayed them.

Catholic Emancipation was a significant event in constitutional history, for it marked the further decline of the royal prerogative. George IV, like his predecessor, had resisted any Catholic concessions and had insisted that the Whigs who joined Canning's Government would have to accept emancipation as an "open question" within the Cabinet. Ministers were free to express their individual opinions, but they were to respect the principle that His Majesty's Government, as a body, would neither encourage nor suppress the demand for emancipation. Hobhouse noted the factor of royal influence during the emancipation debates of 1827. "Anti-Catholic members," he commented, "were, in great part, men, who, if the King said a word, would vote for the Catholics." [60] The imminent danger of civil war in 1829 made Peel and Wellington insist upon the Cabinet's unity in order to obtain emancipation without delay. The King yielded to necessity when he saw himself confronted by a united Cabinet and a parliamentary majority. The precedent was not lost upon the Whigs when Lord Grey formed a Cabinet pledged to parliamentary reform and later when he advised the King to dissolve Parliament following the bill's defeat in committee.

The political world awaited Wellington's answer to the reformers, which came when the Parliament met on November 2. He stood firmly not only against a Tory-sponsored bill but also against any parliamentary reform measure whatsoever. Wellington had nailed his colors to the mast, and the Opposition prepared to take up the challenge. A showdown in the Commons on Brougham's reform motion was avoided when the Government resigned after a defeat on the civil list. Wellington then advised William IV to summon Grey. The reluctant King had no choice but to yield to the leader of an opposition now capable of defeating his ministers in Parliament. Even the royal prerogative of choosing the Prime Minister had been further curtailed.

Hobhouse reacted to the dramatic events of 1830 with mixed feelings of anticipation and of skepticism. He did not take seriously Tory claims about returning soon to office. "I think not," he noted, "To me this appears 'le commencement de la fin' as

60. Ibid., 179.

Talleyrand said of Buonaparte's defeat in Russia." But he retained a deep mistrust of the Whigs who had just entered office:

My impressions were that these men are utterly ignorant of the true state of the country, and will persevere deliberating on the miseries of petty political factions till the storm bursts over them, and all is over with them and the country.[61]

Hobhouse's unflattering estimation is in keeping with his emphatic refusals to formally join the Whig party. He reaffirmed his political independence several times at Brougham's dinner party preceding the new parliamentary session. Hobhouse thought the conservative Whigs would block reform as they had in the past, and he wondered if the Tories who joined the coalition could be counted upon to stand with Lord Grey. He thought they might join the conservative Whigs in persuading Grey to abandon parliamentary reform by pointing to the spectres of radicalism and revolution. Hobhouse still felt in 1831 that the Whigs could not be trusted to reform Parliament on their own and that the need still existed for sympathetic outsiders to prod the new Government if it wavered at any time. By 1832, however, Hobhouse had abandoned his ambivalent position toward the Whigs and included himself among the party that had secured parliamentary reform.

61. Ibid., IV, 61.

CHAPTER V

REVOLUTION ABROAD
SPAIN, GREECE, FRANCE

"Good God! What times!!"[1] Hobhouse exclaimed in 1815 after hearing the Commons discuss the Vienna peace terms. Had Britain, he wondered, poured forth her blood and treasure for such results? Everywhere absolutism triumphed, stronger and more sinister than anything the previous century had known. A week earlier he had sat with a group of Polish exiles who lamented their country's repartition, especially after Castlereagh had allegedly said the Poles would be left their language. The Congress of Vienna had ignored Italian and Belgian nationalism; monarchs stood in dread of liberal aspirations everywhere; worst of all the British Government apparently backed the grand design that absolutist rulers had fashioned for the postwar world. So bitterly disillusioned by events in 1815, Hobhouse became a leading revisionist spokesman in the decade ahead. Spain, France, and above all, Greece, provided opportunities to undo the harm he saw.

Hobhouse's concern for freedom abroad was also significant in terms of domestic politics. He saw that here was an issue on which Whigs and Radicals united: Russell, Nugent, and Holland worked alongside Hume, Bowring, and Bentham on committees to champion libertarian movements abroad. Canning stole some of the Opposition's thunder and enhanced his own reputation by defying the European monarchs, but even Canning was vulnerable to Radical or Whig attacks on major issues. He failed to prevent a French invasion of Spain in 1823, and he proved reluctant to recognize the independence of those gallant Greek rebels who aroused sympathy from people of all backgrounds and outlooks. Lastly, a commitment to political liberalism abroad enhanced Hobhouse's own image at Westminster. Just as he had worshiped Napoleon as the agent of liberty throughout Europe, so at this time did Westminster Radicals toast Simon Bolivar, Spanish liberals, the Greeks, and the "cause

1. Hobhouse, diary, March 23, 1815, John Cam Hobhouse, Lord Broughton, Papers, Add. MSS 47232, f. 85.

of freedom throughout the world." At many banquets, Radicals warmly applauded Hobhouse for announcing that he, too, would champion revolution abroad. Other Westminster public men joined him. Major Cochrane, a former M.P., fought in South America; Major Cartwright wrote manuals of arms for the Greeks. Radicals assumed that the cause of liberty was universal, that it was part of a general historical trend that could not be resisted.

Hobhouse was among many who misjudged the aims of British postwar foreign policy.[2] Castlereagh had joined the Quadruple Alliance out of conviction that Britain must be involved in the collective task of restoring the Continent to tranquility, and in 1815 he regarded France as the greatest potential threat to peace. He denied all along that the major powers had a right to interfere at will in the internal affairs of other states, and refused to associate Britain with the repressive policies against German liberals adopted in the Carlsbad Decrees. His famous State Paper of May 5 outlined objections to foreign intervention against the Spanish liberals who had forced a constitution upon King Ferdinand in 1820. At Troppau, he reiterated in a circular that any attempt to coerce a government into returning to the fold of the Holy Alliance "would be in direct repugnance to the fundamental laws" of England.[3] A similar stand was taken by Wellington, who followed instructions Castlereagh had prepared before his death on the eve of the Conference of Verona in 1822, when France was authorized to act against the Spanish liberals.

Because Castlereagh did not appreciate the importance of disclosing to the public any dealings with the foreign rulers he had come to know at Vienna, those eager to know what transpired behind closed doors at the periodic conferences became suspicious. Hobhouse, for one, found it hard to believe that one so strongly opposed to reform at home should countenance liberal aspirations abroad. His own visits to Italy after the war had left

2. See John Russell, first Earl Russell, *A Letter to the Rt. Hon. Lord Holland on Foreign Affairs*, which accused the Government of destroying the European balance of power essential for peace by joining the monarchs on the Continent in the Quadruple Alliance.

3. Sir C. K. Webster, *The Foreign Policy of Castlereagh, 1815–1822*, 321–23; on the State Paper of May, 1820, see *The Cambridge History of Foreign Policy, 1815–1865*, ed. by Sir. A. W. Ward and G. P. Gooch (Cambridge, 1923), II, Appendix A.

him with the impression of a widespread desire to overthrow the hated "Congress Castlereagh system" [4]; most Italians were Carbonaris, eager to throw off Austrian oppression. Mere verbal protests from the British Government failed to stop Austrian armies from marching on Naples and Piedmont in 1820, and similar, seemingly ineffective, steps were in the offing for Spanish liberals. The future augured not at all well unless the Opposition in Parliament forced a change in English foreign policy. Britain, those in the Opposition felt, must proclaim boldly her intention to defend militarily any peaceful regime threatened by an absolutist power.

In Parliament Hobhouse first singled out for attack the Alien Act in order to expose the Government's complicity in the schemes of the Holy Alliance. Introduced by Pitt during the French Revolution, the measure required all aliens to register and provided for their expulsion should they participate in subversive activities. The complex matter of refugees posed a dilemma for the ministers: As guardians of public order, they wanted to safeguard the country against possible trouble from among the twenty-five thousand resident aliens, but by so doing, they risked criticism about denying sanctuary to unfortunate refugees, possibly through prior agreement with the Russian and Austrian police.

Castlereagh defended renewals of the Alien Act in 1820 and 1822 by explaining the necessity of such action in troubled times. There were traitors throughout Europe, he warned, "who were ready, in the accomplishment of their schemes, to set at defiance every principle of humanity, every sentiment that was worthy of man in civilized society." [5] He assured the Commons that the Government had no intention of refusing asylum to foreign refugees; indeed, the Home Office had deported fewer than a dozen aliens since 1812. Hobhouse, who was not satisfied, joined Sir James Mackintosh and other Whigs in assailing Castlereagh's assertion that the aliens constituted a source of danger. He recalled in 1820 that even Edmund Burke, who supported the bill in wartime "to keep out those murderous French atheists," believed the Alien Act would endanger English freedoms in peacetime. His fear was that the day might come when

4. Hobhouse, diary, October 9, 1816, Lord Broughton Papers, Add. MSS 56537.

5. *Hansard Parliamentary Debates*, 2d series, I (1820), col. 777.

Britons would be at the mercy of the Home Office and denied the privilege of demanding specific charges against themselves or of calling in witnesses to disprove any idle gossip about their activities.

Two years later Hobhouse explained that the Alien Act was renewed because of the atmosphere of fear that still prevailed throughout Britain. Ministers encouraged people to think in terms of plots and revolutions; yet Mme. de Staël, in her *Considerations of the French Revolution*, had wisely admonished those who failed to understand the realities of the past or the present. They seemed to her to regard the *ancien régime* as a golden age of security and happiness, to conjure up only the horrors of the French Revolution, and to describe any reformer as a violent Jacobin. The wars were over, and the Jacobins had vanished, but unfortunately, she thought, many frightened Britons equated law and order with such repressive measures as the Alien Act.[6]

Hobhouse's own fears about the Alien Act were more imaginary than real. He might have succeeded in focusing public attention on the measure had the Government applied it more frequently. The issue of foreign refugees, however, was all but forgotten in 1826, when Peel announced he would not request a renewal of the Alien Act. He pointed out that the Home Office had not expelled a single alien during his four years at the Home Office. Hobhouse welcomed the gesture and added that foreign policy had changed greatly in recent years. He alluded to Canning, who had inherited many of Castlereagh's policies but applied them with flair and skill in courting popular favor. The King's speech of 1823 repeated the declaration made at Verona against any foreign intervention in Spain. Then Canning stepped before the Commons to receive the tributes of Brougham, Sir Robert Wilson, Hobhouse, and other Opposition members. Hobhouse could only regret that "the independence of Europe and the liberties of mankind at large" had not been affirmed with equal vigor at Troppau and at the Congress of Laibach.[7] Amid rumors of French military movements toward the Spanish frontier, he urged repeal of the Foreign Enlistments Act in order to assure Spanish liberals of England's support.

The French invasion of Spain that April resulted in a thor-

6. Ibid., II (1820), col. 405–16, VII (1822), cols. 1446 ff.
7. Ibid., VIII (1823), col. 240.

ough investigation of Canning's policy. Canning himself immediately published the documents relating to Spanish affairs, which revealed that he never intended to go to war over the liberal regime there. Instead, Canning had urged the Spanish Cortes to appease the Holy Alliance by amending its Constitution. In the Commons, Hobhouse attacked this timid stand against the French, a policy he found all the more deplorable because Canning had established a reputation at home and abroad for boldly defying the continental powers. Canning should have exploited this reputation by taking a stronger stand on Spain, Hobhouse believed, but instead, Canning had merely told the Spanish Government to amend the Constitution on the eve of invasion, a strategy that Hobhouse found comparable to the man who tells his neighbor to avoid a robbery by giving away his money. Hobhouse then assured the Commons that his constituents would willingly share the cost of war with France. Canning acknowledged Hobhouse as the only M.P. who had "fairly and boldly met" the issue of declaring war, but the nation seemed to Canning overwhelmingly pacifist. He insisted upon pressing the Opposition's censure motion on his Spanish policy to a division, and the Commons voted down the motion by an overwhelming majority.[8]

Parliament had endorsed Canning's policy of nonintervention, but many Englishmen wished to help the beleaguered Spaniards who were fighting bravely against the Holy Alliance, which was, according to *The Times*, "resolved to make itself felt, as well as understood." [9] The patriots met in the London Tavern on June 13 to establish a Spanish committee in charge of raising public funds. Mackintosh, Lord Ebrington, Lord John Russell, Henry Brougham, Lambton, and Joseph Hume were among the M.P.'s who attended the rally. Hume got the meeting under way by proposing Lord Erskine as the committee chairman. Hobhouse later accepted his election to the committee in a speech that was eloquent about "the cause of liberty all over the world" and the Spanish liberals who fought for "all posterity who deserved to be free." [10] He urged the people of England to defy

8. Ibid., cols. 1335–50, 1508; *Annual Register*, 1823, 97 ff.

9. *The Times*, June 20, 1823.

10. Ibid., June 14, 1823; Lady Dorchester, ed., *Recollections of a Long Life, by Lord Broughton (John Cam Hobhouse) with additional extracts from his private diaries*, IV, 127.

the Government during this crisis by actively intervening in Spain. They should contribute money for arms and supplies; they should emulate the example of Sir Robert Wilson, who was going to Spain as a military adviser.

Contributions slowly trickled into the offices of the committee —Thomas Coke, £10; John Willes, £20; J. Cartwright, 20 muskets; £1 "from an Englishman who wishes it were £10,000." [11] Lord Nugent sailed for Cadiz where he hoped to rally the Spanish Army with promises of aid from England. Some committeemen speculated that Canning had approved these voluntary efforts, since he made no efforts to prevent Wilson and Nugent from joining the Spanish Army by enforcing the Foreign Enlistments Act.

The committeemen had just celebrated Lord Nugent's departure when they were shocked to learn about a scandal within their own ranks. Joseph Hume informed Hobhouse in October about the disappearance of £240 from the £1,770 fund. Furthermore, the five hundred uniforms sent to Spain were of such poor quality that they were unusable.[12] It seemed that in the rush to deliver the supplies, no one had thought to inspect the pattern and quality of the cloth. Perhaps it is just as well the Spanish cause remained for most Englishmen what Princess Lieven described as "the object of their good wishes." [13] Even Lord Nugent lost much of his enthusiasm once he reached Spain; from there, he wrote to Hobhouse about the indolence, which was "the overwhelming vice of the whole nation." Nugent could not understand why the Spanish masses remained so apathetic about a cause he so strongly favored.[14] Only slowly did he realize that the constitutionalists represented a small minority; most of the people remained indifferent, even as the French Army marched swiftly through Spain to rout the liberal forces by the end of the summer.

During the following months, Canning paid his respects to the unsuccessful committeemen whose philosophy "professes

11. *The Times*, June 21, 1823.

12. Hume to Hobhouse, September 11, 1823, Lord Broughton Papers, Add. MSS 36460, f. 123.

13. Princess Lieven to General Alexander Benckendorff, April 27, 1823, in L. G. Robinson, ed., *Letters of Dorothea, Princess Lieven, during her residence in London, 1812–1834*, 64.

14. Lord Nugent to Hobhouse, September 9, 1823, Lord Broughton Papers, Add. MSS 36460, f. 117.

the perfection of our species and the amelioration of the lot of mankind." They were truly noble, he thought, especially such men as Lord Nugent and Sir Robert Wilson, who rushed to Spain to play the role of knight-errant,[15] but he himself was the calm, patriotic realist who knew when and where his country's interests were at stake. The cause of a few quarrelsome Spanish liberals was not among them.

The uprising of the Greeks against Ottoman rule during the 1820's commanded such wide sympathy throughout the West that no government could ignore it, and until the European powers could agree upon a common policy that ended the fighting, philhellenes everywhere rallied behind the insurgents. A variety of motives impelled wealthy Greek expatriates, Napoleonic veterans, students, merchants, and public men to send money and supplies and even sacrifice their lives for Greek independence. For some, news of the rebellion conjured up memories of an immortal and splendid heritage. "We are all Greeks," Shelley wrote in 1821, "Our laws, our literature, our arts have their roots in Greece."[16] Obviously, no civilized man could stand by while the lineal descendants of Socrates and Phidias, Sophocles and Leonidas, fought for freedom. Others thought of a Christian crusade against the unspeakable Turks: "For Liberty and the Cross" read the banners held by a contingent of volunteers that left Marseilles for the East. In Paris and Geneva, in cities throughout Germany, Italy, and America, committees were formed to collect funds for the Greeks.

From its very outset Hobhouse warmly supported the Greek rebellion and first mentioned it at the opening of the 1822 session of Parliament. He expressed dismay and disappointment because the King's speech had avoided Greece entirely. Surely no Briton with a conscience could ignore the "Ottoman crescent displayed on bodies of the Greeks whom the Ottoman scimitar had hewn down."[17] Intervention on behalf of the Greeks was in Hobhouse's estimation imperative for the sake of Christianity, civilization, and humanity, but neither in Parliament nor through several public addresses could he arouse public support for the Greeks. The nature of the fighting was too confused, and there

---

15. *Hansard*, 2d series, X (1824), cols. 1272 ff.
16. Percy Bysshe Shelley, Preface to *Hellas*, in *The Complete Poetical Works of Shelley* (Boston, 1901), 319.
17. *Hansard*, 2d series, VI (1822), cols. 32–36.

were reports of atrocities on both sides. "The infatuation of this nation becomes more evident," the London *Morning Chronicle* countered, "who thought to gain independence by treachery and shameful massacres, which their leaders call victories. The Musselman and the Greeks vie with each other in cruelty."[18] Besides, there was every reason to fear that the dismemberment of the Ottoman Empire would enable the Russians to gain a foothold in the Mediterranean. "We are not enemies of Greek independence, but of Russian aggrandisement," the *Morning Chronicle* commented.[19] The possibility of Russian expansion was uppermost in Canning's mind as the Greek rebellion progressed.

Public sentiment in Britain, as elsewhere, changed sharply following news of the massacre or enslavement of nearly 100,000 inhabitants of Chios in 1822. An outpouring of pamphlets raged against the Turks, "a people without pity, without morality, without letters, arts—a very reproach to human nature," and in Parliament, Lord Erskine spoke about "detestable Turkish vices . . . allowed and patronized by a religion of sensuality, which makes the Ottoman Empire a moral pestilence to every nation."[20] Quakers organized refugee relief; rallies occurred throughout Britain; and among the permanent committees established to aid the rebels the one that received the most publicity, as well as a later notoriety, was the Greek committee formed in London in March of 1823. In addition to Hobhouse, the original twenty-six members included Ellice, Russell, Lambton, and H. G. Bennett among the Whigs; a coterie of Philosophical Radicals with John Bowring, who became secretary, Joseph Hume, and Jeremy Bentham himself; and Zachariah Macaulay among the Evangelicals. William Smith, chairman of the Dissenting Deputies, also joined. Several months later, with over four hundred registered in Sir John Bowring's listing, the London committee gained its most illustrious member when Lord Byron agreed to serve as its agent in Greece. "They are going to make to you a solemn request and appeal," Hobhouse had written to his friend in Italy, "to go to Greece at once for

18. *Morning Chronicle*, June 29, 1821.
19. Ibid., May 10, 1821.
20. Rev. Thomas S. Hughes, *Considerations upon the Greek Rebellion*, 9; Thomas Erskine, first Baron Erskine, *An Appeal to the People of Great Britain on the Subject of a Confederated Greece*, 4.

the sake of showing, in the most positive manner, the interest the English take in their cause, and for the sake of getting certain information on which they can depend." He added, "If you go to Greece, I do not see the necessity of your staying long. Just go to headquarters and look about you and come away again; a few weeks in the Morea would be quite sufficient." [21] Byron prepared for the journey to Greece by arranging for credit through his bankers and by obtaining supplies for the trip. His brig *Hercules* finally set sail from Leghorn in July, 1823.

Meanwhile the London committee was busily devising ways to raise funds for Greece. There were banquets, speaking tours, an exhibition of Greek art, and even an elaborate public ceremony, which ended in embarrassing failure when a large balloon, bedecked with streamers and ribbons—a symbol of resurgent Greece—failed to ascend. Hobhouse headed a literary subcommittee that prepared articles favoring the Greeks and answered those injurious to the rebel cause. Dr. Routh, President of Magdalen College, reported that the higher powers at Oxford were not disposed to support the Greek subscription, but from elsewhere funds were pledged to London: The Chancellor at Cambridge, the Duke of Gloucester who was the King's cousin, donated £100; Staffordshire sent £94; Suffolk, £33 5s. 8d.; Liverpool, £400; the Bishop of Norwich announced £150 raised by the Norfolk committee; funds also came from Dublin and Calcutta. By June, Bowring announced that over £3,000 had been contributed to the Greek fund in London; by October, £7,000; and his subsequent financial statement in *The Westminster Review* in 1826 reported a total of £11,241 6s. 8d. raised by English philhellenes. [22] The expenditure of this money proved quite a problem for the committeemen. They were undecided about whether they would purchase supplies in England or send money directly to the rebels as the Greek agents in England wished. They finally chose to spend the money themselves but

---

21. Hobhouse to Byron, June 11, 1823, in John Cam Hobhouse, Proofs of Letters from John Cam Hobhouse to Lord Byron, set up in type in connection with an edition of Byron's correspondence projected by Charlotte Carleton, Baroness Dorchester.

22. Dr. Routh to E. H. Barker, April 24, 1824, London Greek Committee, Papers, K-8; "Greek Committee," *The Westminster Review*, 6 (June, 1826), 131.

failed to keep an itemized list of their purchases. Bowring's sketchy account reported a sum of just over £4,000—one-third of the total fund—spent for war supplies. Printing presses, surgical instruments, medical supplies, and "sundry other objects not immediately warlike" amounted to £1,767 0s. 8d. Jeremy Bentham's plan to educate eight Greek children in England cost £500. The remaining sum was spent on such items as advertising, freight and insurance fees, expense accounts for committee agents in Greece, and a staggering amount of £730 3s. 2d. for "sundry minor expenses." [23] Just what some of them were we can learn from Byron, who wrote to caution the enthusiasts against sending such useless supplies as a shipment of mathematical instruments that the bewildered rebels simply dumped into the sea. Nor could he see any value in a shipment of trumpets; musical instruments might have signaled the charge at Waterloo, but they were of little value for the warriors of Greece. Byron also discouraged Hobhouse's idea of sending a brigade of mercenaries, because the ones already there often fought with the local population.

Byron, whose journey to Greece had a tragic aspect of a man escaping from himself, proved to have a perceptive understanding of the Greek rebellion. He understood how centuries of isolation from Europe and exposure to Ottoman despotism had changed the descendants of the heroes of antiquity beyond all recognition. He found them often suspicious, thoroughly priest-ridden, and exasperatingly undisciplined. Chieftains often appropriated supplies for themselves; fighting men often refused to follow orders; they never thought of sparing a Turkish prisoner until Byron offered an award for every captive taken alive. Then, by the end of 1823, the rebel leaders became embroiled in discord, as the Mavrocordatos civilian or legislative branch of the government disputed power with the military leaders who controlled the executive branch. Byron warned the disputants that he for one would not deceive his countrymen about the real state of Greek affairs should the disunity continue.

Byron's firsthand experiences were in striking contrast to the

23. Accounts in London Creek Committee, Papers, K-11; "Greek Committee," *The Westminster Review*, 131; also Byron to Bowring, October 13, October 16, 1823, in George Gordon Byron, sixth Baron Byron, *The Works of Lord Byron; A New, Revised and Enlarged Edition, with Illustrations: Letters and Journals*, ed. by R. E. Prothero, VI, 285, 293.

views held by the London committeemen a thousand miles away. Their eyes were fixed on "the heroic achievements and the scientific attainments of Greeks in the past"; the spectacle of the present as Greece "reawakened into freedom and light." [24] Such idealists quickly displayed little practical sense in dealing with mundane matters involving a war, and the results were confusion, incompetence, and disillusionment. It seemed to them that they could readily achieve their goal of liberating Greece through the sheer righteousness of their cause. That the Turks did not want to relinquish the country made little impression upon them or upon Col. Leicester Stanhope, later fifth Earl of Harrington, whom the committeemen chose to join Byron as an agent in November, 1823. Bowring was especially enthusiastic about securing the services of a fellow Benthamite, and Stanhope himself informed the Greek committee of Zurich, which he visited on his way to Greece, that the venerable Bentham was busily engaged in framing laws and a constitution for the rebels.[25] Stanhope later presented himself to Byron as a social reformer who anticipated a sweeping rebel victory. The two agents differed in their views toward the Greek leaders, with Byron favoring the more moderate Mavrocordatos while Stanhope sympathized with Odysseus, the leader of the western Greeks who wished to establish a republic. Byron tried to engage in conversation about gunpowder and field artillery, but Stanhope was interested primarily in Lancastrian schools and printing presses. "I am tired of hearing nothing but talk, and constitutions, and Sunday Schools & what not etc., etc.," wrote a weary Byron to the London committee in a last letter, "all excellent things in their time and place, & here also whenever they've means, money, leisure & freedom to try the experiments." [26]

Voluntary contributions scarcely sufficed against the Ottomans, so the London committee suggested raising a loan on the money market. The Greek Government accordingly sent two deputies, Jean Orlando and Andreas Luriottis, to negotiate through the firm of Loughman and O'Brien. The Lord Mayor

24. "Statement of the London Greek Committee," March 23, 1823, London Greek Committee, Papers, K-1.
25. Col. Leicester Stanhope, *Greece in 1823 and 1824*, 7–8.
26. Byron to Bowring, January 28, 1824, London Greek Committee, Papers, K-7.

honored the final agreement by presiding over a public ceremony held at the Mansion House on the evening of February 21, 1824. The committeemen in attendance could well congratulate themselves on having successfully supported a risky business loan to a belligerent party. Of course the terms of the contract were not lenient: In order to obtain £358,000 after deducting interest, commissions, and a sinking fund, the Greeks had incurred a debt amounting to £800,000. Byron was among the three commissioners chosen to see that the funds were delivered into the proper hands in Greece.[27]

The London committee held another public dinner on May 24 to celebrate the arrival of the first installment of the loan in Greece, but Hobhouse recollected that "all were dreadfully put to it for speeches" on the occasion, since news of Byron's death at Missolonghi had reached London ten days earlier. Perhaps no one at the Crown and Anchor that evening felt the loss more keenly than himself. He had only recently sent a letter telling Byron about the many people who inquired after him and awaited his return to England. "You will have, indeed you have, a very handsome fortune; and if you have health," Hobhouse had written, "I do not see what earthly advantage you can wish for that you have not got." [28] The reply to Hobhouse's consoling words came shortly after eight o'clock on the morning of May 14, when a special-delivery messenger awoke him. Anticipating some dreadful news, he opened a note from Douglas Kinnaird informing him of Byron's death. Hobhouse's detailed diary of the following months tells the sequel to the enduring story of Lord Byron—the arrival of the *Florida* in the Downs, the lying in state at the home of Sir Edward Knatchbull on Great George Street, the journey to Nottingham, and the burial services in the church of Hucknall Torkard.

Hobhouse wanted to honor his friend's memory by taking his place in Greece as an agent of the committee, but there were disagreements with Joseph Hume about just what terms the insurgents would have to meet before another installment of the

27. According to the terms of the loan, no money was to be paid out in Greece without the approval of Byron, Stanhope, and Konduriottis, President of the Greek Executive Government. The bonds were quoted at 59 and bore a 5 per cent interest, with the national property of Greece providing the security.

28. Hobhouse to Byron, March 15, 1824, John Cam Hobhouse, Correspondence, John Murray Collection.

loan would be given to them. Also, Burdett and Ellice persuaded him he could contribute more to the Greek cause as a philhellene spokesman in England. Hobhouse therefore turned to writing, collaborating with Bowring on a review of Byron's activities in Greece for *The Westminster Review*.[29] The article described Byron as a man of "powerful and original intellect," of "quick and sensible feelings," and of "restless and untameable spirit." His greatness had made him all the more disgusted with the "formality, hypocrisy, and sameness of daily life." He had gone to Greece out of a desire to assist a people struggling against their cruel oppressors, and no man, the writers said, who appreciated Lord Byron in life could now remain indifferent to the cause for which he died. Bowring and Hobhouse had thus invested Byron's journey to Greece with mythical qualities that provided a guide to future action for others who wished to work for the ultimate independence of the Greek people.

Such an imaginative interpretation of Byron's year in Greece concealed an unwillingness or an inability to deal with the hard facts of the rebellion. A disquieting comment occasionally appeared, as when Bowring and Hobhouse, in explaining how Byron might have ended the internecine quarrels among the rebels, implied that they themselves did not know how to deal with Greece after Byron's death. They made vague and romantic appeals to his memory, instead of suggesting a course of action that took into account the international scene, the problem of rebel disunity, and an evaluation of Greek military resources. The enthusiasm of the London Greek committee did not long survive the death of Byron. The purchasing of guns, the endless details of freight shipments, and the tedious negotiations with the Greek agents all made the cause of Greece seem uninspiring and exceedingly complex. The committeemen may not yet have realized the fundamental error they committed in assuming that human beings endowed with ideals could automatically recreate the world in their own image. The philhellenes gradually drifted away, and attendance at the monthly meetings grew sparser in 1824. "You are, no doubt, aware of the importance of keeping up *life* in the London Committee," one philhellene wrote from Thetford in June, "even though there may be little *blood* in your

29. "Lord Byron in Greece," *The Westminster Review*, 2 (July, 1824), 225–62.

veins." [30] There was no longer a personal involvement, an attachment that Byron's presence in Greece had furnished, and the London committee, which never formally concluded its activities, faded away during the following year.

Hobhouse proved to have the most enduring interest in the Greek struggle. His voluminous correspondence for the next few years documents the time and energy he devoted to Greek affairs, a matter he found "fatal to more than one reputation." In 1826, after a series of rebel reverses during the previous year, he went to the Continent to discuss the Greek situation with other philhellenes. He stopped at Marseilles to confer with Lord Cochrane, the veteran commander of the Chilean and Peruvian navies who had agreed to lead a naval expedition to Greece, and he then traveled to the French capital in October to meet with members of the Paris committee. Benjamin Constant, an old friend, introduced him to General Sebastiani and the Count de Lameth. They arranged a special meeting on November 5 at the home of M. Tenaux, a merchant living on the Place des Victoires. Chateaubriand and the Duke de Choiseul made many inquiries into rumors of mismanagement that had reached Paris. Hobhouse assured the group that with only a modest token of financial support from Paris, the naval expedition being prepared in London would finally steam forward to Greece. His enthusiasm won over the Frenchmen, for they gave Hobhouse a letter authorizing him to act with Colonel Stanhope for the disposal of some funds. He then left Paris, reflecting on how the generosity and unity shown by the Paris committee afforded a painful contrast to the situation at home. [31]

That autumn Hobhouse returned to London to face the public furor over anyone and everything pertaining to Greece. The outcry was touched off by Count Alerino Palma, a visiting Italian philhellene who publicly criticized the London committee for gross mismanagement and dishonesty in handling Greek funds. [32] Foul play had been suspected for some time because of the strange circumstances surrounding two Greek loans—the first in 1824 and a second contracted the following year—that had netted the Greek Government some £1,046,000, with nearly

30. E. H. Barker to Bowring, June 8, 1824, London Greek Committee, Papers, K-8.
31. Dorchester, ed., *Recollections*, I, 266.
32. Count Alerino Palma, *Greece Vindicated in Two Letters.*

an equal amount reserved for interest and security. Why, the questions went, were the expenditures not made public? Why was there the sharp decline of the bonds to a fraction of their value when they presumably had sound financial backing? Why did the Greeks have to negotiate a second loan through the banking firm of John and Samuel Ricardo within a year of the first?

Bowring's reply in *The Westminster Review* tried to exculpate the committee. His details about the money raised by public subscriptions were sparse enough, but he caused concern when he discussed the expenditure of the first loan. Less than half of the £800,000 ever reached Greece in the form of supplies and in specie. The £80,000 reserved for interest payments was perhaps understandable, but then there were such curious items as the £5,300 for "sundry expenses" of the committee, £5,900 for Jean Orlando's private account, and the £50,000 lost by "two young and enthusiastic members of the committee" who went to Greece as agents. Whereas Palma believed the deputies had too little control over Greek funds, Bowring alleged that "almost every evil is . . . to be attributed to their having too much control." Indeed, he said, the deputies Orlando and Luriottis had contracted the second loan of £2,000,000 without ever consulting the London committee. Bowring may have been suggesting a fraud that involved the Ricardo brothers or perhaps a number of jobbers on the London stock exchange. Bowring himself offered no further explanation; he merely stated that the management of Greek aid was so divided "that it has afforded no species of security for the accomplishment of any object proposed." [33]

Bowring's account failed to satisfy the bondholders, who established their own committee of investigation during the summer of 1826. By autumn the investigators had come up with some charges and questions of their own. The Ricardo brothers stood accused of having obstructed their investigation. Did they, the committee asked, wish to conceal the fact that commissions, stock exchange jobbing, and spurious expenditures cost Greece £1,000,000 of the second loan? And just how could the "minor claims" in Bowring's account of this second loan total £12,400? To what extent was the London committee responsible for contracting with the two New York firms of Leroy, Bayard and

Company and G. C. and S. Howland to build two frigates at an estimated cost of a quarter of a million dollars each? Within a year, the committee pointed out, twice the estimated sum had been forwarded to America, and still no ship had sailed for Greek waters. Furthermore, a Yankee arbitrator had charged an extra $45,000 for affirming that the Americans had acted honestly throughout. Investigators in London unfolded more tales of dishonesty or incompetence, until the philhellenic cause compounded great hilarity with some touching general truths for thousands of detached observers. "Poor Greece! Little cause had she to expect such treatment," *The Times* commented during the uproar over Greek affairs in November, 1826.[34]

The fortunes of the Greeks were at their lowest ebb. Mohammed Ali, Pasha of Egypt, had responded to promises of vast acquisitions in the East by coming to the aid of the Turkish Sultan. The Egyptian Army, commanded by his son Ibrahim, had already conquered the Morea peninsula and stood poised for the assault on Athens. The Greeks had one surviving hope for wresting control of the sea—the arrival of a steam flotilla already long overdue from London. In this situation, as in others, disasters plagued the London committeemen who had been responsible for the naval aid. A U.S. consul in Switzerland, Edward Church, had first introduced the idea of a steam fleet to Byron in a letter describing the successful operation of such vessels on Lake Geneva.[35] Byron forwarded the news to Hobhouse, who then brought the matter before the committee. The London group gave its enthusiastic recommendation to the Greek Government, whereupon the deputies in London were authorized to appropriate funds from the first loan. The deputies gave a contract to a Mr. Brent for building a corvette, the *Perseverance;* a naval engineer named Thomas Galloway agreed to provide the machinery for the vessels by mid-August of the following year, 1825.

Largely through the efforts of Lord Cochrane, the shipyards along the Thames soon prepared to launch an armada. Burdett, Ellice, and Hobhouse had advised the deputies to employ Coch-

34. *The Examiner*, October 29, November 12, 1826; John Francis, *Chronicles of the Stock Exchange* (London, 1882), 285–88; *Annual Register*, 1826, 370–75; *The Times*, November 3, 1826.

35. Edward Church to Byron, June 21, 1823, Hobhouse Correspondence, Murray Collection.

rane upon his return to England in July, 1824,[36] and the deputies accordingly made a handsome offer, which was understandably accepted. Of the £150,000 already spent for the fleet, Cochrane's share came to £37,000, plus a £20,000 bonus when Greece achieved independence. Burdett, who held a high opinion of his former parliamentary colleague, guaranteed the payments of money. "Lord Cochrane . . . will be the liberator of Greece," he wrote to Hobhouse, "What a glorious title!"[37] The contract also specified that five additional ships would be purchased and equipped for service. Cochrane himself immediately arranged early in 1825 to have the Ricardo brothers, who disbursed funds from the second loan, sign a contract with the same Galloway who had already agreed to fit out the *Perseverance*. The Greek deputies merely acquiesced in the transaction, which had Galloway preparing five additional ships for Greek service.

None of the six ships under Galloway's supervision had been fitted with steam engines by the summer of 1825, nor did the end of the year and an additional sum of £10,000 bring the job nearer to completion. The steam engines, which gave Galloway no end of trouble, were still a novelty in naval construction, and he explained to Hobhouse that he had to install larger engines because the vessels displaced nearly twice the amount of water he anticipated. Deptford, the area in which ships were built, rattled from occasional explosions of high-pressure boilers. Prudence urged him to cease all work, "but my zeal for the cause of Greece," the engineer declared, "gained ascendancy over my judgement."[38]

Hobhouse had already lost all trust in Galloway's competence, and his optimism was sinking fast whenever he contemplated other philhellene activities. "Twice have I descended amongst Mr. Galloway's infernal forges," he informed Ellice toward the close of 1825, "twice have I mounted into Mr. Wright's aerial garrets (more balloon ascents to publicize the Philhellene cause). I have hopped, waded and paddled from one end to the other of this half-drowned city and the upshot has been a severe cold which now keeps me snivelling . . . like a tipsy washer-

36. Christopher Lloyd, *Lord Cochrane*, Part III, chap. 3.
37. Burdett to Hobhouse, August 3, 1824, Lord Broughton Papers, Add. MSS 36461, f. 226.
38. *The Examiner*, January 6, 1828.

woman." [39] No consoling news came from America; the frigates ordered there were "useless—not to say 'pretty-considerable'— damned—particularly expensive!! The honest yankees will not finish unless they have £60,000 more, making the whole a sum of £220,000 for two frigates!! Is there a corner hot enough for these extortioners?" [40] Perhaps, Hobhouse suggested, the Greeks had best sell the incompleted American frigates for scrap, and he also suggested that Ellice join Burdett and himself in sending a joint communiqué to rebel leaders in Naples, urging the Greeks to hold out until "the promised aid" arrived.

The restless deputies in London were already complaining about the delays. Luriottis asked Hobhouse to hire another engineer because Galloway feared for the safety of his son who was serving the Pasha in Alexandria. Haste was of the utmost importance, and the poor deputies were at their wit's end as endless delays kept the steam flotilla in Galloway's yards during the mounting crisis. "The naval affair was taken entirely out of our hands," lamented Luriottis, "We were not consulted or even informed of the measures taken for fulfilling it." [41]

The Egyptians stormed into Athens while the Greek agents and philhellenes in London blamed one another for the disaster. "I never doubted the villainy of the deputies," Kinnaird informed Hobhouse. [42] Spaniolacki, who was not involved in the loans, accused his fellow deputies of embezzlement. The deputies refused to obey their Government when it ordered them to turn over their accounts to Burdett, Hobhouse, and Stanhope. Luriottis chose instead to publish certain letters to the Greek committeemen, which gave a one-sided story of the naval preparations. *The Times* observed that the Ricardos made no charge against him until they had "fallen foul of a whole body of contractors, dealers, jobbers, and hucksters of the Greek loan." [43] Colonel Stanhope held Cochrane solely responsible for the contract with

39. Hobhouse to Edward Ellice, November 21, 1825, Edward Ellice Papers.

40. Hobhouse to Ellice, December 12, 1826, Ellice Papers.

41. Luriottis to Hobhouse, May 24, 1826, Lord Broughton Papers, Add. MSS 36462, f. 194. See the letters of Orlando and Luriottis during this time in Eugène Dallegio, *Les Philhéllènes et la Guerre de L'Indépendence*.

42. Kinnaird to Hobhouse, October 24, 1826, Lord Broughton Papers, Add. MSS 36462, f. 375.

43. *The Times*, November 14, 1826.

Galloway, upon which Cochrane informed Hobhouse, "In conducting this affair I was associated with yourself, Burdett, Ellice, and the Ricardo Brothers." [44] "Ridiculous!" exclaimed Hobhouse to Samuel Ricardo, who denied his own connection in hiring Galloway before Hobhouse could once again assert, "We merely guaranteed for Cochrane's services—no more!" [45]

The press had another scandal to report at the end of the year. Joseph Hume and John Bowring had purchased many bonds at the original market price, and when the script fell in value, they first prevailed upon the Greek deputies to repurchase the bonds at an inflated price and later requested compensation for losses and interest payment for the bonds they had sold before their value again rose on the market. "The worse, I think, that any man in candour can say against my conduct in this affair," avowed Hume, "is, that I may have evinced an over anxiety to avoid a pecuniary loss, forced upon me by the conduct of others." [46] But Hobhouse did not look upon the matter so lightly: He severed all relations with Bowring and treated Hume with a cool, formal politeness.

Hobhouse could only encourage the Greek Government to persevere in the struggle while its ships remained in London. He repeatedly visited Galloway to admonish the engineer, whom Samuel Ricardo regarded as "the evil genius that pursues us everywhere." [47] Perhaps there yet remained some hope, for Lord Cochrane expressed his delight to Hobhouse upon learning in April, 1827, that "the engines of the *Perseverance* moved!" [48]

That "evil genius" Galloway then surprised everyone several weeks later by pronouncing the steamship ready for warfare. With great fanfare the vessel left England on a voyage to the Mediterranean, which Capt. Frank Hastings described to Hobhouse in a series of angry letters. From Gibraltar came word that "the most lamentable incapacity has been shown by Gallo-

44. *The Examiner*, October 29, 1826; Lord Cochrane to Hobhouse, January 26, 1827, Lord Broughton Papers, Add. MSS 36464, f. 238; Hobhouse to Major Cochrane, January 28, 1827, Lord Broughton Papers, Add. MSS 47226, f. 84–85.

45. Hobhouse, diary, July 8, 1827, Lord Broughton Papers, Add. MSS 56549.

46. *The Times*, November 4, 1826; *The Examiner*, December 3, 1826.

47. Samuel Ricardo to Hobhouse, December 10, 1826, Lord Broughton Papers, Add. MSS 36461, f. 361.

48. Cochrane to Hobhouse, April 17, 1827, Lord Broughton Papers, Add. MSS 36462, f. 97.

way"; the paddle wheels threatened to fall apart, and the feeding pumps only worked when the engines stopped operating. The Captain cursed Galloway two weeks later because his boilers did not supply enough steam, and from Cagliari, Sardinia, Hastings mournfully told Hobhouse that the voyage "threatens to become as tedious as that of Ulysses" because the heavy engines limited the vessel's speed to seven knots per hour. A stop at Naples brought worse news; in barely decipherable handwriting caused by a disabled right hand, the Captain described the general confusion following an explosion aboard ship. The *Perseverance* finally made it to Greek waters and engaged the enemy in several battles. A second ship, the *Enterprise*, left London in 1827 but had to stop at Plymouth because the rudder was too small.[49]

Perhaps *The Examiner* best expressed the reaction of the Greek Government to these scandals, "which well nigh ruined her," when it quoted the proverb "Defend us from our friends, and we will guard against our foes." Bowring also soundly appraised the situation when he pointed to the absence of a central organization in charge of both the collection and the disbursement of Greek funds. "This," he suggested, "is why every man accused found some ground to attack his accusers."[50]

Clear delegation of responsibility would surely have prevented the spread of so many extensive scandals. A separate body, such as the London committee, could have then performed the valuable service of periodically checking the accounts, thereby protecting the public from misappropriation of funds. Bowring realized the sad truth that the Greek cause had remained a part-time concern of the English philhellenes. As consultants for the first loan, Hobhouse, Burdett, and Ellice were honest enthusiasts about Greek independence, but they subordinated their zeal to their parliamentary duties and to their other interests. The three men claimed responsibility only for obtaining the services of Lord Cochrane. Yet in hiring the Commander, they also agreed to his demands for additional ships and implicated themselves in the Galloway episode.

49. Hastings to Hobhouse, June 8, June 24, July 10, October 5, 1826, Lord Broughton Papers, Add. MSS 36462, ff. 253, 305, 331, 360. On Hastings' naval career, see Z. D. Ferriman, *Some English Philhellenes* (London, 1917).
50. *The Westminster Review*, 6 (1826), 127.

Further, the Greek deputies involved in the second loan did not act as the independent agents described by Bowring. The Ricardo brothers did not contract to raise the loan without taking such precautions as holding a share of the bonds for interest payments and security. It would have been most unusual for the bankers to consult only the foreign deputies, who had a limited knowledge of the London financial world. The Ricardos obtained the deputies' consent for occasional expenses, but in most cases, Luriottis and Orlando merely acquiesced in the management of Greek funds by those who felt better qualified to do the job. When the deputies did act alone, as in the case of the American frigates, they were almost defenseless against unprincipled men who wanted only to profit from the Greek war. The Greek cause, all in all, was haphazardly organized and therefore vulnerable to mistakes, fraud, and confusion on an international scale.[51]

Hobhouse made some belated attempts to retrieve the situation by repeatedly urging Galloway to finish his assignment. He also obtained French backing for the Greeks when the funds in England were exhausted. In June, 1827, however, a weary Hobhouse informed Chevalier Eynard, a leader of the Geneva committee, that he was thoroughly disgusted "with anything connected with the Greeks." [52] Such a despairing comment indicated Hobhouse's deep disappointment about the disasters that befell

51. A writer for the *American Quarterly Review* (March, 1827) attested to the corruption surrounding the Greek cause in the United States: "We believe we hazard nothing in asserting, that the general sentiment of our country is that of disapprobation and regret. . . . The only instance in which we could render the Greeks any substantial service has manifestly been perverted by private cupidity to unwarrantable emolument; a profit of 80,000 dollars made out of their distresses, by their mercantile correspondents, the 'diplomatic agents' of the arbitrators; 50,000 dollars extorted for the use of shipyards and personal services of the owner without expending any of their own money; 10,000 dollars, the sine qua non of a captain of the United States' Navy, for superintending an operation in 'a just and sacred cause'; 45,000 dollars imposed on them by arbitrators, for the dedication of a few days to the dispensation of justice." Quoted in Merle Curti, *American Philanthropy Abroad*, 28–29.

52. Hobhouse, diary, June 3, 1827, Lord Broughton Papers, Add. MSS 56552. The bondholders eventually secured a portion of their holdings through an agreement with the Greek Government in 1878. The Government issued new bonds repayable in 33 years at 5 per cent interest. See *The Agreement with the Hellenic Government for the Conversion of the Greek Loan of 1824–1825* (London, 1878).

the philhellenes. He had embarked upon a crusade in 1823 that had humanitarian, religious, economic, and ideological portents for its success. Hobhouse thought that Greek independence provided an excellent cause for uniting various groups of politicians: Many Tories favored the liberation of a Christian people from the Turks just as strongly as did the Radicals who wanted to spread representative governments throughout Europe.

Unfortunately, the philhellenes looked upon the liberation of Greece as an exciting enterprise, a highly emotional romance in which goodness and knowledge fought evil and ignorance. They interpreted the struggle within their own ideological framework, and once aroused, they ignored the practical side of their enterprise. Accusations and abuse, however ill-founded, were the results. William Cobbett furiously attacked the "greedy, usury-loving fools"; *The Times* found the Greek committee guilty of "peculation, indolence, and incapacity"; and the *Quarterly Review* took the opportunity to satirize the Benthamite philosopher who "arranges with equal felicity the dovetailing of a ballot box, and the minute classification into 79 classes, and 651 subscriptions, of the inmates of a jail." [53] Such men were among the members of the Greek committee; they were victims of their own illusions who were unable to deal with such mundane matters as steam engines or financial accounts.

The Greek committee had effectively served the cause of Greece by acting as a pressure group in England. It awakened Englishmen to the realization that the rebellion was much more than a mere skirmish in some distant Ottoman province. The philhellenes confronted Canning, who did not try at first to enhance his popularity by championing the Greek cause before the British public. The Foreign Secretary understood the international implications of the revolt, and foremost in the web of diplomatic entanglements was Russia. Canning did not want Russia to use the Greek war to obtain a foothold in the Mediterranean. While philhellenes sent their arms and international brigades, he preferred a less dramatic policy of dealing with the Sultan through diplomatic agents. He therefore rejected Czar Alexan-

53. *Political Register*, September 29, 1827; *The Times*, October 25, 1826; "Greek Committee," *Quarterly Review*, 35 (1827), 221–36.

der's suggestion in 1824 that a European Congress be called to settle the question of Greek independence.[54]

At first, Canning observed a policy of strict neutrality in Greece, but he soon realized the turmoil that would follow if Russia intervened in the Greek rebellion. The very peace of Europ "hangs on a thread," according to Canning, who impressed upon Bowring that "with the monstrous power of Russia, Turkey and Greece could be overwhelmed."[55] Canning then expressed sympathy for the philhellenes but asked them to await the outcome of diplomatic negotiations just then under way. The fear of unilateral Russian action was especially acute following the accession of Czar Nicholas in 1825, and the Duke of Wellington was sent on a delicate mission to Saint Petersburg. There, he found Nicholas willing to pursue a common policy with the European powers if English mediations at Constantinople ended in failure. Wellington's mission spurred Canning to seek a general European solution, which was arrived at with the London Agreement of 1827. The governments agreed to establish a Greek nation that would owe a nominal allegiance to the Sultan as "Lord Paramount."

Canning's maneuvering was no secret in Parliament. Hobhouse had urged the Foreign Secretary in 1825 to use all his art of persuasion to convince the Ottomans that they could never recover Greece. According to Canning, "The protracted struggle could only weaken the Ottoman Empire," which was indeed "the bulwark against Austria, and most important of all, against the dreaded power of Russia."[56] A High Tory, Sir Robert Inglis, feared the imminent prospect of an Ottoman victory over the Christian Greeks in 1826 and prepared a petition on behalf of the beleaguered rebels. Hobhouse urged Canning to say as little as possible on the subject, fearing that a speech about neutrality would cause Greek resistence to collapse. Canning duly remained silent after Inglis presented his petition, and Hobhouse supplied an answer by simply declaring that the country preferred to await developments.[57]

54. On Canning's diplomacy, see R. W. Seton-Watson, *Britain in Europe, 1798–1914*, chap. II.

55. Bowring to Bentham, January 14, 1824, Jeremy Bentham Papers.

56. *Hansard*, 2d series, XII (1825), col. 88.

57. Hobhouse, diary, May 19, 1826, Lord Broughton Papers, Add. MSS 56550; *Hansard*, 2d series, XV (1826), cols. 1271–73.

The outcome of the prolonged negotiations over Greece came on October 20, 1827, with the battle of Navarino Bay. The Duke of Clarence, himself an admiral and later King William IV, was all for smashing "those bloody Turks," but Admiral Codrington was under more ambiguous orders, which were to cut off Ibrahim's supply route while avoiding an engagement with the Ottoman Navy. The Admiral stood on the deck; a Turkish fire ship made a suspicious movement; a sudden shot pierced the morning air; a few hours later the entire Ottoman Navy was destroyed. The British Government was chagrined by this "most untoward incident" in the bay, but Hobhouse at the start of the 1828 parliamentary session was unable to resist delivering a lengthy panegyric on the glorious "untoward" battle for Christianity and civilization.[58] The Government and his closest political associates finally persuaded him to withdraw his motion of thanks to Admiral Codrington. Greek independence was established, they argued; besides, votes of thanks were reserved only for engagements against the enemy, and surely the Ottoman Empire and Great Britain enjoyed the most cordial of relations.

Canning had always viewed the Greek problem apart from his general policy toward the Continent. Greece was far from the heart of Europe, and conservatives who found in Greek independence a violation of Troppau and the Holy Alliance were consoled by the strength of legitimacy throughout Europe. But the settlement worked out in Vienna was suddenly shattered by the July Revolution of 1830, which reverberated across the Continent.

The Parisian revolt occurred on the eve of general elections in England. Hobhouse was at home preparing an electoral speech when the newspapers brought word of Charles X's ordinances dissolving the Chamber of Deputies and imposing strict censorship. "If the French bear this," he wrote in his diary, "they deserve to be slaves."[59] Then came "the glorious news from France!": The King had fled upon the outbreak of revolution in the French capital. Many insurgents wanted to create a second republic with the venerable Lafayette serving as President. But the joint efforts of Jacques Lafitte, Casimir Périer, and the aged Talleyrand convinced the President-designate of

58. *Hansard*, 2d series, XVIII (1827), cols. 360–87.

59. Hobhouse, diary, July 28, 1830, Lord Broughton Papers, Add. MSS 56555.

the French people's preference for a constitutional monarchy. The issue was settled by August, when Parisians saw their new sovereign, Louis Philippe, accept the crown.

Hobhouse rejoiced over the events. "How happy for you to find realized all the hopes of your youthful patriotism," he wrote to Lafayette upon learning of the revolution. He assured him that "we Englishmen regard all the unparalleled exploits of the Parisian leaders with exultation and pride." [60] That same day he ordered his bankers to transmit £100 to a fund for the families of those who died in the short but decisive conflict.

The Parisian revolt stirred up wild speculation across the Channel as English political circles tried to predict the probable course of the new regime. Charles X reportedly told Lord Nugent that he would be back in Paris before the end of the year. The Duchesse de Berri, Charles X's daughter-in-law, matched his intransigence when she bluntly told Lady Shrewsbury—who passed on the story to Hobhouse's wife—that the English were mad in wanting parliamentary reform. Reports of riots in Paris recalled memories of the terror of 1792, and some people in London already feared for President Lafitte's life.

Hobhouse held English society partly responsible for the difficulties the Citizen King now faced in the France of 1830. "The great mass of those who call themselves the Whig party" found themselves the object of ridicule in a letter from "An Old Subscriber," which appeared in *The Times* of October 7, 1830. The writer deplored the Whigs' failure to support Louis Philippe; only after the French people acknowledged him as their King did the party politicians "send in their tardy trifle to the subscription list, and record their useless sympathy."

The Old Subscriber was Hobhouse,[61] unreservedly sympathetic to the new regime and willing to defend it against a variety of criticisms. Hobhouse's enthusiasm for Louis Philippe's Government was in striking contrast to John Stuart Mill's disillusionment upon seeing the cynical opportunism in Paris.[62] From Westminster, Hobhouse made exuberant claims for the business-

60. Hobhouse to Lafayette, August 5, 1830, Lord Broughton Papers, Add. MSS 36465, f. 231.

61. He recorded this letter in his diary; see Dorchester, ed., *Recollections*, IV, 45–56.

62. See Michael St. John Packe, *The Life of John Stuart Mill*, 100; also Francis E. Mineka, ed., "John Stuart Mill: Letters on the French Revolution of 1830," *Victorian Studies*, I, 2 (December, 1957), 137–54.

men and financial leaders who served as Louis' ministers. He credited them with a selfless idealism and found their wisdom and virtue unparalleled. "The whole of France," in his opinion, "cannot furnish two honester, nor, in many respects, two abler men, than the Duke de Broglis and Monsieur Guizot." Hobhouse found them admirable in never having believed those "extravagant doctrines" followed by the patriots of the first revolution. Instead, they merely wanted to restore the "free constitution which the Charter, considered in its true spirit" promised to the French people.

Hobhouse went on to answer critics of the Orleanist regime after having asserted its respectability. He resorted to some casuistry in arguing against the French radicals who were clamoring for a new assembly elected by universal suffrage. He thought such an election would produce total anarchy because it meant yielding to ignorance and impatience; universal suffrage would never produce statesmen more attached to the true interests of the French people. Besides, "what would the immediate neighbors of France—what would all Europe—have thought of such a beginning?"

Hobhouse next turned his attention to the many delegations of the curious and well-wishers who flocked to Paris during the year. He was deeply annoyed by the expedition of John Bowring, an enthusiastic supporter of William Cobbett named Sir Thomas Branthwayt Beevor, and Cobbett's son, James Paul. These self-styled "Ambassadors of the Reformers of England" had honored the people of Paris for their part in the revolution by first holding public dinners at the London Tavern and then by presenting addresses in Paris to Lafayette and to the Prefect of the city.[63] The "Old Subscriber's" feud with Cobbett was long standing. His antipathy toward Bowring stemmed from the scandal involving his speculation in Greek stocks, and he therefore regretted Mill's failure to oust Bowring from the editorship of *The Westminster Review*. Upon hearing that the journal could no longer support the burden of a salaried editor, Bowring had outfoxed everyone by securing the financial backing of the wealthy Col. T. Perronet Thompson, who became the proprietor in 1828.

---

63. *The Times*, August 27, 1830; *Political Register*, September 11, 1830, 342–45.

Hobhouse wanted the French to know something about the "English coadjutors of their own ultra-democrats." The Prefect of the Seine would discover their untrustworthy character if he would count "the silver spoons since the banquet, at which son James and his booby Baronet [Cobbett and Beevor] had the happiness to assist" at the Hotel de Ville. The "Old Subscriber" also hoped that when Louis Philippe granted an audience to "a certain doctor [Bowring]," he took care to "conceal all state secrets which might lead to a speculation in stocks." The *Political Register* praised the Radical delegates upon their return from Paris, but Hobhouse had made it quite clear how much he loathed the "Ambassadors of the Reformers of England" for their "impudence and imposture." He concluded the letter with some advice to "our French Friends," who could well afford to learn some lessons from the Glorious Revolution of 1688. Englishmen at that time "considered incompatible with good order and the very existence of government" the absence of any restraints upon freedom of action and of speech. The July Monarchy had obviously reached the proper limits of such freedoms in Hobhouse's estimation.

The writer had given his blessings as France settled down to experience the first decade of rule by the prudent, honest, and well-meaning ministers of Louis Philippe. Hobhouse did not realize that French radicals regarded the Government as an aristocracy of wealth, an establishment that refused to extend the rights it had won to the rest of the nation. He admired Guizot's policy of limiting the monarchy by having a limited number of bourgeois who were supposedly wise enough or good enough to rule others without their consent. The July Monarchy had reestablished the harmony between wealth and political power that England had obtained through the reform bill. Both nations preserved the aristocracy while recognizing the right of the middle class to participate in government.

The July Revolution inspired other revolts in Poland and in Belgium, whose Provisional Government sent one of its members, Mr. Vanderweyer, to consult with Hobhouse.[64] Hobhouse promised him that he would oppose any efforts by his Government to impose an unsatisfactory peace settlement upon the Bel-

64. Hobhouse, diary, November 4, November 8, 1830, Lord Broughton Papers, Add. MSS 56555.

gian people. The Polish insurrection also enlisted his support during the following year. At a dinner in honor of the Marquis Willopolski, a Polish representative, Hobhouse proposed a toast to "the independence of Poland, violated by fraud, may it be restored by valour, and cemented by liberty." [65] Hume, O'Connell, Henry Bulwer-Lytton, and Thomas Campbell then joined his committee for the relief of Polish refugees. Hobhouse soon learned the sad truth from Lord Grey, who informed him that he considered the Polish cause hopeless and that he would not risk jeopardizing relations with the Czar by receiving the Polish envoy in public. [66]

Hobhouse believed the revolutions in France, Greece, and Belgium attested to the collapse of the Vienna settlement and of the old regime. He confidently expected the inexorable tide of nationalism and liberalism to rush across central Europe and on to the Russian Empire. He did not think that these revolutions implied any total reordering of the social and economic hierarchy, judging from a letter he wrote to Lord Durham, who was at the court of the Czar to clear up questions about Belgium, Poland, and the revolutionary movement in Germany. "I trust that His Majesty and his ministers are satisfied," wrote Hobhouse, "that we inculcate moderation and deprecate a system of unrestrained repression." Having presented his Government's liberal creed, Hobhouse next discussed its essentially conservative foundation:

> We do so, not because we wish to promote the objects of revolutionary agitation, but because we are anxious that they do not gain proselytes, and because we are convinced in this age that moderation is the only way of avoiding a collision which may be fatal to social orders. [67]

Hobhouse's remarks are especially revealing. The first part of his letter paraphrases the Cabinet's instructions to Durham, who was "to make them [the Russians] understand, that though friends to free institutions, we are not promoters of revolu-

65. *Morning Chronicle*, March 10, 1831.
66. Hobhouse, diary, March 10, 1831, Lord Broughton Papers, Add. MSS 56555.
67. Hobhouse to Durham, September 13, 1832, John George Lambton, first Earl of Durham, Papers.

tion." [68] The remaining portion of the letter explains the brand of liberalism Hobhouse favored against the representatives of the old regime. He did not have any egalitarian notions in mind whenever he uttered the abstract term "the rights of the people." He thought more in terms of classes, each one having its valuable functions and rights. England's rulers had strengthened the monarchy and retained deference while enlarging the basis of political power. Continental rulers, by bringing their institutions up to date, could likewise assure the preservation of traditional social ranks, or "orders."

68. Quoted in Stuart J. Reid, *Life and Letters of the first Earl of Durham, 1792–1840*, I, 301–3.

CHAPTER VI

SELECT VESTRIES
BILL OF 1831

The same commitment to political liberalism at home and abroad explains Hobhouse's role in the achievement of vestry reform in England. This, his greatest legislative contribution, placed him alongside Brougham, Parkes, Hume, and others who pioneered in transforming local government at this time. Protest against parochial government was nowhere so well organized and so vehement as in London, including Hobhouse's own constituency, Westminster, where earlier acts of Parliament had invested parish vestries with unregulated powers to tax and to authorize various local expenditures. Throughout the 1820's, ratepayers in various parishes had tried and failed to have these statutes amended or repealed. A London-wide movement to withold the payment of local rates was started in 1829, just as Hobhouse obtained a parliamentary committee of inquiry into select vestries and other vestries throughout the country. It was the prelude to his legislation that followed.

Vestry reform was also the most noteworthy achievement resulting from Hobhouse's and Place's partnership. Place continually urged him to take it up. He plied Hobhouse with advice, gathered evidence of abuses, and introduced him to reformers in the various London parishes. They included James Corder, who had led the successful struggle against the vestrymen of Saint Paul's, and William Beckett of Saint James's, although he despaired of ever seeing vestry government reformed after Parliament had refused to deal with his parish in 1829. At that time, Beckett wrote Hobhouse, "The decision of the House leaves the parishioners without a prospect of ever being relieved from the awful power of the select vestry." [1]

The parishioners of Saint Martin's fared no better in court. Since 1822 a reformer named Robert Fenn had been trying to oust or at least control the select vestry there. His supporters researched extensively into the history of the parish, hoping to find

1. William Beckett to Hobhouse, May 20, 1829, John Cam Hobhouse, Lord Broughton, Papers, Add. MSS 36465, f. 150.

a precedent for inspecting the vestry accounts. They unsuccessfully brought action against the vestry before the Court of King's Bench. The vestry refused all petitions about rate payments, whereupon a group of parishioners assembled outside the church one day while the vestry was in session behind barricaded doors. When the reformers tried to force their way into the meeting, fighting broke out and lasted several hours until the parishioners withdrew.[2] Fenn then came on his own to see Hobhouse and described most vividly the deplorable state of vestry rule throughout Westminister. An outpouring of pamphlets and leading articles in *The Times*, Cobbett's *Political Register*, *The Examiner*, and other journals drew attention to the wide discontent that prevailed. At this point Hobhouse decided to intervene.

Sturges Bourne's measures of 1818 and 1819 furnished him precedents for reforming vestry government. These measures did not apply to numerous parishes governed by "select" or "close" vestries created by Parliament, however, and there was no provision for public inspection of parochial accounts. Reformers pointed out that this lack of public inspection was a major complaint against the small ruling body in select vestries. Then there was the matter of regulating general expenditures. Bourne had provided for a referendum only on a proposed increase in the poor rate. Many reformers objected to his plural-voting clause, which allowed parishioners rated at less than £50 one vote and those whose rates were more than £50 up to six additional votes for each additional rate assessment of £25. The reformers argued that each ratepayer should exercise an equal voice in parish government. They also pointed out that it often proved difficult to implement Bourne's provision for ending chaotic "open" vestry meetings through a parish committee; the old vestry officials, resenting a loss of power, could simply refuse to summon a meeting for elections. A new voting procedure clearly was needed.

Hobhouse brought the issue of vestry government before Parliament in a carefully prepared address in which he emphasized the ways it directly involved "the interests, the comforts, the happiness, and the well-being of society."[3] He referred to

2. *The Times*, April 4, 1828; *An Exposé of the Select Vestry of Saint Paul's, Covent Garden; St. Andrew Holborne; St. Martin's-in-the-Fields* (London, 1829).

3. *Hansard Parliamentary Debates*, 2d series, XXI (1829), col. 891.

the steep rise in the nation's poor rates—from £2,500,000 in 1795 to £7,784,356 in 1828—and suggested that an investigation of parochial government would reveal innumerable instances of corruption and gross mismanagement of Poor Law funds. Hobhouse next turned his attention to London's select vestries and, with Robert Fenn's research before him, gave a detailed account of how the vestry of Saint Martin's had gradually usurped the management of all parochial affairs. Even in 1829, only some twenty vestrymen assembled, although the law specified a vestry of over twice that number. He then catalogued instances of the misuse of parochial funds—Saint Paul's, Saint James, Saint Martin's, Christchurch in Spitalfields, Marylebone. Was it any wonder, he asked, that parishes that had changed from the select vestry had witnessed a gradual diminution of the poor rates and other benefits? Paddington; Saint Matthew's, Bethnal Green; Saint Mary's, Islington; and Saint Luke's, Chelsea were all cases in point. Hobhouse stated that as a general rule, discontent and confusion prevailed in those parishes governed by select vestries, whereas those allowing for popular elections had no such discords.[4]

Hobhouse requested and obtained a parliamentary committee of inquiry, which opened hearings in February, 1829. During the interval, Fenn and Place primed him with information, and Hobhouse on his own was busy contacting witnesses and gathering material on various parishes outside the London metropolitan area. The difficulties besetting Hobhouse's efforts at vestry reform were evident from the time the committee hearings started. He found Hume and O'Connell always preoccupied with other matters, which left him to contend with the more conservative wing of the committee—Bourne, Ross, and Sir Thomas Freemantle. "Lord Althorp, Mr. Warburton, Sir J. Graham did now and then look in," Hobhouse informed Place, "but as I said before the only constant attendants were my opponents."[5] Nevertheless, Hobhouse felt the committee had made out a good case for vestry reform.

The committee did indeed condemn the unrepresentative select vestries but at the same time praised the workings of Sturges Bourne's earlier act, under which the ratepayers elected annu-

4. Ibid., cols. 890–903.
5. Hobhouse to Place, March 23, 1830, Francis Place Papers, Add. MSS 35148, f. 49.

ally a committee to manage poor relief. Hobhouse's committee thus recommended "the introduction of a general measure which shall give to all parishes the power of partaking the benefits of the above named Acts or of some new law founded upon an Elective Principle." The supporting minutes provided an invaluable source of information about the operation of various vestries—approximately twenty in the London area and six elsewhere. The witnesses who led the reform movement in London—Robert Fenn, James Corder, and Leslie Grove Jones—were expected to stress the ratepayers' right to elect the vestry, but even the senior churchwarden of Saint George's, Bloomsbury, told Hobhouse's committee of the parishioners' preference for a system of choosing all local officials, although the select vestrymen were known for their honesty and efficiency.[6] With witness after witness, Hobhouse asked whether the principle of election secured tranquility and also good management in parochial affairs. The response was invariably "Yes"—from John Rawlinson, himself a select vestryman from Saint Giles, Bloomsbury; from Alderman Wood of London, a parishioner in the ward of Cripplegate Without; from Joseph Brotherton of Salford; and from many others.[7] Edward Rushton added that the intermingling of tradesmen with gentlemen and merchants in the elected vestry of Liverpool caused no difficulties at all in the management of the affairs of the parish.[8]

Concerning Bourne's Vestry Act of 1819, Rawlinson felt that the measure worked perfectly well in all parishes, large or small, and that the inconvenience of assembling in open vestry to elect a Poor Law committee was a minor flaw, compared with a close vestry system that gave a few men unregulated control over large funds. Joseph Brotherton emphasized the difficulty of implementation in Salford inasmuch as the overseer of the poor, resenting the closer control exercised by a parochial committee,

6. Two Reports from the Select Committee appointed to inquire into the general operation and effect of the Laws and Usages under which Select and Other Vestries are constituted in England and Wales, *Parliamentary Reports*, 1830 (25.215), IV, 425.569. The churchwarden's comments, ibid., II, 53. Hobhouse's committee sat from May 5 to June 2, 1829, and again from February 16 to March 25, 1830.

7. Testimony of John Rawlinson, February 24, 1830, ibid., II, 35; Alderman Wood, March 5, 1830, ibid., 72; Joseph Brotherton, February 26, 1830, ibid., 48.

8. Testimony of Edward Rushton, February 16, 1830, ibid., 9.

simply refused to summon the annual meeting for elections. As was true in many parishes throughout England, Sturges Bourne's Act had not applied beyond the first years, and Salford had lapsed back to the old open vestry system.[9] The evidence clearly indicated that Bourne's Select Vestry scheme reduced parochial expenditures while in operation: Poor relief in Salford averaged £9,437 between the years 1819–1821, diminished for the next three years to £5,333 under Bourne's Act, and then rose to £8,492 during the period 1825–1827, under the old open vestry system. Liverpool also had a diminution of poor rates once the select vestry scheme was implemented, from £4,715 in 1820 to roughly half that sum in 1828. The weekly cost per head in 1820 was 3s. 5.75d., as opposed to 2s. 9.25d. in 1828. The vestry clerk of Saint Luke's, Chelsea, when asked about the operation of the 1819 Act, replied simply, "Not a farthing wasted."[10]

There was greater disagreement over Bourne's plural-voting scheme of 1818. John Aston Yates claimed there were no longer any objections in Liverpool, and Brotherton said the same for Salford. Edward Rushton, the other Liverpool witness, believed his parish could be just as well managed without plural voting because the same class of people would be elected under a democratic voting procedure. However, several other witnesses sharply criticized plural voting. James Corder of Saint Paul's, Westminster, claimed that "it gave very great disatisfaction"; another parishioner, William Yockney, agreed. The severest criticism came from Robert Whatmore, Vestry Clerk of Lambeth, who declared, "The lower orders of people, they object to it; the middling, I qualify myself by saying the middling class of persons who frequent vestries, do not like it, and they came to a resolution of agreement among themselves they would waive it; it is seldom acted on."[11] On the whole, the committee hearings suggested widespread dissatisfaction about plural voting, but the principle of electing a committee to manage parochial affairs was endorsed for reasons of efficiency and economy.

9. Testimony of John Rawlinson, February 24, 1830, ibid., 35–38; Joseph Brotherton, February 26, 1830, ibid., 48–50.

10. Testimony on Liverpool of John Aston Yates, February 18, 1830, ibid., 12–13; William Cornell of Saint Luke's, May 19, 1829, ibid., I, 82.

11. Testimony of John Aston Yates, February 18, 1830, ibid., II, 12; Edward Rushton, February 16, 1830, ibid., 10; James Corder, March 11, 1830, ibid., 89–90; Robert Whatmore, May 28, 1829, ibid., I, 111–12.

Testimony about the close, or select, vestries in London and elsewhere was devastating. The general picture was one of gross abuse, fraudulent mismanagement, or else utter confusion on the part of small groups of vestrymen who had the parishes at their mercy. Witnesses from Saint Matthew's parish in Bethnal Green claimed the Merceron machine survived through his son-in-law, now a vestry clerk. James Corder reappeared with the vestry minutes of Saint Paul's, from which he detailed yet more corruption from that parish: Fully one-third of the rates collected in 1814 went to Mr. Hodgson and Mr. Gann, proprieters of the Piazza Coffee-house, for venison dinners. The parish church was painted the following year at a cost of £339 18s. 9d. The painter was a member of the vestry. A witness from Saint Bartholomew's in London claimed, "I think you might almost determine where the select vestrymen are by the position of the lamps and the better paving." [12] For a variety of reasons, Marylebone parish was in great debt, even though the rates had doubled between 1824 and 1827. Ever since the death or retirement of experienced vestry accountants, the annual estimates had been haphazardly prepared. William Crawford, a parishioner and magistrate for Surrey, said of the parochial accounts he had examined, "With all the experience I have had in accounts, it cost me a great deal of labour before I could tell what they meant. They have none of the right principles of exhibiting accounts about them." With vast expenses at stake for a variety of municipal services, shoddy bookkeeping must have cost Marylebone's residents dearly. As it was, the select vestry's staff was handsomely salaried. Then, too, an expensive church was built; also, a new watch house, for which land was acquired from a vestryman at an extortionate price of £4,800. Parishioners finally formed a committee to unseat the vestry after the Easter offerings to the clergy were converted into another compulsory rate. The impression given by parishioners and vestrymen who testified before Hobhouse's committee, however, was less one of crafty jobbing as much as an utter inability to cope with either the details or the volume of work the management of Marylebone en-

12. Testimony of Anthony Harvey, March 11, 1830, ibid., II, 98; James Corder, March 12, 1830, ibid., 100–102; Samuel Bagster, March 9, 1830, ibid., 87. The following evidence on Marylebone given by William Crawford, May 5, 1829, ibid., I, 12; Leslie Grove Jones, June 2, 1829, ibid., 132–35; Francis Wills, June 2, 1829, ibid., 131–32.

tailed. The system, not the men, was at fault in the large urban community.

Hobhouse himself presented the committee with financial records attesting to the benefits derived from placing the parish of Walcot, in the city of Bath, under the government of a vestry committee annually chosen by parishioners. Under the close vestry system, the expense of maintaining each pauper averaged £24.4.11 during the years 1820–1822. The cost diminished to about £19 during the next six years, when elected overseers managed the Poor Laws. Total expenditures fell from £9,661 in 1820 to £4,090 in 1826, in part because the responsible vestrymen had halved the number of paupers on relief, thus curbing the nepotism of their self-appointed predecessors.[13] Hobhouse also made effective use of information sent by various friends and relations in Bristol when an alderman and magistrate of that city appeared for questioning. The witness, William Fripp, was a select vestryman of Saint Mary's, Redcliff, one of Bristol's nineteen parishes and the place of Hobhouse's birth. The inquiry read:

In the distribution of these funds [charitable bequests], are you aware of any particular line that is followed by the vestry, or in the distribution what you would consider as altogether quite impartial? —I believe they are so; I took some pains to investigate that, because I had heard that they were not impartial; I gave myself some pains to inquire, and I had reason to find that the information I received was invariably false; I believe they are very impartial.

Are you aware that, generally speaking, the vestries in the city of Bristol are formed out of gentlemen of a political bias and feeling? —That has not been so much the case with the last 20 years, as formerly.

Is it not the case, that, generally speaking, for example your own vestry, is formed out of individuals of a particular leaning? —It is the case, certainly; it is more mixed than it was; the ward over which I preside was what is called a blue vestry, a high church party; the vestry used to contain a great majority of persons of that description.

Did you ever happen to hear that the vestry in your own parish have been in the habit of keeping a sort of record of the manner in which freemen vote for the election of members of Parliament? —I am not aware of the fact.

13. Testimony of John Cam Hobhouse, March 11, 1830, ibid., II, 100.

Did you ever hear it rumoured, that in the distribution of the charities, such freemen who voted in a particular way for members of Parliament were relieved in preference to others? —I did hear it on occasion; I investigated it; I charged a person with it; he proved to my satisfaction that such was not the case.[14]

Hobhouse described a society called the White Lion Club for promoting High Tory views, and how the vestry cooperated with its members. He then continued to question Fripp:

Can you recollect whether the influence of your vestry was then employed for one particular candidate? —I believe it was; I refused to lead the vestry on that occasion; I said I will meet you at any other place, I think the church not proper.

In fact, the select vestry of the city of Bristol was, to a certain extent, made use of for political purposes? —Yes, as far as that goes; the gentlemen of the high church party met in the vestry and canvassed for the member.

Are you aware that the vestry of your own parish would not allow the bells to be rung on the 23rd of last April, the King's birthday? —No.[15]

The hearings over, Place expressed dissatisfaction over Hobhouse's role as chairman, finding him too subdued or influenced by Sturges Bourne and too weak in pressing the Radical point of view.[16] As a result, the committee report published early in 1830 had failed to recommend democratic participation in parochial affairs. But even the most radical of witnesses, when asked, had equivocated about whether everyone should exercise a voice in selecting vestry officials. Leslie Grove Jones believed "that the proper people are rather the lower rate-payers than the higher rate-payers," and Thomas De Vear, a member of the Westminster Committee, believed "some little restriction" ought to be placed on the franchise in large parishes.[17] Place lost no time in plying Hobhouse with advice. "Marylebone parish," he wrote after reading the minutes, "exhibits nearly all the vices of a self-elected body accountable to nobody. That it is composed of re-

14. Testimony of William Fripp, March 11, 1830, ibid., 94–95.
15. Ibid., 95–96.
16. Place to Jones, November 5, 1829, Place Papers, Add. MSS 35148, f. 37–38.
17. Testimony of Leslie Grove Jones, June 2, 1829, *Parliamentary Reports*, 1830 (25.215), I, 133; testimony of Thomas De Vear, May 19, 1829, ibid., 89.

spectable and generally honourable men, no one can doubt, but an irresponsible body, no matter of whom composed, must in time become an evil. Inspection—control, and the power to change hands at short periods is as essential to the due administration of affairs as is circulation of the blood to animal life." [18] Hobhouse spent the next few months preparing a bill for parliamentary approval. He described his chief difficulty as "the necessity of making the provisions apply to all parishes, small as well as large, rural as well as metropolitan." [19] He was also confronted with the problem of preparing a bill that would be acceptable to the unreformed Commons, to those reformers who wished to abolish the close vestry in some way, and to parishioners in such cities as Leeds and Manchester who emphatically opposed any restrictions upon the democratic principle that governed their vestries. Hobhouse tried to explain his difficulties before the parochial delegates from London who assembled at the Freemasons' Tavern to discuss his Vestry Bill. He thought every ratepayer should have the vote, but there was little likelihood of carrying such a measure through the Commons. Under such circumstances he thought it best to introduce a modified plan that would restrict the franchise and establish a property qualification clause for vestrymen. But he gave his assurances that he would never accept a plural-voting scheme.[20]

Place was quick to criticize Hobhouse for abandoning the democratic principle. Hobhouse, he thought, was decidedly wrong in making such concessions to the conservative M.P.'s, for "experience has shown," Place maintained, "that to obtain one's end . . . we must *demand* a great deal more than we can hope to obtain." [21] Place erroneously pinned all the blame for parochial mismanagement and discontent on the privileged classes who failed to understand that government, even on a local level, was an art that demanded the undivided attention of experts. "Of all men none are so likely to fall into error as nobles and gentlemen," Place insisted, "Few of them have any habits of

18. Place to Hobhouse, March 22, 1830, Place Papers, Add. MSS 35154, f. 125.
19. Hobhouse to Place, April 16, 1830, Place Papers, Add. MSS 35154, f. 124.
20. *The Times*, February 17, 1830.
21. Place to Hobhouse, April 18, 1830, Lord Broughton Papers, Add. MSS 36465, f. 94.

business, and scarcely any of them ever take a view of the whole matter in any case in which they interfere." He was confident that steps toward democracy were moves not necessarily toward anarchy, but rather toward stable government, because public election "encourages and promotes discreet conduct." He emphasized that the common man "always selects men of property and character" whenever he could vote. The poor, as well as the rich, wanted their representatives to be men "who by their industry and vigilance have acquired or increased their property, and know its value." In Place's estimation, the best guardians of property were indeed those whom the rich described as "the rabble." [22]

Hobhouse tried to conciliate Radical dogma with political practicality. He thought that the essential issue in the vestry controversy was the replacement of corrupt select vestrymen by the election of honest parochial officials. Place had agreed that even the poorest parishioner had confidence in men of property; therefore, there was no violation of basic aims by establishing a property clause for vestrymen. As for equal and universal suffrage, Hobhouse told Place about the insurmountable parliamentary opposition that compelled him to give his reluctant consent to a limited franchise. He opposed Place's strategy of demanding more than could be expected; such tactics would cause conservatives to reject vestry reform altogether. Hobhouse preferred a compromise plan that all political groups would accept.

The Vestry Bill survived two readings in June, only to be thoroughly mutilated in committee. Hobhouse found Sturges Bourne "the most egregious coxcomb I ever met" [23] for introducing plural voting over Hobhouse's strongest objections. Next came the qualification clauses for vestrymen; the committee so enthusiastically favored the election of propertied men that they doubled the assessment for eligibility in parishes outside of London from £10 to £20. "A very ungracious task and by no means a labour of love," lamented Hobhouse, who saw much of his work undone by the revisionists. At this point, the King's death on June 26 prematurely ended the parliamentary session.

22. Place to Hobhouse, March 22, 1830, Place Papers, Add. MSS 35154, f. 124–25.
23. Hobhouse, diary, June 14, 1830, Lord Broughton Papers, Add. MSS 56554.

Hobhouse reintroduced vestry reform in 1831, after the defeat of the Parliamentary Reform Bill in committee had brought about the dissolution of Parliament and another election. Hobhouse had timed his action well. Popular feeling for vestry reform was at its height in London, and the Whigs depended on popular support in their struggle for the Reform Bill. Ministerial backing was forthcoming. Lord Althorp piloted Hobhouse's bill through the Commons amid the fierce and prolonged political crisis over parliamentary reform.

The bill introduced at the 1831 session was a much more radical measure for several reasons. Place had warned Hobhouse that his Westminster seat was in jeopardy because he had "trifled" in the committee hearings and had failed to introduce a sufficiently democratic vestry bill in 1830.[24] Deputations of Radicals from Marylebone, Saint Pancras, and from several Westminster parishes emphasized the point. Then, too, Hobhouse's thinking on the subject had evolved. He thought the new Parliament would favor a more democratic measure; the Commons clearly wanted the franchise enlarged, and the Lords would be too involved with the Reform Bill to make any amending clauses, such as plural voting.

Lord Melbourne later described Hobhouse's Vestry Bill as having a twofold object: It sought to correct the evils of large tumultuous open vestry meetings, and it tried to end the control of parochial affairs by a select few who met in close vestry. Burdett and Hume found the measure second in importance only to parliamentary reform, and Brougham summed up the bill as "coming close to the bosom of every family." The measure contained a number of significant clauses and introduced some innovations into English political life. First, every person, male or female, who paid rates was designated an elector. Elections would be by secret ballot on the request of any five voters; otherwise, parishioners would vote openly from a list of candidates for office. The bill provided that a poll of any parish with 800 ratepayers or more would be taken after one-fifth of the total number of ratepayers requested the churchwarden to hold an election. The reform would be adopted both when a majority of all ratepayers voted and when two-thirds of the voters favored the change. The precedent for this adoption clause was the 1782

24. Place, Memorandum of Passing Events, Place Papers, Add. MSS 35146, f. 102.

Gilbert Act, which was similarly concerned with local government.

Hobhouse's bill specified that the vestry would be entirely superseded in all its functions by a Board of Control, numbering from 12 to 100, as the governing body of the parish. One-third of the members would be elected each year, but ratepayers were restricted in their choice of board members. Parishes within the London police district, as well as those containing at least 3,000 rated householders, could elect to the Board of Control only persons occupying premises rated at £40 or more, whereas the qualification elsewhere was £10 or more. Lastly, the bill answered two major grievances by providing for the election annually of independent auditors and by requiring an annual statement of parish accounts.

Hobhouse refused any proposed changes to his bill in the Commons. He rejected an amendment of Sir Richard Vyvyan, M.P. from Cornwall, to restore plural voting and announced that the equality of all ratepayers was an essential feature of his measure. He also rejected a clause exempting from the bill any select vestry that controlled a charitable bequest. Sir Charles Forbes of Malmesbury raised the most controversial point of all when he predicted that the vestry bill would be the first step toward universal suffrage for parliamentary elections, but Hobhouse assured the Opposition that his measure simply permitted all ratepayers to exercise a vote in matters that immediately concerned them. Besides, the property qualifications ensured that Boards of Control would be composed of only propertied parishioners.[25]

While Parliament debated the Vestry Bill, parishioners from several London parishes met to consider a course of action should the measure be rejected. They threatened to withhold all tax payments, a defiant assertion of public opinion that William Prothero, M.P. for Bristol, wanted to resist with force if need be.[26] Such a showdown never took place, for the Commons passed the bill on October 6. "Vestry reform," Hobhouse later recalled, "was not a bad pilot balloon for the great act of 1832."[27]

25. *Hansard*, 3d series, V (1831), col. 310, VII (1831), cols. 881–91; VIII (1831), cols. 56 ff., 697–725.
26. *The Times*, September 27, 1831.
27. John Cam Hobhouse, first Baron Broughton, *Some Account of a Long Life*, I, 131.

The Lords gave the measure a second reading a few days after they had vetoed the Parliamentary Reform Bill, and Hobhouse believed the Vestry Bill was surely lost once the peers referred the measure to committee. "The Duke of Wellington seems as eager against my bill," Hobhouse recorded, "as against Lord John Russell's." [28] The Earl of Harrowby, however, summed up the situation by describing his fellow peers as thoroughly distracted by the tumultuous outcry against their recent veto of parliamentary reform. The Earl of Delawarr managed to turn their attention for a short time to his amendment for restoring plural voting, which was defeated by a vote of 54–38 after Lord Melbourne once again explained that equality of voting was an essential feature of the bill. Only a few, unimportant remarks attended the final approval by the Lords of the Vestry Bill a few days later, when the Sovereign arrived to prorogue the Parliament. [29]

Months later, it was pointed out that the "Hobhouse Act" failed to mention those taxes a parishioner was held liable to pay in order to qualify as a voter. A select vestry could conceivably oppose reform simply by levying an exhorbitant new rate and thereby disqualifying most persons. Hobhouse tried to amend his Vestry Act in January, 1832, but Parliament postponed consideration of his motion. [30] An amendment proved unnecessary because vestrymen offered no opposition in the several parishes that quickly adopted the reform. Only eight parishes, [31] including five within London, implemented Hobhouse's measure because the Poor Law Act of 1834 removed a major source of grievance against the vestry—the administration of poor relief. The Municipal Corporation Act of the following year also helped to remove a popular grievance by enabling ratepayers to choose borough councilors. These, in turn, assumed control of many municipal services and functions formerly exercised by the ves-

---

28. Hobhouse, diary, October 14, 1831, Lord Broughton Papers, Add. MSS 56555.

29. *Hansard*, 3d series, VIII (1831), cols. 486–87, 807 ff., 822–36. Hobhouse's bill was Act 1 & 2 William 4, c.60.

30. *Hansard*, 3d series, IX (1832), col. 763.

31. See A return of Parishes in England and Wales which have adopted the Act 1 & 2 William 4, c.60 commonly called Hobhouse's Vestry Act, *Parliamentary Accounts and Papers*, 1842, 569. The report lists St. George, Hanover Square; St. James, Westminster; St. John the Evangelist; St. Marylebone; St. Pancras; Nunkeeling; and Beaumaris.

try. Hobhouse's act did have a lasting effect on local government in London; the Metropolis Management Act (1855) applied its provisions to all parishes and at the same time made the vestry the electoral colleges for members of the new Metropolitan Board of Works. The vestries were converted in 1899 into the Metropolitan Borough Councils.

The Vestry Bill of 1831 was Hobhouse's solution to the controversy over local government, which was particularly vehement in London, Bristol, and other large cities. Vestry protest coincided with the crisis over parliamentary reform because both primarily involved urban populations that found themselves excluded from decision making on a local and national level. Hobhouse took a major step toward making local government more representative by incorporating the ratepayer franchise and secret ballot that Place and other Radicals wished.

Hobhouse did not altogether embrace Radical notions of government. His measure's adoptive clause contrasted with the Benthamite-inspired Poor Law Act of 1834, which unilaterally created Poor-Law districts and a central authority over local officials. Hobhouse's measure also limited the ratepayer franchise by allowing the actual work of parish government to be performed only by those who had a sufficient amount of property. The successful manufacturers, the landowners, or the enterprising urban citizens who were gaining in wealth and numbers were now entrusted with leadership on the parish level, but most people shared in the task of either approving or rejecting the rule of superior social orders. Hobhouse hoped such a mixed government would assure the cooperation between the nation's rulers and its people that he had sought since his parliamentary career began.

CHAPTER VII

A DECADE OF LIBERALISM
AND HUMANITARIANISM

Besides seeking political reform, Hobhouse worked for the reform of the law code and of education. He shared with many public figures a keen interest in the need to make the law code more equitable. Bentham, Romilly, Mackintosh, Fowell Buxton, and, more recently, Peel had publicized the abuses and anomalies in the law and called for their correction. Most justly, the *Quarterly Review* observed in 1821, "The era of legal reform has indeed begun. We find mankind restless and disatisfied, and straining every faculty of mind and body for the improvement of their condition." [1]

Hobhouse's interest in law reform derived partly from his Unitarian upbringing. He believed in a benevolent Deity who ordained a course of human perfectability and well-being; man was supposed to act accordingly by framing laws calculated to promote "the greatest happiness of the greatest number" on earth. The English legal code fell far short of this principle. "It is a maxim in jurisprudence, confirmed by the experience of all ages," Dr. Estlin had written, "that crimes are more effectively prevented by their certainty than by the severity of punishment. The severity of laws (an observation which I fear applies to the Criminal Code of this country) hinders their execution, destroys their effect, and leads to their violation, by encouraging the hopes of impunity." [2] Estlin assumed that crime deserved punishment, but punishment itself was an evil because it inflicted pain. Punishment was justifiable only insofar as it prevented greater future evils or repaired past evils, and in either case, the ultimate aim was not retribution but the reformation of an offender, just as the Unitarian Deity did not consign to eternal punishment even the worst of sinners. Hence, for Hobhouse, a reformation of criminal law must include a classification of punishments ex-

1. "Report from the Select Committee on Criminal Laws," *Quarterly Review*, 24 (January, 1821), 195.
2. John Prior Estlin, *Discourses on Universal Restitution delivered to the Society of Protestant Dissenters in Lewin's Mead, Bristol*, 25–27.

ceeding as little as possible the pain the offender inflicted upon others.

Despite some similarities in language and ideas, Estlin's comments on the law were nowhere as comprehensive and systematic as Bentham's. One mildly rebuked his countrymen for departing from the spirit of the divinity; the other shook Englishmen out of their complacent esteem for their body of laws by explaining how that body was in fact a jumble of chaotic, inapplicable, and irrational statutes that must be entirely replaced. Bentham maintained that Utilitarian principles constituted a universally valid standard for a vastly improved legal system based on a balance of pleasures and pains. To this end he criticized the penal code, the organization of courts, and judicial procedures; he attacked the method of paying judges by fees rather than salaries; he advocated a more impartial method of choosing special jurors; he promulgated the idea that Parliament—the supreme legislative body of the land—should be elected by a broad franchise, thus rendering it responsive to majority interests and welfare.

Hobhouse was aware of Benthamite ideas, for his diary records his having read the *Fragment on Government* (1776) and the *Introduction to the Principles of Morals and Legislation* (1789). He first turned his attention to the dramatic issue of capital punishment, as did most other reformers. He was also interested in the closely related matter of prison conditions, and after Fowell Buxton's graphic description of the horrible conditions existing in various prisons,[3] Hobhouse made his own visit to Newgate in 1818.

He accompanied several members of the Commons who were also there to investigate the case of Spicer and Kelley, two boys who awaited hanging for issuing forged bank notes, and he was shocked by what he saw and heard. "I saw about eleven in one room—all under sentence of death, and four of them for execution on Wednesday," Hobhouse recorded, "the two boys and two holloways for river stealing—they only 19 and 23." In another room he saw "little boys—two on nine years old—condemned to die for stealing and a third of the same age who will be, for stealing a muff." The prison keeper told him that most of the

---

3. Thomas Fowell Buxton, *Inquiry whether Crime and Misery are Produced or Prevented by our Present System of Prison Discipline.*

condemned people in Newgate were under twenty years of age. These youths may well have been the prototypes for Oliver Twist, but they had failed to escape from the Fagins who had forced them into a life of crime. "It is clear that the seduced are taken," the official observed, "the pimps and friends escape." Hobhouse then saw "the cells in which convicts are shut up the night previous to execution," and commented:

Hanging does not seem to discourage crime in the least. The two holloways had a brother hung for the same crime for which they are to die on Wednesday. Havrner, a solicitor of Newgate, seemed to think the application would not save Spicer and Kelley—he said he had known so many innocent people suffer he had written a pamphlet to prove the innocence of Haggarty and Halloway who were hanged for murdering Steele. Browne the keeper told us that much of the motion in the hanged which appeared convulsions to the mob were occasioned by pulling the legs below. Jack Ketch he said was a little drunk the other morning when he hanged . . . two women so badly.[4]

Hobhouse successfully intervened through his cousin Henry at the Home Office to have the lives of Spicer and Kelley spared. A year later he again witnessed criminal justice in operation, this time as a parliamentary prisoner in Newgate:

A man was hanged this morning for an unnatural crime. Had my windows fastened up but could not sleep. They began putting up the scaffold at 4 o'clock. The tolling of the bell at 8 was frightful. I heard the crash of the drop falling and a woman screetch violently at the same moment. Instantly afterwards, the sound of the pye man crying "all hot, all hot." Tis dreadful hanging a man for this practise.[5]

Hobhouse warmly supported Mackintosh's motions to immediately alleviate the criminal code by abolishing capital punishment for several categories of offenses. His highest praise eventually went to Peel for mitigating capital punishment, improving the administration of civil law, and for reforming the method of selecting special juries. "He laid the basis for being a great man, by showing himself to be a good one," observed

4. Hobhouse, diary, February 23, 1818, John Cam Hobhouse, Lord Broughton, Papers, Add. MSS 47235, f. 3, 4.
5. Hobhouse, diary, December 29, 1819, Lord Broughton Papers, Add. MSS 56540.

Hobhouse when Peel proposed further consolidation and amendments to the criminal laws in 1827.[6]

Still, they differed on specifics. Peel approached legal reform in the spirit of Bacon, from whom he once quoted, "The work which I propound tendeth to pruning and grafting of the law, and not to ploughing up and planting it again; for such a remove I should hold indeed for a perilous innovation." His powerful administrative mind thought in terms of the consequences and practical details any changes entailed, and he accordingly warned the Commons in 1823 against rendering impractical the abolition of capital punishments by narrowing too much the scale of minor punishments. Hobhouse, however, felt the system of punishments remained inhumane, just as the old penal code was savage and barbaric. Throughout 1822 he presented various petitions describing the terrible conditions at Ilchester prison, where orator Henry Hunt was repeatedly denied medical treatment after exposure to glaring summer sun and cold winter weather.[7] He denounced flogging as a form of punishment and in 1824 drew the House's attention to the use of treadmill labor, referring to one Somerset magistrate who had written that it was exhausting enough to break down a prisoner's health and that it had caused bodily injuries.[8] Peel responded by telling Hobhouse his own minute inquiry found the treadmill an admirable contrivance for prison work and one little liable to abuse.

There was agreement that a thorough overhaul of the country's prisons and inspection by outside officials could provide safeguards against local instances of brutality and abuse. Peel's Gaols Acts of 1823 and 1824 provided for the establishment of local prisons or houses of correction financed by local taxes and administered by local magistrates, but Hobhouse felt the measures did not demand adequate inspection, as evidenced by the situation allowed to continue at Horsemonger Lane prison, Surrey, where magistrates permitted debtors only one hour a day for receiving provisions and clothing from friends and relatives, many of whom had to journey long distances.[9] Hobhouse did not

6. *Hansard Parliamentary Debates*, 2d series, XVI (1827), col. 645.
7. Ibid., VI (1822), cols. 157, 862, 892, 1235, VII (1822), col. 27.
8. Ibid., X (1824), col. 247. John Cox Hippisley, *Prison labour, and correspondence and communication addressed to His Majesty's principal secretary of state for the Home department concerning the introduction of tread-mills into prisons*.
9. *Hansard*, 2d series, XI (1824), cols. 1493–95.

think governmental powers would be overextended by setting up a central prison inspectorate with a body of salaried officials in the pay of the Home Office. Public opinion in 1824 was prepared to accept only the rudiments of centralization, but in 1824 such a system was instituted.

The creation of a Metropolitan police force was equally controversial at the time Peel first proposed it in the early 1820's. Reformers like Romilly and Mackintosh had maintained that law enforcement was primarily a matter of restoring public support and confidence by changing the severe and unpopular criminal code. They and many others associated an efficient police force with centralized, despotic governments on the Continent. Hobhouse thought differently. He was a member of T. G. B. Estcourt's crime committee of 1828, which presented frightening data on the soaring crime rate: Between 1811 and 1827 convictions for various offenses throughout the metropolitan area of London had risen by 55 per cent, whereas the population had increased by only 19 per cent.[10] Witnesses testified about street robberies, organized gangs of juvenile thieves, and organized prostitution. They told of "flash houses" where thieves, gamblers, and even murderers evaded the law. One solicitor found no protection from the local authorities because he had promised them no reward for any recovered stolen property. Areas such as Wandsworth were terrorized by crime, but the existing police force, the Bow Street patrol, came through only occasionally. Such testimony, as well as the impressive mass of statistics, convincingly pointed to a need for some improvement in law enforcement. Westminster and Southwark alone had seven inadequate police offices, each one independent of the others and all interfering with the small parochial forces that patrolled an area containing a quarter of a million people. The Home Office itself had under its control only four hundred men in 1822, a smaller number than the City of London's force.[11]

Statistics on London to the contrary, Francis Place urged

10. Report from the Select Committee appointed to inquire into the cause of the increase in the number of Commitments and Convictions in London and Middlesex, and into the state of the Police of the Metropolis, and of districts adjoining thereto, *Parliamentary Reports*, 1828 (533), VI, 1.

11. For a discussion of the Police system, as well as other aspects of Peel's reforms, see Norman Gash, *Mr. Secretary Peel; the Life of Sir Robert Peel to 1830*, chaps. 9, 14.

Hobhouse to inform the committee that in fact "no place on earth has improved so much in morals." [12] Place felt the masses in the metropolis had endeavored through self-help to enhance their own self-respect and the image they projected to the rest of the nation. The evidence gathered by various crime committees was unwelcomed because it ignored the tremendous improvement that had occurred among the "industrious lower orders" over the past several decades. Crime statistics made excellent propaganda, and Place was certain that the Tory Government desired to isolate the working class by equating the masses with felons and rioters in the minds of superior social groups. Furthermore, a police force could become a powerful weapon of oppression. Such arguments now carried little weight with Hobhouse, who concurred with the committee's recommendation to establish "an Office of Police acting under the immediate direction of the Secretary of State for the Home Department, upon which should be devolved the general control over the whole of the Establishments of Police." [13] This expression of support for Peel on Hobhouse's part indicated how much his esteem for the statesman had risen over the years. It was another point on which Hobhouse and Place now totally disagreed.

Hobhouse also supported Peel's Juries Regulation Bill of 1825. An antiquated judicial system that permitted the Government and various prosecuting societies to take every unfair advantage of Britons who held unpopular or controversial views was one of Hobhouse's major concerns for years. He thought freedom of speech and the press was never more seriously imperiled than during his earliest years at Westminster. Throughout the borough, from political leaders and Radical writers to newsvendors eking out a precarious living, there were cries of protest over the method of empaneling jurors, particularly in the many trials for libel. Cobbett, T. J. Wooler, and William Hone had previously appeared before the bar, and a campaign of intimidation and punishment accelerated after the Peterloo Massacre and into the following years, until some 120 prosecutions

12. Francis Place, Memorandum of Passing Events, Francis Place Papers, Add. MSS 35146, f. 243.
13. Report from the Select Committee appointed to inquire into the cause of the increase in the number of Commitments, *Parliamentary Reports*, 1828 (533), VI, 30.

for libel had taken place throughout the country by the end of 1821. Some involved charges of blasphemous libel, as in the case of Richard Carlile, who was sentenced in 1819 to five years in Newgate for republishing, among other works, Paine's *Age of Reason*. The most widely publicized prosecution for seditious libel happened in 1819, when Sir Francis Burdett was fined and imprisoned for sending an open letter to his constituents condemning the Peterloo tragedy. At a Crown and Anchor meeting he chaired immediately after the sentencing, Hobhouse declared that "the jury by which the hon. bart. was tried (all honourable men, no doubt) was entirely—or at least with the exception of three or four—composed of members of a Pitt-club: so that their representative was tried by a Pitt-club jury for an offence against Mr. Pitt's principles." [14] A short time later, in 1820, John Thelwall, who had escaped with his neck in the treason trials of 1794, was again called to stand trial for denouncing Burdett's imprisonment in *The Champion*.

Speaking in Parliament against the prosecution of William Benbow, a bookseller in the Strand, Hobhouse noted that although the law left the decision regarding the facts of libel entirely in the hands of a jury, this did not exclude the possibility of obtaining biased jurors and of intimidation by influential groups.[15] How else, he asked, was the Government able to score one success after another other than by corrupting jurors, whose duty it was to check the judge, and by keeping a corps of special jurors who always returned a guilty verdict? The elements of the art of packing, Bentham wrote in 1809, consisted of keeping a corps of "Guineamen" who took their orders from servants of the Crown, by whom they were paid, and of passing over the names of those who were prepared to return an impartial verdict.[16] Libel was "simply an excuse to persecute and punish individuals for saying, in print or otherwise, anything disagreeable to Ministers," wrote Francis Place in 1823, "A jury can be found to pronounce an opinion against the speaker, or writer, or publisher." [17]

14. *The Times*, February 13, 1821.
15. *Hansard*, 2d series, V (1821), col. 1484.
16. Jeremy Bentham, *Elements of the Art of Packing, as applied to Special Juries, particularly in cases of Libel Law.*
17. Place, *On the Law of Libel; with Strictures on the Self-Styled "Constitutional Association."*

Place wrote this comment at the time of John Hunt's indictment for publishing Byron's *Vision of Judgement*, a mock elegy on the late King George III, which appeared in the first issue of *The Liberal* in 1822 and in a later issue of *The Examiner. The Times* took notice of Hunt's indictment when it presented readers with "a singular and very striking instance" of the manner in which special juries "were manufactured in cases of libel, where the Crown is concerned." [18] The newspaper reported that on the day appointed to strike the special jury, the secretary of the so-called Constitutional Association, Charles Murray, gave a friend a list of several persons likely to serve on the jury and asked whether they were favorably inclined to his own "line of politics."

Hobhouse had noted in his diary, in January, 1821, the formation of the Constitutional Association for the avowed purpose of prosecuting seditious publications. Before long it had about 700 subscribers; among them were some 20 peers, including the Duke of Wellington, and nearly 40 members of the Commons. It could also reckon on the support of 6 English bishops and many other clergymen who saw that the press—"that mighty engine for diffusing the light of Liberty and of the Gospel," as the Association's circular stated—had fallen into the hands of "evil" men. The issue of freedom of the press and speech was now joined, with other prominent public figures subscribing to a counterfund for hiring, in Hobhouse's words, "the most eminent counsel to defend the first person prosecuted by them." Among the contributors Hobhouse listed the Marquis of Tavistock, Thomas Coke, David Ricardo, Douglas Kinnaird, Alderman Wood of London, and Burdett.[19] In the months ahead Thelwall and Mary Ann Carlile, sister of Richard Carlile, were provided with legal aid. Hunt, who had once described the Constitutional Association as a "canting crew" whose weapons were "as vile as their object," [20] eluded prosecution by the Association until 1823.

Hobhouse believed Hunt's prosecution was a rigged affair, what with the Association's efforts to obtain a partial jury and Chief Justice Abbott's telling them that "a publication tending

18. *The Times*, May 30, 1823.
19. John Cam Hobhouse, first Baron Broughton, *Some Account of a Long Life*, II, 22.
20. *The Examiner*, May 13, 1821.

to disturb the minds of living individuals by reflecting upon persons who were dead" was indeed a libelous offense.[21] Hunt explained to his readers the ways he found the system of selecting jurors liable to abuse. Prior to his trial, an official known as the Master of the Crown Office named 48 persons from the freeholders book; each party then struck off 12 names from the list before the sheriff summoned the remaining 24. According to Hunt, the Master admitted that he had the power of packing juries by the following procedure:

He turns over the pages, reads aloud any name he may fix upon, which is taken down by the parties attending: he usually takes one or two names in a page; but sometimes passes over many pages without taking any. He is asked by the defendent why he thus selects, and upon what principle he makes the nomination; and he explains, that in the first place he only takes such as are designated esquires in the book, and of these names . . . choosing any one his eye may light upon, unless he knows some reason why that one is unfit, and then he passes him over, reserving the objection, however, entirely in his own breast.[22]

Abbott, in June, 1824, sentenced Hunt not to banishment, not to imprisonment, but to a relatively small fine of £100 and to give bail amounting to £3,500 for *The Examiner*'s future good behavior. As Hunt himself observed, the trial ended more happily than expected, partly because of the utter discredit that had befallen the Constitutional Association, the result of proceedings in courts of law, as well as its unfounded attacks upon respected public men, especially Alderman Waithman of London.[23] Hunt's trial was the last in a series that had brought public disfavor upon the courts and the prosecuting societies. A year later Peel's Juries Bill brought a long-overdue change in legal procedure by establishing the use of registration and secret balloting in choosing select jurors for criminal cases and for cases in which the Crown was a real or nominal party. By then, the

21. *Hansard*, 2d series, IX (1823), 572; *The Times*, January 16, 1824.
22. *The Examiner*, May 27, 1821; May 18, 1823; see also "Mr. Cottu and Special Juries," *The Westminster Review*, 1 (January, 1824), 146–71.
23. Henry Hunt to Leigh Hunt, June 19, 1824, Henry Hunt Papers, Add. MSS 38108, f. 523. See William H. Wickwar, *The Struggle for the Freedom of the Press, 1819–1832*, which details the libel laws and the fight against them during this time.

Constitutional Association and other agents of the public good were in disrepute. Also, the Government had realized that prosecutions helped to publicize blasphemous and seditious concepts that were best ignored.

The spirit of the age that made for greater freedom of expression also encouraged many philanthropical institutions to raise public morals and well-being. Hobhouse thought highly of such work. The Royal Humane Society, The Society for the Suppression of Mendicity, and the Philanthropic Sons of Saint Andrew regularly received his donations. He became a vice president of The Eclectic Society of London for promoting learning and the arts in East London. Self-improvement societies flourished in Westminster, and in 1825 The Western Literary and Scientific Organization began offering a series of lectures in "Science, Political Economy, Philosophy, History, and Polite Literature." Hobhouse gladly donated £25 to an organization that he described as "enabling all to participate in that knowledge which was the most useful and the source of prosperity for all." [24] Its members elected him a vice president, along with Douglas Kinnaird and Dr. George Birbeck. Within a year it had a membership of almost two thousand citizens who enjoyed the use of a private library in Leicester Square.

Hobhouse had first met Dr. Birbeck a few years earlier at a meeting held at the Crown and Anchor Tavern to consider establishing a Mechanics' Institute in London. Thomas Hodgekin, editor of *Mechanics' Magazine*, originated the idea of forming a London institute after he learned about the success of the Glasgow school.[25] Francis Place was especially helpful in obtaining support from Brougham and Burdett, but Hobhouse at first had some reservations about the project. He thought its founders entertained some wild notions about producing men of genius in every field, whereas "no great composition," he informed Place, "acknowledged by the world to bear the stamp of genius, has been produced under the auspices of an institution." [26] Hobhouse later supported the institute after Place assured him its founders were indeed practical men whose modest goal was to improve the working class.

24. *Morning Chronicle*, November 11, 1825.
25. See Chester New, *Life of Henry Brougham to 1830*, chap. XVII.
26. Hobhouse to Place, November 19, 1823, Place Papers, Add. MSS 27824, f. 25.

Perhaps the most impressive example of this extensive "march of intellect" was the founding of London University. The idea of such a nondenominational institution had been proposed for some years by Thomas Campbell, the poet and literary critic. A central figure in realizing Campbell's ambition was Isaac Lyon Goldsmid, the wealthy London financier. It was Goldsmid who aroused Brougham's interest in the project, and soon Brougham presented a plan of procedure before Hobhouse and other guests at a dinner party in January, 1825. The group then formed a provisional committee to solicit £100 shares from the public and to prepare a deed of settlement for the university.[27]

Hobhouse fully agreed with the university's essentially practical aims as Campbell and Brougham had stated to the public.[28] Higher education helped preserve social stability; it provided for the growing body of "middling rich" a training necessary to prepare them for future leadership as Britain adjusted to the revolutions in science and technology. Idleness and ignorance were the alternatives. London University was also a major step toward emancipating higher education from religious discrimination, a significance not lost upon Hobhouse, who recalled his own Westminster and Cambridge days. He cautioned Brougham about the opposition that any project for nonsectarian education would surely encounter from Church of England circles, especially from Evangelicals like Wilberforce. He was mistaken, for no serious opposition arose. The University Council itself provided an illustration of prominent public figures from many backgrounds all cooperating in the worthy cause. Brougham and Mackintosh reflected the influence of Scottish public education, George Grote and James Mill represented the Utilitarians, and four peers represented the aristocracy. There were an equal number of Dissenters, and Zachary Macaulay represented the influential Evangelicals.

Hobhouse saw great political significance in such cooperation. Humanitarian reasons alone vindicated a policy of forming a broad political alliance that included reformers of various backgrounds and classes. Hobhouse believed that mankind was basically good and capable of progress but that benign change

---

27. H. H. Bellot, *University College, London, 1826–1926*, 1–32; also New, *Life of Brougham*, chaps. 18, 19.

28. Campbell to Brougham, *The Times*, February 9, 1825; Henry Peter Brougham, *Practical Observation of the People* (London, 1825).

rarely came from the masses. Rather, it was accomplished through a few good and great men. He therefore disapproved of "a foolish letter" he received from Francis Place within a few months of the opening of University College. Place denounced the aristocracy, whose unrivaled power made them the worst predators in a corrupt structure of authority. "Now the aristocracy is exposing its folly every day and its malice every week . . . in Parliament, on the Bench, in Sessions, and on the Game Laws," [29] he charged; Whig and Tory nobles "sassed at the people's 'march of intellect,' " they derided the Mechanics' and other institutes, and they supported philanthropic societies out of selfish motives. The aristocracy could not govern the country much longer, Place concluded, for the great moral and intellectual improvement of the masses had prepared them for assuming charge of the nation.

Hobhouse urged Place to reconsider his severe pronouncements:

I think you are rather severe upon our great and small vulgar —and I also think you are wrong in saying they *laugh* at the March of Intellect. I find all who talk with me think it no laughing matter at all. Quite the contrary—some, like Lord Eldon call it the rogue's march and think it a time to which one day . . . 100,000 tall fellows with clubs and pikes will march against Whitehall. Others regard it as a very beneficial change in the condition of their fellow creatures and labour incessantly to bring it about. Look for example at the Society for Promoting Useful Knowledge and look at the members of London University—and look moreover to the patrons and friends of mechanics and other institutions all over England, I may say all over Europe.[30]

Hobhouse saw social and political anarchy in Place's democratic vision of the future. All standards would be obliterated, he thought, and there would no longer exist men of "pure minds and cultivated intellects" to provide sound and wise leadership. He urged Place not to expect that the aristocracy should always be doing something and produce immediate results. Furthermore, he ought to distinguish between the aristocrats who served the nation and a minority who deserved criticism for

29. Place to Hobhouse, December 19, 1827, Place Papers, Add. MSS 35148, f. 5.
30. Hobhouse to Place, December 21, 1827, Place Papers, Add. MSS 35148, f. 6–8.

failing to live up to the high ideals of their class. Most deplorable of all, to Hobhouse, was Place's failure to realize that the aristocracy's consciousness of the community's welfare overlapped any diversity of interest, social position, or economic class that tended to divide a society. Enlightened men had common goals and principles; they would eventually attain the economic, political, and humanitarian reforms the country needed.

Place's immediate reply re-emphasized his contrary views:

No my dear sir, I am neither too hard nor too hasty. I do look at London University and at every other matter and thing connected with "the march of intellect" and these are the things to prove my case. Our "London Mechanics Institution," the most useful society on the face of the earth, is a conclusive proof of my opinion. When this was started, and before aristocracy had time to be alarmed, I could have obtained money from a great number of them. When it had been a short time in existence I could obtain none. . . . I have many letters from aristocracy, shuffling, or speaking out plainly, some very anxious—all disliking the "march of intellect"; and you will see how from all but *Charitable* Institutions, aristocracy will gradually withdraw. Friendly Societies—see how aristocracy is working at these valuable clubs, endeavouring to get them out of the hands of the people, and to make them charity concerns.[31]

Hobhouse had argued that well-intentioned public men would abandon humanitarian concerns should their efforts be met with dissatisfaction and distrust; Place maintained that such suspicion was warranted. Hobhouse held that the present political system could only impede, not prevent, social progress; Place held out no hope under the present corrupt political framework, but he was prepared to wait a long time observing the "working of events." Once again, on the many philanthropic and humanitarian activities throughout the decade, Place and Hobhouse had irreconcilable views.

Hobhouse's humanitarianism, which underlay his interest in penal and educational improvements, was also the driving force behind his efforts to shorten the working day and to enforce better conditions in the factories. He established through his various legislative proposals a reputation as the leading parliamentary spokesman of state intervention in factory labor during

---

31. Place to Hobhouse, December 23, 1827, Place Papers, Add. MSS 35148, f. 9.

the 1820's, before various reformers had built up mass senti-ment throughout the country for such measures. For some years Hobhouse had hoped that Sir Robert Peel would sponsor a fac-tory bill. Peel's father's Act of 1819 had provided steps in the direction of factory regulation by forbidding the employment of children under nine years of age in the cotton mills and by re-ducing to twelve hours the workday of those under sixteen years. The Act fell short of recommendations made by the 1816 parliamentary committee of inquiry and was far less reaching than improvements suggested in Robert Owen's *Observations on the Effect of the Manufacturing System* (1815), which pro-posed to limit the hours of labor in any factory to twelve a day, including mealtime. Owen had also hoped to prevent the em-ployment of children under ten years of age and to reduce to six hours the workday of children under twelve. Hobhouse tried to interest Peel in amending his father's bill, but the Home Secre-tary proved unwilling to undertake any remedial legislation that would further extend the role of the state in economic affairs. Eventually, John Doherty and other union leaders in charge of delegations from Lancashire and Yorkshire prevailed upon Hobhouse to act on his own. His proposals of 1825 foreshad-owed in a low key the controversy that would attend future, more radical measures.

Hobhouse contended in 1825 that Parliament had already recognized the principle upon which his bill rested—the protec-tion of those factory workers who could not protect themselves.[32] Such was the aim of Peel's earlier measure, an aim that had been shamelessly evaded because witnesses were not compelled to testify before factory inspectors,[33] and hence only two convic-tions had resulted during these many years. To make the 1819 Act effective, Hobhouse proposed to give magistrates the power of summoning witnesses and to prevent any magistrate who was the proprietor of a mill or who was the son or father of a mill owner from acting as an inspector. He then defended with con-siderable force a clause reducing to eleven hours the workday

32. *Hansard*, 2d series, XIII (1825), cols. 643–45.
33. According to the 1819 Bill the justices at quarter sessions appointed a magistrate and a clergyman as inspectors. On the factory reform movement, see J. T. Ward, *The Factory Movement, 1830–1855*, Samuel Kydd [Alfred], *The History of the Factory Reform Movement from 1802 to the Enactment of the Ten Hour Bill in 1847*, and Raymond G. Cowherd, *The Humanitarians and the Ten Hour Movement in England*.

for children under sixteen years of age. When Edmund Hornby, M.P. for Preston, claimed such legislation would cost the nation "two millions and a half of productive revenue," Hobhouse indignantly retorted that "it would be better to give up the cotton industry altogether, than to draw such a sum out of the blood, and bones, and sinews of these unfortunate children." He dwelled upon the worst features of factory labor, with children forced to work fifteen or sixteen hours a day and obliged to take their meals in the dust and down of the cotton. It would surely be the height of human callousness to ignore the wretched children working in the cotton mills. "They scarcely bore any resemblance to their fellow-creatures," Hobhouse observed, "after being so long subject to this torture. Their skins were literally the colour of parchment." [34]

Hobhouse's critics pointed out that child labor was bound up with other features of the factory system that he had ignored entirely. They claimed that any restrictions upon the employment of children would place English cotton goods at a disadvantage in foreign markets, and they emphasized the impossibility of limiting the working hours of children without similarly reducing the labor of adults, so interdependent was their work. Regulation, they claimed, would hinder, not help, the working masses because its net effect would be to close down some factories and deprive children of work altogether. Such arguments, grounded as they were upon the inexorable laws of political economy, provided moral, as well as scientific, justification for a policy of nonintervention, made it necessary to defend in bolder and broader terms the superiority and natural beneficence of factory regulations to society as a whole. This, Hobhouse failed to do, largely because he was influenced by that body of liberal thinking that opposed state encroachment upon the free play of English capital and labor.

Doctrines of political economy consequently blunted the force of Hobhouse's humanitarianism. He was a reformer because in his mind the realities of human experience did allow for some exceptions to general rules, unlike such Radicals as Hume or Roebuck, who held that scientific laws of the Classical Economists could never be qualified. Thus, Hobhouse would remedy a specific evil of child labor, but he still had misgivings about tampering with adult labor: One belonged to the category of

34. *Hansard*, 2d series, XIII (1825), col. 645.

"those who could not help themselves," the other to the category
of a "free agent" in an unregulated economic order. Hobhouse's
1825 provisions were consequently less far reaching than those
favored by philanthropic manufacturers from Lancashire and
Yorkshire, among them John Wood, Matthew Thompson, and
John Rand, who favored regulating adult labor as well. Finally,
at the end of May, Hobhouse announced that at the suggestion
of others, he was abandoning the "eleven hours" plan to which
Peel had declared himself opposed. His measure as passed
lessened child labor in the cotton mills by some three hours a
week and prohibited their working between eight P.M. and five
A.M. or during mealbreaks.[35] Four years later he successfully
sponsored a bill to facilitate enforcement by specifying that it
was not necessary to include the names of all the partners of a
firm summoned in pursuance of his 1825 Act.[36]

Not until the early 1830's did factory reform become a popular crusade, with able leaders who addressed and shocked a
conscience-stricken public. By then, Michael Sadler had sav-
agely attacked "the accursed manufacturers" in his earliest
essays. In October, 1830, the *Leeds Mercury* heralded the new
era of factory reform when its editor, Edward Baines, published
Richard Oastler's famous letter entitled "Yorkshire Slavery."
The Industrial Age had found another Evangelical who exhorted
Britons to blush for shame at the spectacle of thousands of children toiling long hours in the factories.[37] A new reform movement quickly swelled, backed by another leading northern
journal, the *Leeds Intelligencer*, and by mill owners of Bradford who met in November to draw up a petition calling for additional regulations of factory labor. Hobhouse then agreed to
introduce legislation after Lord Morpeth, a Yorkshire M.P.,
presented the petition to Parliament. Within months, mill
owners elsewhere had backed reform, and throughout the northern towns "Short Time Committees" of workmen and trades-

---

35. The hours were lessened through a shorter Saturday workday. Hobhouse's bill is 6 Geo. 4, c.63. See *Hansard*, 2d series, XIII (1825), cols.
1008–11; A Bill to make further Provisions for the Regulation of Cotton
Mills and Factories, and for the better Preservation of the Health of Young
Persons employed therein, *Parliamentary Papers*, 1825 (283) (832), I.
297.303.
36. A Bill to amend the Law relating to the Employment of Children in
Cotton Mills and Factories, *Parliamentary Papers*, 1829 (259), I. 483.
37. See Cecil Driver, *Tory Radical, The Life of Richard Oastler*.

men sprang into existence. Reformers awaited the parliamentary discussions.

Hobhouse had a bill ready in February. It was a more sweeping measure than his 1825 Bill, which applied to only cotton mills. His present proposal barred all children from any textile mill before the age of nine. Anyone under eighteen years of age would work an eleven and one-half hour day, plus an eight and one-half hour Saturday for a total of sixty-six hours. Other clauses provided for mealtimes, sanitation, the prohibition of night work, and the posting of regulations in the factory. As might be expected, the bill provoked a determined opposition once its provisions became known in the north. The master worsted-spinners of Halifax were enraged by the clause forbidding night work, declaring they could never remain in business with restrictions against making up lost time owing to accidents, stoppages, or insufficient water power. In 1831, the *Mercury* featured letters from "Vindex" arguing the case against additional regulations. Hobhouse was accused of inhumanity by desiring to lower the wages of those factory children who contributed to the well-being of working-class families. "Vindex" also maintained that working conditions in the factories compared most favorably to those experienced by the agricultural laborers. Indeed, he said, measures had best be directed against landlords in the south, where the countryside was ablaze! Many letters from "practical men" poured into Baines's office to join "Vindex" in a chorus of protest against the misguided efforts of the M.P. from far-off Westminster.

At first the opinions of the protesting mill owners made little impression on Hobhouse. "It would give me much pain to see the Bill opposed by well-meaning and fair antagonists," Hobhouse informed Baines, "but as to parties interested in upholding present abuses, I not only am prepared for their attacks, but I should think I have attempted nothing useful if I did not encounter them." [38] Then Hobhouse began to waver after pressure groups from throughout the country plied him with advice and presented various objections. It was the powerful lobby of mill owners, not the workingmen's delegations, that finally gained ascendancy. He granted to silk manufacturers the right to employ children at the age of seven; he conceded an extra half-

38. Quoted, ibid., 79.

hour a day for delays due to loss of water power; he then cut by two hours the definition of night work; next he exempted some parts of the woolen industry from the regulations. Finally, before his bill came up for a vote in the Commons, Hobhouse restored a twelve-hour day. At this point, Parliament was dissolved on April 22, following defeat of the parliamentary reform bill in committee.

Hobhouse reintroduced his amended factory bill after the general elections. The controversy continued throughout the summer as delegates from Scotland tried unsuccessfully to get their part of the Kingdom excluded. Fellow M.P.'s buttonholed Hobhouse in the lobby of Saint Stephens, he was buffeted by mill owners and factory workers alike, and letters from all parts of the country continued to pour into London. Hobhouse finally resolved the issue late in the evening of September 28–29 by accepting the amendments demanded by his critics.[39] He pared down the measure so that it applied only to the cotton factories where children under eighteen years of age received a twelve-hour workday. The Act as passed also prohibited night work for all persons under twenty-one. One innovation was a clause requiring employers to keep a record book for reporting the length of each working day.

Even so limited a reform provoked some indignant criticism. "The bill out Herods Herod," wrote one anonymous manufacturer, "I protest against this threatened invasion of the rights of the parent over the child as an infringement of the liberty of the subject, and a direct violation of the homes of Englishmen." A long list of specific objections to Hobhouse's bill followed, and the letter ended by proposing the "real remedy" for factory workers—free trade and cheap corn.[40]

Cries of betrayal and disappointment arose from many industrial towns of the north. The younger Edward Baines, who had long since severed ties with Oastler, informed readers of how deeply he regretted Hobhouse's last-minute about-face. "I remonstrated with John Hobhouse in private, my colleague Mr. Strickland protested in public," a disappointed Morpeth wrote from Castle Howard, "but we both found, as might naturally

39. The debate does not appear in *Hansard* because the recorder had left the Commons around midnight, just before Hobhouse spoke.

40. *A Letter to Sir John Cam Hobhouse, Bart., M.P. on the "Factories Bill."*

have been augured from his humane and liberal principles, that Sir John Hobhouse was not acting from any alteration in his own views, but from the discovery of the opposition directed against his bill.[41] George Strickland, who confirmed Morpeth's account in the *Leeds Mercury*, expressed a belief that Hobhouse should have risked his original bill by an open division of the Commons.

Sir John Cam Hobhouse's bill for shortening the hours of labour in all factories is lost! Yes, the bill, on which you had fixed your fondest hopes, is vanished! Aye, my friends, that bill which had enlivened the hearts of your poor factory children, which had for once implanted the gleam of hope in their hearts, and taught them to chaunt in songs of praise the name of Hobhouse—is abandoned by its author! [42]

So wrote Richard Oastler after the news from London reached him. The *Leeds Intelligencer* accompanied his statement with some unsparing criticisms of Hobhouse and of the Yorkshire M.P.'s. "Hobhouse's stubborn virtue forsook him," the paper noted, "he submitted, mangled his Bill, and violated a duty which he had made a merit of imposing upon himself."

Baines invited Hobhouse to send his own explanations, part of which he published in the November 5 issue of the *Mercury*. Hobhouse explained that the silk trade was first in asking to be excluded from his measure: "I consented; and afterwards an opposition arose from almost the whole body of Scotch members, who insisted on the exclusion of Scotland from the provisions of the Bill. These gentlemen being supported by the Board of Trade, I should have been inclined to listen to their suggestions, in order to secure so much good for England." Hobhouse then explained that other M.P.'s insisted upon excluding Scotland, and another source of opposition came from the woolen interests of England's West Country. At this point, according to the account, the workingman's delegates told Hobhouse to confine his proposals to the cotton factories in order to secure a minimum measure of improvement. He held out for his original bill until

41. Edward Baines, letter to editor, *Leeds Mercury*, October 29, 1831; Lord Morpeth, letter to editor, *Leeds Mercury*, November 5, 1831; George Strickland, letter to editor, *Leeds Mercury*, November 19, 1831.
42. *Leeds Intelligencer*, October 20, 1831.

the Scotch flax factors, who "were my biggest opponents," threatened to oppose any reform whatsoever.[43]

Oastler was not at all satisfied with the published excerpts of Hobhouse's letter. He therefore addressed to him a series of questions, which the *Leeds Intelligencer* published along with Hobhouse's letter of reply. Oastler wanted to know more precisely the opinion of the Board of Trade on factory reform. He also wanted to understand the role played by the Yorkshire manufacturers in determining the final outcome of the bill. Hobhouse did not answer any of Oastler's specific questions; he chose instead to present his opinions in a letter of November 16 on the possibility of passing any strong factory legislation. He had encountered immense difficulties, and only those people who knew nothing about carrying a contested measure through an unreformed Parliament, he said, would censure his altered bill. A stronger proposal would have earned him immediate praise, but it would have met a crushing defeat. Hobhouse explained that he did not want to sacrifice an attainable good for the sake of a fleeting popularity; he therefore altered his bill to ensure some measure of success.

He also dismissed as utopian the movement for a ten-hour bill, which now found a parliamentary supporter in Michael Sadler:

Those acquainted with the real state of the question, so far as parliament is concerned know very well that nothing can be more idle than the talk of the possibility of limiting the hours of daily labour to ten for five days, and to eight on Saturday; and I own I am surprised by Mr. Sadler's answer to the Huddersfield deputies that the worthy member for Aldborough should appear to concur in views so extravagant, and which can only end in disappointment.[44]

The man of practical experience had spoken, and it now remained for visionaries like Sadler, Oastler, and Lord Ashley to contest his opinions. Oastler expressed his gratitude for Hobhouse's exertions but regretted his having yielded to the "cold, calculating, but mistaken Scotch philosophers." Sadler began the greater parliamentary struggle by introducing a ten-hour

43. Hobhouse, letter to editor, *Leeds Mercury*, November 5, 1831; Driver, *Tory Radical*, 96–97; Kydd, *History of Factory Reform Movement*, 138–41.
44. *Leeds Intelligencer*, November 26, 1831.

bill before the end of the year. Hobhouse was greatly impressed by how skillfully Sadler dramatized the issue of child labor, both in Parliament and with the committee hearings. A committee member himself, Hobhouse remained skeptical about a ten-hour bill's chances of success. Perhaps the skeptic omitted too much when recollecting in later years his own part in the factory-reform movement. He briefly wrote about the infinite pains he took "to reconcile the views of the masters and the workmen on the matter; and it was not until after much correspondence and repeated interviews that I brought the parties to something like a compromise." [45] However, his explanations to Oastler in 1831 indicate that Hobhouse, generous-minded though he was, felt he had no alternative than to modify his bill and take what he could get from a hostile Parliament.

He had been given advice to do so by the same Whig leaders who later obstructed Sadler's proposal. Poulett Thompson, who would later try to modify the factory regulations that existed, was frankly hostile. Also, Hobhouse saw that his efforts to protect child labor had become involved with a growing movement to get shorter hours for adults. The workmen of the Leeds Short Time Committee had frankly admitted that limiting child labor would provide the opening wedge for restricting the hours of adults, "hence the objection of the manufacturers and the reason for our support of the Bill." [46] Thus, the specific humanitarian issue of child labor had become overshadowed by a dispute between manufacturers and workers that embittered political life in many industrial towns, and Hobhouse informed Oastler how much he regretted "to perceive that the discussions on the Factory system are mixed up with the party system of Yorkshire, and more especially of the town of Leeds." [47] Hobhouse wished to end a situation already difficult and increasingly distasteful. Besides, he too was reluctant to interfere, however indirectly, with adult labor. To him, the improvement of their working conditions was more a matter of reducing taxes, abolishing the Corn Laws, and self-help in an open economy.

45. Lady Dorchester, ed., *Recollections of a Long Life, by Lord Broughton (John Cam Hobhouse) with additional extracts from his private diaries,* II, 130.

46. Leeds Short Time Committee to Hobhouse, March 25, 1831, *Leeds Mercury,* April 2, 1831.

47. *Leeds Intelligencer,* November 26, 1831; see also Driver, *Tory Radical,* 96–97, and Kydd, *History of Factory Reform Movement,* 138.

Because Hobhouse's radicalism was mainly concerned with political goals, the political situation in 1831 was uppermost in his mind. He had observed how the Parliamentary Reform Bill divided public men who otherwise remained in agreement on other matters. Sadler's and Oastler's brand of Toryism espoused factory measures and denounced the parliamentary reform proposed by Lord Grey's Government, and Hobhouse believed a major disaster could occur if the Tory opponents of parliamentary reform effected an alliance with the manufacturing interests opposing factory reform. The reform bill, as well as the factory bill, would then be lost, or at least delayed. Hobhouse therefore amended his factory bill to assure its quick passage. His hasty action conveniently disposed of the secondary matter of factory reform, enabling politicians to turn their undivided attention to an issue he found more important— the Parliamentary Reform Bill of 1831. That measure, which affected the entire nation, was rejected by the Lords two weeks later.

CHAPTER VIII

HIS MAJESTY'S
MINISTER

Hobhouse participated in the struggle to enact into law the Parliamentary Reform Bill of 1832. By this time, his work attracted the attention of Whig leaders, who invited him to join the Government. The period of the Reform Bill marked an end and a beginning in Hobhouse's career—the erstwhile Radical now declared himself to be a Whig.

Lord Grey's accession to office in November, 1830, set the stage for the prolonged crisis over parliamentary reform. Hobhouse found Brooks's and Holland House filled with jubilant Whigs discussing the distribution of offices and speculating about future policies. "Very different are the sights and sounds of the country," he wrote about the agrarian riots that swept through many counties that autumn.[1] He was shocked to learn that "Captain Swing's" rioters had entered Alexander Baring's Grange, an estate he had often visited. Perhaps, he thought, the rural riots foreshadowed an uprising in London itself, where rumors of a conspiracy forced a cancellation of the royal visit to the City. Even more ominous was the fluttering tricolor displayed by workingmen in December as they marched by Saint James's Palace to support reform. The successful July Revolution in Paris was obviously infectious. Hobhouse had mixed feelings of expectation, anxiety, and uncertainty as Parliament reconvened in February.

The question on everyone's mind was just how far the Government would go in reforming Parliament. Hobhouse, for one, distrusted Whig intentions and wrote in his diary for February 1:

Received an invitation from Lord Althorp to dine with him at a Parliamentary dinner on February 2. Determined not to go, as I considered it a meeting of Members notoriously supporting

1. Hobhouse, diary, November 21, 1830, John Cam Hobhouse, Lord Broughton, Papers, Add. MSS 56555; Lady Dorchester, ed., *Recollections of a Long Life, by Lord Broughton (John Cam Hobhouse) with additional extracts from his private diaries*, IV, 72.

the Administration, amongst which number I do not choose to
to be ranked. I am a friend but no follower . . . so I wrote to
Lord Althorp and told him that my absence in the country
would prevent me having the honour of dining with him. So
long as I am independent I will be wholly so!

His doubts about the Government's intentions vanished on
that celebrated March 1 when Lord John Russell outlined the
provisions of the Parliamentary Reform Bill to a packed House
of Commons. "Never shall I forget the astonishment of my
neighbors," Hobhouse commented, "Indeed all the House
seemed perfectly astounded; and when he read the long list of
the boroughs to be wholly or partially disfranchised there was a
sort of wild ironical laughter." [2] Hobhouse then hurried over to
Charing Cross to get Francis Place's reactions. He found him
generally pleased with the bill, although it did not grant the vote
to the working classes and would, in the case of a democratic
constituency like Westminster, actually diminish the number of
voters. Place believed the £10 household-qualification clause
would be only a temporary restriction until a reformed Parliament extended the vote further. Meanwhile, the Government's
plan to abolish an estimated 168 seats was sufficient reason for
supporting the bill, if only as a first installment toward future
reforms. A redistribution of seats would permit a large influx
of new members from the industrial towns, and Place assumed
these M.P.'s would be well disposed to the goals of Westminster
Radicals.[3]

Hobhouse gave his unqualified support to a reform bill that
was roughly similar to those he had favored in the past, among
them Lambton's motion of 1821 for enlarging the franchise and
Russell's proposals of 1822 and 1826 for assigning additional
seats to the counties and industrial towns. He thought Russell
had taken "a great step" [4] toward renewing the old alliance between the Whigs and the people by coming out so strongly for
reform in 1822. This, in addition to Lambton's previous motion
and declarations of support from Milton, Landsdowne, Holland,
and other peers, gave Hobhouse hope that the Whigs could one

2. Dorchester, ed., *Recollections*, IV, 87.
3. Ibid., 88; Graham Wallas, *The Life of Francis Place*, 258.
4. Hobhouse, diary, April 23, 1822, Lord Broughton Papers, Add. MSS
56544; Dorchester, ed., *Recollections*, II, 183.

day command sufficient will and strength to carry parliamentary reform. It was the task of independent M.P.'s like himself to so rally public opinion behind this issue of "paramount importance" that other Whigs would follow the lead of party liberals. Hobhouse believed any change would be an improvement, so he supported O'Connell's motion of 1830 for universal suffrage, claiming that like Fox, he disliked the approach but welcomed the innovation.[5] On other occasions he emphasized that parliamentary reform would strengthen existing institutions because it would widen the basis of power in the state. The present parliamentary system, he explained in 1821, "encouraged a perpetual struggle between the governors and the governed" because it enabled the ruling clique to ignore with impunity the needs and wishes of most people. Force and fraud often took outrageous forms, as when the Duke of Newcastle interfered in the Newark election of 1829. Some voters had ignored warnings that he, as their landlord, considered their franchise his property. They voted for Serjeant Wilde, a rival to the Duke's nominee, whereupon they received prompt notice to quit their holdings. Such incidents as these undermined public respect for the parliamentary process and ultimately for law itself. Clearly, "the House did not represent the people, but a certain number of persons, who had appropriated the franchise of the country."[6]

The arguments against reform were many. One maintained that quality and ability would perish in a government chosen by the untutored multitude. Hobhouse maintained that this supposition arose from a complete ignorance of the ruling few "as to the real character of the people, who are, in fact, not so degraded and blind as they think, or as they wish."[7] He also tried to dispel fears that popular government endangered property. "The poor are to the full as much interested in the preservation of the laws of property as the rich. They are more so," he argued, "A wealthy man may protect himself either in anarchy, or under a despotism, by the power of his purse and of his previous influence; a poor man has no friend but the laws."[8] He mentioned the French National Assembly during the revolution

5. *Hansard Parliamentary Debates*, 2d series, XXIV (1830), cols. 1235–40.
6. Ibid., XXII (1830), col. 1113.
7. Ibid., V (1821), col. 423.
8. Ibid., col. 416.

as a case in point. Only church lands and the estates of royalist *emigrés* were confiscated; the same kind of holdings had been confiscated in England during the time of Henry VIII and the Long Parliament. France loomed large in discussions of reform, for conservatives conjured up memories of the Terror as one example of a popular government that had sharply descended to anarchy and violence. Hobhouse trusted the day would come when this argument would be as obsolete as it was senseless. He recalled that Burke himself had taken the "incontrovertible" position that "the people have no interest in disorder" in France or elsewhere.

A far more subtle argument, one often raised by John Wilson Croker and other Troy writers, maintained that comparisons with other systems of government were irrelevant because government ought to be changed in accordance with the history and habits of a nation. Denison of Newcastle thus voiced contempt during the 1826 debates for those who mentioned France and America. Bourbon France was ruled by property; America, by population. One was too restrictive; the other totally lacking in talents, principles, and character, because opposition parties were stiffled by the tyranny of the masses. Neither nation could serve as a model for England, which enjoyed the blessings of a perfect, mixed constitution with its principles of "balances and counterpoises." Hobhouse replied that France was ruled by a royal despot who had no aristocracy or propertied interest to oppose him. When Hobhouse addressed himself to Denison's remarks on America, he echoed the Radicals' idea, often found in *The Westminster Review*, of America as an idyllic new world. He pointed to the federal structure and the ingenious system of checks and balances that prohibited any one group or party from enslaving others. Furthermore, American institutions were not of such a peculiar origin as to render them inapplicable to the system of English government. "Whatever is free, whatever is popular, whatever is essentially representative in their government," Hobhouse asserted, "is English." [9] The great battle of American independence was to him a vindication of the principles of the Cokes, the Pyms, and the Glorious Revolution of 1688. Englishmen who desired to know what the parliamentary

9. Ibid., XV (1826), cols. 668, 683; Hobhouse's speech, ibid., cols. 679–705.

principles of their forefathers were only needed to look at the practice of their American contemporaries.

Hobhouse's views on just how much England's government should be altered in order to make it more participatory changed appreciably during the decade. He gave a wide latitude to the numbers deserving the franchise when he spoke in 1821 of a reform sufficient to reconcile "the populace to the happier part of the nation by giving them common rights, and affording them a consciousness of possessing that equal protection from the government." [10] His later terminology was more restrictive, with "the populace" or "the mass of the people," phrases he earlier used, replaced with "deserving numbers" or "propertied interests" in discussions of the franchise. By 1831 Hobhouse could welcome the Whig bill as a perfect compromise: It contained drastic but necessary clauses to redistribute seats and preserved the principle of a propertied franchise.

Hobhouse told Lord Durham that he would help the Government in every way possible. He recognized a twofold threat. One came from the Tory Opposition; the other, from popular violence that would bring anarchy or start a backlash against reform. Westminster, the home of Parliament itself, had to be orderly at all costs. Hobhouse saw he could fulfill a vital role as intermediary between his constituents and the Government and, should tensions mount, as a spokesman for public order.

He presented reform petitions from wealthy Saint George's parish, Westminster, and from Saint Margaret's. [11] He noted that the second came from the parish in which the House of Commons was situated and that Jeremy Bentham's name was appended to it. Also, on March 3, he made a major speech urging Peel, who had initiated so many beneficial changes during the past decade, to add another by supporting parliamentary reform. He declared the demand throughout the country was irresistible, and the measure proposed moderate. Hobhouse did not think that by the reform bill, or any other plan of reform, "the complexion of the House, as to the members returned to it, would be much changed. The motives however that sent men into it would be totally different." [12] Because the new M.P.'s would

10. Ibid., V (1821), col. 416.
11. Ibid., 3d series, III (1831), col. 449.
12. Ibid., II (1831), cols. 1282–1302.

consult the interests of the nation, not those of a small minority, reform would facilitate the functioning of the King's Government.

The reform bill passed its first reading uncontested, but its second by only one vote. The Tories, led by Peel, continued their determined resistance following the Easter recess. Lord Grey countered by persuading the Monarch to dissolve Parliament after the Commons adopted General Gascoyne's motion against the proposed decrease of 30 English and Welsh seats in the Commons. "All his candour, all his moderation, all his trimming, shifty policy disappeared," recorded Hobhouse of Peel's efforts to address the cheering House as the thundering cannons announced the approach of William IV on the afternoon of April 22. "He displayed his real vexation, and true feelings of disappointment and rage, in a harangue of sound and fury, signifying nothing but his own despair . . . the Black Rod cut short his oration just as he seemed about to fall into a fit." [13]

Hobhouse confessed his speeches "were a bit peppery" during the general elections, "but they suited the taste of the day." [14] Perhaps at Covent Garden, where people cheered when he spoke of boroughmongers "who are so fond of preaching about good manners and who presented a miserable example of impotent rage, of detected cunning, of defeated malice driven to despair." [15] Peel seemed to be such a man, and Hobhouse went on to censure him for attempting to bribe voters by contributing £50,000 to a party fund. The affront did not go unchallenged; Sir Henry Hardinge told Hobhouse a week later that Peel found the speech "not warranted by any latitude of free discussion" and would await him at Dover with pistols. Fortunately, the affair of honor between the two men was settled peacefully through their two representatives after Lord Dacre informed Sir Henry Hardinge that Hobhouse had intended no personal insult. Peel agreed to let the matter drop after Hobhouse disavowed the *Morning Chronicle*'s account of the speech. "Had we met, the issue would have done no good to Peel in any possible way," observed Hobhouse, and he then added wryly, "Had any mischief happened to him, what would have become of the Party?

13. Dorchester, ed., *Recollections*, IV, 106.
14. *The Times*, April 27, 1831; Dorchester, ed., *Recollections*, IV, 109.
15. *The Times*, April 27, 1831.

Had any happened to me, what would the reformers have said?" [16]

The sweeping majority of 136 votes on a second reading of the reform bill in the new Parliament confirmed the Government's victory. Throughout the summer, the Tories took up each clause in order to wring some concessions from the Government. Hobhouse protested such delaying tactics as deliberate obstructions to the wishes of an overwhelming majority. He also warned the Lords in August not to imitate the Tories in the Commons lest they wished to provoke a violent reaction against themselves.[17]

Hobhouse absented himself from most of the endless debates to attend his ailing father at the family house on Berkeley Square. Sir Benjamin Hobhouse's long life finally came to an end in the early morning hours of August 12, whereupon his eldest son became the second Baronet.

The reform bill's passage through the Commons several weeks later transferred the nation's attention to the Lords. Hobhouse urged his constituents to act with "prudence, temperence, and wisdom," because any acts of violence would only furnish the peers with a pretext for rejecting reform. He then exhorted the Lords to approve the bill swiftly in order "to prevent tumult, bloodshed, and revolution, and to preserve the Government as by law established." [18] Most of the peers remained unmoved by the vote in the Commons and by the many petitions and warnings addressed to them. On October 8 they rejected the reform bill by a majority of 41 votes. Reformers throughout Britain were both astonished and furious when they learned the size of the majority against reform. A disappointed Hobhouse could only advise the protesting citizens of Westminster to remain patient while the Government tried to win the reluctant peers over to reform. He was especially concerned about the imminent

16. Peel objected on two counts. One was the *Morning Chronicle's* report of Hobhouse's speech, which referred to Peel's political activities as a reflection of "nature in its lowest and most debased state." Hobhouse denied ever saying such a thing. He also disavowed intending any personal insult when he referred to Peel's contribution to a Tory electoral fund. See Sir Robert Peel Papers, Add. MSS 40402, f. 23, 33; Dorchester, ed., *Recollections*, IV, 110–11.

17. *Hansard*, 3d series, V (1831), cols. 698–706.

18. *The Times*, September 22, 1831.

danger of violence and therefore found Macaulay's speech on the following Monday much too fiery and intimidating. A life-long friendship began with Hobhouse, the senior M.P., taking the liberty of cautioning Macaulay, the young orator, against delivering any more violent speeches that referred to "the rule of the sword."[19]

Hobhouse then joined his fellow Londoners on Wednesday when they demonstrated in favor of the reform bill. Various parish delegations headed the procession, which left Portland Place at one o'clock to proceed down Regent Street and on to Pall Mall. Placards reading "Englishmen and fellow trades-men—It is to you Ministers look in the present crisis for support! Be firm! Be peaceable!"[20] lined the route, but an occasional red cap of liberty stood out among the vast throng surrounding Saint James's Palace, where Hobhouse presented various re-form petitions to the King. Throughout the following weeks, Hobhouse, fearing that London be the scene of such riots as those that had occurred in Bristol, urged the people to remain calm while the Government planned the next course of action. George Grote reflected the apprehension of many reformers at this time when he advised Lord Grey against making any major concession to the Tories. Grey assured him that he contem-plated no such betrayal of reform; he merely intended to add some "improvements" that would give the peers "an excuse for repairing the error of their last vote."[21] Several days earlier Grey had replied in the same vein to the expressions of public confidence forwarded by Hobhouse. "It will be our most anxious wish to merit a continuence of these sentiments," he wrote Hob-house, "by a steady consistent, and persevering conduct, directed to the accomplishment of a real reform in the representation of people, not less efficient than that which has been so lately re-jected. A bill to this purpose will be offered to Parliament im-mediately on the opening of the next session."[22] Hobhouse read the assuring note at various parish meetings throughout West-minster. Francis Place was especially pleased to receive word of

19. Hobhouse, diary, October 10, 1831, Lord Broughton Papers, Add. MSS 56556.

20. *The Times*, October 13, 1831.

21. G. Grote to Grey, October 14, 1831, Grey to Grote, October 18, 1831, Francis Place Papers, Add. MSS 35149, f. 111, 112.

22. Grey to Hobhouse, October 15, 1831, Lord Broughton Papers, Add. MSS 47226, f. 138–39.

the Prime Minister's replies; he had doubted Grey's sincerity about reform ever since the awkward deputation Place had submitted on October 12 had received a cool reception at Downing Street.

The reform bill rested in limbo throughout the rest of 1831 while the Government tried to win over Tory waverers. As tensions mounted, Hobhouse declared that a postponement of Parliament would constitute "some fatal error in judgement" as public order could not be maintained indefinitely.[23] He was relieved when Parliament reconvened on December 6.

The second week in January, 1832, was an important time in Hobhouse's political career. He was walking toward Brooks's on January 13 when he heard the news of Sir Henry Parnell's dismissal as Secretary at War for not voting with the Government on a Russo-Dutch loan. Lord Althorp summoned Hobhouse to Downing Street the following day to offer him the vacated post. Hobhouse at first demurred, but encouragement from Place, Durham, and Melbourne helped overcome his reservations. He took the oaths and kissed hands at Saint James's; the ceremony preceded the formality of his return by Westminster on February 8. Two days later, Sir John Cam Hobhouse, His Majesty's Secretary at War, took his seat on the Treasury bench in the Commons.

During the latter part of January, Lord Grey had assured William IV of Hobhouse's "moderate and just" views during the past year. "He has, it is true, been formerly engaged in active schemes of popular contention," Grey recalled, but Hobhouse now merited high office because he "disapproves of many of the measures of the candidates for popular favour." The only difficulty Grey foresaw was "the chance of an opposition . . . in Westminster from Mr. Place and the violent party, who are angry with him for having refused to belong to the *Union*."[24] Grey was referring to the National Political Union that Place and others had organized the previous October to support parliamentary reform. The union was in fact created to prevent any popular resort to force.

Burdett had accepted the presidency, partly to control its activities, but Hobhouse, who was admittedly more cautious

23. *The Times*, November 21, 1831.
24. Henry Grey, Earl Grey, ed., *The Correspondence of King William IV and Earl Grey*, II, Letters 336, 341.

than usual after "the dreadful Bristol riots," opposed this or any other popular organization that posed the threat of force. Worse yet, according to Hobhouse's ideas, Burdett had added prestige to a group whose very existence encouraged more unions during such troubled times. Hobhouse refused to join, and warned Burdett that he had mounted a tiger from which he could never dismount. What had he to gain, Hobhouse wondered, from associating with "Francis Place the tailor and some of his utilitarians such as E. G. Wakefield the abductor, Erskine Perry, Major Beauclerc and the young men with Rogers, Wakely, and the true cut throat set?"[25] Burdett finally agreed he had had enough of political unions after a November meeting at Lincoln's Inn Fields was thrown into confusion by a rival and more radical National Union of the Working Classes, commonly called "The Rotundists," which favored the ballot and universal suffrage. "There was no having to do with any-body but gentlemen of education," Burdett wrote upon resigning; an approving Hobhouse added a postscript, "To be sure he is right."[26] A day after the meeting at Lincoln's Inn Fields, Lord Melbourne issued a proclamation against disorders. A few weeks later the Government tried to suppress all political unions led by unauthorized committees or councils. Following Lord Althorp's communication with Joseph Parkes, Parkes persuaded Joseph Attwood to postpone a plan for consolidating and expanding the Birmingham union.[27] Hobhouse thought the Government had acted wisely; it remained for the ministers to pursue reform with equal vigor.

William IV found Hobhouse's disapproval of the political unions a sufficient recommendation for having him join the Government. Lord Durham, however, who was most instrumental in securing Hobhouse's appointment, gave many other reasons for his enthusiastic endorsement. Above all, a ministerial appointment for Hobhouse would be "gratifying . . . to a numerous party . . . to whom as yet you have shown no

25. Hobhouse, diary, November 4, 1831, Lord Broughton Papers, Add. MSS 56556.
26. Ibid., November 13, 1831, Lord Broughton Papers, Add. MSS 56556.
27. Althorp to Parkes, November 18, 1831, Joseph Parkes Papers; see also Jessie Buckley, *Joseph Parkes of Birmingham and the part which he played in the radical reform movement from 1825–1835*, 85–86.

attention" he wrote to Grey.[28] Durham had in mind the large
electorate of Westminster and other metropolitan boroughs
in which the voters' loyalty to the Government was essential
in maintaining order. Hobhouse's Radical affiliations, his position as M.P. for democratic Westminster, and his long-standing
dedication to parliamentary reform would assure the people of
the Government's determination to carry the reform bill, so
surmised the *Morning Post*, which interpreted Hobhouse's appointment as a compliment to the reformers of Westminster and
a "striking proof of the sentiments of the King upon this great
subject." [29] The Tory cause was all but hopeless, or so thought
Lord Hardinge, who pointed out to Lord Ellenborough that
Hobhouse's appointment "shows the ministers are sure of the
King and mean to use him to make peers to carry the bill." [30]

Lord Hardinge thought that the situation indicated that the
Government was considering the possibility of creating peers in
order to carry the reform bill. Such a step was especially distasteful to Lord Grey, who regarded any wholesale addition to
the peerage as a betrayal of his aristocratic ideals and class.
Lord Ellenborough had accurately surmised that Hobhouse
had asked no questions about the matter of creating peers, "intending probably to give up the office if he found the Government played, what he would call, false." Hobhouse was indeed
surprised when Lord Howick confided to him that his father was
most decidedly adverse to swamping the peerage.[31] Hobhouse
could not account for Lord Grey's unwillingness to ensure passage of the reform bill. Perhaps, he thought, Grey "took up
reform as a toy which he might break or lay down again";
perhaps "he looks upon it as a mere trick of state for the
preservation of power." [32] Hobhouse's renewed suspicions about
the Whigs were not eased when Burdett advised his resignation because the Government was so reluctant to create peers.

28. Durham to Grey, March 8, 1831, Charles Grey, second Earl Grey,
Papers.
29. *Morning Post*, February 2, 1831.
30. Lord Ellenborough, diary, February 9, 1831, in Arthur Aspinall, ed.,
Three Early Nineteenth Century Diaries (*Extracts relating to the Reform
Act of 1832 from the diaries of Sir Denis Le Marchant, E. J. Littleton, Baron
Hatherton and E. Law, Earl of Ellenborough*), 191.
31. Hobhouse, diary, February 11, 1832, Lord Broughton Papers, Add.
MSS 56556; Dorchester, ed., *Recollections*, IV, 174–75.
32. Dorchester, ed., *Recollections*, IV, 176.

Had Hobhouse resigned, the revelation of ministerial disunity at this critical time could have had disastrous consequences for the reform bill.

The ministers were attempting to resolve uncertainties and differences of opinion during February and March. Anxiously, Hobhouse went to Lord Althorp on February 12 and told him he must have some positive assurances about carrying the reform bill. Althorp tried to put him at ease by emphasizing Grey's determination to reform Parliament, but in the manner he thought best. The Cabinet was by this time thoroughly worn out by the political crisis. Hobhouse heard that the excitable Durham had actually announced his immediate resignation at one point.[33] He and Russell gave details about the Cabinet meeting of March 11 when Lord Grey convinced his colleagues to defer any creation of peers. "It is a measure of extreme violence," he wrote Althorp, "there is no precedent for it in our own history, the case of Queen Anne's Peers not being in point, it is a certain evil, dangerous itself as a precedent, and with all these objections, in my opinion, very uncertain of success." [34] Grey also warned the Cabinet that a wholesale creation of peers would inflame the Opposition to mutilate the reform bill in committee.

Although Lady Holland urged Hobhouse to insist upon the creation of peers because his appointment was "a guarantee for strong measures," [35] he had decided to remain with the Government, at least until the reform bill's second reading in the Lords. His resolution gave him some cause for worry; however, "I should be reckoned only a dupe," Hobhouse ruefully informed Lord John Russell, "if the peers defeat the government."

Hobhouse once again addressed the Commons just before the Lords prepared to discuss the Government's bill in April. He advised the peers to think upon the fate that had befallen the French aristocrats who had haughtily refused to bow to the popular will in 1789. He found Mme. de Staël's *Considerations on the French Revolution* particularly relevant to the decision at

33. Ibid., 178–81, 197–200; G. M. Trevelyan, *Lord Grey of the Reform Bill*, 332–35.
34. Grey to Althorp, March 11, 1832, Grey Papers.
35. Hobhouse, diary, March 24, 1832, Lord Broughton Papers, Add. MSS 56556.

hand in England. Mme. de Staël had described how much time was lost in 1789 when the estates argued over voting procedures; time ran out on the Old Regime while its rulers engaged in wretched quibbling, in endless discussions of privileges. Hobhouse then quoted from Mme. de Staël's work:

Privileges are sacred only when they contribute to the public good; in order to preserve them, it is indispensable that we should have recourse to reasoning, and they cannot be really stable except when consecrated by public utility. But the majority of the noblesse contented themselves with these words, "It was so formerly." It was in vain that they were told that former circumstances had brought about the events of former days, and that present circumstances had produced these of their own times.[36]

Hobhouse urged the peers to learn a lesson from the past: The nobility of eighteenth-century France could not hold onto all their extensive privileges, and the French aristocracy had refused to grant concessions until it was too late. Their ruin was the result, and the country was plunged into terror and turmoil. "Will the Peers of England preserve their reputation and their leadership?" asked Hobhouse at a Westminster rally early in April.[37] He added, "The people await their decision." The answer to Hobhouse's question came on April 13, after the Lords had debated the reform bill for five days. He heard the newsmen shouting the news of the Government's victory in the Lords by a majority of nine votes. "Well done Lord Althorp's calculations," wrote Hobhouse, overjoyed, "and well done Lord Grey's adherence to his own persuasion that he could safely risk this great struggle without a creation of Peers!"[38] Lord Melbourne gave him an account of the memorable scene later in the day but also expressed his belief that all was not yet over.

The events following Parliament's Easter recess bore out Lord Melbourne's belief. The Lords tried to reassert their power and prestige by agreeing to Lord Lyndhurst's amendment to

36. *Hansard*, 3d series, XI (1832), col. 737. Hobhouse quoted from Mme. de Staël, *Considerations on the French Revolution*, chap. XVII.
37. *Morning Chronicle*, April 8, 1832.
38. Hobhouse, diary, April 14, 1832, Lord Broughton Papers, Add. MSS 56556; Dorchester, ed., *Recollections*, IV, 213.

postpone consideration of the disfranchising clauses of the bill until after they voted on the enfranchising clauses. Lord Grey considered this maneuver an attempt to sabotage the measure, and he therefore resorted to the ultimate weapon of asking the King to create fewer than fifty peers. On Wednesday, May 9, Hobhouse learned about William IV's refusal to create peers and the subsequent resignation of the Government.

The events throughout the week decided the issue. While Hobhouse and other ministers went to resign at Saint James's, other reformers prepared to resist a Tory Government. A deputation from the Birmingham Political Union reached London on Saturday. Place and Parkes agreed on a program of refusing to pay taxes and of encouraging a rush on the banks for gold. According to Place, Hobhouse stopped by and, seeing the placard "Go For Gold" on a table, pointed to it and said "That's the settler, that has finished it." [39] Hobhouse brought the good news that Wellington had given up trying to form a government in the face of overwhelming public opposition. Thus, Grey's Government was restored to office on Tuesday, May 15.

By Friday, the only remaining reason for doubting the reform bill's final passage was Wellington's refusal to forswear all active resistance in the Lords. Grey prepared to deal with the situation by calling a Cabinet meeting at noon. Hobhouse thought the Government must act immediately to create peers, and he thought a letter from Place concerning his conspiratorial plans would help overcome any ministerial hesitation. The time had come to gain victory by posing the threat of force.

Actually, such concert as there was between Parkes's Birmingham Union and London was aimed at preventing a resort to force. Parkes had persuaded his organization to abandon the quasi-military preparations that Attwood had projected after the Bristol riots, but Place's letter was a convincing argument against delaying reform. "So many men of known character and military have entered heartily into the scheme," Place asserted, "that their names when published will produce great affect in every desirable way. If the Duke comes into power now, we shall be unable to 'hold to the laws'—break them we must, be the consequences whatever they may, we know that all must join

39. Place Papers, Add. MSS 27794, f. 84–86, gives Place's account of the reform bill crisis.

with us, to save their property, no matter what may be their private opinions." [40]

Hobhouse presumably forwarded the letter to the Cabinet, although he makes no mention of the document. He had requested information from Place on other occasions, only to pocket his replies. In all likelihood Hobhouse showed the letter to Durham when they conferred on Friday morning, when Durham informed him that the issue was no longer one of resisting a Tory Government but of obtaining the King's promise to create peers. The Cabinet unanimously favored the action. Grey and Brougham then went to Saint James's Palace and received the King's "full and indisputable security" for the reform bill. Althorp announced the King's consent to create peers before a crowded and expectant Commons. His announcement dissolved any further opposition in the Lords, and on June 7, when the Lord Chancellor gave the royal assent, the Parliamentary Reform Bill became law. The political crisis was over and a new era had begun.

"There is nothing definite and determinate in politics except Radicalism," wrote John Stuart Mill to his friend Carlyle just before the Lords passed the reform bill, "and we shall have nothing but Radicals and Whigs for a long time to come." [41] Parliamentary reform was indeed an outstanding victory for Whigs and working-class Radicals who had actively supported "the Bill, the whole Bill, and nothing but the Bill." An atmosphere of cordiality and unanimity prevailed among the victors throughout the following month, and Hobhouse joined the other ministers in accepting toasts of gratitude and messages of acclaim. Celebrants crowded the Westminster Committee's citadel at the Crown and Anchor, the town houses of the wealthy, and the Guildhall to welcome the new political system of their making.

The Radicals, however, did not long rest content with their recent success. A City of London grand festival to honor the ministers coincided with the July 11 meeting of the National

40. Place to Hobhouse, May 18, 1832, Place Papers, Add. MSS 27794, f. 278–80; see also Place Papers, Add. MSS 35149, f. 149–51, and Henry Ferguson, "The Birmingham Political Union and the Government, 1831–32," *Victorian Studies*, 3 (March, 1960), 261–76.

41. Mill to Carlyle, May 29, 1832, in Hugh S. Elliot, ed., *The Letters of John Stuart Mill*, I, 31.

Political Union. Francis Place outlined a Radical program of future reforms to the latter group, including a shorter duration of Parliament, the ballot, and equal electoral districts. He spoke about financial, legal, and church reforms and abolition of the Corn Laws, and he concluded his address by demanding the abolition of slavery throughout the Empire.[42]

Place's program for the future portended trouble for Hobhouse, who was entirely engrossed at this time with his ministerial post. He found the War Office suffering from every ill that could beset an administrative body. As Secretary at War he had acquired a poorly defined responsibility for military affairs, a duty he shared with the Secretary of State for War and Colonies, and the Commander-in-chief, whose power derived from the Crown. The triumvirate had to contend with various separate departments, such as the Board of General Officers, which clothed the cavalry and infantry, or the Master General and Board of Ordinance, which were in charge of allocating arms and supplies. The Commissariat, a civilian department of clerks responsible to the Treasury, ineffectively provisioned the Army abroad because it had no power to move supplies. The Treasury did not expedite matters, because it frequently referred questions of military expenditures to the Comptrollers of Army accounts, who then passed on their recommendations either to the Secretary at War or to the Commander-in-chief. A Cabinet resolution concerning military matters could conceivably produce a state of absolute chaos if the administrators disagreed with one another. Shortly before he vacated the War Office, Hobhouse joined Lord John Russell and the Duke of Richmond in recommending the formation of a commission to examine the entire subject of military organization and expenditures. Among the items they suggested for future investigation was the nature of the office of Secretary at War. They recommended the creation of a central board over which he would preside.[43] Russell later tried to press home the importance of administrative improvements. "It is found by experience that separate and independent authorities lost time by perpetual communications," he informed Lord Melbourne,

42. *Morning Chronicle*, July 12, 1832; Westminster Committee, *On Pledges to be Given by the Candidates.* See also S. Maccoby, *English Radicalism, 1832–1852*, 63–64.
43. War Office, Box 44, file 10, March 4, 1833, Public Record Office.

"with not infrequent wrangles and disputes." Such was the case with the Admiralty Board, and it was "the case with the many and anomalous bodies which form the army." [44] The recommendations and warnings went unheeded; only after the appalling muddle and confusion during the Crimean War did the labyrinthine administration of military affairs become a public issue.

Hobhouse's duties went unchallenged when he presented the quarterly estimates to the Commons, for the legislature held the Secretary at War in sole charge of recommending appropriations. Hobhouse decided to press for a reduction of the armed forces in the interests of retrenchment, and his year in office is a testimony to the controversial nature of such a proposal. For one, he was empowered only to look after military pay and finance, while the size and cost of the Army came within the province of the Secretary for War. Nevertheless, Hobhouse in February, 1832, presented to Lord Hill a project for reducing the size of the armed forces. Lord Althorp informed him shortly afterwards of the Commander-in-chief's displeasure over a civilian meddling in military affairs. Indeed, Hobhouse seemed in direct opposition to every other authority. Lord Goderich took his complaints to Grey: He felt that Hobhouse, as Secretary at War, had tampered with his general control over the state of all armed forces at home and abroad. Grey quickly dismissed the proposal to reduce the colonial force and sided with Hill in opposing a reduction of the Home Army by some 5,000 men. [45] Hobhouse then decided to present specific proposals for retrenchment to his superiors. He sought the King's approval at the royal levee of March 14 for his plans to make Sandhurst self-supporting and to move the Knightsbridge Cavalry to Maidstone. William IV remained silent on the matters and frowned when Hobhouse requested future support in any encounter with the Commander-in-chief. The monarch bristled over his suggestion to leave vacant the Lieutenant-Governorship of Berwick, and he proceeded to fill the post, despite Hobhouse's directive to the contrary.

Hobhouse found his job especially unpleasant. In the usual course of events he first conferred with Althorp, then disputed

---

44. Russell to Melbourne, September 29, 1843, in Rollo Russell, ed., *Early Correspondence of Lord John Russell, 1805–1840,* II, 48–49.

45. Dorchester, ed., *Recollections,* IV, 185–86, 193–94.

with Lord Hill. The Prime Minister was next to object to Hobhouse's recommendations. "We are all committed equally with Hobhouse to a reduction of the army," Grey informed Althorp, "when it can be done with safety. But that is the question." [46] Hill, of course, had lost no time telling others that Hobhouse's proposed economies threatened national security; he could then sit back to enjoy another success over his civilian "colleague." "I foresee that the two sides of the archway at the Horse Guards will be in acknowledged hostility," Hobhouse commented earlier, "and either my Lord or I must go out, that is clear." [47] He did succeed in reducing the pension warrant and prevailed upon Hill and Goderich to do away with wagon trains, inspectors of clothing, and the Army Medical Board. After tempers flared when Hobhouse questioned the need for a fifth Major-General on the home establishment, relations rapidly deteriorated to the point where Hobhouse acknowledged in 1833 the incredible "turmoil, intrigue, and perpetual discord" between the Horse Guards and the War Office. [48]

It was the timeless issue of dedicated men whose backgrounds and outlooks were utterly different. Lord Hill presented the martial spirit of an old veteran; he invoked potential trouble in Ireland or in some part of the Empire to justify a large peacetime army. Hobhouse reflected a civilian Englishman's distaste for a standing army that had in the past pointed its swords and muskets against the mobs of Westminster. He could enjoy the panoply of the regimental salute to His Majesty in Hyde Park; he found the scene even more impressive when the Horse Guards drew to attention outside of Wellington's residence to receive their new colors from William IV. Hobhouse finally balked at the ceremonies on a "hot, tiresome day" in June when he went over to Chelsea Hospital to watch the ubiquitous Iron Duke preside over another military reception. "The whole affair was contrived to contrast military pomp with civilian insignificance," in Hobhouse's estimation, "and also to prevent any of us Reformers from innovating upon these favorite establishments." [49]

46. Grey to Althorp, January 6, 1833, Grey Papers.
47. Dorchester, ed., *Recollections*, IV, 247.
48. John Cam Hobhouse, first Baron Broughton, *Some Account of a Long Life*, II, 335.
49. Hobhouse, diary, June 28, 1832, Lord Broughton Papers, Add. MSS 56557; Dorchester, ed., *Recollections*, IV, 245.

The question of military discipline posed another problem for the Secretary at War. The Duke of Wellington was among the first who tried to correct Hobhouse's humanitarian sentiments by sending him a pamphlet favoring military flogging. Sir Francis Burdett supported his parliamentary colleague by asking Lord Grey to permit some modification in the use of corporal punishment. The Prime Minister agreed that everyone's feelings rebelled against the practice of flogging in the armed forces, but he found "such things are unfortunately unavoidable from our corrupt nature" and refused to endorse any mitigation of punishment.[50]

Flogging became an absorbing item of public interest during the summer of 1832. Henry Hunt introduced a motion to suspend flogging for one year, and reformers accused Hobhouse of betraying his humanitarian ideals when he opposed it.[51] Joseph Hume reintroduced the subject a few weeks later when he moved for the return of papers relating to the trial of Private Alexander Somerville.[52] Somerville had been court-martialed for insubordination and sentenced to receive a hundred lashes. His defenders claimed that the charge was a mere pretext, that his real offense was writing a letter to a Birmingham newspaper, *The Weekly Dispatch*, in which he asserted that his Scots Greys regiment would never take up arms against Britons who demonstrated in favor of the reform bill. His commanding officer ordered the private to mount an untamed horse and, when he refused, charged him with insubordination and accordingly had him court-martialed. The commander then harangued his regiment on the impropriety of any soldier who expressed political opinions and encouraged mob violence.[53]

According to *The Examiner*, Hobhouse was "infamous" for refusing to believe all the stories about the commanding officer's brutality, but Hobhouse satisfied Hume and other critics by obtaining a court of inquiry, which eventually censured the officer and granted Somerville an honorable discharge.[54] Hobhouse's support of the investigation went unnoticed; instead, many people who knew nothing about the turmoil and discord

50. Grey to Burdett, March 2, 1832, Grey Papers.
51. *Hansard*, 3d series, XIII (1832), col. 892.
52. Alexander Somerville later became a noted Anti–Corn Law propagandist and a pamphleteer.
53. *The Examiner*, July 8, 1832.
54. War Office, 4, 84.372; 3, 174.136.

among the administrators wondered why he, as Secretary at War, did not put an immediate end to military flogging. The offices involved, however, would permit only a restriction of flogging to certain defined misdemeanors. By December, Hobhouse himself was thoroughly annoyed with the task of supporting the Government at the expense of his own views on military matters. "I foresee the impossibility of holding office, Westminster, and character together," reads a discouraging entry in his diary before the end of the year.[55]

A public feud with Joseph Hume partly accounted for Hobhouse's pessimism. Their enmity arose over the first parliamentary elections in Bath, where the Radical reformer sponsored a candidate to rival John Cam's brother, Henry Hobhouse. Hume had explained that he interfered in the election only at the request of a reform association in the Somerset town, and Hobhouse could only blink in astonishment when Hume announced that he wished to promote the cause of reform by helping a candidate who was in no way connected with Lord Grey's Government.[56] Hume therefore supported John Arthur Roebuck, a young Radical who was then associating with the Westminster committeemen.

The Bath election itself was especially interesting since two of the rival candidates tried to outbid each other in establishing the reputation for being reformers. The campaign developed into a public discussion of the "condition of England" question in 1832. Religious beliefs also played a part in the contest, since Roebuck had announced his opposition to the Anglican establishment.

Hobhouse and Burdett arrived in Bath to attend a political meeting on September 12. Hobhouse's address was a paean to Lord Grey's Government, whose reform bill, he said, was the triumph of the democratic principle that had "made England what she is, which has tended, and which will further tend to her renovation." He contrasted the state of England in 1830— "a nation aflame"—with the confident, hopeful nation of two years later. Burdett then praised Westminster's role during the

---

55. Hobhouse, diary, December 21, 1832, Lord Broughton Papers, Add. MSS 56557; Dorchester, ed., *Recollections*, IV, 264.

56. On the controversy, see *The Times*, September 17, October 4, October 8, 1832; *Morning Chronicle*, September 25, September 26, 1832; *The Examiner*, October 7, 1832; *Bath Herald*, October 9, 1832.

reform crisis as a "bright and brilliant beacon light in the midst of the darkest period in our history." Only the candidate, Henry Hobhouse, avoided generalities by discussing the abolition of slavery, of certain taxes, and the payment of church tithes.[57]

Joseph Hume came to town two days later to support Roebuck. He enumerated many abuses worthy of condemnation by reformers. Slavery, flogging, the Septennial Act, and municipal corporations headed Hume's list; the Corn Laws, taxes on houses and windows, the civil list, payment of church tithes, and monopolies all followed. Hume then discussed the ballot, law reform, and the need for establishing a system of nondenominational public education. Roebuck then had his chance to comment generally upon the many abuses "which fettered the energies of Englishmen."[58]

This first Bath election ended with Henry Hobhouse's defeat. Neither the prestige of Lord Grey's Government nor Hobhouse's own local family connections could offset the popularity of radical reform among the people of Bath. Roebuck's election also reflected the strong wave of anticlericalism after the Anglican hierarchy had opposed parliamentary reform.[59]

Hobhouse had campaigned for his own return to Parliament in Westminster's first contested election in over a decade. This time he had to battle against all the influence Place could muster. Place decided that Hobhouse had forfeited his right to represent Westminster because of his dispute with Hume, who was in Place's estimation a model reformer. It was the latest and the most serious in a list of grievances Place had compiled for over a decade. The list was long: Hobhouse had declared himself "an extravagant reformer" when first chosen to represent Westminster; he proved a lukewarm, even a hostile, spokesman on reform once in office; he served the Whigs better than his constituents; and he was servile to the high and mighty, condescending to the tradesmen he represented. He "did himself serious injury in the opinion of many"[60] the day after Russell introduced the reform bill by moving the adjournment of a Westminster meeting that had been called to support annual parliaments and the ballot. He practiced "true Whig tactics"

57. *Bath Herald*, September 15, 1832.
58. Ibid., September 29, 1832.
59. Hobhouse received 1848 votes; Roebuck, 2001; and Palmer, 2516.
60. Place Papers, Add. MSS 27789, f. 276–78.

by posing as the champion of the people only so long as they kept their place. Then he had refused to join the National Political Union. "Hobhouse is not a reformer," Place wrote, "Hobhouse has himself from his own mouth satisfied me that he is not a reformer." Furthermore, "all that has been done, all that is doing on the part of Mr. Hobhouse is of the same kind exactly—and in the same bad spirit, as was shown by the 'sham reformers' and the tricky Whigs against us in Westminster." [61] Place then published his grievances against Hobhouse:

What was good for the people in 1819 is good for them now; what Sir John recommended then, should be the rule now; what he deprecated in the Whigs then, he is now practising himself to the very letter. There is one difference only between those whom he then so properly reprobated and himself, and that is, that they never treated the electors as their dependents, and never pretended to treat them with such perfect indifference as Sir John does now. The electors must be much changed for the worse if they do not assert their own dignity, and reject the man who has so shamelessly deserted them. [62]

Place asserted Hobhouse and the Establishment sought "to avoid taking steps towards enabling the people to reap any of the advantages they reasonably expected from the Reform Bill." It was necessary, then, to safeguard against the likes of Hobhouse by insisting on pledges from future candidates, and Place ended his letter by describing the widespread desire in Westminster to replace Hobhouse with Colonel De Lacy Evans, who had served briefly as M.P. for Rye and had a distinguished military record in Europe and North America. [63]

A delegation of electors had gone to Hobhouse's residence at Richmond on November 18 to obtain his pledge to vote for shorter parliaments, the ballot, and repeal of certain taxes. They received only his blunt refusal. He let it be known that a statesman's past conduct afforded the only reliable pledge for the future, [64] and he for one would not suffer the humiliation of pledging his honor on the dotted line. Burdett likewise refused

61. Place to Jones, n.d., Place Papers, Add. MSS 37949, f. 289.

62. Francis Place, *A Letter to the Independent Electors of Westminster*, 15.

63. Evans fought in the Peninsula campaign and was decorated for action during the attacks on Washington and Baltimore. He returned to Europe in time to resist the French charge at Waterloo.

64. *Morning Chronicle*, November 20, 1832.

to pledge when asked. Thus, both Westminster M.P.'s spurned the concept of the mandatory, rather than the senatorial, role in the Commons that Westminster Radicals demanded. They were representatives, not delegates, and would continue to vote on each issue as they thought best.

Electors from the parishes of Saint Paul's, Saint Clement Danes, and Saint Mary's met at the Crown and Anchor Tavern to discuss action against Hobhouse. Thomas Proud, a tradesman in the Strand, catalogued all the grievances Place had already mentioned and added Hobhouse's failure to end military flogging.[65] "No!" the audience shouted when asked whether the Hobhouse of 1832 was the Hobhouse of 1820; the time had come to replace him. Meanwhile Colonel Evans toured the parishes. He unfolded a plan for reducing the size of the Army; he promised at the Salopian Coffee House to separate church and state, to repeal various taxes, and to end the East Indian monopoly. With great flourish he added Polish independence to his political platform while speaking in Saint Anne. He then informed Burdett of his willingness to unite against Hobhouse, only to receive word that Burdett thought Evans's election would entirely discredit Westminster.

Sir Denis Le Marchant did not think Evans looked like a fit representative for an English constituency. Althorp's private secretary came away from the nomination ceremonies on December 8 with the impression of a tall and thin man "with very sallow complexion, and jet black hair & whiskers. One might almost have mistaken him for an Italian assassin."[66] His listeners cheered as he spoke about how Hobhouse had abandoned radicalism and reform. His reference to the Somerville Case drew hisses and the waving of cat-o'-nine-tails. The ferocity of the Westminster electorate astonished Hughes, the American ambassador, who watched as the crowd prevented Hobhouse from speaking by shouting and hurling mud at him.[67] Before the day was over Hobhouse's headquarters in Lisle Street had been wrecked.

65. Westminster Committee, *Public Meeting of the Electors of Westminster, held in the Great Room of the Crown and Anchor on Thursday, the 28 November, 1832.*

66. Le Marchant, diary, May 9, 1832, in Aspinall, ed., *Three Early Nineteenth Century Diaries*, 284.

67. Dorchester, ed., *Recollections*, IV, 263–64.

The elections resulted in Burdett's and Hobhouse's victory as they received 3680 and 3517 votes to Evans's 1173. It seems as if Place more than met his match for electioneering in Thomas De Vear who organized a committee of voters loyal to the incumbents. Evans's radicalism was too frightening for moderate voters in most parishes. Clearly, the election was a sign of Hobhouse's and Burdett's move toward conservatism and away from radicalism, for their victory was ensured by the large plurality gained in wealthy Saint George's parish, whose residents had so staunchly supported Lamb in 1819 and 1820.

Victorious, Hobhouse once more turned to military matters. He found Grey still opposed to any reduction in the size of the Army because of the threat of violence in Ireland. Hobhouse then announced his intentions to settle the controversial matter of flogging before he introduced another mutiny bill in Parliament. Lord Hill again raised objections, but Hobhouse, whose indecisive stand in the past had made things difficult for himself, now made flogging, as well as Army reductions, points of honor and summoned Althorp's support. "We must also consider who the Secretary-at-War is," Althorp wrote Grey, "We have great advantage from being connected with a man of the Popularity and Character of Hobhouse and in proportion as this advantage is great will be the discredit which his retirement will produce. I feel this so strongly that even if I thought he went too far in his proposals . . . I should be very much inclined to adopt them." [68]

The showdown never came; instead, Althorp summoned Hobhouse at the end of March to offer him the post of Chief Secretary for Ireland, which Stanley had recently vacated. Hobhouse accepted immediately, and the next day Stanley was telling his successor about Irish affairs as the two strolled about Saint James's Park. Hobhouse found out that the state of Ireland was worse than usual. Daniel O'Connell was again rallying his people against the policies of the English Government; Irish Volunteers were unswerving in their demand for the abolition of the Protestant Establishment; Lord Stanley had obtained an Irish coercion law in order to cope with the violence sweeping the impoverished Irish countryside; and Lord

---

68. Althorp to Grey, January 5, 1833, John Charles, Viscount Althorp, Papers.

Anglesey, the Lord Lieutenant, found it necessary to apply coercion in Wexford and Kilkenny.

Hobhouse's appointment caused mixed reactions. High Tories nodded their assent to *The Standard*'s appeal for sparing Ireland "the visitation of a latitudinarian Secretary . . . whose apprenticeship to the trade of a statesman was served in Newgate, and whose writings present texts to justify every form of rebellion." [69] *The Examiner*'s editor, Albany Fonblanque, paid a rare tribute to Hobhouse by describing him as "the very man for Ireland—clever, manly, ingratiating . . . a man, in short, with a head on his shoulders, and a heart in his bosom." [70] The Marquis of Tavistock simply wished the secretaryship would cause no trouble. O'Connell included his own reactions in a letter condemning British policy in general, which appeared in the Dublin papers of April 9:

It is true that we have got rid of Stanley, who was, at least consistent in his opinions—but, then, we have got Hobhouse, who has been a ferocious patriot, and is now a complaisant placeman. I do not know that Ireland can have gained much by the change. Hobhouse, however, has one consolation; he cannot possibly be worse to Ireland than Stanley. [71]

O'Connell's various other declarations had convinced Lord Anglesey that he could be successfully tried for libel. Hobhouse was all for conciliation and informed Lord Grey of his disagreement with the Dublin authorities. [72] Hobhouse agreed that O'Connell was an "arrant bully"; nevertheless, he held undisputed power over Ireland and was the hope of millions of impoverished tenants. His influence, Hobhouse hoped, could be undermined only by attending to the sources of Irish grievances. Had Hobhouse stood up to Stanley, to Lord Anglesey, and to others wishing to rule Ireland with a firm hand, then possibly a conciliatory policy would have emerged, but events decreed that Hobhouse's tenure of office would be all too brief.

69. *The Standard*, March 31, 1833.
70. *The Examiner*, April 11, 1833.
71. *The Standard*, April 11, 1833.
72. Hobhouse to Grey, Grey to Hobhouse, April 19, 1833, Lord Broughton Papers, Add. MSS 36466, f. 441, Lord Broughton Papers, Add. MSS 36467, f. 109. (The first letter is misplaced in the collection.) See also Lord Anglesey to Hobhouse, April 17, April 19, 1833, Lord Broughton Papers, Add. MSS 36467, f. 100, 114.

The issue of the house and window taxes provided the turning point in Hobhouse's political career. Westminster residents had formed another committee specifically to repeal these and other taxes. Hopes ran high because Lord Althorp had promised to remove the assessments as soon as possible, and Burdett and Hobhouse had given strongest possible assurances to vote against the taxation in question.[73]

Hobhouse was among the many people who were totally surprised when Lord Althorp told the Commons in late April that he could not consent to a motion of Sir John Key, an M.P. from the City of London, to repeal the house and window taxes. He pleaded the reduction of the malt tax by 50 per cent as reason for changing his opinion. Hobhouse's reaction was decisive and immediate. He wrote a formal letter of resignation to Lord Grey, explaining that such action was necessary because he had promised support of tax reduction to his constituents and because he was unwilling to hold office with a Government he could not support in Parliament. Hobhouse then went one step further; he persuaded Burdett to move a new writ for Westminster while he applied for the Chiltern Hundreds. London learned the next day about Hobhouse's resignations from his Westminster seat and his Irish Secretaryship.

"Sir John Hobhouse's resignation of his seat for Westminster is one of the most extraordinary things which ever took place," declared a *Morning Herald* editorial.[74] "But why," the paper continued, "in ceasing to be Secretary for Ireland, he should cease to be member for Westminster, we do not at all comprehend." Neither could many other people, including his colleagues in the Government who had advised him to resign only his office. Althorp was particularly bewildered because a few days before Hobhouse told him all resignations were inexpedient.[75] Only *The Times* found in Hobhouse's resignations an example of "a purity of principle for which we should in vain look for a parallel"; the newspaper included the explanation that Hobhouse had written from his Berkeley Square residence and that many constituents found obscure:

73. *Morning Chronicle*, November 30, 1832.
74. *Morning Herald*, May 2, 1833.
75. Sir Denis Le Marchant, *Memoir of John Charles Viscount Althorp, Third Earl Spencer*, 465.

I could not vote for Lord Althorp's resolution this evening, against a proposal which I knew was supported by my constituents, therefore, I have resigned my office as Chief Secretary for Ireland; for, if I could give my vote at all, you had most certainly a right to that vote.

But I could not accede to a motion which, however responsible in itself, would, mixed if successful, be, in my opinion attended with the most fatal results.

I have therefore resigned into your hands the trust so long confided in me; for I know you would not think that any act of mine which would disgrace me could be of any essential service to you.[76]

Hobhouse frequently resorted to such lofty sentiments when something was on his mind. Le Marchant thought he could not really tell why he resigned; he suspected a great deal of rationalizing behind Hobhouse's statement, because "his real motive was to escape from his office, which he felt to be far beyond his powers. The little business he had done in the House he had done feebly, whilst his temper was unequal to the demands made upon it by the constant attacks of the O'Connell tribe." [77]

Hobhouse's tortuous statement expressed the dilemma of a man who felt a dual allegiance to his colleagues in the Government and to his Westminster constituents. Many voters had noted how their representative had acquiesced in the wishes of the Government on military affairs. The Radicals had severed all ties with him for failing to pledge himself to universal suffrage, annual parliaments, and the ballot, and they had threatened Hobhouse's parliamentary seat during the last election by proclaiming his general indifference to the interests of the electorate. Lord Althorp now brought matters to a head by reversing his decision to repeal the house and window taxes, a repeal that Hobhouse and his constituents had advocated for over a decade. Hobhouse, the M.P., realized that he could not support the Government without entirely undermining his already waning popularity among the voters of Westminster, but Hobhouse, the Minister, believed he would be encouraging fiscal

<hr />

76. *The Times*, May 1, 1833.
77. Le Marchant, diary, May 3, 1833, in Aspinall, ed., *Three Early Nineteenth Century Diaries*, 326.

irresponsibility by "acceding" to John Key's motion that had followed the lowering of the tax on malt. A financial deficit would surely be the result. Caught as he was between two equally distasteful alternatives, Hobhouse chose to resign.

Le Marchant's rather caustic remarks shed some more light on Hobhouse's abrupt resignations. The Irish Secretaryship had enabled him to escape from "that detestable War Office," [78] but it was also the graveyard of English politicians. His predecessor Stanley was trying to nurse his own wounded reputation back to health in another job. Stanley had willingly left behind the militant Volunteers and the angry, marauding peasantry who had made the Irish office a disastrous post to hold. A cautious Hobhouse refused to take up the challenge on both private and public grounds. His wife's rapidly deteriorating health left him little time or inclination for public matters.[79] Besides, he foresaw more of the administrative chaos and ministerial disagreements that he had experienced during the past year. Lord Grey had disregarded his views on flogging and military reductions and seemed prepared to overrule his objections to O'Connell's arrest and Irish coercion, which left Hobhouse to bear the brunt of attacks on an Irish policy he could not publicly disavow. He therefore resigned his office. Burdett thought the action quixotic, but Hobhouse asserted he would do it again, if it were to be done again.

He took his family to stay with his brother Henry at Send Grove, near Guilford. Westminster was in utter turmoil as voters passed numerous resolutions censuring or approving the resignations. Some quickly turned to Colonel Evans, who accepted the nomination, but Hobhouse's staunch supporters— Thomas De Vear, Henry Bulwer-Lytton, and Paul Methuen, M.P. for Wiltshire—succeeded in making him stand again for Westminster. The Tories nominated a third candidate, Bickham Escott, in hopes of drawing enough votes from Hobhouse to win. He described nomination day in Covent Garden:

After some hesitation I agreed to stand again for Westminster, and on May 7 I went to Covent Garden with Lord Ebrington, Duncombe, Stanley, and other Members of Parliament, to-

78. Dorchester, ed., *Recollections*, IV, 297.
79. Lady Hobhouse was showing advanced signs of the tuberculosis, which killed her within another two years. The symptoms were especially alarming at this time.

gether with a large body of friendly electors. But the moment I got into the Market the disturbances began; and it was not without difficulty, not to say danger, that I got within the rails of the church portico. The people were ferocious, and if they had got me down, I should never have risen again. . . . Fearon, the American traveller, said that he began to suspect we had given more reform than the civilization of the people would bear.[80]

The first day's polling saw Colonel Evans in the lead by some 250 votes. Hobhouse's supporters tried to persuade Escott to withdraw, but his patron, the Tory Lord Lowther, refused to help one associated with parliamentary reform in any way. The High Bailiff mounted the hustings the second day to announce Evans's upset victory by 2,027 votes to Hobhouse's 1,875. The election results by parishes were as follows:

	Evans	Hobhouse	Escott
St. Martin	457	285	93
St. James	391	343	97
St. George	270	697	339
St. John	246	89	52
St. Margaret	234	182	50
St. Clement Danes	223	116	95
St. Paul	31	37	4
St. Anne	142	110	17
St. Mary	26	8	10
Ward of Savoy	7	8	1
	2,027	1,875	738

The Radical press exulted in Hobhouse's defeat. William Cobbett declared Westminster was once more a bright example to England, and the *Morning Advertiser* rejoiced because "the fetters of tyrannical faction have been broken asunder." [81] *The Times*, however, admonished the Tories for their part in Evans's victory. "We suspect, indeed," an editorial declared, "that the day is not very distant when the Tories will bitterly regret the triumph which they have assisted in accomplishing for a party whose hatred of them . . . is deep, malignant, incurable." [82] Hobhouse reacted serenely to his defeat: "I never felt more self-

80. Dorchester, ed., *Recollections*, IV, 309–10.
81. *Morning Advertiser*, May 11, 1833.
82. *The Times*, May 11, 1833.

satisfied in my life, never more certain that I have acted as became me, and in a way which would finally be creditable to myself and useful to the public." [83] A week later he left London to rejoin his family in the country.

His friends attributed the defeat to Bickham Escott, who captured enough conservative votes to throw the election to Evans. Some political observers emphasized his failure to obtain Government support for repealing the unpopular house and window taxes. Others assigned Hobhouse's defeat to the general apathy that greeted his third appearance on the hustings in little more than a year. However, Colonel Evans did not win his election in 1833 by popular default alone. Francis Place's open defiance of Hobhouse the previous year heralded the fact that he had become too conservative for many Radicals. Parliamentary reform seemed to exhaust Hobhouse's interest in further reform. He found it a convenient halting point after a decade of change and political turmoil; they wished to reap the full benefits of 1832 and were disillusioned because the tempo of reform had slackened. Hobhouse seemed an Establishment figure. He was unwilling to fight the fight against unpopular taxes, monopolies, municipal government, the Corn Law, and the ecclesiastical establishment. He had refused to serve as a popular delegate and to pledge to the Radical program brought to him. Memories of a recent defeat over parliamentary reform and visions of more reforms in the future brought Tories and Radicals together to defeat Hobhouse, a statesman who went too far for many conservatives and not far enough to suit the Radical supporters of Colonel Evans. Thus, Westminster renounced Hobhouse, while the Tory satirist, Mackworth Praed, wrote the adieus of the constituency he had served for 13 years: [84]

> We're parted for ever, John Cam, John Cam,
> We're parted for ever, John Cam,
> You can't think—Oh Heavens!
> With tall Colonel Evans—
> You can't think how happy I am, am,
> You can't think how happy I am.

83. Hobhouse, diary, May 10, 1833, Lord Broughton Papers, Add. MSS 56557.
84. *Morning Post*, May 13, 1833.

Chapter IX

THE MELBOURNE YEARS

Hobhouse's retirement was brief. A year after his resignations came a Cabinet appointment in Lord Melbourne's newly appointed Government. He retained this post in Russell's Government. In 1833–1834, Westminster had rejected him, but the Whig aristocracy came to his rescue. His involvement with reformist causes ceased; henceforth, he voiced opposition to change in Whig counsels. The Radical of old, the man who once provoked Parliament into ordering his imprisonment, re-emerged in Victorian England a conservative minister, a favorite at Court, and before his retirement, a peer.

Within months after leaving Westminster, Hobhouse received invitations to stand for Bridgewater, East Somerset, Marylebone, and Devizes; Macaulay urged him to consider the Leeds seat he would soon vacate by going to India.[1] Other constituencies sought the services of a man identified with the Great Reform Bill. He withheld any commitment for the time being, preferring instead to watch political events unfold while remaining at Basildon Park, the Berkshire property he had rented for a year. Early in 1834 it was apparent that dissension had so intensified that Lord Grey's Government was falling apart. Ireland was the insurmountable stumbling block; one wing of the Cabinet urged coercion while the other recommended concessions to win over the Irish leaders and their followers. Russell finally upset the coach in May by suggesting the appropriation of some Irish church revenue for secular purposes, thereby causing the resignations of Stanley, Graham, Ripon, and the Duke of Richmond. Grey then resolved to restore order to Ireland by renewing the Coercion Bill scheduled to expire at the end of the parliamentary session. This time he ran into trouble because Littleton, Hobhouse's successor as Irish Secretary, had disarmed O'Connell's opposition to the Government with promises that the Cabinet would drop the clause in the Coercion Bill concerning the prohibition of public meetings.

1. Lady Dorchester, ed., *Recollections of a Long Life, by Lord Broughton* (*John Cam Hobhouse*) *with additional extracts from his private diaries*, IV, 326, 328.

Brougham, who had instigated the negotiations, had also hood-winked Althorp into the agreement by falsifying the facts of the negotiations. Grey flatly refused to accept any amendments, and when an unaltered bill was presented to the Commons, O'Con-nell accused Brougham, Littleton, and Althorp of deceit. Al-thorp, who had disliked the terms of the Coercion Bill all along, handed in his resignation. Deprived of his leader in the Com-mons and anxious to return to his Northumberland estate, a weary Grey also chose to resign.

The King wished to form a coalition government that in-cluded Stanley, Wellington, and Peel, but the King's wishes did not make it any more palatable for the Tories to join those Whigs with whom they had recently fought so bitterly. William IV was left with no other choice but to accept another Whig Prime Minister. Lord Melbourne finally filled the office as the only man acceptable both to the King and to various sections of the party. Hobhouse was kept abreast of developments through friends in London, and although the new Cabinet was not so strongly liberal as Durham predicted, Althorp and Rus-sell remained Chancellor of the Exchequer and Post-Master General respectively. Durham was altogether excluded.

Hobhouse was summoned on July 16 to London, where Al-thorp told him that Melbourne wanted him to accept the posi-tion of First Commissioner of Woods and Forests, with a seat in the Cabinet. That evening he met Melbourne, who dispelled his reservations about Ireland with assurances that the ban on public meetings would be dropped. Hobhouse then consented to join a government that he assessed as "the best, which, under the circumstances, could be found." The next day it was an-nounced he would stand for the Nottingham seat vacated by Lord Duncannon's removal to the Lords.

Hobhouse's career was now anchored to a Midland com-mercial, financial, and industrial center of approximately 50,000 inhabitants.[2] The city had expanded rapidly during the early nineteenth century because its machine lace and hosiery in-dustries thrived. Prosperous lace manufacturers and merchant hosiers joined the old trading and banking families to form a ruling circle that was solidly Whig. Nottingham contained many features of English political life which survived parlia-

2. See Roy A. Church, *Economic and Social Change in a Midland Town: Victorian Nottingham, 1815–1900.*

mentary reform. It was renowned for corruption, violent elections, and intimidation. The 3,000 artisans, small tradesmen, and hosiery framework knitters who had been enfranchised before 1832 sold their votes at a high price, and the wealthier, enlarged electorate proved just as venal afterwards. A pattern of violent protest, evident throughout the eighteenth century and during the Luddite uprisings, revived in 1831 when mobs burned down Nottingham Castle because the Duke of Newcastle had rejected parliamentary reform. A strong Chartist movement arose in the area before the decade closed.

Many Nottingham voters and residents embraced Chartism because industrial conditions peculiar to their city affected them so adversely. Many of the city's machine lace workers benefited from belonging to an expanding and technologically advanced industry based upon the factory system and utilizing a high proportion of skilled labor. By contrast, most of the hosiery workers were victims of a stagnant, technologically backward industry. The basic unit of production remained the framework knitter who rented or owned frames, which were outmoded. These workers suffered from cyclical or seasonal fluctuations of trade and from the loss of overseas markets to French and German competitors. The economic woes of most hosiery workers resulted from a situation much different from that of the Lancashire and Yorkshire handloom weavers. The struggling handloom weavers declined in numbers. They were victims of a growing factory system that benefited the industry as a whole. The framework knitters, on the other hand, performed the outwork for a hosiery industry suffering from technological backwardness, a situation not remedied until the latter half of the nineteenth century, when the factory system was introduced. Furthermore, the attraction of the frame rent as a steady source of income had encouraged an increase in frame workers and an overinvestment in a trade beyond what the market demand warranted. As a result, major slumps in the industry produced growing numbers of unemployed and intensified radicalism in the Nottingham area.

Hobhouse had his first taste of Nottingham radicalism when he opposed William Eagle, a local barrister who declared himself for the ballot, triennial parliaments, the abolition of the Corn Laws, and the reform of the town corporation. This 1834 contest did not pass as smoothly for Hobhouse as the voting results would suggest.[3] He informed Burdett after the first day's polling on July 24 of the "most horrible difference" between Westminster and "infernal" Nottingham. "I am just as ill-used in one place as the other," he related, "but the electors here are a totally different body of men."[4] Perhaps Hobhouse's memory of Westminster contests had dimmed after a year, whereas the tumult at Nottingham was both vivid and unexpected. Benjamin Boothby, an iron founder who had seconded Eagle, charged Hobhouse with political apostasy for failing to support the ballot or abolish military flogging. "We are not Old Sarum!" the crowds heckled at "the man sent down from Downing Street."[5] The election over, Hobhouse returned immediately to London, where he resolved to stand for another constituency at the earliest opportunity. It came sooner than he expected; Lord Melbourne's first Government ended soon after it began.

Althorp's transferal to the Lords upon his father's death in November had deprived the Government of its leader in the Commons and furnished William with a pretext for getting rid of the Whigs. Melbourne had given the King his lead by describing the difficulties the loss of Althorp occasioned. William was undoubtedly disappointed when the Prime Minister came down to Brighton not with any offer of resignation in hand, but with the intent of making the necessary arrangements to carry on the Government. He strongly rejected the suggestion that Russell be Althorp's successor. Further negotiations the next day proved fruitless, whereupon Melbourne received his dismissal. Back in London he related the events to an indignant Cabinet. "Nothing could have been more cavelier than our dismissal," was Hobhouse's immediate reaction to Burdett, "nothing more uncaused or uncalled for except in courtly imaginations. One or two of us (I amongst the number) have long had suspicions that all was not right at headquarters, but not a soul guessed at the opportunity which would be

3. Hobhouse won by the handsome majority of 1015 votes; he received 1581 votes while Eagle received 566. Thomas Raikes reported, "Sir John Hobhouse has gained his election for Nottingham amidst great popular clamour against him." *A Portion of the Journal Kept by Thomas Raikes Esq. from 1831 to 1847*, I, 270.

4. Hobhouse to Burdett, July 24, 1834, Letter 52, Sir Francis Burdett, Correspondence.

5. *Nottingham and Newark Mercury*, July 26, 1834.

taken." [6] He described the interval during which Peel sped back from Italy as the time "to prepare the stage and arrange the actors and scenery." It was necessary first to refute Tory commentators like John Wilson Croker, who had asserted in the *Quarterly Review* that "the Cabinet has been dissolved by its own internal and irreconcilable dissensions." [7] Thus, William had remedied a situation harmful to the country by dismissing in November a Government whose most sanguine members did not expect to survive beyond the new year. Hobhouse's reply in the *Morning Chronicle* stressed how unanimity and mutual trust prevailed in Melbourne's Cabinet. He did not challenge the royal prerogative but suggested that William IV had acted most inopportunely. By dismissing the Whigs, the King had managed to "throw the country into ferment and recall into active operation the political unions." [8] The King's highhanded action seemed to invite serious repercussions. Weeks later Hobhouse told Greville that the restoration of Melbourne's Government was impossible because "they [the late Government] could not look the King in the face again, nor he them, after such a clear intimation on his part that he disliked them, and dreaded their principles." [9] What, then, could be done to end the impasse, with a partisan King and the Tory-dominated Lords aligned against a hostile Commons?

Already Hobhouse and other Whigs were preparing the groundwork for reversing the royal action. A first step was preserving an Opposition majority in the Commons after Peel decided upon the dissolution of Parliament and a general election in December. Toward this end, Hobhouse, along with Edward Ellice and Thomas Drummond, formerly Althorp's secretary, established themselves as electoral agents at London's Cleveland Square. Besides dispensing funds to various candidates, the trio tried to discourage contests between Whigs and Radicals in various constituencies. [10] They were disappointed when

6. Hobhouse to Burdett, November 19, 1834, Letter 53, Burdett Correspondence.

7. John Wilson Croker, "Personal History of Louis Philippe, Postscript," *Quarterly Review*, 52 (1834), 569–72.

8. *Morning Chronicle*, November 18, November 19, 1834.

9. Charles Fulke Greville, diary, January 15, 1835, in Lytton Strachey and Roger Fulford, eds., *The Greville Memoirs, 1814–1860*, III, 144.

10. Edmund Temple to Hobhouse, December 29, 1834, Lord Breadelbane to Hobhouse, January 6, 1835, John Cam Hobhouse, Lord Broughton, Papers, Add. MSS 47227, f. 98, 116.

the results came trickling in; Hobhouse had confidently predicted an Opposition plurality of at least 150 seats, but instead, the Tories scored impressive gains in most counties and in a great number of boroughs where local party organizations, modeled on London's Carlton Club, had actively canvassed and organized the voters. Hobhouse himself fell victim to the Tory resurgence in Bristol. He had his name placed on the nomination list but found that the appeal of a native son mattered little as he placed last behind the vigorously campaigning Tories, Miles and Vyvyan, and the losing Whig, Baillie.[11] He was fortunate in having the Whig corporation of Nottingham propose his candidacy, which virtually assured his victory at the polls in an uncontested election. Hobhouse, as did many other Whigs, made a point of presenting a Radical image at Nottingham. In a widely publicized address, he stressed support for many reforms favored by Radicals; the redress of all nonconformist grievances and municipal reform were cited as matters requiring immediate attention. Hobhouse also declared that the Whigs would consider the ballot, triennial parliaments, and "an entire reform in the Church of Ireland—a reform which would cut at the root of the great abuses which render that country a by-word." [12]

The election results could only be precisely determined when the Commons met and voted. A dilemma confronted the Whig leaders during this interval: They could likely return to office by combining their diminished ranks with the Radicals, who had advanced in Strength and with O'Connell's followers—a "miscellaneous multitude" as Stanley termed such a union. The Whig patricians did not seem prepared to pay the price of countenancing distasteful Radical reforms and of associating with the likes of O'Connell. Grey, Auckland, Anglesey, and Holland loathed such tactics; Spencer and Lansdowne feared the Radicals but welcomed the prospect of ousting Peel; Melbourne was uncommitted and inclined toward reconciliation with Stanley. Nevertheless, the impending showdown in the Commons over the Speakership started the momentum toward an Opposition entente reached through the Litchfield House

11. *Bristol Gazette*, January 15, 1835. The election results were Miles, 3709; Vyvyan, 3312; Baillie, 2520; Hobhouse, 1808.

12. *Nottingham and Newark Weekly*, January 10, 1835; see also *The Times*, January 13, 1835.

Compact. Russell's commitment to lay appropriation provided the basis for agreement among the various Opposition groups, and Hobhouse and Duncannon among the Whigs played instrumental roles in the complex interplay among politicians that preceded the first Litchfield meeting of February 18, one day before Parliament was to elect a Speaker.

If anything, leading Whigs allowed Hobhouse and other party subordinates to proceed with the Litchfield meeting for want of an alternative. With Duncannon's encouragement, immediately after the general elections in January, Hobhouse had pressed upon Melbourne the need for uniting Opposition groups behind Russell. After urging Melbourne to persuade Abercromby to run for Speaker, Hobhouse wrote:

Thompson & myself agreed yesterday that we ought to get together all the members returned by reformed constituencies a few days previously to the session—& that the best mode of doing this would be by having a dinner—say on the 19th of Feb', the day on which the writs are returnable.

Our plan is to write to every M.P. who can be called a Reformer telling him that such a scheme is in agitation & that if he wishes to attend he will signify his intention to Mr. Drummond at Cleveland Square. If the answers do not give a certainty of a large attendance the dinner may be abandoned & notices sent to every assenting member accordingly. If the promises of adherence are encouraging we can then appoint time place president & proceed with the business.

There is much to be said both for & against this project—& as I before said, there ought to be more, if not wiser heads than those which now consult together in Cleveland Square to settle a point of so much delicacy.[13]

A week later, on January 25, Hobhouse and Thompson met Melbourne and Russell at Brocket Hall to discuss the measures already underway. Both Whig leaders were hesitant, so Hobhouse reported:

Poulett Thompson & myself told him [Russell] of the measures we had taken for the cooperation of the Radical party under Henry Warburton, & of the Irish under O'Connell. Melbourne

13. Hobhouse to Melbourne, January 19, 1835, Melbourne Letters, Box 12, Royal Archives. See also Duncannon to Hobhouse, January 16, January 24, January 31, 1835, Lord Broughton Papers, Add. MSS 47227, f. 146–47, 156–57, 160–61.

& Russell had no objection to union with Warburton & his friends; but they thought union with O'Connell & his Irishmen inexpedient, unless these gentlemen could promise to act with them in Government as well as in Opposition. We had a great deal of talk on this subject. Thompson and myself were not alarmed by the O'Connell alliance; but our two friends demurred, & we did not come to any definite conclusion that evening. Of the two, Russell seemed to me to hesitate the most. We decided, therefore, that a vigorous opposition should be made in both Houses at the opening of the session.[14]

Hobhouse had suggested as an intermediary between the Whigs and other Opposition groups some moderate Irishman familiar to Whig society, perhaps one of the Grattons. However, Hobhouse found himself and Warburton, the Radical whip, assuming the role of intermediaries between Russell and O'Connell. Warburton had received a batch of invitations to Litchfield House in the form of a circular letter sent out in Russell's name, and either he or Hobhouse forwarded some to O'Connell for distribution to his followers. There remained the chance that O'Connell would misconstrue the invitation inasmuch as Russell, preferring to remain in the background and leave the details to party subordinates, had not written personally. Hobhouse interceded by having O'Connell informed that his attendance was a matter of import to Russell, who was told of the action taken. "I have taken care that it should be known (through Warburton) that the circulars are considered a sufficient notification," Hobhouse wrote, "and that no slight or disrespect was intended." [15] Russell later accepted Duncannon's advice to forward a gracious reply acknowledging O'Connell's note that he and his supporters would attend the meeting of all reformers at Lord Litchfield's house in Saint James's Square.

14. John Cam Hobhouse, first Baron Broughton, *Some Account of a Long Life*, III, 87–88.
15. Hobhouse to Russell, February 3, 1835, quoted in Sir Spencer Walpole, *Life of Lord John Russell*, I, 220. Walpole suggests that Russell did not know about the circular sent to O'Connell until the latter replied favorably. It seems unlikely, however, that Warburton had acted entirely on his own; he more likely got the circulars to O'Connell after Duncannon or Hobhouse, who may have delivered them, notified him of Russell's approval. See A. H. Graham, "The Litchfield House Compact, 1835," *Irish Historical Studies*, 12 (1960–1961), 209–25; also Abraham D. Kriegel, "The Politics of the Whigs in Opposition, 1834–1835," *Journal of British Studies*, 7, 2 (May, 1968), 65–91.

The Opposition unity forged at a series of Litchfield House meetings held together throughout the crucial weeks preceding Peel's resignation. The day after the February 18 meeting saw the Opposition win the contested election to the Speakership, with Abercromby's ten-vote majority over Tory Charles Manners Sutton attributable to the Irish representatives, who reversed Sutton's lead from the English, Welsh, and Scottish M.P.'s. Peel held on, hoping to swing over some votes on the issue of Irish church revenues, whereupon Russell carried a motion to the effect that the Commons could only accept a measure including lay appropriation. Peel's resignation then forced the King, in Hobhouse's words, "to accept the bitter pill of his own compounding" by asking Lord Melbourne to form another government. Hobhouse did not believe the country had seen the last dismissal of a Government by the Crown, after observing William's cold demeanor throughout the swearing-in ceremonies at Saint James's. He knew of "not a single step taken to prevent the recurrence of a similar danger and disgrace," [16] and he could only hope that the events following the November dismissal had clearly demonstrated that the King could not choose a Government in face of an Opposition majority in the Commons.

The prospects facing Lord Melbourne's second Government were not inviting, dependent as it was upon Radical and Irish support and confronted by a hostile King and House of Lords. It survived over six years and, after two parliamentary dissolutions, ushered in the reign of Queen Victoria. Lord Melbourne needed all his arts of persuasion and easygoing assurances during these years to keep his Cabinet together. Some members proposed bold new measures to stem the increasing sentiment against the Government; others threatened resignations should these measures be enacted. Hobhouse became a member of such divided counsels by accepting the Presidency of the Board of Control for India, the office Pitt had created to supervise the Home Government's interests in the colony. He retained this post throughout the Melbourne and Russell governments.

His appointment was designed to reinforce Radical support for the Government by including a member who had formerly identified with them. It was also an expression of Melbourne's

16. Dorchester, ed., *Recollections*, V, 35.

confidence in Hobhouse's loyalty to himself. He had refused office to more prominent party members, such as Durham and Brougham, because he reckoned them troublesome colleagues. The question remained about whether Hobhouse, fresh from his involvement with the Irish-Radical pact, would incline toward the liberal or conservative wing of the Cabinet. His work on behalf of the Litchfield Compact was similar to his earlier role at Westminster when he urged the Whigs to once more become the popular party. Hobhouse told Melbourne upon accepting office that the Cabinet was not as liberal as before; to which the Prime Minister retorted that others told him it was too Jacobinical.[17] Their exchange suggested differing approaches to policy, with Hobhouse favoring reforms and Melbourne continuing to be chiefly concerned with keeping reformers within manageable bounds. Melbourne did not fail to take into account the strong backlash from Howick, Tavistock, and other Whig exclusionists that had caused Russell to modify his reformist stance at the first Litchfield meeting.[18] The Whig aristocracy had in fact successfully avoided specific commitments to Radical groups. The Whigs had avoided any binding claims, such as the ballot or triennial parliaments, and they were not obliged to include O'Connell in the Government. Ultimately, Melbourne played a trimmer's role, yielding to reformers here and seeking understandings with conservatives there, while tacking along a course that seemed safe enough within the political context of the time. Certain measures he would accept, if only to avoid an unpleasant showdown with a determined majority in the Cabinet whose views had overwhelming outside support. These were tactical concessions, however, not parts of a grand design to resolve the predicament of the Whig aristocracy's relationship to Radical groups. Hobhouse, Duncannon, Thomson, and other party subordinates may have wished to broaden the base of the party, but they lacked either the will or the strength to do so.

Both wings of the Cabinet did agree to support some important measures during the early years of the Melbourne Government. "This second great measure of the Whig or Liberal Ministry," as Hobhouse termed the Municipal Corporations Bill,

17. Ibid., IV, 34; Norman Gash, *Reaction and Reconstruction in English Politics, 1832–1852,* 173. See also W. T. M'Cullagh Torrens, ed., *Memoirs of the Rt. Hon. William Second Viscount Melbourne,* II, 108.
18. See Kriegel, "Politics of the Whigs in Opposition," 82–91.

survived a stormy passage through the House of Lords in 1835. Earlier, he spoke out against Peel's property qualification clause. "When you are founding a measure on a great popular basis," he advised the Commons, "you should carry out your principle to the full." [19] Hobhouse then came up with the specific example of the £40 qualification for parochial officials in his own Vestry Bill, a clause he now thought had had no positive consequences whatsoever. He also voted for the remedial measures of the following year—Church administrative and fiscal reforms, legal recognition of nonconformist marriages, and a reduction of the newspaper tax.

Despite such solid accomplishments, the Cabinet found little cause for optimism as the 1836 session ended. Its majority in the Commons was slim, the Court remained decidedly hostile, and the Lords were wrecking with impunity other Government proposals. They had rejected once more lay appropriation of Irish church revenues, and their drastic emendations had forced the Government to abandon Irish municipal reform. The fate befalling Irish legislation was not for want of Government firmness. Indeed, at the time he resumed office, Lord Melbourne had dismissed the King's plea of conscience about the oath he had taken at his Coronation by insisting on the "need to come to a distinct understanding" in terms of the mandate Russell had received for lay appropriations. Russell and Hobhouse had defended the tithe bill in the Commons; [20] Melbourne and Duncannon fought unsuccessfully in the Lords. Russell then sought to rescue the Government from its quandry by breaking out of the narrow constitutional confines imposed by the peers' veto. His Cabinet memorandum of June, 1836, by proposing the creation of sufficient peers to tame the obstructing Upper House, was a projected step toward establishing a more popular Government. Melbourne refused to countenance such a step because it was certain to cause the resignations of most Cabinet members.

Hobhouse focused attention upon the constitutional issue involved when the Commons once again debated Irish municipal reform in February, 1837. "Shall this country be governed by a

---

19. *Hansard Parliamentary Debates*, 3d series, XXIX (1835), col. 111.
20. Melbourne to the King, April 15, 1835, in Lloyd C. Sanders, ed., *Lord Melbourne's Papers*, 273; *Hansard*, 3d series, XXVII (1835), cols. 529–39.

majority of the House of Lords against a majority in the House of Commons," he asked, "or shall it be governed by a majority of the House of Commons against a majority of the House of Lords?" [21] He then implied that the Government intended to resign if the Lords again vetoed the legislation at hand. He viewed the Irish Municipal Corporations Bill as a popular question, one of local rights, and while its rejection would be the triumph of the former principle he had enunciated, such action would also provoke a violent reaction in Ireland. Hobhouse then asked the Tories whether they would once more resort to coercion after Melbourne's ministers "should be relieved of our thankless servitude here."

In the following extract from his diary, Hobhouse exaggerated the impression his comments had made, but he also gave a more accurate expression of his own feelings at the time:

I heard that what I had said of the happy day that was to release us from our thankless servitude had given rise to rumours of our immediate relinquishment of office. The comment on this from our opponents was somewhat flattering; for they were pleased to say that I was honest and truthspeaking, and really did wish to leave office. This was true, so far as the desire to leave office was concerned; not so much, however, from any dislike of office, as because I did not see how we could retain it now, without loss of character, and, consequently, of influence. If we were to go out on losing our Irish Corporation we would be spared the embarrassment, not only of the Tithe Bill, but the Canada Bill, and the proposals of our Radical friends, which were sure to damage us, though very unjustly, with our constituents. I was aware that this was only a party consideration; but I thought that, even so far as the advancement of good principles were concerned, our speedy retreat was highly expedient. [22]

Russell renewed the threat of resignation when he spoke during the Irish Municipal Bill's third reading in April, but Melbourne easily prevailed over the Cabinet members—Russell, Spring Rice, Duncannon, and Hobhouse—who had favored such action. Did they wish, he asked, to charge the political atmosphere with a crisis over the veto power of the Lords? In that event, O'Connell had a drastic proposal to establish an elective

21. *Hansard*, 3d series, XXXVI (1837), cols. 380–87.
22. Dorchester, ed., *Recollections*, V, 65; Hobhouse, diary, February 11, 1837.

chamber. Were they willing to dilute the peerage by a wide-scale addition of members, as Russell had prescribed in 1836, the year before? [23] If so, could they be certain that the newly created peers would remain responsive to liberal views, especially when the Government that had placed them might not survive for very long afterwards? Having been made aware of such difficulties and deadlocks, Hobhouse agreed to seek other alternatives. [24]

A solution came through political tactics operating within the existing constitutional framework. The issue was not between Lords and Commons, as Hobhouse had outlined, but between two parties, each controlling separate chambers. The politicians, therefore, reached an accord that allowed for the passage of some contested bills and the modification of others. The Government had O'Connell's consent to drop lay appropriation, and Peel and Wellington urged the peers to table, rather than reject, the Irish Municipal Bill, a first gesture toward a more conciliatory policy.

Irish affairs remained a touchy issue for the Melbourne Government, dependent as it was upon the support of O'Connell's following. Thus, Hobhouse's and Russell's remarks about resignation at the beginning of 1837 were last-minute feints; the two men were probing for a Tory surrender on the Irish reforms for which they had been leading parliamentary spokesmen. Two years later Hobhouse was among the Cabinet members appointed to rally Government supporters against Lord Roden's hostile motion regarding Irish administration. "The miserable state of Ireland was not attributable to the present government," he declared, "but its causes might be traced to the oppressive manner in which the Irish people have been treated ever since England obtained dominion over them, down to the accession to office of the present administration." [25] Although he knew that the broad dimensions of the Irish problem suggested further and more effective reforms for the future, he, for one, had

23. See Rollo Russell, ed., *Early Correspondence of Lord John Russell, 1805–1840*, II, 144–45, 185–87.

24. Gash, *Reaction and Reconstruction*, chap. II; Dorchester, ed., *Recollections*, V, 69. Hobhouse thought of Irish affairs in general when he noted that "Lord Melbourne, at this jointure, was of the greatest service, and led the party in the Lords in a way that showed he was worthy to lead it."

25. *Hansard*, 3d series, XLVII (1839), cols. 368–71.

thoroughly wearied of "tiresome Irish matters" by the time an amended Irish Municipal Bill became law in 1840.[26] As far as he was concerned, a well-intentioned Government had devoted enough time to Ireland.

By 1840, the tired Cabinet had found its staunchest supporter in Queen Victoria. In 1837, Hobhouse had noted that in the Cabinet "there was more gloom on the faces of all than might have been expected" [27] over the passing of William IV, the energetic, patriotic King who never overcame his antipathy toward the Whigs, but he was quickly drawn into the courtly idyll that sprang up between the young, uncertain Queen and the worldly, aristocratic Melbourne, who enjoyed his new role of royal confidant and mentor. "Lord Melbourne always sat next to Her Majesty," Hobhouse wrote after his first stay at Windsor Castle, "and it was most gratifying to observe her demeanor with him; it was that of a child to a parent." [28] Perhaps on certain occasions, when he joined them for dinner at Buckingham Palace or played chess at Windsor, Hobhouse may have reflected upon the shifting nature of human relationships. He, who once had been scorned by the Whigs, was now highly esteemed by their most eminent member. "Hobhouse is a man of immense knowledge and acquirements," the Prime Minister told the Queen, "there's nothing he don't know." Victoria agreed he was indeed "a very agreeable man." [29] In 1839, however, politics suddenly intruded upon the Court when the Government resigned after the meager majority it received for suspending the Jamaican Constitution. Then arose the question of the royal Household —Victoria firmly refused to part with even one of her Whig ladies. Hobhouse never thought about the constitutional niceties of the situation. He only knew that the Whigs must come to the young Queen's rescue, and when Lord Howick proposed that a Cabinet minute should be sent recommending further negotiations with Peel, he gallantly protested that he would sooner cut off his hand than sign such a negotiation. The matter was

26. Hobhouse, diary, June 19, 1840, Lord Broughton Papers, Add. MSS 56563.

27. Dorchester, ed., *Recollections*, V, 79. Hobhouse's account of Victoria's accession, ibid., 76–88.

28. Ibid., 97.

29. Queen Victoria, diary, October 2, 1839, in Viscount Esher, ed., *The Girlhood of Queen Victoria; a selection from Her Majesty's diaries between the years 1832 and 1840*, II, 258.

resolved; the Cabinet decided to support the Queen by remaining in office.[30]

The Melbourne Government had been reprieved, but it remained a matter of concern for Ministerialists, as well as a point of attack for critics, that Hobhouse had become a negligible force in the Commons. Francis Place, always prodding him with new or unfinished business during his Westminster days, described him in 1836 as "live lumber." At the same time, Joseph Parkes concluded that "Hobhouse, for all his Parliamentary illuminations, is burnt out to the socket," and Lord Duncannon bluntly told Melbourne in 1838, "Hobhouse is not considered as adding any weight to your Government." Greville included him in an unfavorable assessment of the Cabinet members: "John Russell is without support; Rice is held cheap and is ineffective; Palmerston never utters except on his own business; Thomson and Hobhouse never on any business; and Howick alone ventures to mix in the fight." [31]

The changes in the Cabinet after the Whigs resumed office in 1839 did not bring all the changes desired by Greville and other commentators. Instead, Howick retired in disgust over the "fatal mediocrity of his colleagues." Conservative Spring Rice vacated the Exchequer by going to the Lords, and cautious Sir Francis Baring succeeded him. An able economist, Poulett Thomson, had turned down the offer in favor of the Canadian Governor-Generalship. Clarendon, Labouchere, and Macaulay buttressed the liberal wing of the Cabinet while Hobhouse retained his post, despite persistent rumors to the contrary. Both Melbourne and the Queen wanted him there, and further changes entailed additional electoral contests, a risky venture at that point.

There were also imperial and foreign affairs to consider. By this time, Hobhouse had worked out with Palmerston and Lord Auckland a master plan to thwart the supposed Russian designs on India by occupying Afghanistan. He also shared with Lansdowne and Holland a privileged position of receiving Palmer-

30. Dorchester, ed., *Recollections*, V, 1951; Hobhouse, diary, May 11, 1839, Lord Broughton Papers, Add. MSS 56560.

31. Parkes to Durham, May 1, 1836, in Stuart J. Reid, *Life and Letters of the First Earl of Durham, 1792–1840*, II, 82; Lord Duncannon to Melbourne, October 20, 1838, in Sanders, ed., *Lord Melbourne's Papers*, 381; Greville, diary, February 5, 1838, in Strachey and Fulford, eds., *Greville Memoirs*, IV, 19; Torrens, ed., *Memoirs of Melbourne*, II, 107–8.

ston's dispatches concerning the conflict between Mohammed Ali, Pasha of Egypt, and his Ottoman suzerain, Sultan Mahmud II.[32] By 1840 a Cabinet majority had swung round to Russell's view that Palmerston had acted too much alone in handling the crisis in the Middle East. Clarendon and Holland especially favored some understanding with the French, perhaps by amending the agreement with other European powers limiting the Pasha's holdings to Egypt and Syria. Russell again threatened to resign unless Palmerston was made to do so, but Hobhouse stood by the Foreign Minister throughout the crisis. Just as British armies had stepped forward to protect India from outside aggression, so too must British strength enforce a European settlement over Mohammed Ali and his French ally. The issues at stake were global, as Palmerston had outlined while asking for Hobhouse's support at the next Cabinet meeting: "I tell my colleagues that if we give way now it will be to the menaces of the French, & that if we so yield when backed by all Europe, all Europe will treat us henceforth like a nation afraid to fight; France will take Morocco and Tunis . . . Russia will do what she likes in Asia, & the disputed territory will be laid hold of by the United States."[33] This time Hobhouse had backed the winning man. Palmerston's prestige soared, especially at the end of 1840. At that time, the annihilation of Egyptian forces in Syria had brought on a settlement that confined Mohammed Ali to his hereditary Egyptian domains, thereby thoroughly humiliating the French Government.

At home, the Government had to deal with mounting economic distress, Chartist disorders, and a growing Anti–Corn Law League. Liberal support waned, whereupon Melbourne made some gestures that were conciliatory but short of fully endorsing reformist demands. He withdrew his opposition to the ballot and made it an open question. He made the Corn Laws another open question in order to permit the Government to ascertain the feeling of Parliament without losing the support of protectionist Whigs. Melbourne had no intention of champion-

32. Sir C. K. Webster, *The Foreign Policy of Palmerston, 1830–1841*, II, 40.

33. Palmerston to Hobhouse, September 29, 1840, Lord Broughton Papers, Add. MSS 46915, f. 221. The Afghan occupation was considered an outstanding success at this time. Hobhouse believed that concessions in one part of the world would encourage enemies elsewhere; thus, Afghan and Middle Eastern affairs were related.

ing free trade, but Russell moved in that direction by tacking a moderate fixed duty on corn to Baring's 1841 budget, which already included proposals to lower duties on sugar and foreign lumber.

Hobhouse thought Russell's action was inopportune. "You are bringing forward three great measures, and raising all the great interests against you," he advised Russell, "without being sure of carrying either of them."[34] Russell was able to convince most of the Cabinet to take the gamble for several reasons. There was an immediate need to balance the budget, and Hume's 1840 committee on import duties held out such a promise because a greater volume of trade would more than offset the loss of revenue from lower tariffs. In political terms, the urban free-trade vote would more than compensate the Government for losing the support of some protectionists or colonialists. A bold fiscal policy was needed to restore public confidence in the Whigs.

The attempt failed. A debate on the sugar duties ended with the Government's defeat by a majority of 36. Melbourne favored resigning at the May 13 Cabinet meeting, but his colleagues urged that action be deferred until the Commons voted on the Corn Laws, which Russell had scheduled for June 4. That day, however, Peel carried his motion of confidence against the Government by a majority of one. Hobhouse argued against the motion by cataloguing all the Whig reforms of the past several years.[35] The sporadic laughter in the Commons ceased when he turned to the Tories and the serious divisions within their ranks: Catholic and Irish reformers sat next to vehement critics; members supporting parliamentary reform, the Corn Laws, or the gold standard sat next to erstwhile foes. Peel, the party leader, had abandoned a stated position in the past, and Hobhouse predicted he would repeal the Corn Laws upon assuming office. Such action would undoubtedly make the Tories a more popular party, but it would cause irreconcilable divisions and cost Peel his position as party leader.

Would the Government now resign or dissolve Parliament? Hobhouse held out for the former: News from Nottingham and elsewhere indicated a resurgence of public support for the Whigs. Melbourne finally acceded to that wing of the Cabinet

34. Dorchester, ed., *Recollections*, VI, 19–20.
35. *Hansard*, 3d series, LVIII (1841), cols. 836–56.

favoring dissolution. Their optimism proved unfounded, for the July elections ended with a decisive Tory victory. Defeated 360–269 on the address to the new Parliament, the Government at last resigned. Victoria braced herself for a Peelite Ministry; Melbourne, though pained at leaving her services, met his downfall with a usual coolness his colleagues found distressing. Hobhouse experienced great relief that the Government had fallen. "I walked home and got to Berkeley Square by half-past three in the morning," he recorded, "most happy that this long agony had ended at last." [36]

Why had the Whigs lost the leadership they once held so securely? Observers pointed to the re-emergence of the Tory party under Peel's skillful leadership, an inevitable reaction against a group in power for eleven years, the slow erosion of support because the Government made either a wrong move or no move at all. Lord Campbell stressed Whig inconsistency when he commented, "They wavered between the two extremes of their supporters, by turns disgusting both; and they committed several palpable blunders by which their influence was rapidly undermined." [37] A case in point, Campbell said, was Russell's attitude that the ballot question in 1838 was a final concession the country could expect from the Whigs. This was a "double mischief" because conservative supporters deserted the Government for accepting another innovation while others charged that the Whigs had ceased to be reformers at all. Each year the Ministry had grown more infirm because its members could not resolve whether to lead an oligarchic or popular government.

Hobhouse was no help to the Government because he, too, shared the dilemma of Whiggism. He had urged the Whigs throughout the 1820's to identify with the people by championing popular causes that would put right the ills within the state. He assumed that there was a natural community of interest among all those willing to end unjust privilege, monopolies, and restrictions. This approach lingered as he tried in 1835 to align the Whigs with Irish and Radical groups, but the resurgence of Whig conservatism turned the Litchfield Compact into little more than a maneuver to oust Peel, not a union of politicians

36. Dorchester, ed., *Recollections*, VI, 29.
37. The Hon. Mrs. Hardcastle, ed., *Life of John, Lord Campbell*, II, 151–53; Gash, *Reaction and Reconstruction*, 183–90.

with a broad reform program. Hobhouse accordingly adjusted his reformist political views to the facts of political life. Aristocratic influence remained strong at a party level and in both Houses of the reformed Parliament. Radicals were by contrast few in numbers in the Commons. Furthermore, the 1837 election confirmed a growing conservative mood in the country as Radicals lost seats while Tories and moderate Whigs gained. To be sure, Hobhouse still favored some measures that would help to maintain a tenuous liaison with liberal groups, but reform put stresses upon a mixed constitution, with oligarchic power successfully checking whatever popular causes were brought before Parliament. Were the Whigs prepared to impose further changes upon the Constitution, the issue Hobhouse posed in 1837, or to strike out along a popular course by championing the ballot or an expanded suffrage, reforms that could conceivably transfer too much power to the masses? Hobhouse stood opposed but had no alternative policy. Instead, he immersed himself in the administrative details of his Indian Office and tried to perpetuate the *status quo* with the Whigs in power. "I am sure you will agree with me," he wrote Lord Holland, "that the lawful use of patronage is to keep the party together as long as we can by distributing favors, not to unworthy persons, but to those worthy persons who are politically serviceable in one way or another." [38]

The ballot question illustrates how and why Hobhouse's liberalism waned. He had supported Hunt's ballot motion of 1830, voted against three later motions of Grote's, and with Melbourne's ban lifted in 1839, he absented himself from the voting on this "open question," which lost, 335–217. He announced in 1830 his strong support of the ballot. "Without it, they [the reformers] could do nothing," *The Examiner* stated, "with it they could accomplish almost anything; and [Hobhouse] would even consent to let the right of voting remain as it was, if he could get election by ballot." [39] In 1835 he favored making the ballot an open question. He approached Russell, who refused. As Hobhouse remembered it:

Later I told Melbourne I thought it ought to be an open question; as well as one or two other questions. He rather combatted

38. Hobhouse to Holland, October 1, 1836, Henry Richard Vassall Fox, third Baron Holland, Papers, Add. MSS 51569, f. 83.
39. *The Examiner*, July 25, 1830.

this, and talked of the mischief of disunion, adding, "Do not let us break up of ourselves."[40]

Hobhouse then voted against Grote's motion, as he did the following year:

I did not consider myself at liberty to vote for any essential change in the system, after being a party—and an active party, too—in carrying our Reform Bill; but I confess then, and I confess now, that I have never heard Mr. Grote's arguments answered satisfactorily. Little interest was excited either in Parliament or the country, by this question.[41]

In 1838 he added:

At the House of Commons today Sir Robert Peel, speaking on the question of the ballot, made what I considered the true objection to that measure—namely, that it would take away influence over the vote which preserves the representative system, in our country, from being of too democratic a character. To this opinion I incline. I think the Ballot before the Reform Bill, and without it, would have been a good measure; but I am not prepared to say the same of it after, and with the Reform Bill. Accordingly, I have never voted for it since the carrying of that measure, although our Liberal friends have always done me the honour to fancy that I have made a sacrifice of my opinions and conscience for the sake either of friendship or of office, and consequently they treated me this time, as they did the last, to an ironical cheer as I walked up the House with the majority, and they confined this distinction to me alone. Never mind.[42]

The Reform Bill was decisive in Hobhouse's thinking. Before its passage he took Hunt's position that the ballot offered voters protection against intimidation at the polls. He believed that the voice of the people must be freely heard, but after the Reform Bill, he accepted Peel's position that the ballot would elevate "the fever of the moment, the popular cry" that often deadened the influence of reason. Peel had stood in the way of reform in 1832 because he foresaw further popular concessions once the principle of change was admitted. Hobhouse had favored reform

40. John Cam Hobhouse, first Baron Broughton, *Some Account of a Long Life*, III, 131–34.

41. Dorchester, ed., *Recollections*, III, 245.

42. Ibid., V, 120–21.

in 1832, but he later supported Peel to prevent those whom he considered enfranchised undesirables from voting freely or entering Parliament. He would not vote for "any essential change in the system" because, like Russell in 1835, the Reform Bill was a final measure. It sufficed to reconcile both the middle class and the working class to aristocratic rule. Another reform would constitute a breach of faith with those who had supported the Great Reform Act as a permanent settlement. "Finality Jack" Russell had proposed the ballot in 1838 as the final political change the nation could expect from the Whigs. Hobhouse thought it was one change too many.

Not surprisingly, Hobhouse took a hostile stand against the working-class protest that grew during the 1830's. During the 1834 London demonstration protesting the transportation of the Tolpuddle laborers who had administered secret oaths, he declared, "Notwithstanding this display of physical force has passed off quietly, a repetition of such scenes is not to be tolerated and I trust something will be done to prevent it." [43] With law and order affirmed, Hobhouse later consented to remit punishment for the "misguided" men, but he thought that John Frost deserved no such clemency after leading a Chartist march on Newport in 1839. Hobhouse and Melbourne agreed that stern measures were needed to resist Chartist revolutionaries, and Hobhouse recalled, "I remarked that, as the object of the Chartists was to knock us on the head and rob us of our property, we might as well arrive at the catastrophe after a struggle as without; we could only fail and we might succeed." [44]

By 1841, Hobhouse's reformism was exhausted. He contended for a political settlement in opposition to the Radicals, who felt their interests had been betrayed. He was insensitive to the harsh lot of the poor, partly because he assumed that the reforms of his Westminster years sufficed to usher in an age of prosperity that would be enjoyed by all. Instead, the extent of poverty and suffering grew—the result of a downturn in the economy. He was apathetic, even resentful to urgent social distress, as if it were an unwarranted intrusion upon the privileged life he led in London. He cared little that Nottingham newspapers were hostile or that working-class leaders were urging voters to reject

43. Ibid., 232.
44. Ibid., 240.

at the next opportunity an M.P. who was so indifferent to their misery.

A brief glimpse of Hobhouse in society during his later political career reflects the comfortable niche he had made within the nation's ruling circles. Exclusive society had again opened to him before his well-connected marriage in 1828. He had rejoined the Holland House circle and was even received at Almack's. The ducal surroundings at Devonshire House struck him in 1827 as "a scene of magnificance which I have never before seen." [45] He enjoyed to the full a social ascent that a Cabinet office made possible in Victorian England. Accounts of concerts and balls at Buckingham Palace and of occasional dinners there, some with only Lord Melbourne as the other guest, crowded his diary. The society of the rich and the up-coming intermingled at Baron de Rothschild's in Piccadilly Terrace where Hobhouse sat next to Disraeli, who "spoke with that sort of confidence which sometimes belongs to men of genius, and sometimes to very impudent pretenders." [46] The Russell Cabinet would occasionally hold informal sessions at Hobhouse's Berkeley Square residence. He rarely entertained large numbers there, but on one occasion in 1849 he included the Duke of Wellington among the two hundred guests invited to his first open house. He much preferred to have close friends or small groups stay at Erle Stoke Park, his country place in Wiltshire. "This place is as handsome as man could desire," William Makepeace Thackeray reported, "the park beautiful, the cuisine and drinks excellent, the landlord most polite and good natured, with a very winning simplicity of manners and bonhommie and the small select party tolerably pleasant." [47] It was impossible for one to recognize in the reposeful, comfortable Hobhouse of mid-century the public man who had once stirred up so much controversy. He suggests something about his political outlook late in life with an account of a morning spent at Macaulay's in 1857:

I breakfasted with Macaulay—his other guests were Ld. Stanhope, Ld. Grenville, Ld. Glenelg, Mr. Senior, M. De Tocque-

45. Ibid., III, 207.

46. Hobhouse, diary, June 16, 1844, Lord Broughton Papers, Add. MSS 43746, f. 172.

47. Thackeray to Mrs. Brookfield, December 26, 1850, Letter 734, in Gordon N. Ray, ed., *The Letters and Private Papers of William Makepeace Thackeray.*

ville & an American gentleman. We had a very agreeable morning. De Tocqueville, a small thin black eyed & black haired middle aged man, was very pleasing and contributed his full share to the talk. Macaulay was eloquent in *broad* French which he spoke intrepedment. He remarked that there had been no addition to the domestic animals since the creation or within historic knowledge. I said there was no mention of cats in Homer. He agreed but said there was a mention of them in the century before Christ. . . . It was a fine sunny morning and we walked on the lawn. De Tocqueville eulogized our gardens & our country life which however he said was perhaps a little too much accomodated to the very wealthy. In France the country life was slower & more retired. We did not talk politics at Macaulay's but I took Glenelg & Senior & Tocqueville in my carriage & then we then had some conversation on the state of England. Mr. Tocqueville found it wonderfully improve materially and otherwise—happy, tranquil, prosperous. I remarked he was right and that we owed much of our happiness to our Queen. Had a bad sovereign been in the throne in 1848 there might have been an outbreak. Tocqueville assented, but added that there was a union here between the upper and lower classes not to be found in France—and whilst that lasted we need fear no revolution. He said the difference between France and England was that in the one all the useful & good works were works of the Government—in England mostly of individuals.[48]

48. Hobhouse, diary, July 6, 1857, Lord Broughton Papers, Add. MSS 43760, f. 134–35.

CHAPTER X

POLITICIAN AND PEER
1842-1852

Although it relieved him of his Cabinet responsibilities, the fall of Melbourne's Government did not remove Hobhouse from the cares of public life. Within a year came the news confirming the annihilation of the Anglo-Indian Army in Afghanistan. There was lurid press coverage of the expedition into Central Asia that had brought death to several thousand soldiers in Himalayan Mountain passes and of the probable fate of hostages, among them women and children, who had been captured by merciless Afghan warriors. Journalists, politicians, and the public at large accused Hobhouse and other Indian authorities of incompetence and deception. In all, 1842 was just about the most unpleasant year in his long political career; time after time, he rose from the Opposition benches to answer those charges, and he also had to face a Select Committee of the Commons on charges of electoral bribery and intimidation at Nottingham. It was a wretched time for one who prided himself as a man of principles.

Hobhouse had always felt that Nottingham was a comedown after representing Westminster, the home of Parliament itself and an area renowned for its "purity of elections." Nottingham had a full measure of the corruption that persisted in English postreform politics.[1] By the system of "thumbing," a worker risked being fired unless he voted as the employer thought fit. Others were abducted and plied with liquor during the "cooping" period prior to the elections. Those who were not victimized exploited others. Thomas Wakefield, an influential Whig electoral agent and local manufacturer, told parliamentary investigators about the "basket money" that Nottingham voters expected from him as elections drew near.[2] Larger bribes were paid off from the money distributed to each ward as a matter of

1. See Norman Gash, *Politics in the age of Peel: a study in the techniques of parliamentary representation, 1830–1850*, 130, 140–44, 234–35, 258–63; *The Examiner*, August 6, 1842.
2. Report from the Committee on Election Proceedings, *Parliamentary Reports*, 1842, V, 163–73.

course. Such blandishments having failed, there was the practice of hiring "lambs" to rough up voters and candidates and destroy property. A Nottingham candidate led a hazardous and expensive life at voting time. But Hobhouse found satisfaction in the fact that the parliamentary seat he gained in the uncontested 1834 election remained secure three years later when he decisively defeated the Tory candidates, Plowden and Twiss.[3] Besides, he had a capable agent, Wakefield, whose work on the scene left him with the simple task of delivering a speech or two in the market square and making a few visits to local committee rooms before returning to London, where he stayed until just before the next election. Hobhouse, however, began to worry as the economic recession during the closing years of the decade intensified the discontent among Nottingham's poor and unemployed. Chartists kept gaining fresh recruits. Local Anti-Poor Law feeling erupted at the by-election of April, 1841; in that election, which was caused by the death of Sir Ronald Ferguson, John Walter, the Tory editor of *The Times*, defeated Sir George Larpent, who was associated with the unpopular Whig measure. Hobhouse made a forboding and sanctimonious appraisal of his own situation a month later:

I must say that no one can have given a more impartial opinion than myself, for I shall not go back to Nottingham, and have a great repugnance to looking elsewhere for a seat. After representing Westminster for so long, and maintaining, I trust, there, and even at Nottingham, a character somewhat above the ordinary level of politicians, I think I should lower myself by dropping down to some notoriously venal constituency, or even by standing a contest for some larger place upon the only terms on which such battles are now fought; for as a Minister I should have no chance at any town where ultra-radical or anti poor-law pledges would be required. The upshot, therefore, may be that I may have no seat, and may retire from office. The general rumor, indeed is that I am to be made a Peer, which is not true, and to which, even if it were offered to me, I have many, I will not say, insuperable, objections.[4]

3. Hobhouse received 2053 votes; Ferguson, 2056; Plowden, 1397; and Twiss, 1396.
4. Lady Dorchester, ed., *Recollections of a Long Life, by Lord Broughton (John Cam Hobhouse) with additional extracts from his private diaries*, VI, 21; Hobhouse, diary, May 7, 1841, John Cam Hobhouse, Lord Broughton, Papers, Add. MSS 56564.

A flurry of correspondence preceded the 1841 general elections. Hobhouse wanted to know the precise positions on the issues he and Larpent, the other Whig candidate, would take, and he rejected a proposal to pay some of Larpent's expenses for what promised to be an unusually costly contest.[5] It was also rowdy, beginning with Hobhouse's opponents parading around town with a cart bearing a man flogging another, a gibe against Hobhouse's retention of corporal punishment while he was Secretary at War. That evening, a gang of bludgeon men roamed the streets attacking his supporters, and on nomination day, the troops were called in to quell the rioting and violence. "I was informed by my friends," Hobhouse later told the parliamentary committee, "that it was not safe for me to walk about, except well guarded, and indeed I was not permitted to do so; and when I did go out by myself, or rather with one or two friends, I was obliged to go by back streets, circuitously, in order to save my life." [6]

Onlookers heard Walter introduce Hobhouse and Larpent as "two game cocks, ready clipped and weighed, their spurs tipped with gold." [7] The allusion was not lost upon the multitude, for both Whig candidates were returned at incredible expense. "Indeed," Hobhouse observed, "had the means by which it was procured been as pure as the cause was good, there would have been just reason for unmingled satisfaction." [8] He and Larpent expended an estimated £12,000; Walter and T. S. Charlton, the Tory candidates, placed at the bottom of the polls after spending nearly another £5,000—a total of some £17,000 lavished upon the 5,400 voters of Nottingham.[9] Within a year Parliament had received two petitions on behalf of Walter praying that, on grounds of corruption, the election should be declared void. A third petition was thereupon submitted as a counterclaim on behalf of Hobhouse and Larpent. Because another election would

---

5. Hobhouse to Wakefield, April 28, June 7, 1841, Wakefield to Hobhouse, June 5, June 8, 1841, Commonwealth Relations Office, Home Miscellaneous Series, 840, f. 107, 136–38. (Subsequent references to the Home Miscellaneous Series in the Commonwealth Relations Office are cited as HMS.)

6. Report from the Committee on Election Proceedings, 157.

7. *Nottingham Mercury*, July 7, 1841.

8. Hobhouse, diary, July 2, 1841, Lord Broughton Papers, Add. MSS 56564.

9. Report from the Committee on Election Proceedings, 77–84, 88; Gash, *Politics in the age of Peel*, 130.

be enormously expensive, the litigants worked out a private agreement just before the appointed parliamentary committee began hearings. They discreetly agreed to drop all petitions arising out of the election and to pay £1,000 to the petitioning parties as reimbursement for their expenses; within four days, one Nottingham seat was to be vacated, and Walter would stand unopposed by leading Whigs in the borough. Finally, Hobhouse signed a promissory note for £4,000 that was deposited in a London bank and that would be forfeited if two referees found the terms of the agreement violated.[10]

Larpent resigned his seat the day before Roebuck reopened his campaign for electoral purity by telling the Commons that several discreditable compromises had followed the 1841 elections. He was substantially accurate in alleging that the Nottingham petitioners had dropped their charges in order to stave off an investigation into the gross bribery they all had practiced. With Peel's backing, a select committee was appointed on May 9 to inquire into compromises at Nottingham and elsewhere, not with the aim of deciding upon the legality or illegality of the transactions, Roebuck averred, but "to elicit and lay before the House all the facts rather with a view to expose the evils of a system, than by any direct expression of their own opinion to inculpate individuals." Hobhouse's parliamentary seat was not at stake, only some embarrassment and lost reputation. Testifying in June, he explained that both the London security note and the reimbursement of £1,000 to the petitioners came from his own pocket. He and Larpent also paid £7,000 each for election expenses, but Hobhouse denied having communicated with anyone about how the money was used. When asked if he knew that a large sum of his money was employed to purchase votes, he replied, "Most assuredly not!" which left an incredible conclusion that after seven years he was unaware of the bribery in Nottingham. He had in fact queried his agent Wakefield about the rising costs of representing his constituency: £1,800 in 1834; £4,000 in 1837; £7,000 for his share in 1841.[11] The interstices of Victorian politics had little room for electoral purity, a principle Hobhouse once vowed to uphold at Westminster.

10. Report from the Committee on Election Proceedings, 146–50; Gash, *Politics in the age of Peel*, 258–59.
11. Report from the Committee on Election Proceedings, 145; Hobhouse to Wakefield, June 4, 1837, HMS, 843, f. 120.

Nottingham politics may have been distasteful, but Hobhouse was not above acting in accord with the prevailing assumptions of his times.[12] He retained his seat for another five years, but only once did he address Parliament on an issue affecting Nottingham. In 1846, he spoke in opposition to Thomas Duncombe, M.P. for Finsbury, who proposed to curtail night work for adults and abolish child labor in all lace-making establishments—the larger factories, as well as domestic work shops where hand-operated machines were commonly used.[13] Earlier parliamentary reports had painted a grim picture of working conditions in the trade, especially for children, who were employed at all hours of the day or night in ill-ventilated, damp, and overcrowded workshops. In "these wretched places," read the second report, children were "treated as if they were mere brute animals"; most working-class children of Nottingham reportedly suffered "from Scrofola, indigestion, and defective eyesight" after exposure to such conditions at an early age.[14] Hobhouse, once the leading parliamentary spokesman for factory reform, stood opposed to Duncombe's corrective legislation because he felt that the protests of more than twenty-five lace manufacturers should not be ignored. Indeed, he had excluded regulation of that industry from his 1831 bill for the same reason. Also, the accounts he had received from Nottingham and elsewhere suggested that conditions were not as bad as the interventionists alleged. They had reported scenes of appalling demoralization, whereas he knew of one large factory employing more than two hundred children that

12. Thomas Hobhouse, his half-brother, deplored Roebuck's inquiry and pleaded existing practices or assumptions in one letter of June 3, 1842: "Why appoint a committee to inquire into the existence of a practice which is admitted to be of many years standing by Sir Robert Peel himself?" He later adds that it is wrong to stigmatize as "corrupt compromises" certain "arrangements which violate no law of the land nor privileges of the House of Commons and which have an easy explanation in the expenses and uncertainty of the trial of controverted elections." Lord Broughton Papers, Add. MSS 36471, f. 203, 367, 377, 392.

13. Hansard Parliamentary Debates, 3d series, LXXXVI (1846), cols. 930–33.

14. Appendix to Second Report of Commissioners for inquiring into the Employment and Conditions of Children (Trades and Manufacturers) with Reports and Evidence from Sub-Commissioners, Parliamentary Reports, 1843 (431), XIV.XV, 8; see also Roy A. Church, Economic and Social Change in a Midland Town: Victorian Nottingham, 1815–1900, chap. IV.

had only two charges of misconduct brought against it in an entire decade. Even if universal feeling favored factory legislation, Hobhouse declared, Duncombe's proposals, which would curtail adult night labor, as well as all child labor in the factories, were still too broad. Because such a multiplicity of purposes could adversely affect working conditions, the regulations might check the extension of advanced steam power to the smaller lace establishments, thereby making their goods less competitive on the world market and causing greater unemployment. Having advanced these and other prudent considerations, Hobhouse was relieved to see that Duncombe's bill of 1846 was not enacted.

The severe economic recession that afflicted Nottingham the following year was instrumental in Hobhouse's electoral defeat. By spring, at least 1,000 people were in the workhouse that Nassau Senior had earlier described as positively the worst he had ever seen, and at least 3,000 people received outrelief. Local authorities alerted the yeomanry to the danger of serious rioting over prices that put food beyond the means of most impoverished workers. Their despair gave way to hope when Feargus O'Conner returned to Nottingham in 1847 to rally the dissatisfied to the Chartist cause. Its appeal had not been lost upon other local politicians. During the by-election of 1842, Joseph Sturge, the Quaker reformer, had acquired support from Chartists and prominent Radical Whigs by including five of the Charter points in his platform. He narrowly lost a contest that was later voided when bribery charges were proven against the victor, John Walter. The vacant seat next went to Thomas Gisborne, the Whig candidate who had given his enthusiastic endorsement to all points of the Charter. His radicalism, however, did not survive his victory at the polls, and the local Whig-Chartist alliance that began so promisingly ended with O'Conner's public repudation of Gisborne.[15]

O'Conner was urging Nottingham voters to show their disgust with the Whigs by casting out the two standing "do-nothing kid glove reformers." From London, Hobhouse sent inquiries to Wakefield about the threat Chartism posed in the coming election. Wakefield's reply suggested that Hobhouse would have to use every available means to hold his seat against mounting opposition. He refused. Mindful of his own narrow escape in

15. See Church, *Change in a Midland Town*, chap. VI.

1842 and of Walter's subsequent unseating because of bribery, Hobhouse sent word that "nothing would induce me again to pay more than the legal expenses of an election and that, if more than these are expected from me, I will at once retire from the town."[16]

Hobhouse stood for Nottingham on his own terms and lost decisively. He finished last, receiving 974 votes. Gisborne, who also was not returned, received 1,081 votes. The younger John Walter, with 1,840 votes, topped the polls, but his program was never revealed because he failed to appear in London. Chartists everywhere cheered the news that O'Conner, who had gotten 1,830 votes, had gained a parliamentary seat by placing second. *The Times* was at a loss to explain the Tory-Chartist victory in a traditionally Whig stronghold, "as surprising an occurrance as could possibly arise from the mere movements of human opinion and feeling."[17] The pro-Tory *Nottingham Journal* attributed the Whig defeat to Nonconformist abstentions, a form of protest against the Anglican Church's control over education, which a recent Government proposal upheld.[18] Hobhouse, however, thought his defeat was a simple matter of his refusing to bribe voters. "I persisted in the determination," he told Grey, "and the consequence was, that those who did what I would not do came in."[19]

The more fundamental reasons escaped him. Hobhouse's lackluster election campaign offered no solution for present difficulties, only reminders of past achievements. He cited his own factory legislation of 1831 and his role in parliamentary reform, "one of the greatest changes in civilized society,"[20] but the idle workers and men who had small businesses were interested less in constitutional issues or past performances than in solving immediate bread-and-butter questions. O'Conner, claiming to understand the needs and wishes of the people, vigorously campaigned against the two wealthy Whigs. Their past voting record he found most questionable; Hobhouse had supported Poulett Thomson's 1836 bill lowering the age qualification from

16. Hobhouse to Wakefield, March 22, 1847, HMS, 845, f. 87.
17. *The Times*, July 31, 1847.
18. *Nottingham Journal*, July 29, 1847.
19. Hobhouse to Lord Grey, August 2, 1847, Lord Broughton Papers, Add. MSS 43751, f. 10.
20. *Nottingham Mercury*, July 30, 1847; *Nottingham Journal*, July 29, 1847.

13 to 12 years for children receiving the protection of an eight-hour day,[21] he and Gisborne had opposed extending factory legislation to lace workers, just recently Hobhouse had absented himself from voting on the ten-hour day, and Gisborne had opposed the 1847 measure altogether. O'Conner then proposed a property tax and increased land ownership for workingmen. Nonconformists were pleased that he favored church disestablishment and nonsectarian education. Local Tory voters overlooked these Radical proposals in their desire to avenge the electoral agreement violated by those prominent local Whigs who had petitioned Parliament to unseat Walter in 1843. His son had now reaped the rewards from the Tory-Whig feud in Nottingham.

Local politics and economic distress had brought about a stunning Whig defeat at Nottingham, and there was talk about replacing Hobhouse in the Cabinet. The senior John Walter had suggested such action in July, 1846, when he learned that Hobhouse had been reappointed to the Indian Board of Control. *The Times* announced that Russell had made a serious error by again inflicting upon India the minister associated with an earlier disaster. The post called for an able administrator and statesman, and *The Times* observed:

But can any person say that even an approximation to the requisite standard is to be found in the gentleman now selected for this appointment? If Sir John Hobhouse contributes neither a serviceable following nor acknowledged ability to the resources of the newly-formed Cabinet, in what quarter are we to search for his peculiar qualifications—what proof is offered of his capacity for an office so mightily influential for good or evil? Unfortunately, all the evidence of his unfitness—evidence which, as far as it goes suggests most strongly the impropriety of the appointment. The name of Sir John Hobhouse is connected with the greatest disaster that ever befell our arms in the East.[22]

Russell had in fact hesitated on Hobhouse's appointment, but Hobhouse was a member of an old team, and sacrificing him to critics meant making a hard task harder by adding a new, untried member to the Cabinet. Russell preferred an unpopular but

21. *Hansard*, 3d series, XXXIII (1836), col. 788.
22. *The Times*, July 4, 1846. Hobhouse's diary for June 27 and July 2, 1846, reports on Russell's reluctance to give him his old Cabinet post. Lord Broughton Papers, Add. MSS 43749.

loyal colleague to a rash, ambitious newcomer who might cause offense. Besides, Hobhouse was useful because the Whigs could cite him as proof to the nation that the party awarded high office even to those formerly associated with radicalism. At least Hobhouse was "safe"; he was still a favorite at Court; and Palmerston gave strong backing to one who saw eye to eye with him on Indian and foreign affairs. After all these considerations another parliamentary seat was found for him at Harwich.

It was one of the smallest and most corrupt constituencies in the country. Le Marchant was dismayed after spending £1,000 on less than 300 voters and yet finishing last in the 1841 election.[23] The triumph of two Tory candidates made it clear that government patronage, which had weighed most heavily when Harwich was a treasury borough, had been supplanted by direct bribery as a decisive factor at the polls.

Hobhouse by 1848 was an old hand at dealing with constituencies open to the highest bidder. He nevertheless felt some caution was called for, especially when J. C. Herries, the experienced Tory politician, had maintained a hold on the borough for nearly two decades before unsuccessfully seeking a less expensive seat elsewhere. He was also aware that a parliamentary inquiry which might result in Harwich's disfranchisement, a fate that had recently befallen Sudbury. Although Wortley, the chairman of the standing committee, upon being sounded out by Palmerston, felt that electoral practices at Harwich did not warrant any investigation, Le Marchant advised Hobhouse not to see any voter without a witness lest trumped-up charges be preferred against him later. Bribery assumed more sophisticated forms during the contest, which Hobhouse won by 132 votes to John Manners Sutton's 127. Hobhouse paid £120 14s. for 142 dinners, the regatta cup cost another £50, the financial needs of the local Mechanics' Institute needed attention, and after the support Hobhouse received from the Eastern Counties Railroad Company, so did the matter of a steam-packet service to Rotterdam.[24] Even with all the concerns and costs, however, the constituency that Hobhouse retained throughout his remaining years in the Commons was far less costly than Nottingham.

23. Gash, *Politics in the age of Peel*, 259, 452–55.

24. On the Harwich election see Palmerston to Hobhouse, March 23, 1848, Le Marchant to Hobhouse, March 24, 1848, Lord Broughton Papers, Add. MSS 36471, f. 436, 439, 447, 456, 466, 467.

His role in Russell's Cabinet was suggested in Prince Albert's appraisal of the Government upon its inception in 1846. "There is the *Grey* party," he wrote, "consisting of Lord Grey, Lord Clarendon, Sir George Grey, and Mr. Wood; they are against Lord Lansdowne, Lord Minto, Lord Auckland, and Sir John Hobhouse, stigmatising them as old women. Lord John leans entirely to the last named gentleman." [25] The divided Whig councils amounted to a reshuffling of Melbourne's Government, with the same problems confronting its members as before. Radicals once again stood on the left, urging government retrenchment and parliamentary reform as part of a forward, popular policy. Within the Cabinet itself Clarendon called upon the Whigs to "constitute a government fairly representing the industrial mind and conservative progress of the country." [26] He thought that this could be achieved by incorporating Peelites and Free Trade Radicals, rather than the aristocratic and landed interests. Hobhouse stood squarely among the Cabinet group favoring a standstill policy that, by keeping institutions intact, would preserve aristocratic favor and quite likely win over the Peelites. Russell himself was ambivalent about recruitment and policy; he would set out toward the Radical camp and then stop abruptly because his colleagues protested or because he feared that any Radical movements would reunite Peelites and Protectionists against the Government. Thus, Cobden's appointment was considered and abandoned, and consequently he and Hume instituted a separate Radical party of over fifty members. More of Russell's time and effort went to recruiting the leading Peelites, who remained independent supporters and occasional critics. As Clarendon had forewarned, the attempts to conciliate too many irreconcilable interests gradually lost Russell what support he had. Once again a Whig Government shifted about until it lost all momentum.

Russell fell back upon various tactics he had tried before. Such was his 1850 proposal to create a number of life peers in order to nullify the hostile majority Stanley and Brougham commanded in the Lords. This time Hobhouse refused to join the

25. Albert, Memorandum, July 6, 1846, in Arthur C. Benson and Viscount Esher, eds., *The Letters of Queen Victoria; a selection from Her Majesty's correspondence between the years 1837 and 1861, published by the authority of His Majesty the King*, II, 102.
26. Quoted in Norman Gash, *Reaction and Reconstruction in English Politics, 1832–1852*, 193, from Sir Herbert Maxwell, *The Life and Letters of George William Frederick, fourth Earl of Clarendon*, I, 265–67.

war cry against the peers. In one of his rare moments of force he voiced his total disagreement with those Cabinet members who felt the House of Lords needed reforming after having sunk very low in public estimation. Russell's rash proposal, Hobhouse declared, would "entirely alter the character of the House of Lords, and, *pro tanto*, change the constitution of the country." [27] Similar considerations weighed against Russell's halfhearted recommendations to reform Parliament. "I was very much struck by this second proposal of organic change," Hobhouse observed early in 1851, "without any apparent necessity, except the unfounded expectations of some weak men may be called a necessity." [28] A year later he again "urged the folly of being forced to do what we thought wrong, because half a dozen writers in newspapers urged us to do it. I did not believe the people generally cared about the Bill or called for reform." [29]

At midcentury, Hobhouse was more than ever certain about the solid strength of the existing political structure in which he held authority. He had the satisfying knowledge that England alone had been spared revolutionary upheaval in 1848. The early events of that momentous year naturally filled him with alarm, beginning with the "dreadful" news in February of Louis Philippe's abdication. Hobhouse disassociated the deposed French monarch, whose only apparent offense was his refusal to threaten the rights of his propertied subjects by making the ballot available to the masses, from Guizot, the Premier who Hobhouse thought condemnable for his hostile foreign policy and for prohibiting the Reform Banquets organized by discontented Parisians. Metternich's downfall the following month was "marvellous news," heralding as it did "the rise of Germany and the freedom of Italy." [30] By April, Hobhouse was afraid that the revolutionary tide might reach England, and he anxiously recorded "the expectation of some struggle or disastrous event," perhaps in Ireland or even in London, where the impending Chartist meeting could conceivably produce an insurrection that would reduce the capital to "havoc and destruction." [31] He and other members of the Cabinet studied large maps of the city

27. Dorchester, ed., *Recollections*, VI, 262–64.
28. Ibid., 267–68.
29. Ibid., 294.
30. Ibid., 211.
31. Ibid., 212, 214.

while Wellington discussed the key points at which troops could intercept Chartist mobs. Henry St. George Tucker, chairman of the board of directors of the East India Company, reported plenty of muskets, bayonets, and cutlasses to repel any attack upon India House.[32] On the day of the procession, Hobhouse made his way to Cannon Row, where he found the staff upset over the absence of arms or troops there. He later described his own reactions:

> I cannot say I felt quite easy, separated as I was from my children, and recollecting that my door had been chalked, as also had Lord Grey's and Labouchere's and my brother Tom's. Lord John Russell had a force of constables in his house. I sat down to office business, not expecting, but thinking it by no means improbable that I should hear discharges of musketry or cannon from the other side of the river. Indeed, the slamming of doors made me start once or twice, and I looked at Westminster Bridge to see whether it was crowded.[33]

That afternoon brought the welcomed news that the meeting had broken up and the procession abandoned, thus ending "this far feared Monday, the events of which Lionel Rothschild said were more important for England than the most glorious victory she had ever gained!" The mood of doubt and uncertainly continued to linger, and Hobhouse became convinced "that our institutions want reforms and that the conditions of the labouring classes requires careful attention." [34]

Such concerns were quickly forgotten during the political tranquility and unparalleled prosperity the 1850's brought. Hobhouse now assumed an almost Podsnappian pride for an enduring Constitution that made England blessed to the direct exclusion of other countries as there might happen to be. In June, 1850, Palmerston's address to the Commons, which was much more than a defense of his support of Don Pacifico, understandably held Hobhouse spellbound—perhaps "the most effective and extraordinary speech I ever heard in my life." [35] It was an eloquent expression of Hobhouse's own beliefs that liberty was compatible with order, that individual freedom was reconcilable with obedience to the law, and that British honor and universal

32. Henry St. George Tucker to Hobhouse, April 8, 1848, HMS, 852, f. 1.
33. Dorchester, ed., *Recollections*, VI, 215.
34. Ibid., 220.
35. Ibid., 257.

justice were synonymous. The Great Exhibition the following
year provided the material counterpart to the new mood Palmerston had evoked. "All former apprehensions were forgotten,"
commented Hobhouse, after observing "the good conduct and
good temper of the thousands within and the hundreds of thousands without" the Crystal Palace. He was deeply moved by
those opening-day ceremonies, with the "rapturous reception of
the Queen and the Duke of Wellington as the procession walked
through the long avenue of happy human beings." [36] And he had
no reason to doubt that the material progress so vividly evident
on this occasion would remain unbroken, provided the nation
continued to entrust authority to the enlightened minority. A
leap in the direction of democracy was at this point in his political career outside the ken of Hobhouse's political understanding.

At the Crystal Palace ceremonies he sat to the right of the
royal family as Baron Broughton of Broughton de Gyfford, the
title conferred upon him by the Russell Government in which he
served. Hobhouse assessed what the peerage meant in terms of
his political position at the time:

I did not ask for this. I accepted it, not for the sake of being in
the House of Lords, but of being in Parliament. I should not
have secured this otherwise. I cannot stand for a county—I am
a Free Trader; I could not be a candidate for a large town constituency—I am not a radical; nor for a small constituency, for
I will not repeat my Nottingham delinquencies; I could not be
again returned for Harwich on the honourable terms of the
last election. A dissolution would have left me in private life;
to avoid this I have to go to the House of Lords, where I may
not be altogether useless to my party and my country! [37]

Although his elevation to the House of Lords had rescued
Hobhouse from a political no man's land, his days of office were
numbered. He was given a year's reprieve at the Board of Control only because Sir James Graham was unwilling to join the
shaky Russell Cabinet as Hobhouse's replacement. Hobhouse
thus participated in the many Cabinet deliberations that Palmerston's foreign policy occasioned throughout 1851. In November,
the objections of his colleagues and Russell's formal prohibition
caused the Foreign Minister to give up his proposed reception of

36. Ibid., 279–80.
37. Ibid., 271.

the Hungarian patriot, Kossuth. A few days later, Palmerston again offended the Court by graciously accepting the addresses from Finsbury and Islington Radicals in which the Austrian and Russian rulers were described as despots, assassins, and odious tyrants. In this situation, he got strong backing from Hobhouse. When Lord Grey proposed to send a Cabinet memorandum to the Queen repudiating Palmerston's actions, Hobhouse protested; he "looked on the whole complaint as a continuation of the *set* made against Palmerston. I *had* disapproved his intention to receive Kossuth as strongly as any one, but this was quite a different matter." [38] It was one thing to offend Continental monarchs by officially welcoming a revolutionary leader; it was another to deny the Foreign Minister's right to receive opinions from Englishmen on the subject.

The Cabinet agreed that Russell himself should speak to the Queen and smooth over matters, the only practicable choice in view of Palmerston's immense popularity. That popularity did not continue much longer, because shortly afterwards Palmerston managed to affront his admiring public, as well as the Court and Cabinet, by expressing his sincere approval of Louis Napoleon's *coup d'état* to the French ambassador. Liberals were deeply shocked that the man who had established a reputation for opposing Continental autocrats now welcomed the resurgence of Bonapartism across the Channel. This time, Palmerston had gone too far without consulting his colleagues or informing the Court. Hobhouse learned of his dismissal on Christmas Eve; apparently, Russell and Victoria had rid themselves of Palmerston without endangering the Government or making the offender a martyr.

Hobhouse soon thought otherwise. He foresaw the Government's fall early in 1852 as the sensation caused by Palmerston's dismissal superseded concern over Louis Napoleon's plebiscite election. Lord Grey likewise surmised at the next Cabinet meeting that Palmerston would prove a formidable opponent. In an unsuccessful bid at strengthening his Government, Russell finally asked Hobhouse to step down from the Board of Control and make way for Fox Maule. Hobhouse accordingly retired from the Government that February. He was honored at Windsor and invested with the Order of the Bath at a Buckingham

38. Ibid., 289-90.

Palace ceremony: "H. M. smiled when she gave me her hand to kiss for the third time in the ceremony: a very unusual honour, as I was told!" [39] Upon this parting note Hobhouse's active political career ended; however, his contemporary and favorite, Lord Palmerston, contemplated no such retirement. Within two months of his dismissal he had brought down the Russell Government over the Militia Bill. For well into the next decade, Hobhouse watched approvingly from the sidelines as Palmerston left behind his Whig colleagues of old and rose to undisputed power and prestige.

39. Ibid., 301.

CHAPTER XI

PRESIDENT OF THE BOARD OF CONTROL

Many early nineteenth-century English liberals, among them Benthamites like James Mill and Whigs like Macaulay, were vitally involved with justifying and improving the British Empire in India. Hobhouse, as President of the Board of Control during the Melbourne and Russell ministries, was similarly concerned with India. He had to decide whether he would encourage Indian self-government as he had for people elsewhere, how he would view the ultimate purposes of British rule in India, whether he would encourage Anglicization or Indian traditional culture, and which forces or other individuals involved in Indian administration would influence him. Finally, he had to deal with the most complex problem of the conflict implicit in Pitt's concept of dyarchy whereby the East India Company and the Crown ruled jointly. British policy toward India in the decades preceding the Great Mutiny was bound up with the issues Hobhouse encountered.

Hobhouse's office dated from Pitt's India Act of 1784, which created a body of six commissioners empowered "to superintend, direct and control all acts, operations and concerns which in any wise relate to the civil or military government or revenues of the British territorial possessions in the East Indies." [1] The commissioners originally included a Secretary of State, the Chancellor of the Exchequer, and four Privy Councillors—an arrangement intended to give the Government a decisive voice in Indian affairs. In time, the Board's duties were entrusted to the President, and the other five commissioners gradually assumed ex officio status. In 1833, the President was required to have the signature of only one ex officio commissioner, in addition to his own, for all important documents prepared by the Board. There was also a

1. Quoted in B. B. Misra, *The Central Administration of the East India Company, 1793–1834*, 30, from 24 Geo. 3, c. 25, s. 6; see also Peter Auber, *An analysis of the constitution of the East India company, and of the laws passed by Parliament for the government of their affairs, at home and abroad*, 60–85.

sizable staff to deal with its growing amount of business. It consisted, in Hobhouse's day, of two chief secretaries, usually Members of Parliament, a number of assistant and junior clerks, and assistant secretaries for each of six departments—Secret and Political, Revenue, Financial, Public, Military, and Judicial. The selection of the Board's personnel was to some extent a family concern, with one or another of Hobhouse's brothers acting as private secretary to the President. Some staff members were especially influential inasmuch as Hobhouse often consulted them about points of detail and broader matters of policy. Thus, William Cabell, assistant secretary in the Secret and Political Department, become a key figure in the ill-fated Afghan expedition of the late 1830's. James Wilson, editor of *The Economist* and chairman of the council of the Anti–Corn Law League, played an important part in Indian commercial and business matters from the time Hobhouse appointed him chief secretary in 1848.

Hobhouse's duties and responsibilities were manifold. He was the Cabinet spokesman on India and a chief consultant for the Governor General at Calcutta. Even so, his Cabinet colleagues could overrule a decision reached by the Board, or an Indian official could act independently or even contrary to London's expressed wishes. It was difficult to coordinate action in times of emergency because three months elapsed before an Indian authority received the Government's reply to one of his inquiries. Even if the various parts in the unwieldy administrative machinery worked smoothly, voices of dissent might arise in Parliament, perhaps from Evangelicals protesting idolatry or from spokesmen on behalf of commercial interests. Hobhouse had the task of responding to these criticisms or demands. Of course he faced the business of daily administration, with letters dictated to many officials and private communiqués addressed to important Indian authorities. Also, he had to reply to inquiries about the availability of assignments in India: A nephew of the Marquis of Anglesey desired an artillery appointment; Henry Labouchere wanted a cadetship for a relative; Sir Francis Baring, the Earl of Carlisle, and the Countess Grey all put in good words for their friends; Sir Charles Wood suggested a legal post for John Arthur Roebuck.[2] There were the irksome tasks of bestowing military honors and arranging the pay scale of troops. Not

2. HMS, 847, f. 69, 81, 97, 181.

the least of Hobhouse's concerns was his relations with the East India Company.

The company no longer held the powers and privileges that existed during its eighteenth-century heyday. It was denied of all commercial functions in 1833, and its surviving administrative capacity was subject to various restrictions or procedures prescribed by Pitt's India Act. These were interpreted with ever-widening latitude, to the periodic dismay of the twenty-four directors who constituted the company's executive body. The Board had access to all company papers and held the right of approving or rejecting dispatches the directors prepared for India. Hobhouse's predecessor, the younger Charles Grant, had obtained judicial backing when the directors protested alterations he had made in a dispatch involving a commercial firm's claim against an Indian prince, an area previously held to be beyond the Board's scope. The President could also order the directors to prepare drafts on various subjects, and cases of default after two weeks gave him the power to send out a dispatch in the company's name. Provisions in Pitt's Act also covered "secret" matters that required confidential communication between the Board and authorities in India. In such instances the President sent a dispatch to a secret committee of three directors who were compelled to forward the document and were barred from divulging its contents. During the 1820's, Lord Ellenborough made every conceivable item of Indian administration a "secret" matter. The directors thus found themselves in the unenviable position of being responsible legally for a wide range of Board decisions. Henry St. George Tucker, a company director and chairman, quite accurately summed up the diminished power of the company in 1833 when he described its role as "a screen between the Government and the British People." [3]

Hobhouse lost no time in asserting his authority over the directors. The issue of replacing Lord William Bentinck as Governor General arose shortly after Hobhouse assumed the presidency. Previously, the directors had successfully upheld their right to approve a ministerial candidate. They accordingly accepted in 1835 Lord Heytesbury, upon the recommendation of

3. John W. Kaye, ed., *Memorials of Indian Government selected from the papers of Henry St. George Tucker*, 47. The waning power of the company is traced in C. H. Philips, *The East India Company, 1784–1834;* see also Misra, *The Central Administration of the East India Company.*

Peel's short-lived Government. The parties involved then learned that Hobhouse had cancelled the appointment because His Majesty's current Government would be held responsible for an official not of its own choosing. Next, without any prior consultation with India House, the Government persuaded the King to accept its own nominee, Lord Auckland. The directors received the news with "utmost surprise and concern"; obviously, they thought, party politics was taking precedence over their privilege of vetoing a Government nomination. However, the series of recent reverses had drained any willingness on the part of the directors to resist, and they finally acquiesced in sending Lord Auckland to India.[4]

The directors' power waned further as Hobhouse advanced his own position in Indian administration throughout the following years. He channeled communications directly to his own office by repeatedly urging higher Indian authorities to address all communiqués only to himself. As an extra precaution he ordered the secret committee to forward papers to his own office immediately upon arrival, thereby depriving the three directors of copies for their files.[5] Hobhouse even went so far as to deny the secret committee's right to record protests or dissents against orders he forced upon them. It would "create and perpetuate differences amongst parties," he argued; besides, the secret committee, "being compelled by law to give their formal signature to dispatches . . . have therefore no responsibility from which it is proper to relieve by the expediency of recording adverse protests."[6] Tucker, who was then chairman, responded that he found Hobhouse's reasoning both spurious and dangerous, for he was reducing a group of legally responsible directors to the status of "mere unreflecting automata."[7] Hobhouse impatiently terminated further discussions by announcing that so marked a difference of opinions made it unbecoming on his part to prolong them. His peremptory dismissal underscored the subordinate role the directors then held in Indian administration, a situation

4. Hobhouse to the King, May 1, 1835, John Cam Hobhouse, Lord Broughton, Papers, Add. MSS 36473, f. 13–14; William IV to Hobhouse, May 2, 1835, Chairman to Hobhouse, May 6, 1835, HMS, 833, f. 4, 8.
5. Hobhouse to Dalhousie, May 7, 1850, Lord Broughton Papers, Add. MSS 36469, f. 17–18; HMS, 859, f. 275–79.
6. Hobhouse to Tucker September 9, 1846, HMS, 850, f. 86.
7. Tucker to Hobhouse, September 8, 1846, HMS, 850, f. 21.

Hobhouse summed up in this revealing draft of a letter for Lord Dalhousie's edification:

In fact the Court of Directors and the Secret Committee are but formalities: the former may be compelled at any time to write what the President of the Board chooses; the latter *always* do sign what the President sends them for transmission to India. All that either one or the other can do when they dislike a dispatch, is to protest; and if they wish to make the dissents public, to get some meddlesome gentleman to move for the production of them either in the Court of Directors or in Parliament. But even then the President has the power of refusing to give any papers connected with the Secret Committee; and, if the Government has a majority in Parliament, may easily dispose of any motion to that effect.[8]

The system of checks and balances was operating against the directors, but they were not entirely subservient to the Government. There were occasions when they could muster up enough strength to check a course of action the Government proposed. Tucker occasionally reminded his colleagues about the effectiveness of passive resistance and public protests. James Weir Hogg, another chairman and member of the secret committee, often threatened to bring a disputed issue before the Tory Opposition. The directors found some consolation in retaining the power of recall, a privilege they exercised in 1844 against the Governor General, Lord Ellenborough. And no Government risked the charge of corrupt influence by tampering with the company's ultimate control over patronage. Its role had declined greatly, but the company still remained a factor in Indian administration.

In taking leave of the directors before sailing for India in 1835, Lord Auckland told them how much he welcomed "an opportunity of doing good for his fellow creatures, of promoting education and knowledge, of improving the administration of justice in India, of extending the blessings of good government and happiness to millions of her people."[9] His pronouncements were attuned to an age when Indian authorities saw themselves entrusted with the task of renovating along Western lines a land long sunk in despotism and superstition. Liberals, humanitarians, and Evangelicals—while differing in their approaches to

8. Hobhouse to Dalhousie, October 30, 1849, HMS, 859, f. 213–14.
9. *The Times*, July 16, 1835.

Indian reform—all applauded those measures recently enacted during the viceroyalty of Auckland's predecessor, Lord William Bentinck: the improvement of administrative systems and financial affairs, the prohibition of such repugnant customs as suttee and female infanticide, the abolition of corporal punishment in the sepoy army, and Bentinck's exercise of only a nominal control over the press, which was a prelude to the curtailment of censorship.[10] Macaulay found him a staunch supporter when he began his duties in 1833 as legal member on the Supreme Council. By the time Hobhouse assumed the presidency, however, opposition to some recent changes had arisen. William IV, for one, urged immediate censure and public disavowal of the curtailment of flogging. He also joined the directors in protesting the abolition of press censorship by Sir Charles Metcalfe, the acting Governor General. Hobhouse prevailed upon the Cabinet to await Auckland's opinions on these matters before taking action. This recurrent feature of Indian administration, whereby the home authorities stood aside and allowed a man on the scene to arbitrate or decide vexing issues, in this instance served the cause of reformers. Auckland informed Hobhouse that he could trace no injurious effects from the two recent changes, and he urged the Cabinet to follow a consistent policy by allowing them to remain.[11]

Hobhouse had also "earnestly entreated at Lord Melbourne's desire" that Auckland "keep Babington Macaulay a little more quiet." Any headlong rush into further legal and other reforms would ensure endless disputes with the directors and Parliament, "to say nothing of the King," Hobhouse added, "who somehow or another has been taught to take a very lively and troublesome interest in Indian affairs." A dispatch from Calcutta likewise expressed misgivings about Macaulay. "He has always loved to provoke than to conciliate the antagonists . . . in the council," Auckland reported, "and his great defect is exaggeration with which, when provoked to controversy, he states his own views

10. On Bentinck's work in India, see George D. Bearce, "Lord William Bentinck: the Application of Liberalism to India," *Journal of Modern History*, 29 (September, 1956), 234–46.

11. John Cam Hobhouse, first Baron Broughton, *Some Account of a Long Life*, III, 158, 180; Hobhouse to Auckland, November 7, 1836, HMS, 837, f. 180.

and opinions." [12] Auckland did absolve him from the many faults ascribed by British residents who were in a furor over the so-called Black Act of 1836, one of Macaulay's major steps toward establishing equality of law in India. The measure had placed all British residents outside Calcutta under the civil jurisdiction of provincial company courts in which Indian judges might preside. Auckland warmly endorsed the change, as did various board, company, and Indian advisers with whom Hobhouse consulted. John Stuart Mill's eloquent memorandum saw the very existence of the Empire in India dependent upon preserving "the character of being more just and disinterested than the native rulers and being united among ourselves." Hobhouse included his own opinions in an abstract of a speech he prepared in defense of the principle of equality of the law. "The natives indeed needed protection," he noted in his speech before the Commons, "and it was right the settlers should be warned before hand under what law they were to live." Furthermore, the English petitioners were actually seeking "to bribe odious privileges and distinctions—to make discriminations of race." [13]

Macaulay requested Hobhouse's support in the education controversy, which had raged for a number of years. He saw disputants at Calcutta clearly divided into conservative and reform camps, the former including "the most distinguished of the servants of the Company" and the other having "the ablest, most active, and most public-spirited of the young men." The issues resolved themselves into one great choice: "Newton or Ptolemy, the Vedas or Adam Smith, the Mahabharat or Milton, the sun around the earth or the earth around the sun, the medicine of the middle ages or the medicine of the nineteenth century!" [14] A few weeks later the directors presented their views in a draft dispatch that Mill had prepared to refute Macaulay's famous

12. Hobhouse to Auckland, June 30, 1836, HMS, 833, f. 101–3; Auckland to Hobhouse, June 20, 1836, Lord Broughton Papers, Add. MSS 36473, f. 70–78, and HMS, 836, f. 106–8.
13. Mill, Memorandum, January, 1838, Lord Broughton Papers, Add. MSS 36468, f. 401–7; see George D. Bearce, *British Attitudes Towards India, 1784–1858*, 292. Hobhouse's comments, Lord Broughton Papers, Add. MSS 36468, f. 411–15; see also *Hansard Parliamentary Debates*, 3d series, XLI (1838), cols. 1145–54.
14. Macaulay to Hobhouse, September 14, 1835, Lord Broughton Papers, Add. MSS 47227, f. 176–77.

minute on Indian education. Hobhouse's point-by-point critique left no doubt about where he stood in the controversy. He did not think Macaulay had acted rashly, because "some changes are more safe by being sudden." The superseded system did not work well; it merely reared a group of scholars who were not qualified for any "useful occupation" and encouraged the printing of many volumes "which never have and never will leave the warehouse." With the new system, many natives could elevate themselves above the level of their countrymen under a program that appropriated all educational funds for Western learning. Contrary to the claims in a company dispatch, Indians would not find themselves uprooted or degraded by imposing upon them an alien culture; rather, they would leap at the opportunity to acquire education through the medium of English. Hobhouse concluded that the dispatch was mistaken in its facts and inconclusive in its reasoning. He so informed Calcutta and announced he would stand by Macaulay, whose minute "bears the stamp of genius."[15]

A Western education, then, was assumed to have special virtues in producing learned men for the India of the future. Hobhouse felt that similar standards must apply to British civil servants in order to render them, in conjunction with trained Indian personnel, effective agents of progress. He therefore introduced in 1838 an entrance examination at Haileybury, the company's training college, which projected his age's, as well as his own, image of a gentleman; such a one should be conversant with all fields, knowledgeable in the elements of "mathematical science," able to translate portions of specified classics, thoroughly familiar with the Scriptures (the Archbishop of Canterbury appointed the examiner), and thoroughly grounded in British history and geography. Otherwise, Hobhouse left untouched the long-established system of nomination and ignored Macaulay's proposal to accept into the civil service, after examinations, a quarter of the candidates selected by the directors.[16]

15. "Recent Changes in Native Education," October 5, 1836, Commonwealth Relations Office, Revenue, Judicial, and Legislative Committee, Miscellaneous Papers, 9; Hobhouse to James Carnac, December 12, 1836, HMS, 837, f. 118; Hobhouse to Auckland, December 5, 1836, HMS, 837, f. 114–21.

16. India Register, XXIV, 18–23 (1838); Board to Court, 11, July 6, 1836, February 3, 1837, f. 151, 279; Hobhouse to Board, August 14, 1837, HMS 838, f. 130.

The tempo of reform then slowed, because Hobhouse was inclined to defer more intrusions upon Indian customs or religion until time and circumstances made specific changes necessary. He felt that the remaining limitations in Indian life would in any case be profoundly affected by the social revolution already generated. The blessings of Western learning would set Indians free from ignorance, and good laws and sound government would enable them to improve their earthly condition. Indian and English authorities favored this disposition. Macaulay had returned in 1838 from Calcutta, leaving Auckland wretchedly bored with the details of domestic improvement. The Cabinet grew increasingly reluctant to take any steps that could conceivably provoke the natives against British rule; also, economic recession, Chartist riots, and the Anti-Corn Law League demonstrations absorbed London's attention. Then there was the growing menace of a Russian invasion of India, which the Government decided to forestall by sending an army into Afghanistan. The resources of India thus became entangled in another cycle of wars and imperial expansion.

Evangelicals were not willing to accept the Board's scrupulous concern for Indian customs, even when they were based on terms of expediency. Many influential public men were with them in the struggle against surviving Indian practices they found repellent. Hobhouse's urgent pleas for information concerning Indian slavery indicated the pressure placed upon him by parliamentary abolitionists. In defending the Government's stand, he used a dispatch forwarded by William Hay Macnaghten, Auckland's influential chief secretary, stating in effect that the intolerable evil of Negro slavery must not be confounded with certain deeply rooted Indian customs that compelled various forms of hereditary service. The situation in India called for gradual measures—laws protecting servants against maltreatment, or emancipation in areas that lapsed to British control—until the time was ripe for ending the practice altogether.[17] Hobhouse notified Calcutta that he was willing to reach some compromise with "that fierce and foolish" Evangelical party, whose "fanatical spirit is becoming daily more active at home."[18] He issued a directive to abolish the pilgrim tax at Allahabad and

17. *Hansard*, 3d series, XXXVIII (1837), 1853–54.
18. Hobhouse to Auckland, August 30, 1837, May 9, 1838, HMS, 838, f. 120, 299.

Gya. The temple at Juggernaut was a more complex matter because the British authorities had inherited an obligation to contribute a sum toward its maintenance. Nevertheless the Government's association was terminated in 1838 by transferring superintendence to native officials, who henceforth received only voluntary contributions.

Charges of encouraging idolatry also arose, prompted by the presence of European troops at Indian religious festivals. Although Charles Grant had earlier persuaded the directors to relieve company employees from attending these ceremonies, Hobhouse had preferred to let the order remain inoperative. Sir Peregrine Maitland, Commander-in-chief at Madras, reopened the matter by issuing a circular letter discontinuing the attendance of troops at all native religious ceremonies, whereupon Governor Lord Elphinstone suspended Maitland's order. Maitland resigned, and the Bishops of Madras and London began to marshal support in his favor. Auckland expressed to Hobhouse the dilemma now confronting him: "If I reject the agitation I know the storm which I may raise on one side, if I encourage them even to the limited extent to which I feel with them, a mistrust on the part of the natives." [19] Though Hobhouse counseled a policy of resisting "your saints and our saints," he eventually acceded to continued pressure; upon his initiative, the directors sent a dispatch dated August 8, 1838, ordering the participation of company servants in native religious observances to cease immediately. Even escort duty or the firing of salutes by troops were now held to be beyond the call of duty. Hobhouse, however, could claim some success with the Evangelicals. For one, Bishop Blomfield of London had promised him not to make any more inflammatory speeches about idolatrous practices in India.[20] Also, the vacant bishopric of Madras had gone to a clergyman Hobhouse had warmly supported for reasons he outlined to Elphinstone. "He will not be a missionary Bishop—he will not be a converting Bishop," he wrote, "I mean he will consider his first object to be not preaching the gospel to the heathens but to the Christians of your community." [21] Hobhouse

19. Auckland to Hobhouse, April 9, 1837, Lord Broughton Papers, Add. MSS 36473, f. 128–30.
20. Hobhouse to Elphinstone, March 4, 1841, HMS, 840, f. 75.
21. Hobhouse to Elphinstone, August 30, 1837, Commonwealth Relations Office, Elphinstone European MSS, Box 2G, 14, f. 87.

could feel more assured on the score of religion at Madras, knowing that a scrupulous regard for established Indian observances
would be maintained by Bishop Trever Spencer, his brother-in-
law.

Whatever misgivings he may have had about changing other
customs and organizations, Hobhouse had no qualms about
changing Indian political institutions, as demonstrated by the
important part he played in consolidating and extending British
rule in India from the time of the Afghan expedition to Lord
Dalhousie's viceroyalty of the 1850's. The Afghan invasion itself has been related in sufficient detail [22] to permit only a brief
account of Hobhouse's role in the expedition. For years, he and
Palmerston had pored over sketchy maps to pinpoint the latest
reports of Czarist treachery. Russian aggression had commenced
against the Ottoman Empire; the Czar's armies moved across
Central Asia toward the headwaters of the Indus; Persia was
reduced to a satellite state, and Persian armies were besieging
Herat in western Afghanistan. Worst of all, a Russian agent in
Kabul was reportedly swaying Amir Dost Mohammed over to
his side. Hobhouse was utterly dismayed when Lord Durham,
the envoy to Saint Petersburg, could "discern no hostile designs
upon our Indian Empire." [23] "We have but one formidable rival
in Central Asia—that is, Russia," he wrote Palmerston, "Unless
we are prepared for that great struggle, we had better quit the
field, and await for the attack, which will assuredly not long be
delayed, upon our Indian frontier." [24] After reading a few more
choice dispatches forwarded by the Foreign Office, Hobhouse
was convinced by the beginning of 1839 that the threat of a
Russian invasion was imminent.

By this time the Persian Shah had lifted the siege of Herat,
although Palmerston thought he was "only temporizing." The
vaunted Russian expedition into Central Asia had halted a good
thousand miles from India. Dost Mohammed's parlays with
Captain Vitkievitch, whom the Afghan ruler had studiously
ignored until all hopes of acquiring British support had van-

22. See J. A. Norris, *The First Afghan War, 1838–1842*, an account
that greatly differs from conclusions reached by Sir John W. Kaye, *History
of the War in Afghanistan* (3 vols.; London, 1857–1858).

23. Hobhouse to Palmerston, February 27, 1837, Lord Henry Palmerston
Papers, by permission of the Trustees of the Broadlands Archives.

24. Hobhouse to Palmerston, September 29, 1838, HMS, 838, f. 441–42;
Hobhouse to Palmerston, August 25, 1838, HMS, 838, f. 429.

ished, proved to have none of the hostile designs assumed at Calcutta and London; invaded from the west by the Persians and from the east by the Sikhs, who had recently seized the strategic bastion of Peshawar near the Khyber Pass, Dost Mohammed understandably had sought all possible aid. The British had not been willing because the cornerstone of British diplomacy was the alliance with the Sikh ruler, Ranjit Singh. Auckland had therefore devised a scheme that Hobhouse commended for having "a face of boldness and decision." [25] It also approximated plans formulated by the Cabinet at a Windsor Castle conference in October, 1838: an Anglo-Indian army would march on Kabul to replace the unreliable Dost Mohammed with a puppet ruler—his predecessor, Shah Suja, who was an exile in India. "I think I may safely promise you the full support of the Court and Government in this crisis," Hobhouse wrote Auckland, "Your policy appears to coincide so exactly with our own that we shall be contented to leave all details of operation entirely to your discretion." [26]

By summer the invaders were in Kabul. Hobhouse took time from arranging for the bestowal of military honors to remind the Commons that "the very stations of which the British flag is now flying, were the resting places of the great Alexander, and that since his day, the standard of no civilization has been seen on the banks of the Indus." [27] The exhilaration of victory soon gave way to a more sober appraisal of just what the expedition had achieved. The Afghans' unwillingness to accept the ruler imposed upon them made it apparent that British garrisons must bolster Shah Suja's unpopular regime, and Hobhouse quickly accepted the truth that it is often easier to occupy than to evacuate a country. "There must be no withdrawal of troops," he told Auckland, "no attempt to hold the country by mere good will or fair government." [28] Hobhouse continued to counsel the Indian authorities in such a vein until he left the Board of Control upon the fall of Melbourne's Government in the summer of 1841. His last letter, which reached India toward the end of the year, expressed confidence in the army's ability to crush an uprising near Kandahar. The following February, the news

25. Hobhouse to Palmerston, July 8, 1839, HMS, 839, f. 164.
26. Hobhouse to Auckland, November 5, 1838, HMS, 838, f. 492.
27. *Hansard*, 3d series, LI (1840), col. 1330.
28. Hobhouse to Auckland, January 1, 1841, HMS, 840, f. 4.

reached London of another uprising in Kabul and of the Anglo-Indian army's subsequent annihilation in Afghanistan. Hobhouse seemed unwilling or unable to comprehend the incredible turn of events. He found "dispiriting" and a sign of "lamentable panic" Auckland's pathetic final letter from India detailing the appalling suffering and loss of life.[29]

It was a total disaster. Dost Mohammed eventually returned to Kabul, never fully understanding the motives that had compelled the British to contest his authority, carry him off into exile, and finally restore him on the throne of his poor country. India incurred a large debt, excluding the expense of mounting another expedition in 1842 to retrieve British prestige and prisoners west of the Indus. In Britain itself a stunned and angry public clamored for more information to fit together the bits and pieces of the Afghan puzzle. Had Lord Melbourne's Cabinet ignored the Duke of Wellington's warnings against the expedition? Was the invasion necessary to forestall an imminent Russian threat to India, or was it an unjustifiable act of interference in the internal affairs of an Asian territory? Did the company directors have no prior knowledge of the expedition, as some of them now avowed? An entry in Hobhouse's diary was addressed to this last assertion:

Of course the Conservative press imputed the catastrophe to the authors of the Afghan war. Lord Duncannon told me that he had heard it stated positively as a fact that the Court of Directors had remonstrated with me against the expedition beyond the Indus. It was not so. The Court acquiesced, with only one exception, in the whole transaction; and I never heard even of the one dissent until long afterwards, on the arrival of the bad news. The Secret Committee—that is to say, the Chairman and Deputy Chairman, and the senior member of the Court—fully approved of the despatch which I wrote to Lord Auckland, directing that the expedition should be undertaken; no dissenting vote, that I heard of, was given. I did, indeed, hear afterwards that Mr. Tucker put a dissent on the Court records; but it was not forwarded to me; and when a vote of thanks to Lord

29. Hobhouse, diary, July 3, 1843, Lord Broughton Papers, Add. MSS 43745, f. 164; Hobhouse to Auckland, January 1, 1841, Hobhouse to Carnac, February 4, 1841, HMS, 840, f. 4, 44. See also Commonwealth Relations Office, Board's Drafts of Secret Letters and Dispatches, XIII, 1st series.

Auckland passed the Court there was not a dissentient voice, nor was there any disapproval of his policy uttered by anyone.[30]

Later, there was some thought that the expedition might have been a crime, as well as an act of folly, because the late Government stood accused of deceiving the public about the origins of the war through the carefully edited documents it published in 1839, the so-called garbled dispatches. These blue books rankled in the minds of public men for decades and furnished material for Sir John Kaye's highly moralistic and indignant history of the Afghan war. To understand the nature of the books we must go back to January, 1839, when Palmerston and Hobhouse conferred over just what materials ought to be made public to justify the pending war. "The objection to giving papers," Palmerston declared, "is that our case against Russia is *too good* a one to be made out against a dear ally. It would be a terrible shewing up for Nicholas; not but that he richly deserves it." [31] Hobhouse then weighed the matter in a short memorandum in which he noted that justice could not be done to the Government's policy unless all the documents were produced. Nevertheless, there were considerations involving national security, which he specified. First and foremost, publications of all the documents in full would exacerbate the already strained relations with Russia. Some vital secrets involving Indian defenses might also be revealed. Finally, some papers might "embarrass and weaken" Afghan policy on the eve of war "by raising a premature discussion and create unnecessary alarm in the Public Mind." [32] At this point William Cabell, an assistant secretary at the Board, suggested a presentation of papers that would avoid these objections. Briefly, he proposed to publish a treaty between Persia and the Amir of Kandahar, which was designed to set up a power in Afghanistan independent of the British Government and assisted by Russia. Various dispatches from Sir John McNeill and from Captain Alexander Burnes, envoys to Teheran and Kabul, would draw attention to the danger posed for India. At the same time the Czar could take no offense because his

30. Lady Dorchester, ed., *Recollections of a Long Life, by Lord Broughton (John Cam Hobhouse) with additional extracts from his private diaries,* VI, 55–56.

31. Palmerston to Hobhouse, January 28, 1839, Lord Broughton Papers, Add. MSS 46915, f. 151–52.

32. Undated memorandum among papers for January, 1839, in Lord Broughton Papers, Add. MSS 36470, f. 19–21; see also Norris, *The First Afghan War,* 221–30.

Government had subsequently disavowed the acts of his Persian and Afghan envoys.[33] The Board began shuffling the Afghan papers according to Cabell's plan until Lord Ellenborough, at the end of February, 1839, outlined to the Government precisely how he wanted the documents arranged.[34] He wanted the treaties with the Indian states followed by copies or extracts of Burnes's letters, a copy of Burnes's original instructions, and then correspondence concerning Shah Suja's bid for the Afghan throne in 1834. During the next six weeks Hobhouse and other Board members scrutinized mountains of documents and rushed the evidence through the various stages of publication. The compilation, arrangement, and editing of so much official material within a short time can well explain why the Afghan papers were carelessly or inefficiently prepared. A hard task was bungled, but critics of the Afghan expedition quickly imputed motives of deliberate deception and misrepresentation once the documents were published.[35] Hobhouse from the outset thought it best to publish all or nothing on Afghanistan. Because Parliament and the public wanted facts, the latter course became impossible; delicate matters involving Russia or certain Indian officials likewise prevented publication of all documents in full. If anything, Hobhouse felt that too much was finally included in the Afghan papers, for reasons he explained to Auckland:

The selection has been made in the best manner circumstances would allow, and the documents were carefully looked over by Macneill [sic]; but I have still some misgivings as to the effect their publication may produce in India. Some of your functionaries may complain of the exposure of their views & proceedings, & I confess that nothing but stern necessity justifies the course we have pursued. The choice is we had no choice— the language of Aberdeen & Brougham & Ellenborough & Lyndhurst was such as to render a detailed account of your motives & the causes of them indispensable: and, had we refused the papers, a hostile vote would have extorted them from us.[36]

33. Cabell, Memorandum, February 14, 1839, Lord Broughton Papers, Add. MSS 36470, f. 103.
34. *Hansard*, 3d series, XLV (1839), col. 963.
35. See G. J. Alder, "The 'Garbled' Blue Books of 1839—Myth or Reality?" *The Historical Journal*, 15, 2 (1972), 229–59, which very effectively demolished Kaye's interpretation about deliberate "garbling" in 1839.
36. Hobhouse to Auckland, April 11, 1839, Lord Broughton Papers, Add. MSS 46915, f. 121.

Three years later Henry Baillie, M.P. for Invernesshire, and Disraeli arraigned the Afghan expedition in Parliament. Hobhouse ably defended the late Government's policy and reminded Tory critics that they, too, had applauded the action when it seemed so strikingly successful. He corrected various speakers about points of detail and also elaborated on the Afghan papers, although neither Baillie nor Disraeli had made any accusation of deliberate misrepresentation. Hobhouse wanted to clear the air now that the press had published the late Captain Burnes's letters sharply criticizing the Government's publications:

It has been said that all the documents were not laid upon the Table, and that parts had been omitted. That is true: but there has been no garbling of the papers. Various parts were withheld, and very reasonably so: and if I were still the Minister, and those pages were called for, I should do the like again. To have published all that Sir Alexander Burnes said, would have answered no good purpose. The only object required to be shewn was, what was the cause of the war. I do not mean to say that Sir Alexander Burnes did not maintain opinions different from Lord Auckland; and as I stated the other day, the late Government published three of Sir Alexander Burnes's letters, in which he gave a decided opinion in preference of Dost Mohammed against the pretensions of any other person.[37]

Publication of the Afghan documents in full was delayed until 1859. Hobhouse's carefully prepared defense helped mollify parliamentary concern about the "garbled" dispatches. His case had gained unexpected support from the Tory Government in power. Lord Vesey Fitzgerald, his successor at the Board of Control after Ellenborough left for India, confirmed in 1842 the substantial accuracy of the blue books. Peel flatly opposed publishing more papers because such action would endanger England's good relations with Russia. Peel again settled the issue the following year when Joseph Roebuck, Hobhouse's old rival at Bath, unsuccessfully moved for another inquiry into the dispatches.[38]

Only after John William Kaye and other authors had written about mutilated and emasculated official letters did a motion pass the Parliament to have the dispatches published in full. The

37. *Hansard*, 3d series, LXIV (1842), col. 1301 ff.; see also cols. 460–96.

38. *Hansard*, 3d series, LXIII (1842), col. 1151; LXIV (1842), cols. 517–23; LXVII (1843), cols. 182–91.

presentation of all the documents in 1859 was indeed illuminating, but not for the reasons Kaye and other investigators had alleged. Clearly, the Home Government was at no point a mere accessory to Auckland's unbridled ambitions, as Kaye had maintained. Kaye, who had succeeded John Stuart Mill as secretary of the Political and Secret Department of the new India Office, had indicated that in 1839 letters to Burnes had been suppressed, but the 1859 publication of all documents verified that the Government had in fact published them in either of two collections. One of the letters did suggest disagreements with the Indian authorities, as Hobhouse had emphasized to the Commons. Another letter, which contained a rebuke to Burnes for disobeying instructions, was suppressed in parts not because it damaged the Government's case for the Afghan expedition, but because the London authorities did not want to damage the career of a young and talented official.[39] Also, several letters published in 1839 did paint Dost Mohammed in a good light, and Kaye tried to enhance his case for garbling by omitting some of these letters in his edition. Hence, full publication turned the tables on the critic.

Hobhouse did not try deliberately to deceive the public in 1839, but he incurred public censure precisely because he did not follow his original inclination to publish all or nothing. Some of Burnes's abstracts were incomplete in themselves, with no indication about where the omissions occurred in the text. One deletion especially argued against deposing Dost Mohammed. In a note to Macnaghten of June 2, 1838, Burnes had written, "It remains to be considered why we cannot act with Dost Mohammed. He is a man of undoubted ability, and has at heart high opinions of the British nation; and if half you must do for others were done for him, and offers made which he could see conduced to his interests, he would abandon Persia and Russia tomorrow." [40] Hobhouse had rightly argued that other published

39. See Alder, "The 'Garbled' Blue Books," 255–56. Alder also discusses Burnes's dispatch of January 26, 1838, to Macnaghten, which critics maintained was a prime example of forgery because the deletion of a first paragraph made it appear that Burnes had expressed his views, not the Government's. A later paragraph establishes the fact that Burnes had just expressed the Government's opinions.

40. Burnes to Macnaghten, June 2, 1838, in The Indian Papers restored by Sir J. W. Kaye, Parliamentary Papers, 1859 (Session 2), XXV, 252. See also Norris, The First Afghan War, chap. 17 and Appendix I, a comparison of the papers presented in 1859 and the 1839 edition.

letters revealed that Burnes held Dost Mohammed in high favor, but critics of Palmerstonian diplomacy in 1860 wanted to exploit the distrust of Palmerston's colleagues further. The Afghan papers were "garbled," and M.P.'s asked who had done the actual editing. The veteran Palmerston left the question unanswered in 1861 when he defended everything connected with Afghan policy. The information is supplied by an entry in Hobhouse's diary, which states that "part of the papers were prepared at Foreign Office and a part at India Board" and that McNeill and Cabell were involved with the actual editing. Hobhouse then concluded that Palmerston had presented a "triumphant" restatement of the case for invading Afghanistan, a move he himself never doubted was necessary to protect British India.[41] Also, Palmerston sought to create satisfactory conditions for British commercial expansion into various regions of the world, and the march on Kabul could thus be viewed as an essentially defensive measure to provide security for the valuable Indian Empire.

India was also linked by trade to the China coast, chiefly through the illicit sale of opium. Poppy cultivation provided an income of £2.5 million for India in 1836–1837 alone, which prompted Auckland to comment, "I depend upon the smuggler, and the inveterate habits of the Chinese for keeping it up until other resources come into play."[42] Then in 1838 the Imperial Governor at Canton took steps to root out the opium trade altogether, starting with the seizure and destruction of stock worth more than £2 million. The final breach came after English warships fired upon a fleet of junks sent out to seize a group of English sailors wanted for trial in a Chinese court. "You must not be startled at having to make war on the Empire of China, for to this it comes," Hobhouse wrote Auckland, "We thought, after due deliberation that we had no alternative; and, with that opinion, we have adopted the course now announced to you."[43] Once more Hobhouse and other Cabinet members found themselves in the role of armchair strategists, subordinating expensive but dull reforms to more expensive but exciting battles in distant places. He and Melbourne thought a few decisive engagements by a British squadron would make the Emperor open the

41. Hobhouse, diary, March 24, 1861, Lord Broughton Papers, Add. MSS 43763, f. 133–34.
42. Auckland to Hobhouse, April 9, 1837, HMS, 838, f. 150.
43. Hobhouse to Auckland, November 4, 1839, HMS, 839, f. 220.

ports of China to foreign trade; Palmerston was for seizing some Chinese property; and Macaulay was reportedly the most belligerent of all in recommending that the entire China coast be blockaded.[44] Everyone, however, agreed the commencement of hostilities must be made a matter of timing, for reasons Palmerston outlined to Hobhouse toward the end of 1839:

> I have seen many people about China, and from all our manufacturers and commercial houses—the result is that though they urgently require us to take vigorous measures, they anxiously wish that those measures shall not commence till March next; & that nothing should happen to interrupt our commerce in China until that month, when the trading season will finish, and their current transactions will be closed.[45]

"Opium is a sad business," Hobhouse wrote Auckland in 1840, "but I am pleased to say fanaticism at home is dying on the subject."[46] He then referred to the China debates of the previous April, describing the Opposition's motion attributing the outbreak of hostilities to the Government's want of foresight and precaution as "a mere party matter, brought forward without the slightest care for China." Actually, Graham's motion skirted the controversial subject of opium but gave Gladstone and others the opportunity to denounce the iniquitous trade, and Hobhouse privately recorded that "we were fortunate in being able to keep our party together on this occasion."[47] During the debates Palmerston had emphasized the Government's efforts to settle differences through negotiations, Macaulay dwelled upon the wrongs inflicted on the British flag, and Hobhouse, after explaining that the Government could not stop Englishmen from smuggling opium at their own risk, saw that, unfortunate as it might be, British gunboats, opium, and progress seemed necessarily conjoined. He had to trust that

> if we did enter upon this expedition with honour and justice on our side we should be able to carry it out not only to the profit of our own nation but that of every civilized power of the world. That we should do so in a way to vindicate our own honour and

44. Dorchester, ed., *Recollections*, V, 43.
45. Palmerston to Hobhouse, October 14, 1839, HMS, 839, f. 225.
46. Hobhouse to Auckland, September 28, 1840, HMS, 839, f. 439.
47. Dorchester, ed., *Recollections*, V, 130; Hobhouse, diary, April 7, 1840, Lord Broughton Papers, Add. MSS 56562.

to improve the relations of this great empire [China] with all others in the universe, and at the same time, in doing good to ourselves, do good also to the general interests of humanity.[48]

The Government's majority was slim, but a month later Lord Stanhope moved to abolish the opium trade by outlawing the cultivation of the poppy in India. "It will cost money to disconnect the government from the cultivation and from all sale of opium," Hobhouse reminded Melbourne, and he wearily added, "Even if banished from India it would take root in Scinde and the Punjaub." Furthermore, "no good can be done by public discussion and far less by parliamentary resolutions which must necessarily be premature, and tending only to embarrass the executive government both in India and at home." [49] Hobhouse then advised Melbourne to put Stanhope off by announcing that the Government's attention was already directed to the opium trade. It was, in a sense, for a month later Hobhouse cautioned Auckland about his public dispatches, because a public outcry "has been raised against your wicked wish to poison a third of the whole human race, merely to fill your own coffers." [50]

The spring of 1841 brought word of the terms Admiral Elliot had accepted: Hong Kong and an indemnity, but no provisions for opening China to foreign trade. The terms were accordingly rejected by the Melbourne Government.[51] By 1842 Hobhouse could derive some satisfaction from seeing that the Tory Government had been able to open several Chinese ports to the produce of Britain and India. He himself would once more become closely involved with imperial expansion and economic welfare upon his return to the Board of Control.

48. *Hansard*, 3d series, LIII (1840), 898.
49. Hobhouse to Melbourne, May 9, 1840, Melbourne to Hobhouse, May 8, 1840, HMS, 839, f. 226, 327.
50. Hobhouse to Auckland, June 4, 1840, HMS, 839, f. 364.
51. Dorchester, ed., *Recollections*, V, 227, VI, 13–14.

CHAPTER XII

THE INDIAN EMPIRE
1846-1852

Imperial expansion, Indian social reform, and economic development were among Hobhouse's chief concerns after he returned to the Board of Control during the Russell Government. The impetus for change came more than ever before from Calcutta, not London. Forceful, unusual men often determined a course of action in India, which had also been the situation in the 1830's. There was Sir Charles James Napier, who became Commander-in-chief of British military forces. Known as "The Elephant," Napier looked bizarre with his huge black beard and matted hair. He could be cruel or kind, megalomaniacal or humble, depending on his mood. But the towering figure in Indian administration after 1848 was James Andrew Broun Ramsay, first Marquess of Dalhousie, the Governor General. Dalhousie had shown an enormous capacity for work since his early years in Scotland. In 1843 Peel appointed him Vice-President of the Board of Trade, and two years later he succeeded Gladstone as President. A brilliant man, he had little patience for administrative delays and no tolerance for opposing viewpoints. Almost immediately upon his arrival in India, Dalhousie sent Hobhouse communiqués about irrigation and roads, railways and telegraphs, annexations and military expeditions. It promised not to be a quiet time for Hobhouse.

The Afghan disaster checked only momentarily the extension of British rule in India, which continued up to the time of the Great Mutiny. Imperial expansion during these years was less the deliberate intent of the Home Government than the aim of authorities in India who had absolute faith in the rightness of their action, even to the point of ignoring instructions from London. Such was the case in 1843, when Lord Ellenborough annexed Sind at the mouth of the Indus. The victorious general, Sir Charles Napier, agreed that the army had no right to seize the territory, but he welcomed the move. The Court of Directors condemned this final despoilation of the amirs, but Peel's Cabinet ultimately acquiesced in the *fait accompli.*[1] Only after Lord Ellenborough overplayed his hand by attacking the state of Gwalior did the Government and the company agree to recall him, naming his brother-in-law, Sir Henry Hardinge, as succeeding Governor General.

The northwest frontier still held the attention of Indian authorities when Hobhouse returned to the Board of Control upon the fall of Peel's Government in 1846. Earlier in the year, the Sikhs had chosen war as the only means of defending themselves against British encirclement, which seemed to presage the fate that befell Sind. Hobhouse thought Lord Hardinge had made a grave error in not annexing the Punjab after the Sikh defeat, and he so informed the retiring Governor General, adding that he "would not let a moment pass after your departure" without extending British rule into the area.[2] He was gratified to learn that Hardinge's successor, Lord Dalhousie, was in complete agreement with the views he presented to the Cabinet. "I never entered into that part of Lord Hardinge's policy which was founded on the expectation that a strong and friendly Sikh Government could ever be established in the Punjaub," Hobhouse informed Lord John Russell, "I always felt sure that on the first favourable occasion an attempt would be made to shake off the British yoke; and that we should be obliged to become in name what we are now in fact, the Masters of the Province."[3] The resumption of hostilities at the end of 1848 bore out Hobhouse's predictions, but the Cabinet, beset with memories of Afghanistan, still refused to authorize any annexation when the Sikhs surrendered the following year.

Dalhousie meanwhile awaited orders from London. He received a puzzling earlier communiqué from Hobhouse indicating that "general feeling is against annexation; although the conviction is equally general, that we cannot abandon the country and . . . render our North West frontier perpetually insecure and subject to constant alarm."[4] Further dispatches were equally ambiguous. One spoke of annexation as "an extreme measure"; another advised Dalhousie to "review the question in all its

1. Robert A. Huttenback, *British Relations with Sind, 1799–1843; an anatomy of imperialism*, chap. 5.

2. Hobhouse to Hardinge, January 24, 1846, HMS, 853, f. 181.

3. Hobhouse to Lord John Russell, October 7, 1848, HMS, 847, f. 18.

4. Hobhouse to Dalhousie, November 24, 1848, HMS, 859, f. 76–82.

bearings, and inform us of conclusion to which you have arrived, before you announce your final arrangement." [5] Hobhouse could give no clear lead about a course of action while the Cabinet remained deadlocked over the future status of the Punjab. He and Palmerston continued to press for annexation; Russell and Grey, backed by the company directors, remained opposed. Auckland also warned that Britain would have to station an army of at least 50,000 men should the Sikhs be deprived of their independence.[6] Dalhousie finally took matters into his own hands by announcing he would annex the country. "Disallow my act, reverse my policy," he wrote to Hobhouse, "You will disgrace me, of course, but do not let that stand in your way. I shall submit quietly to the consequences now: well satisfied that the disgrace will be but temporary; that time and events will right me." "I can hardly believe that you would choose to take any decisive step without previously consulting the Home Authorities" was Hobhouse's hurried reply, which arrived in India several weeks after Dalhousie had carried out his unilateral action in May. It was another *fait accompli*, with the Cabinet declining Dalhousie's challenge and Hobhouse finally informing him that he indeed had the option of annexation if he thought it necessary for the general interest of India.[7]

Dalhousie's relations with the Home Government had deteriorated to the point where he seriously contemplated resigning. Before leaving for India in 1847, he had expressed to Hobhouse and others his anxiety over leaving Lord Gough in command of the Indian Army. Actually, the matter of replacing the aged veteran had concerned the Cabinet for the past several years. Opinion favored Sir Charles Napier, but in view of Sir James Outram's bitter exposé of Napier's "tyrannical" treatment of the Sind amirs and the company's vehement opposition to one who had so flagrantly disregarded any civilian authority, the appointment was dropped.[8] Wellington's recommendation to

5. Hobhouse to Dalhousie, October 6, 1848, May 7, 1849, HMS, 859, f. 56, 157.

6. Auckland to Hobhouse, October 30, 1848, HMS, 846, f. 30.

7. Dalhousie to Hobhouse, April 7, 1849, Hobhouse to Dalhousie, May 7, May 24, 1849, HMS, 856, f. 132, 157, 164.

8. Sir James Outram, a political agent in Sind, had written *The Conquest of Scinde, a Commentary* (London, 1846), which sharply attacked Napier and was sympathetic to the amirs. Hobhouse wanted to remove Outram from his post, but Macaulay, among others, dissuaded him from doing so. See Macaulay to Hobhouse, August 7, 1846, HMS, 844, f. 43.

promote Napier to Field Marshal was likewise discarded in the interest of preserving unanimity at the highest military level.[9] At one point Hobhouse told Dalhousie that either by his own accord or by compulsion Gough would soon make way for a younger man, but papers continued to shuffle as the Cabinet and the company wrangled over the question of a successor. Hobhouse finally informed Dalhousie of the Government's decision to retain Gough as Commander-in-chief until further notice. Somewhat lightheartedly he added that in case of another military campaign, "the honour and glory will belong to this brave and most fortunate veteran." [10]

The next campaign in 1849 led to Chillianwalla, where the intrepid Gough ordered a charge against the Sikhs that ended in victory but cost more than 2,000 casualties. "The impression made upon the public mind has been stronger than that caused by the Caubal [sic] massacre," Hobhouse reported. "The result has been that, in 8-and-40 hours after the arrival of the mail, it was determined to send Sir Charles Napier to command the Indian army." [11] Hobhouse received the Government's and the Queen's endorsement for a letter deploring Dalhousie's alleged communiqués to various confidants and to company directors about Gough's retention, whereas one decisive word on his part would have sufficed to have him removed. Dalhousie found "insolent and ungentlemanlike in the worse degree" [12] Hobhouse's concluding remarks:

When you accepted the Government of India you made a stipulation scarcely, as I thought at the time necessary, that your political conduct, on your return to England, should, in no degree, be compromised by your connexion with Lord John Russell's Cabinet; but I am sure you never intended that condition to apply to your proceedings whilst corresponding with the present Government, and I am equally sure that you would scorn any public functionary, so circumstanced, who contemplated the defence of his own character by preparing a case against his associates or employers.[13]

9. Hobhouse to Russell, September 3, 1846, Lord John Russell Papers, 30/22, 5c.
10. Hobhouse to Dalhousie, July 6, 1848, HMS, 859, f. 28–29.
11. Hobhouse to Dalhousie, March 7, 1849, HMS, 859, f. 121.
12. Dalhousie to Sir George Couper, May 1, 1849, in J. G. A. Baird, ed., *Private Letters of the Marquess of Dalhousie*, 67.
13. Hobhouse to Dalhousie, March 7, 1849, HMS, 859, f. 122–26.

Dalhousie repeatedly protested his innocence, maintaining that he never wrote, publicly or privately, about Gough's command. Indeed, he tried to make the best of his continued appointment.[14] Relations with the Cabinet remained strained for over another year. He regularly corresponded on terms of "elaborate courtesy" with Hobhouse while privately confiding how much he despised the man. However, tensions between the two gradually eased with the mutual discovery that they shared similar aspirations concerning future British rule in India.

Hobhouse was soon reporting the final deposition of the Koh-i-noor diamond somewhat in terms of his and Dalhousie's mutual victory over the directors. Sir Archibald Galloway, the company chairman, opposed surrendering the jewel to Queen Victoria because all treaties with Indian states were made in the company's name. Besides, he maintained, the diamond did not come under the definition of booty because the British Government had continued to recognize the Sikh state throughout both wars. Galloway could not enforce his views against Hobhouse and other members of the Cabinet. The presentation of the diamond at Buckingham Palace during a rehearsed ceremony therefore symbolized what was in fact the company's subordination to Her Majesty's Cabinet. "It was distinctly understood that the Court were merely the recipient of the jewel en transite to the Sovereign," Hobhouse reported to Dalhousie, "and when the chairman placed it in Her Majesty's hands, he read from a paper approved by me, and shown before hand to the Queen, that it was *delivered* to H.M. The word *presented* was cautiously avoided." [15]

Hobhouse was also pleased to send word that the Cabinet's intransigence over annexing the Punjab did not suggest an unwillingness to accept any "just and honourable accession of territory," such as the Mahratta state of Satara. "I have a very strong opinion," he concluded, "that on the death of the present prince without a son, no adoption should be permitted, and this petty principality should be merged in the British Empire." [16]

14. Dalhousie to Hobhouse, March 6, 1849, HMS, 859, f. 82; Dalhousie to Couper, May 18, 1849, in Baird, ed., *Private Letters of Dalhousie*, 71–74.
15. Galloway to Hobhouse, May 26, 1849, John Cam Hobhouse, Lord Broughton Papers, Add. MSS 36480, f. 41; Galloway to Hobhouse, May 28, July 6, 1849, HMS, 852, f. 60, 68; Hobhouse's communiqué to Dalhousie, July 8, 1850, HMS, 859, f. 298.
16. Hobhouse to Dalhousie, May 24, 1848, HMS, 859, f. 11.

Hobhouse was encouraging imperial expansion through "lapse," which Dalhousie applied extensively during his time as Governor General to native states whose ruling family had been appointed by British authorities. The doctrine held that the Crown acquired the state in default of natural heirs in the ruling family. Accordingly, upon the death in 1848 of the appointed Apa Sahib, Satara set the precedent for later acquisitions. Dalhousie's action was not contested in London, where Hobhouse had already gained the Cabinet's approval and where the Court of Directors, after recommending a future course of preserving most native states, also sanctioned the annexation.[17]

However, the directors rejected decisively by a vote of 19–4 Dalhousie's proposal to abolish the Mogul Dynasty upon the death of the King of Delhi, and all of Hobhouse's enthusiastic persuasions failed to alter their decision. The directors believed the deposition would incite the Moslem population to fight for the preservation of a throne symbolic of their former conquests and supremacy. Hobhouse repudiated their views in the following memorandum, an especially revealing statement on his own mid-century attitudes toward India:

We might, it appears to me, permit this mock Sovereignty to be upheld for an indefinite period without much injury to any one, except so far as the encouragement of vicious habits and degrading sensuality may be considered injurious to public morals.

The obscene mysteries of the Palace of Delhi might indeed be subjected to police regulations and a supervision hitherto not employed & some respectability might be attached to the imperial puppet; but not enough to make him, as some appear to apprehend, at all dangerous.

To my mind nothing can be more ridiculous than to anticipate a general rallying of all Indian Mohametans round the King of Delhi under any conceivable circumstances. And this conviction induces me to make light of the principal argument by those who contend against the suppression of the dynasty. I do not believe there could be the slightest danger arising from the discontent of our Mohametan subjects . . . such fears are founded on the prevalent and oft repeated assertion that our power in India is an Empire of opinion: some men of the high-

17. Hobhouse to Russell, January 13, 1849, Russell Papers, 7E. The directors' vote was 16–6.

est reputation and greatest experience have sanctioned this saying. To me it seems utterly devoid of all foundation, or even claim to any attention.

The subjugation of India was obtained by the sword. By the sword alone can it be secured. The wisest institutions, the most humane policy, would, of themselves, fail to give stability to our dominion: nothing but a general conviction of the utter hopelessness of all attempts to throw off the yoke secures the obedience of the many many millions who peacefully submit to bear it; and if our rule were 10 times more just and more productive of happiness than it now is, or, perhaps, can ever be, there would be the same necessity for the terror of the sword as now.[18]

Thus the liberal empire of opinion of the 1830's had evolved in Hobhouse's mind into an empire of force by mid-century. Munro, Macaulay, and John Stuart Mill among earlier liberals had held that imperial rule was justified only if used to prepare India for eventual self-government. It was an article of their faith that force must be tempered by benevolence because Europeans were essentially the guardians of a less-fortunate people. Further, Europeans should always try to preserve the respect of Indians by maintaining high standards of impartial justice and honest government. However ungenerous their estimation of native character and institutions, earlier reformers never doubted that Indians would quickly appreciate the benefits conferred by Westerners. Hobhouse implied that the gap between Indians and Englishmen had widened, not narrowed, during recent decades. Much of his earlier imaginative sympathy and idealism had given way to a hardheaded acceptance of fact: An age of steam and iron made India's backwardness more apparent, the incapacity of her impoverished people for assuming self-government more obvious. Hobhouse's mid-century attitudes toward India reflected in large measure his opinions about the Victorian social and political structure. Before 1832 he and other middle-class liberals had invoked broad principles concerning all mankind to justify such changes as an extended suffrage or parlia-

18. Hobhouse, Memorandum on the Delhi Political Draft, September 1, 1849, HMS, 851, f. 39; H. S. Tucker, Statement, November 28, 1849, Commonwealth Relations Office, Appendix to Court Minutes, IX, f. 297–309; Galloway to Hobhouse, December 1, 1849, HMS, 852, f. 106; Dalhousie to Hobhouse, December 21, 1849, Lord Broughton Papers, Add. MSS 36476, f. 393–406.

mentary reform. The application of these principles had been attempted in India and had provided a reform tradition that had been still strong when Hobhouse first held the Board's presidency. The reform impulse then abated. In England the propertied classes saw anarchy in any further extension of the privileges they had recently won. The way to elevate the people was not by enfranchising them en masse, but by bestowing the vote as a reward for self-help and self-improvement. By applying similar standards to India, it could be safely assumed that her impoverished masses would remain disqualified from ruling themselves. Earlier liberals envisioned limitless change and possibilities for India; Victorian liberals stressed difficulties and dangers.

Hobhouse, when he implied that the Indian masses would always resist change, denied earlier assumptions about their eagerness to acquire British values, skills, and institutions. As early as 1840 he had referred to "the slow and tedious process" of Indian improvement, "at most points resisted by the natives."[19] He later attributed the Great Mutiny to "the general improvements such as electric telegraphs, railroads, post offices, missionary schools and educational movements" that had threatened deeply rooted traditions.[20] Hobhouse never went so far as to think that Indian backwardness was inherent; rather, he thought it was the product of a long and unfortunate history. Therefore, the Mogul Dynasty, a symbol of all that had withheld the fruits of civilization from its domains, could no longer be tolerated by him or other British authorities.

Hobhouse's memorandum about the King of Delhi also suggested that the preservation of empire had become an end in itself, with India an important entity in the imperial structure. He was aware of strategic, as well as commercial, considerations. The Afghan war had alerted him to the vast resources of military strength in India, which could be mustered for the inevitable showdown with the Russian Empire—for the time when "the sepoy and the cossack" would clash. The resurgence of the competition for empire was already under way in his opinion, and Britain would be "forced to quit the field" if she did not have the

19. Hobhouse, diary, June 8, 1840, Lord Broughton Papers, Add. MSS 56562.
20. Hobhouse, diary, June 27, 1857, Lord Broughton Papers, Add. MSS 43758, f. 271.

strength her overseas possessions provided.[21] Thus, India must remain ruled "by the sword" in order to provide not only potential military support, but also a potential source and market for commercial enterprises. The economic upswing in the later 1840's, which coincided with the repeal of the Corn Laws, caused English manufacturers and investors to take a closer look at the prospects India afforded, especially since British rule seemed permanent. James Wilson's influential *Economist* stated the belief that opportunities were excellent: India was "better adapted than any other country" for the production of tropical raw materials, read one typical article in 1847, "while its dense and illustrious population would seem to offer an illimitable demand for our manufacturers." [22] Wilson's board appointment the following year involved him in the creation of conditions under which trade and industry could flourish to the advantage of Englishmen and Indians alike. Fresh from chairing the council of the recently triumphant Anti-Corn Law League, Wilson became a key figure in applying free-trade policy to India. His past association with many northern manufacturers and shipping magnates made him an especially valuable agent for promoting investment in India. Dalhousie, who believed that the strongest bonds of understanding between East and West could be forged through technology and capital, welcomed Wilson's appointment. So did Hobhouse, who found in the man described as "the most efficient chairman in England during his day" [23] one admirably equipped for handling the details of commercial policy.

Free trade and investments were at that time crucial to India's economic future, or so thought the Board and the Home Government. Together the two groups easily overcame any resistance by the company directors to specific measures. For example, when the directors in 1849 proposed regulations for Indian joint-stock banks, among them the publication of accounts and lists of shareholders, the Board announced that it felt no confidence in the efficacy of Government regulations designed to promote sound private banking. It distinctly avowed the principle that "the employment of capital should be left perfectly free and un-

21. Hobhouse, diary, December 4, 1853, Lord Broughton Papers, Add. MSS 56566.

22. *The Economist*, August 28, 1847, 982.

23. George J. Holyoake, *Sixty Years of an Agitator's Life*, II, 226.

fettered."[24] Hobhouse also dismissed company objections to extending Indian coastal trade to foreign nations on a reciprocal basis.[25] At one point Henry St. George Tucker, company chairman, tried to resist the movement toward free trade by recommending an opposite policy of protecting every branch of native industry. He said that sugar had been one of India's most promising exports until free trade transferred "the government revenue, the landlord's rent, the tenant's profits, and the interests of capital from our own people to the degenerate Creoles of Cuba and the slave catchers of Brazil!!"[26] Such arguments carried little weight among ministers who were bent on ending economic regulations and restrictions, and by 1852, *The Economist* could report:

Internal customs and transit duties have been entirely abolished: with very slight and unimportant exceptions the old and somewhat onerous export duties have been abandoned. Coasting trade first, and latterly the foreign navigation, have been rendered perfectly free. The old salt monopoly has been abandoned, and the trade converted into one in which all who please can engage in the import of foreign salt. In short, the whole tendancy of Indian legislation for the past twenty years has been to remove restrictions of every kind from trade and industry.[27]

There were other encouraging reports of progress. Wilson thought that British investors were becoming less wary about risking their money in India. Assam tea, a Government enterprise that was later turned over to private hands, got a big boost when the Queen announced she was highly pleased with the flavor. Hobhouse foresaw improved commercial relations with Siam and Cochin-China after Palmerston discussed negotiations taking place.[28] At Bombay, Lord Falkland was assured by an experienced cotton planter that a large portion of the Mahratta country could increase its cotton production sixfold, and at a

24. Board of Control to East India Company, October 12, 1849, Commonwealth Relations Office, Letters from the Board of Control to the East India Company, E/2/44, f. 102–3.

25. February 6, 1849, Commonwealth Relations Office, Minutes of the Revenue, Judicial, and Legislative Committee, 1848–1850, VI, 149.

26. Tucker to Hobhouse, January 29, 1848, HMS, 845, f. 437–38.

27. *The Economist*, April 24, 1852, 445.

28. Letter 1398, December 18, 1849, Commonwealth Relations Office, Board's Drafts of Secret Letters and Despatches.

comparatively trifling expenditure on irrigation and roads. "Everything is going on steadily," he wrote Hobhouse a year later, "Our merchants here are beginning to establish agencies up the country, for the purpose of buying cotton."[29] *The Economist* reported Indian economic development well under way at mid-century, with cotton, silk, indigo, hemp, rice, and sugar production all having shown sizable increases in the past decade. This growth was a mere prelude to the phenomenal progress India would experience once railroads linking her mines and plantations to coastal ports were completed.[30]

Railroad construction was in fact one of Hobhouse's chief concerns from the time he resumed the Board's presidency in 1846. Negotiations between the East India Company and promoters of two railroad lines had already begun in earnest, but several more years would elapse before all parties concerned could agree on terms. From the outset Hobhouse had many misgivings about the practicability of Indian railways; he had earlier given enthusiastic support to projects for steamship service to India,[31] but building railroads struck him as a hazardous enterprise, even on an experimental basis, because passenger and freight traffic allegedly would not cover operating expenses. Building costs seemed prohibitive in jungle country plagued with hot sun, torrential rains, and insects and vermin. For these very reasons the promoters of the Great Eastern Railway wanted the East India Company to assume responsibility for any risk of loss by giving a guarantee of a minimum annual dividend of 5 per cent on shares amounting to £5,000,000. The company was prepared to accept these terms, but throughout the negotiations it was at the mercy of the Board, which took a keen interest in every detail of railroad construction. Hobhouse sanctioned at first only a fifteen-year guarantee of 4 per cent on a sum limited to £2,500,000 for constructing a line extending 140 miles from Calcutta toward Allahabad.[32] Influential railroad

29. Falkland to Hobhouse, April 30, 1850, January 3, 1851, HMS, 857, f. 40, 198.

30. *The Economist*, October 19, 1850, 1149.

31. *Parliamentary Papers*, 1837, VI, 10–25 (371–386). Hobhouse strongly recommended steamship service to Madras, Calcutta, and Bombay.

32. President to Chairs, December 11, 1846, HMS, 850, f. 124. Railroad negotiations and documents are found in L/PWD/2, Railroad Home Correspondence, Series A & B. See Horace Bell, *Railway Policy in India*, and Daniel Thorner, *Investment in Empire: British Railway and Steam Shipping Enterprise in India, 1825–1844*.

promoters, including Rowland M. Stephenson and Sir George Gerard de Larpent, a powerful figure in London financial and commercial circles, then publicly and privately campaigned against the Board's stand. Finally, Hobhouse agreed to raise the guarantee to 5 per cent for a period of twenty-five years. Further delays occurred when the financial crash in the autumn of 1847 left the promoters unable to raise an initial deposit. Negotiations meanwhile continued with promoters of the Great Indian Peninsular Company, many of whom were Lancashire and Glasgow manufacturers interested in building a line from Bombay to near-by cotton fields. More trouble arose in early 1848 when railwaymen demanded an unconditional assurance of profit, in addition to the guaranteed interest for shareholders. At this point the East India Company proposed returning the deposits of both companies and terminating negotiations altogether. Once more the railway promoters went into action, this time by sending spokesmen on their behalf to Hobhouse's office in early February, 1847. It was a formidable deputation: Cobden, Bright, several other Midlands M.P.'s, representatives from various Lancashire commercial associations, Baron Rothschild, and Sir Isaac Goldsmid.[33] James Wilson, who had recently joined the Board, then negotiated a compromise that became the basis for the contracts that were signed in August. Essentially, the agreements involved private enterprise along with public aid and risk: The East India Company guaranteed a 5 per cent interest to be paid on all capital deposited with it for ninety-nine years. Also, in the event the railroads incurred a net loss after they were built, the owners could turn over the lines to the Government and receive compensation in full.

"Our error," Hobhouse later wrote Dalhousie, "if we have erred, is that we have given too much assistance, and not left the work to private enterprise. It would have been far better, either not to interfere at all, or to have taken the whole upon ourselves, and left it to your government to plan, execute, and conduct the Railway and everything connected with it."[34] He clearly disapproved an accord forced upon him by irresistible economic and political pressure groups, and he did not like private enterprise extracting so many services from the state. Dalhousie, who

33. *The Times*, February 8, February 9, 1849.

34. Hobhouse to Dalhousie, August 22, 1850, Commonwealth Relations Office, Letters from the Board, E/2/43, f. 314.

had struggled to impose some degree of state control when serving at the Board of Trade, thought these contracts were an improvement over the schemes launched during the earlier English "railroad mania." Under the clauses of the new contracts, the Government had much supervision and control over Indian railroads during and after construction; it had the right to choose or alter the routes for each line, to approve all railroad expenditures, and to set schedules, rates, and fares. The Board proceeded to apply these prerogatives during the early stages of construction, often over strong objections from the East India Company's directors. Hobhouse refused to sanction any of the railroad companies' past liabilities becoming a charge on the capital paid into the Treasury. The directors approved, but he rejected as too costly and ill planned a tender for constructing the Calcutta line. He also asserted the Government's right to appoint an ex-officio director to represent the East India Company at railway board meetings. He repeatedly by-passed the directors and dealt directly with the railway companies about the details of construction.[35] "It is the proper function of the Court to originate and of the Board to control," the directors protested, "and there is nothing in the case of the Indian Railways to make it an exception from the rule." Hobhouse's term of office drew to a close just as it had begun—by his asserting that the Board of Control alone was "invested by law with the power of controlling and altering in any way they pleased." [36]

Other features of Indian administration during Hobhouse's few remaining years at the Board centered around the career of Joseph Drinkwater Bethune, who arrived at Calcutta in 1848 as a legal member of the Supreme Council. His primary task was to emend Macaulay's long-neglected penal code for promulgation. But after Dalhousie sent word that the Council Board was at the point of civil war, Hobhouse wrote to temper Bethune's enthusiasm, "I'm informed that you are slashing at Macaulay's code at a furious rate, and are determined it shall be a Benthamite

35. Letter 8496, February 8, 1850, Commonwealth Relations Office, Letters from the Board, E/2/43, f. 200–205; Hobhouse to Galloway, October 15, 1849, HMS, 851, 42–44; Letter 8381, October 20, 1849, Commonwealth Relations Office, Letters from the Board of Control to the East India Company, E/2/44, f. 109–25, October 2, 1849, Commonwealth Relations Office, E/2/44, f. 125–30.

36. Chairman to Board, October 25, 1849, HMS, 852, f. 95–99; Hobhouse to Chairman, October 29, 1849, HMS, 851, f. 135.

Code or nothing." Hobhouse emphasized, "All you are asked to do is, to fit the Code for actual legislation, not to reform and remodel it altogether."[37] Bethune defended himself against charges of seeking to substitute his own, or Bentham's code. "I think even he [Macaulay] would, on reflection, discard 'voluntary culpable unmitigated homicide' in favor of 'murder'; 'lurking house trespass' for 'housebreaking,' " retorted Bethune, asserting that he merely attempted to revise the archaic, Benthamite language in Macaulay's code.[38] Meanwhile he revived the controversy over the "Black Act" by proposing to place British residents under the criminal, as well as the civil, jurisdiction of the company courts where Indian judges presided. Then there was Bethune's incoherent minutes on a marine mutiny bill. "Indeed," Hobhouse wrote, "if you will look again at your minutes, I am certain you will regret not having drawn your liquor a little more 'mildly.' "[39] Hobhouse also alluded to Bethune's "jovial escapades" while presiding at a Saint Andrew's Day dinner. Bethune replied that he was "ill-obliged to drink, and unable to eat." Furthermore, even if "I had sung 'God Save the Queen' the papers would have been as ready . . . to taunt me with singing a blasphemous song."[40] By 1850 Bethune was at odds with Dalhousie, the Legislative Council, and the entire British community at Calcutta. "I am sorry to find that you are in hot water again, or rather that you have not yet got out of it," Hobhouse observed, "for it seems to me that you have been more or less in that condition since your arrival in India."[41]

Hobhouse found Bethune's activities in India a welcomed respite from the tedium of administrative details. Even as late as 1851 he wrote a thoroughly exasperated Dalhousie that Bethune was "a very good fellow and a very wrong-headed functionary."[42] He agreed there were times when Bethune totally lacked tact or understanding. Bethune dismayed Indian officialdom by going through channels—his sister spoke to Lady John Russell, who spoke to one of Victoria's ladies in waiting—about royal patronage for a women's teachers college in India. "You must, I

37. Dalhousie to Hobhouse, July 11, 1850, HMS, 857, f. 93–95; Hobhouse to Dalhousie, October 6, 1850, HMS, 859, f. 330.
38. Bethune to Hobhouse, November 23, 1850, HMS, 857, f. 193.
39. Hobhouse to Bethune, August 24, 1848, HMS, 859, f. 46.
40. Ibid.; Bethune to Hobhouse, April 8, 1850, HMS, 857, f. 308.
41. Hobhouse to Bethune, January 25, 1850, HMS, 859, f. 164.
42. Hobhouse to Dalhousie, January 24, 1851, HMS, 859, f. 358.

think, on reflection, admit that to employ the services of a *Lady in Waiting*, for the purposes of Government is somewhat more suitable to the days of Mrs. Masham than to the present times," Hobhouse wrote disapprovingly.[43] In November, 1850, Bethune proposed to remove restrictions against the remarriage of widows. "Saint Paul says 'it is better to marry than to burn,' " he wrote to Hobhouse, "but we won't let them burn, and their friends won't let them marry, and the necessary consequence is, that, flesh being frail, these unhappy creatures commit every kind of debauchery." [44] The abolition of polygamy was the next item, until Hobhouse declared that the Government would be very reluctant to intrude upon such a strongly established native custom. In March, 1851, he received a reply concerning India's educated vanguard who were "in a very strange state of transition"; they were inclined to tradition by their upbringing, but intellectually accepted Western customs and mores. Therefore, the Government would find more effective than any legislative fiat a policy of awarding stipends and offices in Indian administration to those natives who had renounced "the palpable evils sanctioned by their culture." [45] Dalhousie was also deluged with suggestions from the man he described as "more devoid of judgment than anybody I ever knew," and at his request Hobhouse reprimanded Bethune for stepping out of line. Social innovations, Hobhouse had written in November, 1850, must not be attempted "without strong evidence that the wishes of the people point in that direction." [46] A friendlier though condescending letter reached India a few months before Bethune's death in 1851:

I can easily understand how a man of your experience, and long connexion with legislative duties, when placed in the high position which you now occupy, should turn his mind to effecting some great and beneficial change in the condition of the many, many millions in whose happiness, present and future, he feels he ought to be deeply interested—& I am sure that the shorter the period allowed for devising, considering, & carrying out such measures, the more eager you must feel for the early adoption of them:—I must, at the same time, confess

43. Hobhouse to Bethune, October 6, 1850, HMS, 859, f. 330.
44. Bethune to Hobhouse, November 23, 1850, HMS, 857, f. 191.
45. Bethune to Hobhouse, March 8, 1851, HMS, 857, f. 252–53.
46. Hobhouse to Bethune, November 23, 1850, HMS, 859, f. 191.

that I greatly doubt the expediency of endeavouring, by any overt act, to change the whole texture of society amongst a vast mass of human beings, who, as long as anything has been known of them, have been most strongly, and superstitiously, attached to their own institutions.[47]

Some significant features of Indian administration and policy emerge from Hobhouse's presidency, which began prior to Lord Auckland's viceroyalty and ended in 1852 during Lord Dalhousie's. The reform impulse was still strong when he acted decisively to implement parts of the liberal program bequeathed by Bentinck and Macaulay. Otherwise, he preferred to move cautiously in reforming along Western lines most areas of Indian life. Change, while desirable, must not disturb the smooth functioning of the administrative machinery over which he presided, especially when it threatened to provoke the Indian masses against their British masters. Hobhouse had no reservations about changing Indian political institutions, as evidenced during the controversy over the Mogul Dynasty. At the beginning of his term, he viewed Britain as the paramount power among the many territorial governments on the vast subcontinent. British rule, having expanded considerably during his presidency, was now throughout all of India, a fact that could be emphasized by abolishing a native dynasty that once held a similar position. At the time when imperial defense justified the Afghan conflict, Hobhouse found himself in the role of an armchair strategist, but during his second administration, he turned to the task of making India an important economic entity in the imperial structure. British commercial interests welcomed free-trade policies while also advocating new services from the state, such as aiding railroad construction. Hobhouse maintained that these enterprises must remain either entirely private or public, and he temporized in the negotiations until formidable pressure groups overrode him. His office was always subject to the opinions and interests of commercial circles, the Cabinet, and various administrative officials. He thus played the essential role of a co-ordinator, making known various views others held within the world of Indian officialdom. Clearly, he was able to assert authority most strongly against the East India directors. It is equally clear that Hobhouse did not subscribe to doctrines

---

47. Hobhouse to Bethune, January 20, 1851, HMS, 860, f. 1.

of anti-imperialism or separatism while presiding over Indian affairs. In his efforts to expand, consolidate, and defend British India, he figured as an ardent champion of Empire at a time when anti-imperialist sentiment is said to have prevailed. Moreover, his encounter with India infused an authoritarian strain into Hobhouse's Victorian liberalism, evidenced by his dealings with East India Company directors or by his dispatch on the Mogul Dynasty, which anticipated the theories of James Fitzjames Stephen a generation later. Just as Hobhouse's liberal views narrowed during his presidency, so too did the delicate balance between encouragement and force in India gradually incline to the latter. By mid-century, the British guardian had evolved in his thinking into a stern master whose rule must continue indefinitely. Administrative changes reflected the new attitude. In 1858 Hobhouse, then Lord Broughton, supported strong one-man rule in India, to the point of defending the Viceroy's privilege of withholding from other officials any information he chose to forward to London. He also protested the creation of any Indian advisory council lest, as he informed the peers, the administrative duality that existed be perpetuated to the detriment of India. Only clearly defined and firm leadership, he felt, could sustain and strengthen the Empire after the Great Mutiny of 1857.[48]

48. *Hansard Parliamentary Debates*, 3d series, CLI (1858), 1561–67.

CONCLUSION

An end to the Napoleonic wars enabled England's public men to turn their undivided attention to the political ideas and institutions bequeathed by their eighteenth-century forebears. An unprecedented task confronted the Government—the remaking of a venerable Constitution to meet the demands and needs of a rapidly changing society. The Industrial Revolution had altered the basis of power: It had displaced the growing population into the cities and towns; it burdened statesmen with the responsibility of checking and guiding the economic and social consequences. Conceptions and functions of government, which had sufficed for a rural England, had become antiquated.

Especially during his early career at Westminster, Hobhouse felt the nation's rulers must concern themselves much more urgently with popular grievances. He could not observe such evils as child labor in the factories or an unduly harsh criminal code without thinking that there were immediate and effective remedies. Throughout the 1820's he was the leading parliamentary spokesman for state regulation of factory labor, and he strongly supported various legal reforms. He constantly maintained that any restraints upon individual conscience lay outside the reach of civil authorities. He championed liberal regimes abroad after Europe reveled in Napoleon's final exile. His Select Vestries Bill of 1831, besides including such innovations as the ballot and suffrage for all ratepayers, male or female, was a major step toward establishing local government on a representative basis.

The "paramount object" of his career was parliamentary reform. Hobhouse urged Whigs at Brooks's to take it up; he consulted with Lambton on a reform motion in 1821; he advised Grey through his friend Ellice on the necessity of embracing reform without delay.[1] His efforts proved rewarding because various Whigs told him they had converted to reform. It is difficult to estimate the extent of Hobhouse's influence on the

1. Lady Dorchester, ed., *Recollections of a Long Life, by Lord Broughton (John Cam Hobhouse) with additional extracts from his private diaries*, II, 139–40; see also ibid., 145–70.

Whig party as a whole, but it seems reasonable to assert that a man of his socially respectable background, a participant in the fashionable life at Brooks's, Holland House and elsewhere, increased the appeal of parliamentary and other reforms. It is significant that *The Times*, commenting on his Cabinet appointment in 1832,[2] coupled Hobhouse's name with the King's as if radicalism and royalty stood united behind a bill all parties and groups could support.

Hobhouse ardently supported the Whig bill because it preserved the legitimate influence of property and freed Parliament from the strangle hold of aristocratic patronage. He assumed that any problem arising in the future would be readily solved because the conscientious members of a reformed Commons would have interests identical with those of the nation at large. The year 1832 was the dividing point between a very turbulent past and a most promising future; 1832 was also the year that the Radical M.P. declared himself to be a Whig. He joined the Establishment of property and rank; Sir Francis Burdett did likewise some years later, though as a Tory.

The influences that shaped Hobhouse's outlook were varied— a background of commercial wealth that wanted a greater voice nationally; a Unitarian upbringing that made him aware of legal and social restrictions against some Englishmen; his father's earlier liberalism bred in an age of enlightenment; the ideals proclaimed by French revolutionaries and by Napoleon, for whom he had naïve hero-worship; and a Whig creed that, although far from democratic, invoked popular support to protect and expand the liberties of the people. He thought it possible for men to bring their institutions into harmony with a universal natural order created by a benevolent Deity who had decreed the evolution toward a more comfortable, humane, and decent life on earth. This outlook accorded with the notion of benevolent change propagated in an age of revolution. Hobhouse believed that the discrepancy between mankind's limitless potential and his present shortcomings was partly because the ruling class had failed to make special interests consonant with general interests. Yet progress was certain, he thought, providing such essentials as honesty and benevolence were applied, rather than merely used as slogans or devices of programs. Hobhouse's

2. *The Times*, February 2, 1832.

simple moralisms, his belief that a perfect English constitution had once existed and should be restored, and his assaults upon party, corruption, and patronage were all voiced by reformers before him. Hobhouse's politics often revealed less of an innovator's approach than the approach of one thoroughly imbued with a reform tradition of the past. The eighteenth century was by no means dead; many of its ideas lingered.

The nature of Hobhouse's radicalism during his years at Westminster reflected his own interpretation of the word. He established his extremist reputation during the disputed 1818 election when he declared himself to be an "extravagant reformer" and "a leveller." He himself interpreted radicalism in the literal sense of reaching an understanding of fundamentals, or vital principles, in order to "strike at the root" of major evils. His radicalism rejected programs. He refused in 1819 to profess his faith in the Radical panaceas of universal suffrage, annual parliaments, and equal electoral districts. He likewise eschewed Place's program of 1832, and he did not join a Radical party that sought to direct liberal M.P.'s in the reformed Parliament. Radicalism defined in terms of programs or groups, however, can be misleading and beset with difficulties. Marx's scientific socialism led to an industrial utopia; William Cobbett hankered after a legendary preindustrial past. Tories like Oastler and Shaftesbury were moved by their sense of moral purpose or indignation over specific abuses—feelings Hobhouse shared whenever he spotted political corruption or else heard about such events as Peterloo. Hobhouse did not share a Radical disposition for scientific explanations and hypotheses. In fact, he thought Benthamite Radicals spent too much time devising rational schemes and attempting to define the conditions for improving society. He eventually found a closer affinity with Macaulay, who criticized the Philosophical Radicals for attempting to deduce a science of government.

If anything, Hobhouse's radicalism was an approach or an attitude to things, but as John Derry has observed, Radicals were often confused, contradictory, and ambiguous in their attitudes.[3] Hobhouse saw the contradictions inherent in Whiggism, which claimed revolutionary origins but rested on aristocratic power, which extolled the people but would not submit to

3. John Derry, *The Radical Tradition; Tom Paine to Lloyd George*, 406.

popular leadership. Still, he hoped to educate the party, to make its members aware that changes were urgently needed. He later hoped to reconcile the Whigs to his Radical candidature. He failed, not because great differences of opinion divided them, but because the Whigs felt personally affronted by the Westminster Committee. For over a year Hobhouse believed himself mistreated by his Whig friends and felt disillusioned by a party he had tried to serve. He condemned party politics, but once in Parliament he joined "His Majesty's Opposition," which at the time was composed mainly of Whigs. He soon realized that party enabled him to propose more effective alternatives to Government legislation. The fact that influential party members had unequivocally supported reform helped pave the way for Hobhouse's *rapproachement* with the Whigs. Besides, the Radical program enunciated by Hunt, Cartwright, and others could conceivably undermine the property basis of English society. To Hobhouse, Whiggism seemed to ensure that radicalism would be kept within bounds.

Hobhouse's social views underwent no change throughout his political career. Even in 1819 he was just as paternalistic as the Whigs he severely censured. He appealed to the working masses not in terms of their interests as workers, but in terms of their community of interests with other and higher classes of society. He was never underprivileged and only for a brief time felt the sense of an outsider ostracized from Whig circles and imprisoned by the Government. Unlike a Paine or a Marx, he never felt entirely estranged from the society he knew; hence, he wished to introduce reforms within the existing social structure and sought a consensus among various reformers. His radicalism belonged to the tradition that had as its spokesmen men of wealth or rank, like Wyvill, Fox, Byron, and Burdett. He discovered that Whigs and Radicals had many points of agreement on foreign affairs, legal and educational reforms, Catholic Emancipation, and removing restrictions against personal freedoms.

Westminster Radicals ultimately found Hobhouse's radical Whiggism untenable. He had faith in a tempered aristocracy; they scorned aristocratic patrons and predators. He assigned leadership to men of rank and property in a reformed England; they believed the future belonged to the masses who were preparing to become their own masters. He upheld the senatorial concept of the House of Commons; they maintained he was a delegate of the people. He thought the Reform Bill of 1832 sufficed to restore a harmony between the rulers and the people; they saw it as only a first installment of a larger reform program. Hobhouse became more concerned with arresting the tempo of change; Place pressed on for more changes, which he outlined to the National Political Union. Hobhouse's refusal to pledge to any Radical demands—although he had done so in 1819—incurred the opposition of Place and the electors who supported Colonel Evans. Sir John Cam Hobhouse, His Majesty's Minister, had risen in the political world, but disagreements with the Westminster Radicals and with his colleagues in the Cabinet, as well as the opposition of Tories, cost him his Westminster seat.

Consolidation likewise replaced innovation as the dominant motif while Hobhouse presided over Indian affairs during the Melbourne and Russell ministries. Some changes along Western lines had obvious merits in terms of advancing India to an age of steam and iron, but he thought that change must in no way disturb the smooth functioning of the administration under his command. The rule of force replaced the rule of opinion as his rationale for British India: India's subjects remained immutable to Western standards because of complex historical circumstances; therefore, Britain had best remain master of a subcontinent incapable of self-government. Earlier traces of Hobhouse's liberal ideals, which accorded with the work of Bentinck and Macaulay in India, gradually receded until by mid-century, he considered India the adjunct to British global power. At the same time, Hobhouse saw no need at home for eliciting through democratic concessions any further support for those in power. Britain's ruling classes had survived Chartist demonstrations and had escaped the revolutionary tumults that swept Europe. They had clearly mastered the processes of change by assuring for all the best of all possible worlds.

Hobhouse did not record any reaction to the Darwinian controversy. He was horrified by atrocities on both sides during the Indian Mutiny, sent his condolences to the American ambassador when President Lincoln was assassinated, and lived after Disraeli's uncertain "leap into the dark." At the age of 79, he went by invitation to the Queen's reception at Buckingham Palace where he "made my bow to Her Majesty who gave me one of her most gracious smiles." [4] He died in 1869, exactly fifty years after first standing as the Radical candidate for the borough of Westminster.

4. Hobhouse, diary, April 27, 1865, John Cam Hobhouse, Lord Broughton, Papers, Add. MSS 56568.

BIBLIOGRAPHY

I. PRIMARY SOURCES

MANUSCRIPT COLLECTIONS

John Charles, Viscount Althorp, third Earl Spencer. Papers. Althorp, Northamptonshire.

George Eden, Earl of Auckland. Papers. Additional Manuscripts 37689–37713, British Museum, London.

Dukes of Bedford. Papers. Bedford Settled Estate Papers, London.

Jeremy Bentham. Papers. University College, London.

Henry Peter Brougham, first Baron Brougham and Vaux. Papers. University College, London.

Sir Francis Burdett. Correspondence. MS English Letters d. 96, Bodleian Library, Oxford.

George Gordon Noel, Baron Byron. Papers. Additional Manuscripts 42093; Ashley Manuscripts 4730, 4744, 4745, 5160–5165, British Museum, London.

John George Lambton, first Earl of Durham. Papers. Lambton Castle, County Durham.

Edward Ellice. Papers. National Library of Scotland, Edinburgh.

Charles Grey, second Earl Grey. Papers. The College, Durham.

Edward John Littleton, first Baron Hatherton. Papers. County Record Office, Staffordshire.

John Cam Hobhouse. Correspondence. Mr. John Murray, 50 Albermarle Street, London.

———. Correspondence. Trinity College Library.

———. Diary. January 3, 1814–July 1, 1814; March 29, 1815–April 5, 1816. Berg Collection, The New York City Public Library, New York.

———. Proofs of Letters from John Cam Hobhouse to Lord Byron, set up in type in connection with an edition of Byron's correspondence projected by Charlotte Carleton, Baroness Dorchester.

———, Lord Broughton. Papers. Additional Manuscripts 36455–36483, 42093, 42230–42235, 43744–43765, 46914–46915, 47222–47235, 56527–56571, British Museum, London. Add. MSS 56527–56571 were acquired by the British Museum from Sir Charles Hobhouse, sixth Bart. in 1971. These were unfoliated at the time of my researches. The remaining volumes, other than those now in the Berg Collection, The New York City Public Library, were bequeathed to the British Museum by Lord

Broughton upon his death (Add. MSS 47231–47235 and 43744–43765). Hobhouse's own edition of his memoirs was earlier called *Some Account of a Long Life;* later, his daughter, Lady Dorchester, edited and published *Recollections of a long Life, by Lord Broughton (John Cam Hobhouse) with additional extracts from his private diaries.*

Henry Richard Vassall Fox, third Baron Holland. Papers. Additional Manuscripts 51569, 51663–51664, British Museum, London.

Henry Hunt. Papers. Additional Manuscripts 38108, British Museum, London.

London Greek Committee. Papers. K–1–K–13, National Library of Greece, Athens.

William Lamb, Viscount Melbourne. Papers. Royal Archives, Windsor Castle.

Lord Henry Palmerston. Papers. Broadlands Archives, Historical Manuscripts Commission, London.

Joseph Parkes. Papers. University College, London.

Thomas Love Peacock. Papers. Additional Manuscripts 36815–36816, British Museum, London.

Sir Robert Peel. Papers. Additional Manuscripts 40402, 40525–40540, 40551, 40593, British Museum, London.

Francis Place. Papers. Additional Manuscripts 27789–27809, 27823–27827, 27837–27850, 35144–35154, 37142–37145, 37154, 37949–37950, British Museum, London.

Lord John Russell. Papers. Public Record Office, 30/22, London.

Sir Robert Wilson. Papers. Additional Manuscripts 30095–30144, British Museum, London.

Sir Walter Scott. Papers. National Library of Scotland, Edinburgh.

OFFICIAL SOURCES

Hansard Parliamentary Debates, 1st series (1818–1820), 2d series (1820–1830), 3d series (1830–1863).

Report from the Select Committee appointed to inquire into the Origin, Management, and Present State of the Arigna Iron and Coal Mining Company, with any Special Matter touching the conduct of any Members of this House. *Parliamentary Reports,* 1826–1827 (234), III, 37.

Report from the Select Committee appointed to inquire into the cause of the increase in the number of Commitments and Convictions in London and Middlesex, and into the state of the Police of the Metropolis, and of districts adjoining thereto. *Parliamentary Reports,* 1828 (533), VI, 1.

Two reports from the Select Committee appointed to inquire into the general operation and effect of the Laws and Usages under which Select and Other Vestries are constituted in England and Wales. *Parliamentary Reports*, 1830 (25.215), IV, 425.569.

Papers showing the result of Inquiries as to the effect of the tread-wheel in the Prisons where it has been established. *Parliamentary Reports*, 1825 (34), XXIII, 567.

Report from the Select Committee appointed to inquire into the means of establishing a Communication by Steam with India by way of the Red Sea, and to whom the several Petitions on that subject were first referred. *Parliamentary Reports*, 1837 (539) VI. 361.

A return of Parishes in England and Wales which have adopted the Act 1 & 2 William IV, c.60 commonly called Hobhouse's Vestry Act. *Parliamentary Accounts and Papers*, 1842, p. 569.

Report from the Committee on Election Proceedings. *Parliamentary Reports*, 1842, V.

Comparative Account of the Population of Great Britain in the Years 1801, 1811, 1821, 1831. *Parliamentary Accounts and Papers*, 1831 (348), XVIII.

Correspondence relating to the Affairs of Persia and Afghanistan. *Parliamentary Papers*, 1839, XL.

The Indian Papers restored by Sir J. W. Kaye. *Parliamentary Papers*, 1859 (Session 2), XXV.

Commonwealth Relations Office: Court Minutes; Appendix to Court Minutes, Copies of Dissents, 6–10; Letter Books from the Board of Control, 11–18; Board's Drafts of Secret Letters and Despatches; Minutes of the Board of Control, 1–7; Letters from the Board of Control to the East India Company, 11–15, 39–44; Board's Copies of Letters from the Board of Control to the East India Company, E/2/39–E/2/43; Bengal Secret Letters, 22–37; Home Miscellaneous Series, vols. 833–862; Revenue, Judicial, and Legislative Committee, Miscellaneous Papers, 7–9; Railway Home Correspondence, A, 3; East India Railway Co., L/F/5/124; Elphinstone European MSS, F 87, Box 2G, 14; Board's Records of Secret Despatches to India; Collections to Railway Letters Received from Bombay, L/F WD/3; *India Register*, 1835–1852. India Office Library.

Home Office. Internal Disturbances, 41, 42, 193. Public Record Office.

War Office. 3, 4, 1832–1833. Public Record Office.

Electoral papers, advertisements, and Letters of St. Margaret and St. John elections, 1818–1820. Archives Department, Westminster Public Library.

Order for the Procession on the Chairing of Sir Francis Burdett and John Cam Hobhouse. Broadside 6.95, Guildhall Library.

NEWSPAPERS

The Alfred and Westminster Gazette, 1819.
Bath Herald, 1832–1833.
Black Dwarf, 1818–1820.
Bristol Gazette, 1833–1835.
Bristol Mercury, 1833–1835.
The Globe, 1818–1820.
Gorgon, 1818–1820.
The Leeds Intelligencer, 1821–1833.
The Leeds Mercury, 1830–1833.
Morning Advertiser, 1830–1833.
Morning Chronicle, 1818–1834.
Morning Herald, 1818–1820.
Morning Post, 1819–1833.
Nottingham and Newark Weekly, 1835–1839.
Nottingham Journal, 1846–1848.
Nottingham Mercury, 1841–1848.
Nottingham and Newark Mercury, 1834.
The Standard, 1833.
The Times, 1816–1858.

PERIODICALS

Annual Register, 1818–1850.
The Economist, 1846–1852.
Edinburgh Review, 1815–1840.
The Examiner, 1816–1830.
Political Register, 1810–1829.
Quarterly Review, 1818–1840.
The Repository, 1818–1819.
The Westminster Review, 1824–1836.

ARTICLES

"Affairs of Spain," *Quarterly Review,* 28 (1822), 538–41.
"An Englishman's Letters on Napoleon," *Edinburgh Review,* 26 (February, 1816), 215–23.
"Greece and Russia," *The Westminster Review,* 2 (1824), 453–71.
"Greek Committee," *The Westminster Review,* 6 (June, 1826), 113–33.
"Greek Committee," *Quarterly Review,* 35 (1827), 221–36.

"Law of Libel and Liberty of the Press," *The Westminster Review*, 3 (April, 1825), 285–321.

[John Wilson Croker.] "Letters from Paris," *Quarterly Review*, 14 (February, 1816), 445–52.

"Local Government in the Metropolis: a sketch of Municipal Institutions of London," *The Westminster Review*, 25 (April, 1836), 96–110.

"Lord Broughton's *Recollections of a Long Life*," *Edinburgh Review*, 133 (April, 1871), 287–337.

"Lord Byron in Greece," *The Westminster Review*, 2 (July, 1824), 225–62.

Macaulay, Thomas B. "The Utilitarian System of Governments," *Edinburgh Review*, 99 (October, 1829), 99–125.

———. "The Utilitarian System of Philosophy," *Edinburgh Review*, 98 (June, 1829), 273–99.

"Mr. Cottu and Special Juries," *The Westminster Review*, 1 (January, 1824), 146–71.

"Recollections of Dr. John Prior Estlin," *Monthly Repository*, 12 (October, 1817), 573–74.

"Report from the Select Committee on Criminal Laws," *Quarterly Review*, 24 (January, 1821), 195–217.

"State of Parties," *Edinburgh Review*, 30 (June, 1818), 181–206.

"Universal Suffrage," *Edinburgh Review*, 31 (December, 1818), 165–203.

BOOKS AND PAMPHLETS

Auber, Peter. *An analysis of the constitution of the East India company, and of the laws passed by Parliament for the government of their affairs, at home and abroad.* London, 1826.

Bentham, Jeremy. *Elements of the Art of Packing, as applied to Special Juries, particularly in cases of Libel Law.* London, 1821.

Blaquire, Edward. *The Greek Revolution; its origins and progress.* London, 1824.

Brooke, James. *The Democrats of Marylebone.* London, 1839.

Buxton, Thomas Fowell. *Inquiry whether Crime and Misery are Produced or Prevented by our Present System of Prison Discipline.* London, 1818.

Erskine, Thomas, first Baron Erskine. *An Appeal to the People of Great Britain on the Subject of a Confederated Greece.* London, 1824.

———. *A Letter to an Elector of Westminster.* London, 1819.

———. *A Preface to the Defences of the Whigs.* London, 1819.

———. *A Short Defense of the Whigs.* London, 1819.

Estlin, John Prior. *Discourses on Universal Restitution delivered* to the Society of Protestant Dissenters in Lewin's Mead, Bristol. Bristol, 1813.

———. Evidences of Revealed Religion, and Particularly Christianity, Stated, with Reference to a Pamphlet called "The Age of Reason." Bristol, 1796.

———. Familiar Lectures on Moral Philosophy. 2 vols. London, 1818.

An Exposition of Circumstances which gave rise to the election of Sir Francis Burdett, Bart . . . . and of the Principles which governed the Committee who conducted that election. London, 1807.

Galt, John. The Ayrshire Legatees. London, 1821.

Gordon, Thomas. History of the Greek Revolution. 2 vols. London, 1832.

Hippisley, John Cox. Prison labour, and correspondence and communication addressed to His Majesty's principal secretary of state for the Home department concerning the introduction of tread-mills into prisons. London, 1823.

Hobhouse, John Cam, first Baron Broughton. A Defence of the People in Reply to Lord Erskine's Two Defences of the Whigs. London, 1819.

———. Essay on the Origin and Intention of Sacrifices. London, 1809.

———. Historical Illustrations of the Fourth Canto of Childe Harold: containing Dissertations on the Ruins of Rome; and An Essay on Italian Literature. London, 1818.

———. Italy: Remarks Made in Several Visits from the Year 1816 to 1854. 2 vols. London, 1859.

———. A Journey Through Albania and other Provinces of Turkey in Europe and Asia to Constantinople during the years 1809 and 1810. 2 vols. London, 1813.

———. A Letter to the Independent Electors of Westminster, 26 February 1820. London, 1820.

———. Proceedings in the House of Commons and in the Court of King's-Bench, relative to the Author of the "Trifling Mistake," together with the argument against parliamentary commitment, and the decision which the judges gave without hearing the case . . . Prepared for the press by John Cam Hobhouse. London, 1820.

———. Remarks on the Exclusion of Lord Byron's Monument from Westminster Abbey. London, 1844.

———. The Substance of Some Letters written by an English Resident at Paris during the late reign of the Emperor Napoleon. 2 vols. London, 1816.

————. *A Supplicatory Letter to Lord Viscount Castlereagh, K. G. on the bills introduced into Parliament for preventing seditious meetings.* London, 1819.

————. *A Trifling Mistake in Lord Erskine's Recent Preface.* London, 1819.

Hughes, Rev. Thomas S. *Considerations upon the Greek Rebellion.* London, 1823.

Kaye, John W. ed. *Memorials of Indian Government selected from the papers of Henry St. George Tucker.* London, 1853.

A Letter to Sir John Cam Hobhouse, Bart., M. P. on the "Factories Bill." London, 1832.

Martineau, Harriet. *A History of the Thirty Years' Peace.* 4 vols. London, 1877–1878.

Palma, Count Alerino. *Greece Vindicated in Two Letters.* London, 1826.

Place, Francis. *A Letter to the Independent Electors of Westminster.* London, 1832.

————. *On the Law of Libel; with Strictures on the Self-Styled "Constitutional Association."* London, 1823.

————. *Reply to Lord Erskine by an Elector of Westminster.* London, 1819.

Russell, John, first Earl Russell. *A Letter to the Rt. Hon. Lord Holland on Foreign Politics.* London, 1819.

Stanhope, Col. Leicester. *Greece in 1823 and 1824.* London, 1825.

Westminster Committee. *On Pledges to be Given by the Candidates.* London, 1832.

————. *Public Meeting of the Electors of Westminster, held in the Great Room of the Crown and Anchor on Thursday, the 28 November, 1832.* London, 1832.

Westminster Committee appointed to manage the Election of Mr. Hobhouse. *An Authentic Narrative of the Events of the Westminster Election which commenced on Saturday, February 13 and closed on Wednesday, March 3, 1819.* London, 1819.

AUTOBIOGRAPHY, BIOGRAPHY, DIARIES, AND LETTERS

Aspinall, Arthur, ed. *The Diary of Henry Hobhouse, 1820–1827.* London, 1947.

————. *The Letters of George IV, 1812–1830.* 3 vols. Cambridge, 1938.

————. *Three Early Nineteenth Century Diaries (Extracts relating to the Reform Act of 1832 from the diaries of Sir Denis Le Marchant, E. J. Littleton, Baron Hatherton and E. Law, Earl of Ellenborough).* London, 1952.

Baird, J. G. A., ed. *Private Letters of the Marquess of Dalhousie.* London, 1910.

Bamford, Frances, and William Arthur Wellesley, seventh Duke of Wellington, eds. *The Journal of Mrs. Arbuthnot, 1820–1832.* 2 vols. London, 1950.

Bamford, Samuel. *Passages in the Life of a Radical.* 2 vols. London, 1842.

Benson, Arthur C., and Viscount Esher, eds. *The Letters of Queen Victoria; a selection from Her Majesty's correspondence between the years 1837 and 1861, published by the authority of His Majesty the King.* 3 vols. New York, 1907.

Bowring, John, ed. *The Works of Jeremy Bentham.* 11 vols. Edinburgh, 1843.

Brougham, Henry Peter, first Baron Brougham and Vaux. *The Life and Times of Henry, Lord Brougham Written by Himself.* 3 vols. New York, 1871.

Byron, George Gordon, sixth Baron Byron. *The Works of Lord Byron; A New, Revised and Enlarged Edition, with Illustrations: Poetry*, edited by E. H. Coleridge, 7 vols.; *Letters and Journals*, edited by R. E. Prothero, 6 vols. London, 1898–1904.

Cartwright, F. D., ed. *Life and Correspondence of Major Cartwright.* 2 vols. London, 1826.

Colchester, Lord, ed. *A Political Diary, 1828–1830 by Ellenborough, Edward Lord.* London, 1881.

Dorchester, Lady, ed. *Recollections of a Long Life, by Lord Broughton (John Cam Hobhouse) with additional extracts from his private diaries.* 6 vols. London, 1909–1911.

Elliot, Hugh S. *The Letters of John Stuart Mill.* 2 vols. London, 1910.

Esher, Viscount, ed. *The Girlhood of Queen Victoria; a selection from Her Majesty's diaries between the years 1832 and 1840.* 2 vols. London, 1912.

Ginter, Donald E., ed. *Whig Organization in the General Election of 1790; selections from the Blair Adam papers.* Berkeley, 1967.

Gooch, G. P., ed. *Later Correspondence of Lord John Russell.* 2 vols. London, 1925.

Gore, John, ed. *The Creevey Papers.* New York, 1963.

Grant, James. *Random Recollections of the House of Commons, from the year 1830 to the close of 1835.* London, 1836.

Grey, Henry, Earl Grey, ed. *The Correspondence of King William IV and Earl Grey.* 2 vols. London, 1867.

Griggs, Earl Leslie, ed. *The Letters of Samuel Taylor Coleridge.* 4 vols. Oxford, 1956.

Hardcastle, The Hon. Mrs., ed. *Life of John, Lord Campbell.* 2 vols. London, 1881.

Hazlitt, William. *Complete Works of William Hazlitt*, edited by P. P. Howe. 21 vols. London, 1930–1934.

Hobhouse, Benjamin. *An Address to the Public, in Answer to the Principal Objections Urged in the House of Commons against the Repeal of the Test Laws.* London, 1790.

———. *To the Patriotic Societies in London and its Neighborhood.* London, 1792.

Hobhouse, Charles P. *Account of the Family Hobhouse and Reminiscences.* Taunton, By the Author.

Hobhouse, Henry. *Hobhouse Memoirs.* Taunton, 1927.

Hobhouse, John Cam, first Baron Broughton. *Some Account of a Long Life.* 5 vols. London, 1863–1865.

Holland, Lord Henry. *Memoirs of the Whig Party during my Time.* 2 vols. London, 1852–1854.

Holyoake, George J. *Sixty Years of an Agitator's Life.* 2 vols. London, 1892–1893.

Jennings, Louis J., ed. *The Croker Papers. The Correspondence and Diaries of the late Rt. Hon. John Wilson Croker, 1809–1830.* 2 vols. New York, 1884.

Le Marchant, Sir Denis. *Memoir of John Charles Viscount Althorp, Third Earl Spencer.* London, 1876.

Maxwell, Sir Herbert. *The Life and Letters of George William Frederick, fourth Earl of Clarendon.* 2 vols. London, 1913.

Mineka, Francis E. *The Earlier Letters of John Stuart Mill, 1812–1843.* Toronto, 1963.

Moore, Thomas. *Memoirs, Life, and Journals of Lord Byron.* 3d. ed. London, 1860.

Morpurgo, J. E., ed. *The Autobiography of Leigh Hunt.* London, 1949.

Quennell, Peter, ed. *The Private Letters of Princess Lieven to Prince Metternich, 1820–1826.* London, 1937.

Raikes, Thomas. *A Portion of the Journal Kept by Thomas Raikes Esq. from 1831 to 1847.* 4 vols. London, 1856–1858.

Ray, Gordon N., ed. *The Letters and Private Papers of William Makepeace Thackeray.* 4 vols. Cambridge, Mass., 1946.

Reid, Stuart J. *Life and Letters of the first Earl of Durham, 1792–1840.* London, 1906.

Robinson, L. G., ed. *Letters of Dorothea, Princess Lieven, during her residence in London, 1812–1834.* London, 1902.

Russell, Lord John, ed. *Memoirs, Journal and Correspondence of Thomas Moore.* 8 vols. New York, 1853–1856.

Russell, Rollo, ed. *Early Correspondence of Lord John Russell, 1805–1840.* 2 vols. London, 1913.

Sadler, Thomas, ed. *Diary, Reminiscences and Correspondence of Henry Crabb Robinson.* Boston, 1898.

Sanders, Lloyd C., ed. *Lord Melbourne's Papers.* London, 1889.

Smith, Nowell C., ed. *The Letters of Sydney Smith.* 2 vols. Oxford, 1953.

Stavordale, Lord, ed. *Further Memoirs of the Whig Party 1807–1821, with some Miscellaneous Reminiscences, by Henry Richard Vassall, Third Lord Holland.* London, 1905.

Strachey, Lytton, and Roger Fulford, eds. *The Greville Memoirs, 1814–1860.* 8 vols. London, 1938.

Torrens, W. T. M'Cullagh. *Memoirs of the Rt. Hon. William Second Viscount Melbourne.* 2 vols. London, 1878.

Walpole, Sir Spencer. *Life of Lord John Russell.* 2 vols. London, 1889.

II. Secondary Sources

articles and lectures

Alder, G. J. "The 'Garbled' Blue Books of 1839—Myth or Reality?" *The Historical Journal,* 15, 2 (1972), 229–59.

Bearce, George D. "Lord William Bentinck: the Application of Liberalism to India," *Journal of Modern History,* 29 (September, 1956), 234–46.

Brown, Wallace C. "The Popularity of English Travel Books about the Near East, 1775–1825," *Philological Quarterly,* 15 (1936), 70–80.

De Beer, E. S., and Walter Seton. "Byroniana: The Archives of the London Greek Committee," *The Nineteenth Century,* 100 (September, 1926), 396–412.

Erdman, David V. "Lord Byron and the Genteel Reformers," *PMLA,* 56 (December, 1941), 1065–94.

Ferguson, Henry. "The Birmingham Political Union and the Government, 1831–32," *Victorian Studies,* 3 (March, 1960), 261–76.

Foord, Archibald S. "The Waning of the 'Influence of the Crown,'" *English Historical Review,* 62 (1947), 484–507.

Graham, A. H. "The Litchfield House Compact, 1835," *Irish Historical Studies,* 12 (1960–1961), 209–23.

Kriegel, Abraham D. "The Politics of the Whigs in Opposition, 1834–1835," *Journal of British Studies,* 7, 2 (May, 1968), 65–91.

Main, J. M. "Radical Westminster, 1807–1820," *Historical Studies of Australia and New Zealand,* 12 (October, 1965–April, 1967), 186–204.

Minchenton, W. E. "Bristol—Metropolis of the West in the Eighteenth Century," *Royal Historical Society Transactions,* 5th Series, IV (1954), 69–89.

Mineka, Francis E., ed. "John Stuart Mill: Letters on the French Revolution of 1830," *Victorian Studies*, I, 2 (1957), 137–54.

Namier, Sir Lewis. "Monarchy and the Party System." The Romanes Lecture Delivered in the Sheldonian Theatre, May 15, 1952.

Robbins, Caroline. "Discordant Parties; a Study of the Acceptance of Party by Englishmen," *Political Science Quarterly*, 73 (1958), 505–24.

Sutherland, Lucy S. "The City of London in Eighteenth-Century Politics." In *Essays Presented to Sir Lewis Namier*, edited by R. Pares and A. J. P. Taylor, 49–74. London, 1956.

Thomas, William. "Whigs and Radicals in Westminster: The Election of 1819," *Guildhall Miscellany*, 3, 3 (October, 1970), 174–217.

Thomas, W. E. S. "Francis Place and Working Class History," *Historical Journal*, 5, 1 (1962), 61–79.

SELECTED BOOKS

Aspinall, Arthur. *Lord Brougham and the Whig Party*. Manchester, 1927.

———, ed. *The Formation of Canning's Ministry, February to August, 1827*. 3d series. Royal Historical Society Publications, no. 59. London, 1937.

Bain, Alex. *James Mill*. London, 1882.

Baker, Herschel. *William Hazlitt*. Cambridge, Mass., 1962.

Bearce, George D. *British Attitudes Towards India, 1784–1858*. Oxford, 1961.

Bell, Horace. *Railway Policy in India*. London, 1894.

Bellot, H. H. *University College, London, 1826–1926*. London, 1929.

Black, Eugene. *The Association, British Extraparliamentary Political Organization, 1769–1793*. Cambridge, Mass., 1963.

Brock, W. R. *Lord Liverpool and Liberal Toryism*. Cambridge, 1941.

Brown, Philip A. *The French Revolution in English History*. London, 1918.

Buckley, Jessie. *Joseph Parkes of Birmingham and the part which he played in the radical reform movement from 1825–1835*. London, 1926.

Butler, J. R. M. *The Passing of the Great Reform Bill*. London, 1914.

Cecil, David Lord. *Melbourne*. New York, 1954.

Christie, I. R. *Wilkes, Wyvill and Reform; the Parliamentary reform movement in British politics, 1760–1785*. London, 1962.

Church, Roy A. *Economic and Social Change in a Midland Town: Victorian Nottingham, 1815–1900.* New York, 1966.

Clark, George Kitson. *The Making of Victorian England.* London, 1962.

———. *Peel and the Conservative Party.* London, 1929.

Cole, G. D. H. *A Short History of the British Working Class Movement, 1789–1947.* 4th ed. London, 1960.

———. *The Life of William Cobbett.* London, 1924.

Cone, Carl B. *The English Jacobins: Reformers in Late Eighteenth Century England.* New York, 1968.

Cowherd, Raymond G. *The Humanitarians and the Ten Hour Movement in England.* Boston, 1956.

Curti, Merle. *American Philanthropy Abroad.* New Brunswick, 1963.

Dallegio, Eugène. *Les Philhéllènes et la Guerre de L'Indépendence.* Athens, 1947.

Darvall, F. O. *Popular Disturbances and Public Order in Regency England.* London, 1934.

Davis, H. W. C. *The Age of Grey and Peel.* London, 1929.

Davis, Richard W. *Dissent in Politics, 1780–1830: The political life of William Smith, M.P.* London, 1971.

Derry, John. *The Radical Tradition; Tom Paine to Lloyd George.* London, 1967.

Driver, Cecil. *Tory Radical, The Life of Richard Oastler.* New York, 1946.

Feiling, Keith. *The Second Tory Party, 1714–1832.* London, 1938.

Foord, Archibald S. *His Majesty's Opposition, 1714–1830.* Oxford, 1964.

Fulford, Roger. *George IV.* London, 1949.

———. *The Trial of Queen Caroline.* New York, 1968.

Gash, Norman. *Mr. Secretary Peel; the life of Sir Robert Peel to 1830.* Cambridge, Mass., 1961.

———. *Politics in the age of Peel: a study in the techniques of parliamentary representation, 1830–1850.* London, 1953.

———. *Reaction and Reconstruction in English Politics, 1832–1852.* Oxford, 1965.

George, M. D., ed. *Catalogue of Political and Personal Satires preserved in the Department of Prints and Drawings in the British Museum.* 11 vols. London, 1949–1956.

Grego, Joseph. *History of Parliamentary Elections.* London, 1892.

Halévy, Elie. *History of the English People in the Nineteenth Century.* 6 vols. London, 1949.

———. *The Growth of Philosophical Radicalism.* Boston, 1955.

Hamburger, Joseph. *James Mill and the Art of Revolution*. New Haven, 1963.

―――. *Intellectuals in Politics: John Stuart Mill and the Philosophical Radicals*. New Haven, 1965.

Harris, William. *The History of the Radical Party in Parliament*. London, 1885.

Hawes, Frances. *Henry Brougham*. New York, 1957.

Hutchins, Francis G. *The Illusion of Permanence*. Princeton, 1967.

Huttenback, Robert A. *British Relations With Sind, 1799–1843; an anatomy of imperialism*. Berkeley, 1962.

Jackson, J. *The Public Career of Sir Francis Burdett: The Years of Radicalism, 1796–1815*. Philadelphia, 1932.

Joyce, Michael. *My Friend H*. London, 1948.

Keith-Lucas, B. *The English Local Government Franchise*. Oxford, 1952.

Kydd, Samuel [Alfred]. *The History of the Factory Reform Movement from 1802 to the Enactment of the Ten Hour Bill in 1847*. 2 vols. London, 1857.

Lean, E. Tangye. *The Napoleonists: A Study in Political Disaffection, 1760–1960*. Oxford, 1970.

Little, Bryan. *The City and County of Bristol, a Study in Atlantic Civilization*. London, 1954.

Lloyd, Christopher. *Lord Cochrane*. London, 1947.

Maccoby, S. *English Radicalism, 1786–1832*. London, 1955.

―――. *English Radicalism, 1832–1852*. London, 1935.

Machin, G. I. T. *The Catholic Question in English Politics, 1820–1830*. Oxford, 1964.

McKenzie, Robert T. *British Political Parties*. London, 1963.

McLachlin, H. *The Unitarian Movement in the Religious life of England*. London, 1934.

Marchand, Leslie A. *Byron, A Biography*. 3 vols. New York, 1947.

Memorials of Brooks's. London, 1907.

Minchenton, W. E., ed. *The Trade of Bristol in the Eighteenth Century*. Bristol Record Society Publications, no. 20. Bristol, 1957.

Misra, B. B. *The Central Administration of the East India Company, 1773–1834*. Manchester, 1959.

Mitchell, Austin. *The Whigs in Opposition, 1815–1830*. Oxford, 1967.

Moore, Doris Langley. *The Late Lord Byron; posthumous dramas*. London, 1961.

Namier, Sir Lewis. *The Structure of Politics at the Accession of George III*. London, 1957.

New, Chester. *Life of Henry Brougham to 1830*. Oxford, 1961.

———. *Life of Lord Durham*. Oxford, 1929.

Nicholson, Harold. *Byron, The Last Journey, April, 1823–April, 1824*. London, 1924.

Norris, J. A. *The First Afghan War, 1838–1842*. Cambridge, 1967.

O'Gorman, F. *The Whig Party and the French Revolution, 1789–1795*. London, 1967.

Packe, Michael St. John. *The Life of John Stuart Mill*. New York, 1954.

Pares, Richard. *King George III and the Politicians*. London, 1953.

———. *A West-India Fortune*. London, 1950.

Patterson, M. W. *Sir Francis Burdett and his Times (1779–1844)*. 2 vols. London, 1931.

Philips, C. H. *The East India Company, 1784–1834*. Manchester, 1961.

Porritt, Edward, and A. G. Porritt. *The Unreformed House of Commons*. 2 vols. London, 1931.

Quennell, Peter. *Byron: The Years of Fame*. New York, 1935.

Radzinowicz, Leon. *A History of English Criminal Law and its Administration from 1750*. 3 vols. London, 1948–1950.

Ramsay, A. A. W. *Sir Robert Peel*. London, 1928.

Read, Donald. *Peterloo: The "Massacre" and Its Background*. Manchester, 1958.

Robbins, Caroline. *The Eighteenth Century Commonwealthman*. Cambridge, Mass., 1959.

Roberts, Michael. *The Whig Party, 1807–1812*. London, 1939.

Rudé, George. *Wilkes and Liberty*. London, 1962.

Seton-Watson, R. W. *Britain in Europe, 1789–1914*. Cambridge, 1937.

Sheppard, F. H. W. *Local Government in Saint Marylebone, 1688–1835*. London, 1958.

Southgate, Donald. *The Passing of the Whigs, 1832–1886*. London, 1962.

Sutherland, Lucy S. *The City of London and Opposition to the Government, 1768–1774: a study in the rise of metropolitan radicalism*. London, 1959.

Temperly, Harold W. *The Foreign Policy of Canning, 1822–1827*. London, 1925.

Terry, G. P. *The Story of Greater London*. London, 1899.

Thompson, Edward P. *The Making of the English Working Class*. London, 1963.

Thorner, Daniel. *Investment in Empire: British Railway and Steam Shipping Enterprise in India, 1825–1844*. Philadelphia, 1950.

Trevelyan, G. M. *Lord Grey of the Reform Bill.* 3d. ed. London, 1952.

Turberville, A. S. *The House of Lords in the Age of Reform.* London, 1958.

Veitch, G. S. *The Genesis of Parliamentary Reform.* London, 1913.

Vincent, Eric R. P. *Ugo Foscolo, an Italian in Regency England.* Cambridge, 1953.

———. *Bryon, Hobhouse and Foscolo; new documents in the history of a collaboration.* Cambridge, 1949.

Wallas, Graham. *The Life of Francis Place.* London, 1898.

Ward, J. T. *The Factory Movement, 1830–1855.* London, 1962.

Webb, Sidney, and Beatrice Webb. *English Local Government from the Revolution of 1688 to the Municipal Corporation Act.* 11 vols. London, 1963.

———. *The History of Trade Unions.* London, 1894.

Webster, Sir C. K. *The Foreign Policy of Castlereagh, 1815–1822.* London, 1925.

———. *The Foreign Policy of Palmerston, 1830–1841.* 2 vols. London, 1951.

White, R. J. *Waterloo to Peterloo.* London, 1957.

Wickwar, William H. *The Struggle for the Freedom of the Press, 1819–1832.* London, 1928.

Woodward, Sir Llewellyn. *The Age of Reform, 1815–1870.* Oxford, 1962.

PH.D. DISSERTATIONS

Churgin, Naomi H. "Major Cartwright: A Study in Radical Parliamentary Reform, 1774–1824." Columbia University, 1963.

INDEX